SOCIAL MEDIA
FOR FASHION MARKETING
STORYTELLING IN A DIGITAL WORLD

BLOOMSBURY VISUAL ARTS
Bloomsbury Publishing Plc
50 Bedford Square, London, WC1B 3DP, UK
1385 Broadway, New York, NY 10018, USA

BLOOMSBURY, BLOOMSBURY VISUAL ARTS and the Diana logo are
trademarks of Bloomsbury Publishing Plc

First published by Bloomsbury Visual Arts 2017
Reprinted 2019 (twice), 2020

Cover design: Louise Dugdale

A catalogue record for this book is available from the British Library.

Library of Congress Cataloging-in-Publication Data
Names: Bendoni, Wendy, author.
Title: Social media for fashion marketing : storytelling in a digital world / by
Wendy Bendoni.
Description: New York : Bloomsbury Visual Arts, 2017. | Includes bibliographical
references and index.
Identifiers: LCCN 2016012434| ISBN 9781474233323 (pbk. : alk. paper) |
ISBN 9781474233330 (epdf : alk. paper)
Subjects: LCSH: Fashion merchandising. | Internet marketing. | Social media.
Classification: LCC HD9940.A2 .B46 2017 | DDC 746.9/20688—dc23
LC record available at https://lccn.loc.gov/2016012434

ISBN: PB: 978-1-4742-3332-3
      ePDF: 978-1-4742-3333-0
      eBook: 978-1-4742-3899-1

Typeset by Struktur Design
Printed and bound in Great Britain

To find out more about our authors and books visit www.bloomsbury.com
and sign up for our newsletters.

SOCIAL MEDIA
FOR FASHION MARKETING
STORYTELLING IN A DIGITAL WORLD

Wendy K. Bendoni

BLOOMSBURY VISUAL ARTS
LONDON · NEW YORK · OXFORD · NEW DELHI · SYDNEY

CONTENTS

06   Introduction

PART 1

THE DIGITAL LANDSCAPE TRANSFORMS THE FASHION INDUSTRY

01

DIGITAL DISRUPTION OF THE FASHION INDUSTRY

10   Introduction
11   The Fashion Landscape Before Social Media
18   Evolution of the Fashion System
22   Democratization of the Fashion Industry—
      Information Age
25   Case Study: Street Photography Zeitgeist
26   The Fashion Landscape Altered: Four Disruptions
      that Changed the Fashion Industry
28   Blogosphere Takes On The Fashion Industry
35   Style Sharing Communities;
      User-Generated Content (UGC)
38   Interview: Rachel Arthur, Founder and Editor,
      Fashion and Mash
40   The Future of Runway
50   Confirmation of a Trend Through Online
      Engagement
54   Exercises

02

INTRODUCTION TO THE DIGITAL LANDSCAPE

58   Introduction
58   The Environment in Digital Space
64   Social Exploration
66   Case Study: Social Engagement Disruption
67   The Social Structure
68   Case Study: Leveraging Social Currency
69   Case Study: Beyoncé Breaking the Rules and
      Harnessing Social Currency
71   Case Study: Retailers Utilizing Crowd Social Proof
72   Case Study: Urban Chase Turns to Gamification
73   Case Study: Jimmy Choo, Launching Trainers
      with a Scavenger Hunt
75   Social Media Networks
82   Interview: Aliza Licht, Founder and President
      of Leave Your Mark, LLC
85   Case Study: Expiring Digital Content: Snapchat
86   Case Study: Snapchat Takes on the Luxury Market
87   Legally Speaking in a Social Media Space
88   Case Study: The Applicability of US Federal Trade
      Commission Law to Online Advertising
89   Uniting the World
90   Interview: Leila Samii, Global Research on
      Connecting Through Social Media
92   Interview: Misha Janette, Tokyo Fashion Diaries,
      Impact of Fashion Blogging and Social Media
      in Japan
94   Exercises

03

THE RISE OF THE HYPER-CONNECTED CONSUMER

98   Introduction
99   Hyper-Connected Consumers
104   Interview: Dr. Larry Rosen, Professor of Psychology
      of Technology
110   Case Study: Selfies Create Sale Conversions
      by EDITED
111   Evolution of Social Behavior on Social Media
117   Generation Gap Through the Digital Landscape
120   Generation Z: 1995–2012
123   Case Study: Tavi Gevinson, Rookie Magazine
128   Millennials / Gen Y: 1986–1994
131   Generation X: 1965–1985
135   Baby Boomers: 1946–1964
138   Exercises

PART 2
THE BUSINESS OF MARKETING FASHION

04
DIGITAL STORYTELLING

142 Introduction
143 Storytelling in Marketing
148 Case Study: Storytelling Marketing Funnel—
     CHANEL
151 Interview: Raman Kia, Founder/CEO RJK Project
154 Interview: Bumpy Pitch Brand Story
158 Case Study: Brand Voice—Barbie Takes on
     Social Media
159 Case Study: Brand Voice Through a Social Story:
     #LikeAGirl Campaign
160 Interview: Cindy Whitehead
162 Visual Consumption of Content
163 Case Study: The Burberry Dream Team:
     Digital Storytelling
164 Trending Social Stories of the #Hashtag
166 Case Study: #Lovewins—The Rainbow Movement
     Goes Viral
167 Case Study: #TheDress—Is it White and Gold
     or Blue and Black?
168 The Science of Stories: Neurological Response
     to Stories
170 Storytelling Becomes Storygiving
171 Interview: Marketing Storyteller, Mike Monello
     of Campfire Marketing Agency
175 Case Study: Tiffany & Co, Incentive Through
     Love—"What Makes Love True?"
176 Interview: Braden Harvey in his own words
178 Social Good Marketing: Purposeful Stories in the
     Digital Age
179 Case Study: Social Good from Ford Motor Co.
179 Case Study: The Giving Keys
180 Interview: Stewart Ramsey of Krochet Kids
182 Case Study: Fashion Revolution Day: The Power of
     a Hashtag Telling a Story of Human Interest
184 Exercises

05
STRATEGIC MARKETING IN THE DIGITAL AGE

188 Introduction
189 Social Media Marketing Strategy
190 Real-Time Marketing Strategies by Teri Thompson
196 Interview: Trina Albus, founder of Magenta Agency
197 The Social Media Team
198 Influencer Marketing / Marketing Agencies
199 Case Story: Kate Spade Camp
200 Interview: Zoe Waldron, Social Media Strategist
     at HelloSociety
202 Interview: Chelsea Matthews, Founder and CEO
     of MATTE BLACK
204 Interview: Kyle Hjelmeseth, Affliliate and Blogger
     Marketing Tactics
206 Interview: Christopher Griffin, President of
     WWDMAGIC Fashion Industry Trade Shows
208 The Art of the Pitch
208 Hidden Influencers
209 Case Study: Pretty Little Liars (PLL)
210 Case Study: Costume-to-E-Commerce
     Arianne Phillips, Costume Designer
212 Case Study: Authenticity of Modeling Consumers as
     Brand Influencers
213 Digital Curation
216 Fashion On-Demand World
218 Interview: Damian F. Scoglio, Founder and CEO
     of Gandr
220 Interview: Cuit Gonzalez, Brand Engagement +
     Social Media Manager at BCBGMAXAZRIA &
     Herve Leger
222 Case Study: Comics-to-Commerce: Phillip Lim
222 Mobile Interactive Shoppable Storefronts
223 Case Study: Kate Spade Saturday
     Shoppable Window
224 Case Study: Jeremy Berstein, President of
     The Science Project
226 Exercises

06
THE EVOLVING MEASURABLE IMPACT OF SOCIAL MEDIA

230 Introduction
231 The Power of Data
232 Evolution of Fashion Data + Analytics
234 The Future of Fashion Forecasting
235 Interview: EDITED, Katie Smith, Marketing &
     Communications Director
238 Case Study: Think With Google –Shopping Insight
239 Data-Driven Briefs and Personas
240 Case Study: Affinio, India White,
     Chief Marketing Officer
246 The Power of Search
254 Journey Mapping
257 Case Study: Simplified Example of the
     Buyer Journey
260 Exercises

262 Glossary
266 Index
270 Acknowledgments
272 Picture credits

INTRODUCTION

The Author's Inspiration for this Textbook:

The inspiration for this book originated from a conversation on teaching social media in the discipline of fashion marketing. In search of a book, I quickly learned that most books that are available do not cover the topic of social media marketing within the context of the business of fashion. Also how do you write a book on social media without it being dated before it is published? I remember speaking to other professors in search of a similar book, and we all agreed that we did not need another book on the basics of how to use social media, or a single chapter on the general rules of social media. Rather, we needed a book that introduced social media marketing from the fashion industry's point of view, focusing on the raised expectation of consumers in the age of social sharing and real-time content over the Internet. This created an opportunity to create a textbook that would approach the topic of fashion marketing in the digital world by pairing academic research findings with industry-related experiences, content, case studies, benchmark digital movements, and insightful interviews. I pooled together my industry resources from over two decades of professional practice as a fashion marketer as well as mentors in the fashion industry such as Donna Karan's Senior Vice President of Global Communication to the Digital Marketing Director of Condé Nast Digital Marketing. The goal of this textbook is to prepare, inform, educate, and share how the business of fashion operates in the digital landscape with the next generation of fashion marketing, managers, digital curators, and digital strategist. This textbook aims to enable students to gain knowledge about social media marketing efforts (e.g., campaigns, social engagement, outreach programs, content marketing) as well to prepare them to better understand the new digital-savvy consumer.

Approach

This textbook will enable the reader a chance to explore how social media networks continue to alter the world of digital communications and impact the fashion industry's overall marketing efforts. Throughout the chapters of this book, we will analyze the concepts of utilizing and integrating social media platforms to leverage the digital landscape to both reach and understand a brand's targeted audience. Students will closely examine digital communications and experiences through a collection of digital marketing case studies (exclusive to this textbook), interviews (e.g., marketing strategists, marketing directors, brand marketers, digital influencers) and chapter exercises that focus on critical thinking and practical applications. Interviews will help gain insight into the fashion industry and understand the current industry trends in social media marketing in terms of technology, digital influencers, consumers' behavior in the digital age, social media analytics, search engine optimization, and the effects that social media has had on the fashion cycle. Social media driven activation and digital benchmark campaigns in the fashion industry will also be featured to share the idea of new media marketing strategies (e.g., storytelling, story giving, digital curation, social currency, and user-generated content). This analysis will allow the readers to gain insight into the integration of social media through the campaigns and digital strategies behind them.

Additionally, the textbook will highlight how different levels of communication and brand messages require different ways of communicating on a variety of social media platforms, that is, not all brands should communicate the same way, and social media platforms vary on how they resonate with consumers and what type of information is best communicated on these platforms. Marketers must carefully select the right social media strategy to communicate their brand's message across appropriate social media platforms. In this book, we will further investigate four key criteria to assist in the decision-making process of which social media channel best suits the brand's overall message to their target customer. The criteria will include the market level (mass, mid, luxury, etc.), the cohort group (based on the new consumer point of view; how they currently use social media), the gender (comparison of social media behaviors between men and women), and social media channels (Instagram, Facebook, Twitter, Snapchat, etc.). The assignments and exercises in the textbook will give examples of practical applications to content-driven marketing strategy, while also sharing new approaches to applying digital curation to fashion brands.

Part 1: The Digital Landscape Transforms the Fashion Industry (Chapters 1–3)

The business of fashion today operates on the influence of social network communities through an increasing shift in communication and fundamental transformation in real-time content. The first section of this book will examine how the hyper-connectivity between social media and real-time content has altered the fashion system's concept-to-consumption (design-to-commerce) model. Real-time social media communication has evolved from the new digital landscape created during the turn of the new millennium. Before confronting this transformation, it is necessary to review the previous fashion zeitgeist in order to understand the changes in store for the next generation of managers and marketers.

The impact of social media on the business of fashion is not only a concern for marketers—it is also a focus area for designers, buyers, merchandisers, and trend researchers. These new communication platforms (i.e., social media, blogs) have ushered in a world of fashion-on-demand consumerism by allowing innovation to diffuse quickly across markets. Social online communities will continue to transform the digital landscape and disrupt the industry by introducing new fashion cycles, season-less fashion trends, and crowd-sourced commerce. This section will examine how both brands and consumers communicate through social feeds and user-generated content. It will also provide insight into the game changers that revolutionized how brands and retailers shared content with their respective audiences.

In addition, this section will explore fashion marketing's new rules of engagement and how marketers connect with the Internet's social communities (tribes). Content sharing through social feeds has transformed the very nature of how we connect with each other. Hence, understanding consumer behavior within the context of social media will give marketers a better idea of how to approach online consumer behavior.

Notes
Tsu, T. (2015), '6 Cognitive Biases You Can Use to Boost Social Media Marketing', *Keyhole*, October 27. Available online: http://keyhole.co/blog/6-cognitive-biases-can-use-boost-social-media-marketing/

Google Search Statistics (n.d.), In *Internet Live Stats*. Retrieved November 25, 2015 from http://www.internetlivestats.com/google-search-statistics/

Part 2: The Business of Marketing Fashion (Chapters 4–6)

The business of fashion relies on strategy development and storytelling: a brand's strategy must adhere to its story using user-generated content, digital-curation skills, creative branding, and strategic marketing alliances (influence and affiliate marketing). Social media is now the primary avenue for consumers to discover the latest styles, trends, and topics of interest. In the age of social marketing, fashion brands need to connect with their customers and maintain open channels of communication. In this section, we will investigate how the fashion landscape is evolving and how social media is proving to be an effective tool in forming brand communities and raising awareness for social issues. Digital storytelling has shifted today's narrative. Instead of merely pushing their messages onto audiences, brands now rely on their customers to become active participants and share their respective stories.

Social media platforms can change quickly, but what remains unchanged is that consumers need to connect with like-minded communities through imagery, text, and online blogs. The insatiable demand of consumers has forced social media marketers to function as developers of interesting and engaging content. Every day, 400 million "snaps," 500 million "tweets," 55 million status updates, and 400 million Instagram photos or videos are uploaded (Tsu, 2015), making it inherently difficult for brands to stand out in this densely populated space. Currently, Google processes over 40,000 search queries per second on average, which translates to over 3.5 billion searches per day and 1.2 trillion searches per year worldwide (Google Search Statistics, n.d.).

In order to increase their visibility, brands now utilize search engine optimization to direct searching consumers to their respective platforms. Social media platforms continue to surface at a rapid rate, thus applying pressure on marketers to provide meaningful content that will inspire, entertain, and ideally convert online engagement into sales. The era of the conventional customer segmentation is over—today's marketers gain insight from data derived from user interactions throughout the social media space. New, actionable data points and consumer personas have enabled brands and retailers to engage with their audiences like never before, allowing them to customize their social media strategies toward markets of interest.

01

PART 1
THE DIGITAL LANDSCAPE TRANSFORMS THE FASHION INDUSTRY

DIGITAL DISRUPTION OF THE FASHION INDUSTRY

Chapter Objectives
- Explore the traditional fashion landscape before the emergence of social media
- Discover the ever-changing fashion system
- Examine how social media democratized the fashion industry
- Understand the digital disruptions that have forever changed the fashion industry
- Discover the blogosphere revolution
- Understand the strength of the fashion community
- Discover the future of runway
- Study the evolution of fashion intelligence

1.1
Fashion disrupted through consumers' need to consume and share endless "postable moments" in real time.

INTRODUCTION

The business of fashion has undergone a revolution in the digital age of social media. It has democratized, disrupted, and even shifted the business model of the traditional fashion system. Most fashion industry veterans barely recognize the industry from a decade ago and continue to adapt to the emergence of new technologies and their influence on the new fashion consumer. This transition is not limited to marketing and management, but permeates to the core of design itself. While blogs and social media have influenced the speed of fashion-to-market, it is important to examine the way in which the cycle of trends and the adoption of fashion impacts the industry as a whole. In this chapter, we will take a closer look at the fashion industry from the beginning of the digital age (1990s) to the information age of the millennium. To forecast where the "business of fashion" is heading with the fast pace of social media behind it, we must first reflect on the fashion system before the disruption of social media. The traditional methodology of the fashion ecosystem has been rewritten; consumers' need for immediacy in receiving products and their demand for faster accessibility to trends contribute to the shift in the fashion industry. In this chapter, insights will be given into the pre-social media fashion industry and the building blocks of customers' adoption of fashion trends. Consumers' fashion interests derive from a collective response, globalized with the boundless reach of social media.

While this disruption has enabled fashion marketers to become closer to their customers, they have had to first understand the shifts that are affecting the industry as a whole. The fashion industry's entire ecosystem goes to great lengths to ensure that they offer goods and services that coalesce with consumer needs and desires seamlessly. Historical, economic, societal, and technological variables have always had an impact on fashion sales. This is true of any industry; however, today, the fashion industry has embraced this series of impactful disruptions as "business as usual." From the Industrial Revolution to women's suffrage, NAFTA, and the introduction of the Internet to mass consumption in the 1990s, the industry has been forced to adapt repeatedly.

Of these movements, social media's buildup of the "Information Age" and "Online Communities" have proven to be one of the most dramatic shifts to ever affect the fashion industry. In this chapter, we will explore the fashion industry before social media, and how the emergence of user-generated content democratized the industry as a whole. Additionally, the power of online social communities appears to be able to alter a brand's role in the marketplace. It permits a role reversal in which the industry doesn't merit chasing consumer cues and creating content in real-time to attract prospective customers. We will introduce and begin to examine four disruptions of the fashion industry, based on the evolution of the Internet and the impact of social networks on the future of fashion.

" FASHION IS RIPE FOR DISRUPTION… BECAUSE A LOT OF THE WAYS THINGS ARE DONE NOW – FASHION-OF-THE-WEEK SHOWS, BUYERS, VERY POWERFUL EDITORS IN MAJOR FASHION CAPITALS – THESE WERE THE WAYS THAT TRENDS WERE DISTRIBUTED, AND THEY WEREN'T VERY DEMOCRATIC. BUT THE INTERNET DEMOCRATIZES EVERYTHING."
MANISH CHANDRA, FOUNDER AND CEO OF POSHMARK
(*SILICON VALLEY BUSINESS JOURNAL*) (XAVIER, 2014)

THE FASHION LANDSCAPE BEFORE SOCIAL MEDIA

The fashion system before the advent of real-time social media feeds followed predictable boundaries of time and space. Fashion collections were set, styles were anticipated, and fashion venues for the collections were globally established, thus setting the tone for the fashion season. The fashion system was determined and controlled by a method that ran as the exclusive business of fashion through the 1980s and 1990s. Consumers were not privy to previews of designer collections, nor did they have any tools to monitor fashion shows in real time. By the beginning of the twenty-first century, technological advances such as Apple's 2007 smartphone, the iPhone, social media's open-platforms, and Web 2.0 applications began to transform both the creation and marketing of fashion. While this change created a disruption within the fashion industry, it is necessary to understand the fashion system before social media platforms became an active participant in the process.

Social media is "a group of Internet-based applications that build on the ideological and technological foundations of Web 2.0, and that allow the creation and exchange of user-generated content (Kaplan and Michael)." The adoption of social media changed the way consumers communicated and connect in our modern culture, but it also opened doors to a new way to unite globally with others. There are over two billion active users on social media. While it may have began as a way to connect with friends and family it has now evolved as a powerful tool for brands to connect with consumers.

The Fashion System of Yesterday

Before social media, consumers adopted trends at a much slower pace, maintaining a leisurely driven fashion cycle (number of trend adopters over time). Consumers before social media were also more passive recipients, approving (and rarely rejecting) the industry-driven pre-selected collections presented to them in stores. The flow of goods through the fashion system (design concept and retail supply to consumers) shared a similarly moderate pace. However, after the social media movement, highly demanding, digitally connected consumers imposed intense and unprecedented pressures on the fashion system. Social media's real-time content has raised consumers' awareness and measurable participation throughout the fashion pipeline. This movement naturally creates new challenges along with new opportunities for retailers, marketers, and suppliers.

Who kept consumers up-to-date with what was deemed fashionable before social media? How was fashion cycled through society by the industry and its influencers before the onset of Google and fashion blogs? Early on, the fashion system opened with the presentation of collections to industry gatekeepers (influencers), a pre-selected, elite group of fashion editors, collectors, buyers, and celebrities. Fashion is also an expression of personal preference, influenced by other, more prominent, groups (celebrities or publishers of fashion information) who inspire the masses through envy or reliability. Such gatekeepers largely defined fashion-acceptable merchandise (Shoemaker and Vos, 2009). This gatekeeper theory also explains how traditional media such as fashion magazines, movies, or coverage of fashion events filtered "how and why certain information either passes through gates or is closed off from media attention" (Shoemaker and Vos, 2009).

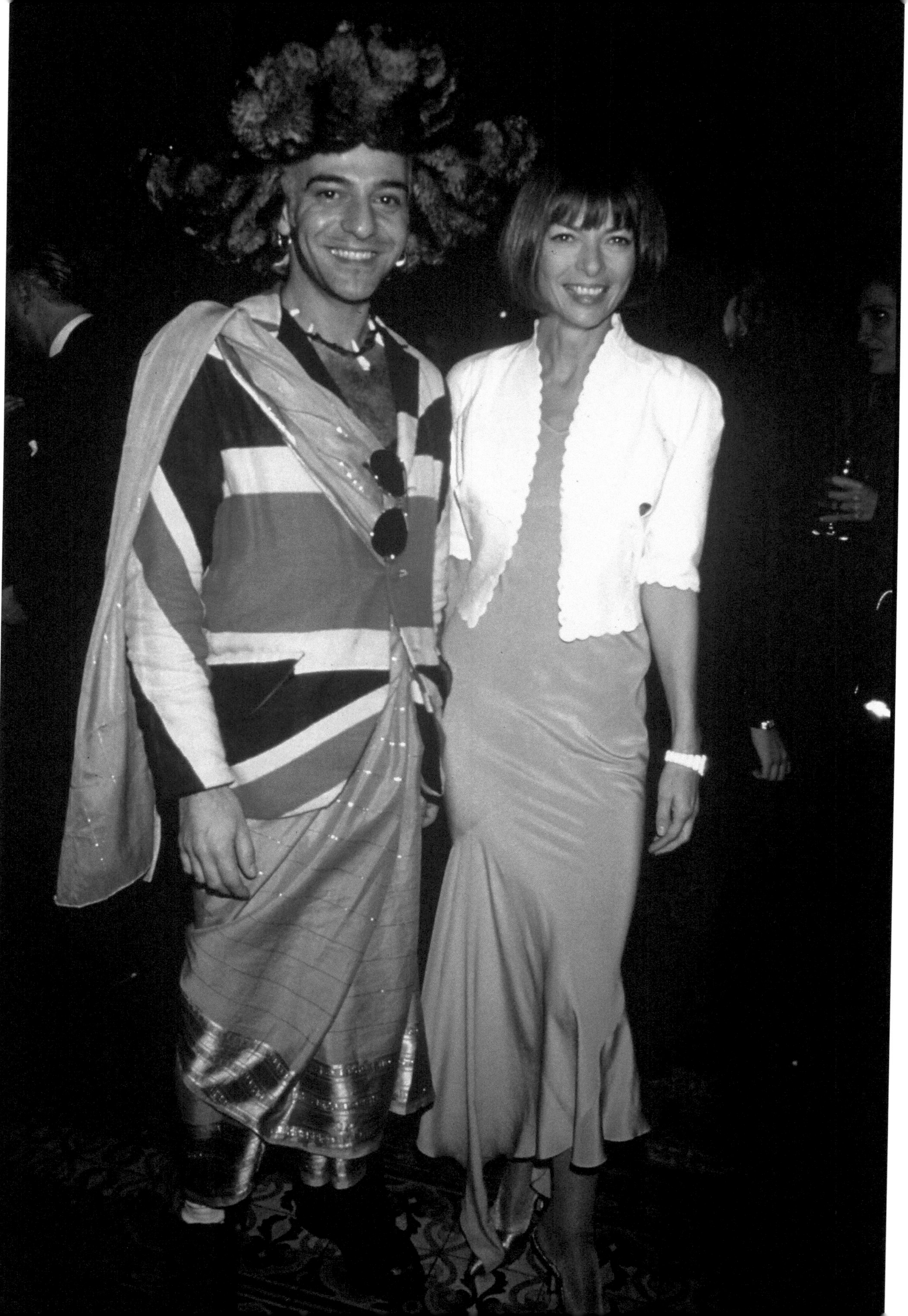

1.2

Fashion Week presentations (sometimes referred to as cat walks in Europe) are based in major world capitals for an exclusive, trade-only audience. These shows featured styles that were thematically aligned with the traditional seasons: resort, fall/winter, and spring/summer. Their primary purpose was to enable the media and consumers to preview a collection before its release for public purchase. Fashion editors gathered insight from shows to align with an editorial calendar in order to begin the storytelling process of the season. Buyers made their purchase decisions based on their interpretations of what they believed their target audience wanted. Retailers incorporated push marketing strategies into the promotional mix (commercials, visual merchandising, catalogs, magazine advertisements, and editorials) to announce the seasonal trends to consumers.

Interestingly enough, both before social media and now, the marketing team is required to execute a highly strategized launch of a newly introduced collection in order to ensure a target market's strong adoption. Delivering the right marketing message continues to require placing advertisements in media outlets, billboards, and retail venues. Marketers craft a strategy around the collection to pique the interest of potential customers in, and in connection to, the goods. In a highly competitive market, each season's campaign seeks to entice the customer to re-invest in a brand by leaving a strong first impression that will hopefully develop into sales conversion. The speed-to-market has to be at a pace that ensures merchandise delivery, once advertisements successfully draw shoppers in.

1.3
One gatekeeper who had a talent for discovering creative talent was Isabella Blow. Blow supported many young, talented designers and believed in them while others did not. Two fashion icons she discovered were Philip Treacy (milliner) and Alexander McQueen. In 1994, Blow attended McQueen's Saint Martins graduate show and bought his entire collection for £5000.

1.2
One example of a traditional fashion gatekeeper is Anna Wintour, the English editor of American *Vogue* since 1988. Through the years, she has worked closely to help young designers through the pages of *Vogue* and Council of Fashion Designers of America (CFDA). Interesting enough, Isabella Blow for a brief time was Wintour's assistant before moving back to England. Photographed here in Paris with fashion designer John Galliano 1993. Wintour was the editor who first discovered Galliano when he first came onto the London fashion scene.

1.4

Historically, the fashion system followed a set, cyclical protocol, which was precisely timed to when the public received access to the collections. In the 1990s, the fashion industry, as a whole, would read reviews of the collections in the only source available, that is, trade journals. This was the platform used by veteran fashion journalists to share their critiques with a voice of approval or rejection of the season's fashion silhouettes, themes, colors, and textures. It is important to understand that this was the fashion industry's first glimpse of runway shows, without the privilege of being seated at the actual events themselves. Within twenty-four hours of these shows, trade publications such as *Women's Wear Daily* (*WWD*), the New York-based trade journal established in 1910, or *Drapers*, the British source of fashion business intelligence established in 1987, would feature extensive coverage of these events.

Alex Badia, *WWD* style director and men's fashion director, stated in an interview for *WWDMAGIC* that negatives of photographs from the early-90s Paris fashion shows would be flown to New York to be developed and sent to press for print the following morning. The final results would then be printed in trade newspapers the very next day, whereas the majority of full collections in an edited trade-only publication (such as Italian fashion magazine, *Collezioni Donna*) would take months to surface. The content published during the early stages was strictly intended for industry use. Trade-only content would have a large price tag attached to it and would be unavailable to consumer-based stores. Through this distribution of content, retailers and editors maintained tight control of the editorial and marketing strategies behind fashion collection launches.

Women's Wear Daily first appeared as an insert in the *Daily Trade Record* (later named DNR), and aimed to supply relevant news to "important men in all departments of women's wear." See "Our Excuse for Being"—a reproduction of the paper's mission statement (Alexrod, 2008).

Zeitgeist

Fashion trends are a reflection of "the spirit of the times" or Zeitgeist. According to Vinken, "the goal of determining a trend is to be able to monitor that it achieves full integration among the majority" (Vinken, 2005). Blumer (1969) agrees that individuals choose among competing styles that connect with the current Zeitgeist.

TRADITIONAL FASHION TRADE PUBLICATION "OUR EXCUSE FOR BEING"
Mission Statement from *Women's Wear*

"It will be the aim of the publishers to present to its subscribers a succinct epitomization of the most important happening and events occurring in the women's wear industry. The scope of the publication will be to cover the factors between the mill and the merchant. There is probably no other line of human endeavor in which there is so much change as in the product that womankind wears. This brings about an enormous amount of traveling, and the result is that important men in all departments of women's wear are scattered everywhere over the earth's surface and lose track of events and happenings, which it will be our purpose to try and chronicle as briefly as possible, so that these men can pick up and at minimum of time and expense keep posts. A knowledge of what has transpired is most important and Women's Wear will aim to do this."

Women's Wear, Vol. 1. No. 1. (June 1910)
The original *Women's Wear* mission statement

1.4
1951, US buyers at the Autumn-Winter fashion show in Florence

Fashion News in Traditional Media

Consumer-directed news about the fashion industry is a new facet of the twenty-first century. While there were a few fashion distribution channels supplying news to the fashion industry in the 1980s and 1990s, it was nothing like today's current stream of content. Traditional coverage expanded with two television programs: CNN's *Style with Elsa Klensch* and MTV's *House of Style* with Cindy Crawford. These shows gave the average consumer a rare glimpse into the world of fashion. CNN's broadcasts on the world of fashion, beauty, and décor came first and aired from 1980 to 2001, while *House of Style* aired between 1989 and 2000 (re-launched in 2012). Fashion loyalists eagerly awaited each episode as models and celebrities shared their personal take on fashion in popular culture. Viewers gained a better understanding of the latest fashion trends, ultimately opening the door for average consumers to access what was once considered secret industry insight.

1.5

1.5
1995 CNN's *Style* television fashion commentator Elsa Klensch (on right) shown here with US fashion designer Donna Karan (on left).

1.6

1.6
1991 MTV's *House of Style* television commentator Cindy Crawford (right) interviews German super model Claudia Schiffer wearing Italian designer Gianni Versace.

" COOL HUNTING IS NOT ABOUT THE ARTICULATION OF A COHERENT PHILOSOPHY OF COOL. IT'S JUST A COLLECTION OF SPONTANEOUS OBSERVATIONS AND PREDICTIONS THAT DIFFER FROM ONE COOL HUNTER TO THE NEXT AND FROM ONE MOMENT TO THE NEXT."
THE NEW YORKERS (GLADWELL, 1997)

The Directional Flow of a Trend before Social Media

Like any successful enterprise, the fashion industry constantly adapts to social and economic changes that impact supply and demand. The fashion system, which encompasses the process of fashion from concept-to-consumption, includes influential consumers whose engagement with fashion novelties pushed trends forward to reach an even wider audience (Rogers, 1995). New trends must be adopted in order for the fashion cycle to evolve. Rogers (1995) defines the diffusion of innovation as "the process by which an innovation is communicated through certain channels over time among the members of a social system" (p. 35). Innovations are initially adopted by a few forward-thinking consumers (innovators), proceeded by the early adopters, early majority, late majority, and lastly by laggards. Before social media, traditional entertainment media (magazines, newspapers, television, movies, etc.), in-store visual merchandising, and word-of-mouth (WOM) set the rhythm of exposure and interpretation of trends. Prior to the rapid increase of user-generated content through social media, a much more gradual adoption process of fashion trends existed locally, nationally, and globally.

Innovative trends that differ from what is currently "in fashion" help keep the fashion cycle (Fig. 1.7) rolling. Consumers search for what is "new" and are not currently part of their respective inventories. The cycle of a trend requires both communication within a social system and a path by which communication migrates to another social group. Before the advent of social media, social circles of consumers embraced such influences as friends, family, acquaintances, and influencers from the print, television, and movie media.

Since the 1980s, fashion forecasters (Doneger Group, Tobé Report, Bill Glazer & Associates, Promostyl), buyers, designers, and retailers have looked to street fashion for inspiration. They began to collect and categorize street fashion shots to interpret and predict future trends from a consumer's point of view. The goal was to find something in the early stages from street fashion, "borrow" it from the early adopter, and share it with the early majority. Fashion forecasters and designers scouted locations around the world, collecting imagery and inspiration wherever they went. In contrast, owing to the prevalence of today's digital fashion communities, such as Polyvore and Pinterest, those forecasters and designers can pull opinions (behavior measured through data) from millions of fashion-minded consumers using the website. They can then share with the user what is popular or "trending" on the website. In chapter 6, we will explore how fashion data is shedding new light on the future of trend forecasting in the digital landscape.

Street fashion was closely monitored by the fashion industry as a runway on the streets. Still, consumers had little access to it on a global scale. Online social communities and outfit-sharing posts were still a decade away from realization. In early 2000, fashion bloggers were not reporting on runway collections, nor were brands live-streaming their runway shows. For example, if Gucci showed a jumpsuit with a seventies flare during Fashion Week, the show rule of "no public access" would still prevail and the generality of consumers would not be able to demand what they had not yet seen. Before social media, shows such as these were exclusive and only a select group of influencers had access to these. The only photographers allowed to shoot the shows were members of the press, strategically located at the end of the runway. The general consumer would have to wait an additional four to seven months in order to preview these looks.

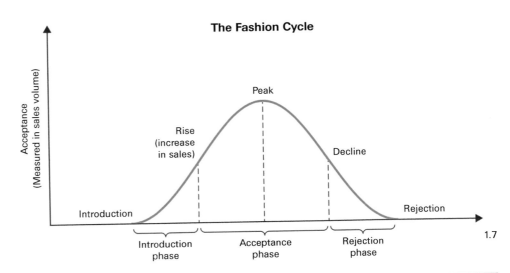

The Fashion Cycle

1.7
The Fashion Cycle (Adapted from https://rampages.us/chandlerbing/2015/07/08/the-process-of-fashion-forecasting-and-what-would-we-do-without-it/)

1.7

THE EVOLUTION OF THE FASHION SYSTEM

The fashion industry has always been fast paced, adopting changing styles and shifting the latest fashion movement through popular culture. The Internet's evolution over the years has been a key contributor to increasing the momentum of fashion information reaching consumers. This shift began as the new millennium approached, with the emergence of a handful of fashion-focused websites, which began producing fashion content online for the fashion-conscious consumer.

1.8

The Transition of Fashion Information

One innovator to join the conversation on the Internet was visionary Parisian designer Jean-Paul Gaultier, who invited viewers for a virtual walk around his online boutique (the first of its kind). Two innovative websites that offered fashion news, FashionNet.com (est. 1995) and theFashionSpot.com (est. 2001), sprang up with an emphasis on Business-to-Consumer (B2C) rather than Business-to-Business (B2B). Susanna Lau of Style Bubble blog, one of the first well-established UK fashion bloggers, shared her view on the world's pre-fashion blogger movement in 2012. In the book titled *Style Feed: The World's Top Fashion Blogs*, Lau remarked that her first connection with fashion and technology occurred upon finishing her degree at university. Lau states, "Everyday I would escape from the lectures and seminars and log on to The Fashion Spot, a community forum where fashion lovers and industry insiders could pour over collections, models, magazine editorials, and personal style. I succumbed to having a second life on the Internet, chatting to people I had never met in person and sharing parts of my life with strangers long before the explosion of Facebook and Twitter" (Oliver & Lau, 2012).

Despite being seemingly trivial in light of today's fashion climate, this change was critical in the evolution of the fashion online community that was designed for the consumer to share and create content across the digital landscape. Lau was not alone in her interest in fashion and the world that surrounded it. New fashion-focused forums, such as LiveJournal, Blogger, and MySpace, attracted an entire generation of creative, style-driven consumers who were given platforms to comment, share, and embrace new discovery media. These social outlets used applications to foray into fashion territories that had not been mapped by the public. As time passed, advances in social media enabled the devoted fashion follower to actively participate in this newfound fashion world of blogs, websites, and social media networks of communities. Participation was key for this success as

1.8
Susanna Lau, founder of StyleBubble.co.uk blog. Lau now works full time on her blog as well as writing for *Elle* and *Dazed Digital*.

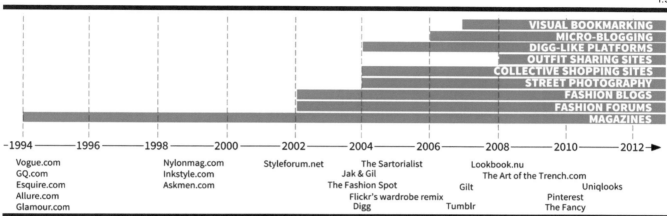

VISUAL BOOKMARKING
MICRO-BLOGGING
DIGG-LIKE PLATFORMS
OUTFIT SHARING SITES
COLLECTIVE SHOPPING SITES
STREET PHOTOGRAPHY
FASHION BLOGS
FASHION FORUMS
MAGAZINES

−1994 ——— 1996 ——— 1998 ——— 2000 ——— 2002 ——— 2004 ——— 2006 ——— 2008 ——— 2010 ——— 2012 ➤

Vogue.com	Nylonmag.com	Styleforum.net	The Sartorialist	Lookbook.nu
GQ.com	Inkstyle.com		Jak & Gil	The Art of the Trench.com
Esquire.com	Askmen.com		The Fashion Spot	Gilt · Uniqlooks
Allure.com			Flickr's wardrobe remix	Pinterest
Glamour.com			Digg	Tumblr · The Fancy

1.9
A Timeline of the Online Fashion World: This figure shows what Dolbec and Fischer captured in terms of the emergence of online fashion media taking action with the adoption of an online presence. Source: Pierre-Yann Dolbec, Eileen Fischer. "Refashioning a Field? Connected Consumers and Institutional Dynamics in Markets." *Journal of Consumer Research*, 2015; 41 (6): 1447 DOI: 10.1086/680671 / By permission of Oxford University Press.

1.10
Worth Global Style Network is a service website that offers faster content compared to traditional forms of media (e.g., newspapers and magazines). While they have a strong presentation merging their company with StyleSight. com, today, they have well-attended presentation, both on and off line, about trends at both the micro and macro level. The photograph shows WGSN during Mercedes-Benz Fashion Week Russia in Moscow, Russia.

well as engaging user-generated content practices of sharing personal style photos or haul videos. Haul videos are a narrative approach of sharing recent purchases (fashion, beauty products, DIY ideas), including details and ideas surrounding the products.

This shift from B2B to B2C fashion insight began to challenge the very foundation of the fashion industry. The industry's initial reaction was to approach the Internet as a commerce hub; however, the dot-com crash of 2000 caused it to begin taking note of how the Internet was transforming into a valued online community for engagement. The fashion industry was trying to remain on the forefront of technology and incorporate new methods of receiving insight, but more consumer-based websites

around the fashion industry were appearing quickly, armed with more insider-based content than others. It reached a point where the fashion industry was lagging behind consumers' tastes, resulting in retailers beginning to fall behind. In 1998, a UK company took note of how the industry needed to modify the way it received content on trends, consumers, and the retail environment. Worth Global Style Network (WGSN) broke into the world of B2B online trend forecasting, providing extensive online content for a subscription fee. The information was developed by a global team of researchers and flooded the website with content that used to take months to provide to fashion channels. Designers, merchandisers, buyers, and marketers began to utilize the content instantly in order to keep up with market speed.

Digital Transformation of the Fashion Industry

The escalation of consumer expectations directly results from increased access to trends through social media feeds. The speed-to-market of fashion developments is nearly impossible to meet. Fashion shows are live-streamed and photographs are immediately uploaded from mobile applications directly onto social media networks from the front row of top runway shows. Consumers have begun to adapt to the fashion-on-demand mentality and don't believe in waiting for a product in the traditional sense (months after the show). Consumers demand instant gratification of their fashion desires with each double-tap on Instagram or newly curated board on Pinterest. The human attention span is shortening, and consumers no longer wish to wait for the release of a collection six months after its debut. Thus, they demand the very latest, instantly. The pressure on the fashion industry to produce at an ever-ratcheting pace continues, which is a growing concern in the world of fashion today.

The notion of "a trend is over before it begins" means that by the time the merchandise is shipped to retailers, consumers will already have moved on to another trend. Still, customers gravitate towards brands that can most quickly provide insight to what is currently trending at that moment. Consumers are traditionally attracted to the "new" factor of fashion trends, but in today's digitally connected world, the FOMO (Fear of Missing Out, detailed in chapter 3) fuels the consumers' drive to "possess immediately" whatever they see on social media platforms.

In 2009, *WWD* reported that the Council of Fashion Designers of America (CFDA) held a town hall meeting with designers, retailers, and fashion journalists to review the entire "hyperactive fashion system" (Feitelberg and Karimzadeh, 2009). Presenters agreed that this shift in the fashion system grew out of the digital communication revolution, which had already begun to refocus fashion weeks and presentations onto consumers' use of social media.

The readiness of the industry to create brand awareness through social media tie-ins at runway shows has, perhaps ironically, contributed to consumers' discarding of trends even before the collection is shipped to the stores. In a CFDA meeting, Donna Karan, Anna Wintour, and Diane von Furstenberg met to brainstorm how they might rescue the fashion industry from this threat. Donna Karan, long a proponent of showing and selling clothes in-season, took the opportunity to challenge the fashion cycle and consumers trying to understand fashion season on the digital landscape provided to them. Seasons are getting pushed together and the industry is trying to incorporate what they have in stores to reflect what consumers are seeing on their social media feeds, but it continues to confuse all parties involved. Karan said, "We should truly focus on the problem and the solution. The consumer has been trained to buy on sale. The clothes in stores are not in season, so she is confused. Why should she go out and spend money early in the season, when in fact come September and October, when the season

" RUNWAY SHOWS DON'T MATCH RETAIL EXPECTATIONS; DESIGNERS CAN'T KEEP UP WITH ORDERS; AND CUSTOMERS CAN'T BUY A COAT IN WINTER. BUT IT'S HARD TO KNOW WHO'S TO BLAME? . . . THE PUBLIC CLICKING ONLINE TO BUY DURING BURBERRY'S LIVE-STREAM RUNWAY SHOW MONTHS BEFORE THE CLOTHES ARE EVEN SEWN? INTERNET SHOPPERS HITTING ON SPECIAL DELIVERY PIECES FROM NET-A-PORTER THAT NO ONE ELSE WILL HAVE AT LEAST FOR THE NEXT TWO WEEKS?"
SUZY MENKES (MENKES, 2013)

1.11
Attendees at the live runway show capture the moment from the POV of their smart phones and tablets to share immediately with their audience. These real-time moments are changing the runway culture forever.

actually changes, the next season is there and it's called resort?" Karan's remarks confirm both digital and social media control over the fashion system and creators' fear of this control. KCD president Ed Filipowski stated that "it's probably a good time…for the industry to come together and look at how we need to adapt to how the landscape has changed." One fact that clearly stirred conversation, if not controversy, was that the speed of the Internet, social media, and blogs made clothes shown on the runway seem dated before their delivery to consumers (Feitelberg and Karimzadeh, 2009).

DEMOCRATIZATION OF THE FASHION INDUSTRY—INFORMATION AGE

Prior to 2006, the fashion industry carefully curated and pre-selected the looks it would share with the public through email outreach, banner ads, catalogs, visual displays, in-store retail merchandising, and other non-digital channels. The momentum behind fashion trends had much to do with the linear business model of fast fashion for mass-market retailers like Forever 21. Fast fashion retailers achieve maximum productivity through efficient planning and manufacturing technologies that increase speed-to-market, and thus the concept-to-commerce process (design, manufacturing, distribution). Some retailers utilized vertical integration (manufacturing, distribution, retail) that ensured the seamless marketing of fashion trends within a month of production, allowing consumers to accept it before more accessible venues cheapened them. Merchandise that are yet to achieve a full cycle of acceptance would be marked down in price to make room for the next on-trend merchandise on the floor. This fashion cycle continues to spin ever faster, consigning trends ever more quickly to the realm of has-beens.

The Evolution of Real-Time Fashion Information

Both the pace and direction of trend adoption hinge on exposure to the public, whether from media or first-hand experience. Access to real-time fashion, through top influencers' social media feeds and live-streamed fashion shows, disrupts the classic mode of diffusing innovation, enabling almost any consumer to view merchandise before it becomes available for purchase. Social confirmation of a trend is now measured through engagement and acknowledgment of social media feeds, trends "liked" and commented on, and those shared by the new digital native gatekeepers (digital influencers and fashion bloggers). The "likeability" of a trend can now be measured and evaluated by consumers through social media feeds. Owing to social media, the transmission of images, video, and text allows fashion-conscious consumers to obtain front-row seats to international runway shows and exclusive launch parties, showrooms, and trade-only events. This in turn has ignited consumers' sense of entitlement to know more about "behind-the-scenes" moments of the fashion industry. Bloggers were the first to share this fashion-privy content, giving the industry no choice but to share information with consumers to compete with this movement. By 2011,

1.12

1.12
In Fall/Winter 2014, Moschino unveiled a collection inspired by fast food chain McDonald's and capturing the move towards "fast-fashion" and the speed of trends at retail.

1.13

1.13
J-Lo's green Versace dress led to the creation
of Google Image search.

the walls were completely torn down and there were more fashion bloggers attending runway shows than members of the press. The democratization of fashion clearly began with the bloggers and the shift in the role of communication in the digital landscape.

High social-media engagement explicitly reveals consumers' desire to discover new trends and to obtain them quickly. Online fashion communities such as Lookbook.nu were founded on the principle that the latest coveted styles, outfit posts, and like-minded fashion insights need to be shared immediately within the community. Exposure to trends on social media platforms can also be measured by social reach and impressions through "likes" and "shareability" on platforms such as Pinterest and Instagram. The fashion industry utilizes the **social intelligence** gathered to create algorithms, enabling it to track trends showing good traction. According to the Future of Retail Report by PSFK research, it was "found that retailers and brands are leveraging intelligent algorithms and social data such as a person's "likes" and "pins," as well as those of their friends, to create a more personal and curated shopping experience for their customers. These automated services, which can also tap into previous transaction history, help simplify the process of shopping by building a user-centric stream of recommendations and available offers focused on delivering relevancy and aiding in the discovery of new products" (Ryan, 2012).

Fashion Influences Technology: A Dress Inspired Google Image Search

According to Google's executive chairman, Eric Schmidt, J-Lo inspired Google Image. Prior to J-Lo's now famous Versace dress she wore to the 2000 Grammy Awards, there was no way on Google to search for images. The former method was to search for keywords and hope that the desired image(s) would turn up. In 2000, J-Lo's dress was the most popular search query that appeared on Google. Thus, Google Image search was born.

" **MORE THAN GOING TO A SHOP AND HAVING A LOOK, YOU FIND SOMEONE YOU FOLLOW ON INSTAGRAM OR A BLOG. IT BECOMES A LIFESTYLE RATHER THAN A TREND. WE'RE MOVING FROM BEING TREND-FOCUSED TO LIFESTYLE-FOCUSED... SOME TRENDS TURN OUT TO BE SHORT-LIVED, WHEREAS OTHERS CONTINUE TO EVOLVE AS THEY ARE MORE ABOUT LIFESTYLE CHOICES AND STYLE, RATHER THAN CONSPICUOUS CONSUMPTION."**
ANNE LISE KJAER, FOUNDER OF INTERNATIONAL TREND FORECASTING AGENCY KJAER GLOBAL (ABNETT, 2015)

Bloggers vs. Traditional Press

Suzy Menkes, the highly acclaimed British journalist and Vogue's International Editor, wrote an article that took on the fashion bloggers' position in the industry and international fashion weeks: "The Circus of Fashion." In this controversial article, Menkes compares and contrasts the fashion industry before and after the arrival of social media, and she touches on the role that fashion bloggers play. This was the beginning of change for fashion week, and through this article, the great debate between fashion bloggers and fashion journalists began. Menkes was formerly the fashion editor/critic for the *International Herald Tribune* but now is the international editor for *Vogue*. (To see the full article, please visit: http://www.nytimes.com/2013/02/10/t-magazine/the-circus-of-fashion.html?_r=0)

1.14
Kenzo's Tiger Sweatshirt

Social Media Changing The Trend Landscape

Ruth Chapple, head of content at Stylus Fashion states, "It's making some trends stick, while long ago we would have been over them more quickly. The Valentino rock stud, which everyone expected to be a one-season wonder, has been going strong for eight seasons. The death of the stud was forecasted long ago, but that was very much a social media trend, where the bloggers made that trend stick. On the other hand, social media can quickly overexpose a trend, and kill its 'edge.'" Kenzo's tiger sweatshirt, Chapple recalled, was "over and done within a month" (Abnett, 2015).

CASE STUDY: Street Photography Zeitgeist
GARAGE Magazine

1.15

1.15
Bill Cunningham viewed the Fall 2016 Collections at New York Fashion Week. While sitting at the front row he would often say, "The best fashion show is on the street."

In a documentary film titled *Take My Picture* by GARAGE Magazine, they explore the fashion street photographer and the blogger influencer movement. This impactful film takes the viewer through the lens of the photographer and the movement known as "Peacocking." Tommy Ton (blog Jak & Jil), Style.com and *GQ*'s street photographer, was interviewed about how he selects who he photographs. Tim Blanks, Business of Fashion Editor At Large, who is being interviewed in the documentary, shares his opinion of fashion bloggers and the real-time content that is being shared by everyone involved. "It's part of reality TV, it's part of 'No secrets about anything' anymore because of Facebook and stuff like that. It's a world where everything is just on display the whole time. Everybody has a blog, everybody has a Facebook account, everybody has this, that or the other thing. 'You're part of the dialog, you're part of the process.'"

Bill Cunningham

In the 1970s, photographer Bill Cunningham snapped candid photos of what ordinary New Yorkers wore in their everyday lives. He happened to take a photograph of the always-stunning silver screen star Greta Garbo, published it in the *New York Times* in December of 1978, and began a new career as the paper's street fashion photographer. In 2010, First Thought Films released *Bill Cunningham New York, 2010*, a profile documentary of the renowned street photographer.

1.16

1.16
Smartphones ready to capture runway
moments as they exhibit the latest styles and
instantly share with millions.

THE FASHION LANDSCAPE ALTERED: FOUR DISRUPTIONS THAT CHANGED THE FASHION INDUSTRY

In the early 2000s, during the beginning of the social
media phenomenon, "business as usual" characterized
the fashion industry. Most fashion leaders appeared
to believe in the notion that "this too, shall pass." Even
brands that joined the conversation had yet to figure out
how social media and bloggers could actually benefit
their businesses and lead to increased sales. Although
the industry's transition seems slow in retrospect, all of
it actually happened within a five-year span (2006 to
2010) and continues to evolve through new business

opportunities and blogger-brand collaborations to
shoppable real-time runway shows. The four elements
that so dramatically changed the fashion landscape are
the following:

1. The Blogosphere
2. Style Sharing Communities + User-Generated Content
3. The changing nature of runway: 360° Videos, Live-
   Stream, Virtual Runway, Shoppable Runway, See
   Now/Buy Now, and Consumer Participation
4. The Confirmation of a Trend through Online
   Engagement: Trend Evolution of Fashion Analytics

These four key factors will be looked at in further detail
in the following sections.

1.17

1.17
Paparazzi at New York Fashion Week
capturing the latest street fashion.

" FASHION IS RIPE FOR DISRUPTION…
BECAUSE A LOT OF THE WAYS THINGS ARE
DONE NOW – FASHION-OF-THE-WEEK SHOWS,
BUYERS, VERY POWERFUL EDITORS IN MAJOR
FASHION CAPITALS – THESE WERE THE WAYS
THAT TRENDS WERE DISTRIBUTED, AND
THEY WEREN'T VERY DEMOCRATIC. BUT THE
INTERNET DEMOCRATIZES EVERYTHING."
MANISH CHANDRA, FOUNDER AND CEO OF POSHMARK
(*SILICON VALLEY BUSINESS JOURNAL*) (XAVIER, 2014)

BLOGOSPHERE TAKES ON THE FASHION INDUSTRY

At the beginning of the twenty-first century, the introduction of blogging ushered in a new online persona and environment: the Blogosphere. In the fashion world, these innovations represented a "changing of the guard" as style bloggers and their followers took a place alongside traditional gatekeepers: fashion editors and celebrities. Fashion bloggers and social media influencers, the new gatekeepers, generate content that directly connects with consumers who are now a part of rapidly growing fashion communities. User-generated content gives a glimpse into "a day in the life" of a fashion influencer or fashion peer, alongside his or her "outfits of the day" (#OOTD). Additionally, they prove more approachable and more credible than the gatekeepers of decades past, and average consumers latch onto their availability and honesty, allowing bloggers to aggregate fashion news and opinions.

1.18

Fashion Bloggers' Role in the Industry

We have seen that the previous rules of style innovation were guided by controlled content, which retailers, magazines, and selective outlets provided to the masses. Bloggers ended this virtual industry dictatorship or, at least, forced its somewhat unenthusiastic evolution, by introducing fashion trends to consumers in real time. Without a doubt, digital influencers have changed the game by creating a direct, impactful link with fashion-conscious consumers. Not only have fashion bloggers contributed a new voice to fashion, but they have also opened the doors to a world that was once trade-only. These new influencers attracted a global following by offering an authentic voice with relatable points of view. Bloggers gained loyal followers from valued insights shared on their blog, involving everything from outfit posts to where to find the best deals on apparel. Tween to twenty-something fashion bloggers share content as if they were speaking directly to their best friends. These communities have opened a two-way conversation between bloggers and commenting readers. As bloggers continued to write about fashion trends, deals, and gossip, they quickly realized that the most inspirational content peeked behind the scenes in the fashion industry. The industry recognized that these bloggers had a strong voice in the blogosphere and wanted a piece of this profitable pie. Thus, a select group of influential bloggers with large audiences has been given behind-the-scenes access to exclusive B2B insight that turned it into B2C content designed to be shared with readers. This single, radically new disruption of the fashion industry would begin to change the dynamics of how and why consumers shop, engage with like-minded individuals, and remain loyal to a pre-selected group of brands.

1.18
@Tania_Sarin started blogging to share her style with a few friends. Today with over 200k Instagram followers and a strong engaging audience, she is a valued influencer in the fashion industry.

The blogosphere began with a community of self-published "web logs" (now known as blogs) by individuals within the self-contained world of the Internet. A blog can be defined as a type of content management system (CMS) that includes social features throughout its platform such as blogrolls, comments, trackbacks, and subscriptions (Zarella, 2015). The first fashion bloggers were young writers and fashion enthusiasts who were looking for a platform to share their opinions and insights about fashion. These platforms enabled bloggers to connect to hundreds, even thousands of like-minded individuals with whom to exchange their views. At first, they shared a practical take on the world of fashion from their perspective and provided advice on topics such as shopping to do-it-yourself (DIY) fashion design projects. That emphasis soon shifted as sponsorship and affiliate programs altered the bloggers' primary motivations.

LiveJournal (1999) was one of the first online platforms that allowed bloggers to speak their minds on fashion industry trends and ideas. Since blogs air individual opinions without the imposition of sponsors or publishers, all consumers could now access a safe platform to share their point-of-view as a matter of simple free speech. During this unique stage of online community development, the term "free" characterized both access and opinion. Readers of blogs quickly realized that bloggers were sharing authentic relatable viewpoints, without the influence of other agendas, and swiftly placed their trust in this platform. These self-published blogs soon built a fresh, engaging, and global dialogue available through any Internet connection. Up to this point, fashion content had normally been paid for through magazine subscriptions, so, the notion of free content provided "by consumers, for consumers" proved revolutionary.

Citizen Journalism

The concept of citizen journalism, sometimes referred to as "street" journalism, puts the public citizen in the active role of being a reporter. This is a volunteer position that enables "real people" to disseminate the news or stories they collect and analyze. The rise of mobile phone reporting in real-time, far outweighs the content that is collected by traditional journalism.

These radical changes in communication allowed users not only to follow and discuss but also to purchase full collections online. The blogosphere had become a platform in which fashion consumers resided as part of a new community that eventually became accepted as legitimate online journalism. The unprecedented personal and interactive approach of blogging sharply contrasts with traditional mainstream media's treatment of consumers as both generic and passive. To their readers, fashion blogs smack of authenticity both in their display of practical tutorials and a "look-at-me" approach.

" SOCIAL MEDIA HAS ALLOWED EVERYONE TO BECOME A FASHION CRITIC. I THINK THE RAMIFICATIONS OF THAT HAVE BEEN BOTH GOOD AND BAD. ON THE PLUS SIDE, AN UNPRECEDENTED NUMBER OF PEOPLE ARE EXPOSED TO FASHION NOW, EVEN FASHION THEY COULD NEVER DREAM OF AFFORDING, AND BY DRAWING PEOPLE INTO THE INDUSTRY, SOCIAL MEDIA HAS HELPED MAKE FASHION A TRUE PART OF POP CULTURE, IN THE SAME WAY FILM, TV AND MUSIC ARE, BECAUSE IT CAN BE 'CONSUMED' ON SOCIAL MEDIA, AT THE SAME TIME IT'S CONSUMED IN REAL LIFE."
BOOTH MOORE, SENIOR EDITOR, FASHION HOLLYWOOD REPORTER/PRET-A-REPORTER

BLOGGER ZEITGEIST – A Timeline

1998

- Open Diary is launched as the first tools to assist users in publishing online journals

1999

- LiveJournal launches to be the first International social network blogging service.

2000

- Daily Candy Newsletter Launches. Popular newsletter site delivers interest insight on new fashion and lifestyle information straight to your email inbox.

2005

- A Shaded View on Fashion (ASVOF) by Diane Pernet is launched. Pernet was one of the first digital fashion reporters for trade publication, French *Elle*, and *Vogue* as well as a fashion editor for JOYCE, Hong Kong.
- Scott Schuman began photographing the street-style of "real people" on the street and posting the photos to his blog, The Sartorialist.

2006

- Julie Fredrickson unexpectedly interviews Anna Wintour for her personal blog at New York Fashion Week.
- Susie Bubble, UK Blogger. Susie Lau, based in the United Kingdom, begins her internationally recognized blog – Susie Bubble. It is featured in *Vogue* UK, *Vogue* US, and *ELLE* US.

2007

- Alix Cherry begins Cherry Blossom Girl in Paris after working for Alexander McQueen and Chloé. The name is an ode to the song "Cherry Blossom Girl" by French band AIR.
- Model, socialite, and blogger Gala Gonzalez begins AMLUL.COM. Gonzalez is considered to be the first Spanish fashion blogger. She posts daily with the goal "display, share, and learn."
- IFB (Independent Fashion Bloggers) First fashion blogging association is founded

Aimee Song starts her personal style blog, Song of Style in college. Today, her blog receives over two million page views per month. She complements her site with an active Instagram account, which boasts 3.4 million followers.

2009

- In the United States the Federal Trade Commission (FTC) publishes regulations regarding bloggers and brand advertising.

2010

- Digital Brand Architects digital agency is launched focusing on creating a brand's voice through digital strategy, social media innovation, online talent agency (bloggers), and influencer marketing. The beginning of bloggers being recognized as an important part of marketing outreach in the digital landscape

2012

- London-based menswear blog, The Gentleman Blogger was founded by Matthew Zorpas. Dedicated to men's fashion lifestyle, street style, and shopping secrets. Zorpas also teaches Luxury Management and Communications at universities in the UK.

2013

- The *Blonde Salad* book by fashion blogger Chiara Ferragni is published.
- Fashion blogger Leandra Medine's launches her new book *Man Repeller*.

2003

- Kathryn Finney of The Budget Fashionista was invited to New York Fashion Week.
- Myspace is launched and joins the newly discovered social network (blogging)
- WordPress is launched enabling easier ways to create blogs and websites

2004

- Bryan Grey Yambao begins blogging using alias Bboy777. Begins using name "Bryanboy" in 2004. Launched from his parent's home in Manila, the Philippines.

- The launch of Flickr, a photo-sharing community, begins and sharing images becomes common practice

by Jennine Jacob to support the blogging community.
- London based, Navaz Batliwalla launches Disneyrollergirl an anonymous fashion insider blog about insider secrets while he was working as a fashion director at a magazine in London.
- The microblogging site Tumblr was introduced to the blogging community; founded by David Karp. Enabling re-blogging of posts.

2008

- Marc Jacob names his Ostrich bag the BB in honor of blogger Bryanboy.
- Tavi Gevinson begins Style Rookie at age 11 from a small town in Oak park, Illinois. Gevinson takes the fashion world by storm while giving a new generation a voice on the Internet.
- Rumi Neely starts her style blog French Toast. She began with her eBay vintage store, Treasure Chest Vintage, also in 2008. French Toast continues to have a

loyal following of receives 5.5 million hits per month.
- Curvy Blogger emerges. Gabifresh and The Curvy Fashionista create a space for the plus-size community through personal style blogs.
- Ari Seth Cohen launches Advanced Style blog to pay tribute to some of the most fashionable older ladies and gentlemen.
- Aimee Song starts her personal style

- Career as a Blogger. According to fashion trade paper Women's Wear Daily, Bryanboy boasts that he has made $100,000 annually as a blogger.
- Tavi Gevinson's bow causes uproar between bloggers and journalists at the Dior 2010 runway show. TWITTER: "At Dior. Not best pleased to be watching couture through 13 year old Tavi's hat" @Grazia._Live.

- Leandra Medine begins The Man Repeller. While studying journalism in college Medine begins her journal with a blog to add some humor to the fashion industry while paying respect to the industry itself.
- CoachxBloggers, a major collaboration between bloggers and Coach, created four custom bags that embodied the blogger's personal style.

2011

- The Coveteur is created as a platform for adventures in style, travel, arts, and culture.
- rewardStyle, an invitation-only monetization platform for top tier fashion, beauty, and lifestyle publishers is launched by Amber Venz Box.

2014

- LiketoKnow.it is launched and changes the way consumers view Instagram (IG). Allows IG users to "like" a photo from their favorite bloggers and influencers to receive ready-to-shop product links straight to their email inboxes.

2015

- Harvard University created the first fashion blogger case study of its kind on how Chiara Ferragni of the Blonde Salad makes $8 million annually from blogging.

2016

- Blogger Squads are formed; key influencers attend the same events as a group and create #SquadGoals.
- WWD Reports that the top bloggers make between one to three million dollars a year.

THE FASHION BLOGGING MOVEMENT

Kathryn Finney of *The Budget Fashionista* was the first fashion blogger invited to New York Fashion Week (Burcz, 2012). According to a 2006 *WWD* article, fashion bloggers began to appear at Bryant Park for New York Fashion Week. In 2006, fashion blogger Julie Fredrickson of *Almost Girl* surprised renowned *Vogue* editor-in-chief Anna Wintour with an interview at the New York Fashion Week. At the time, it was unheard of for a non-industry writer to interview an industry powerhouse such as Wintour. The disruptions in the fashion industry continued and the shift in how fashion was communicated to the public persevered with the rise of the fashion blogger. Fashion bloggers immediately posted reviews from the show tents onto their websites. This too deviated from the norm, since most reviews traditionally appeared in trade publications, usually a day after the actual show. More importantly, these fashion bloggers were unafraid to criticize as well as praise what they had seen. While traditional reviewers regularly panned collections they did not like, their opinions were respected due to their reputations. For instance, Julie Fredrickson of *Almost Girl* wrote, "The John Bartlett men's collection is just slightly odd and is a combination of lumberjack bearded men with Tobias Wolf Old School and was not a look I can really grasp" (Corcoran, 2006). Not all bloggers were as harsh as Fredrikson, but all remained true to their voice in order to ensure that readers received authentic points of view.

> **" FASHION OFFERED THIS INCREDIBLE ESCAPE. AND YOU KNOW LINDA EVANGELISTA WAS LIKE THIS GODDESS… AND I THINK TIMES ARE HARD AGAIN, BUT THE ESCAPE ROUTE IS NOT "YOU BEING TAKEN 'SOMEWHERE,' WHERE YOU NEVER GET TO GO. IT'S 'YOU' BEING 'EVOLVED' NOW, EVERYONE IS EVOLVED."**
> TIM BLANKS, EDITOR-AT-LARGE, THE BUSINESS OF FASHION PREVIOUSLY WAS EDITOR-AT-LARGE OF STYLE.COM, AND THE SITE'S PRINCIPAL SHOW CRITIC SINCE 2006. (GARAGE MAGAZINE, 2012)

Tim Blanks, the editor-at-large of *The Business of Fashion*, spoke freely in the documentary film *Take My Picture* by *GARAGE* Magazine about his point of view of how social media has changed the way behind the scenes content (e.g., photos) at fashion shows is viewed by the consumer: from the fashion industry in the early 1990s "supermodels" (e.g., Linda Evangelista) to how real-time content from fashion bloggers has changed the way content is viewed now.

Between 2006 and 2008, the fashion industry began growing skeptical of self-proclaimed fashion bloggers; they were presumed to lack the expertise that would guarantee quality and credible reporting. However, this cultural sphere, once resisted by established brands and designers, has now been adopted into their corporate communication strategies. This does not indicate that all fashion bloggers are influential; in fact, there are more amateur fashion bloggers than professional or influential fashion bloggers. But today's marketing mix includes digital agencies and in-house digital directors responsible for connecting bloggers with brands in order to create impactful collaborations. These highly influential bloggers now possess a gatekeeper position (level of influence), based on their impressive capability to exponentially grow a brand's social following through engaging social content. In chapter 5, we will take a closer look into the monetization of fashion blogs and their impact on the fashion industry.

In another *WWD* interview during the 2006 New York Fashion Week, buyers and traditional (newspaper and magazine) journalists were asked what they thought about the presence of bloggers. Constance White, style director at eBay, stated, "The impact [blogs are] having is the idea that the whole population is taking control and ownership of fashion. As we used to say at *The New York Times*, "Our jobs are in jeopardy. Everybody's a fashion critic. Everyone can comment on whether Reese Witherspoon should have worn the same dress that Kirsten Dunst wore before" (Corcoran, 2006). Fashion bloggers began inviting their readers to follow them through Fashion Weeks, while allowing them to see daily trend reviews. Influential bloggers (measured by followers and level of engagement) were on the move, and aggressively evolving after their first invitation to designer collection previews, runway shows, and private launch parties.

Fashion bloggers now possess a full access pass to the trade-only side of the fashion industry and represent a new, significant press platform. This enables their followers to legitimize the bloggers as fashion experts who are able to attend industry-exclusive events. When fashion bloggers first began posting their personal style photos, everything they did was "shareable" and readers were given complete access to these posts. These bloggers could have possibly had no inkling as to where blogging would take them, but they were certain that consumer engagement (comments, sharing, liking) fueled their fashion posts. Consumers were no longer being educated about trends directly from brands or traditional media; rather, they were receiving.

1.19
Shows are being captured, shared and instantly consumed on Facebook Live, Snapchat and Instagram Stories.

1.20
Independent Fashion Bloggers (IFB) logo

1.20

First Fashion Blogger Association and Community

To assist bloggers in their role as modern fashion gatekeepers, Jennie Jacobs created a website in 2007 to support the blogger community. It was called Independent Fashion Bloggers (IFB) at HeartIFB.com. The community of bloggers could contribute and share their own knowledge about the blogging industry from affiliate programs to the best data tracking programs.

How Fashion Bloggers Changed the Process of Innovation

Word-of-mouth (WOM) is generated by consumers through social media, from one consumer to another, with the use of social transmission through the vast supply of social media. The spreading of a message through social media characterizes social transmission, which may include verbal and nonverbal communications, actions, behaviors, knowledge, and beliefs.

The WOM movement was spread from social media communities, and was led by blogger communities such as Lookbook.nu and Chictopia. Digitally connected consumers rejoiced in having everything at their fingertips through advances in mobile technologies. Social media platforms have lifted the traditional limitations of consumers' access to global trends by providing them with uninhibited access to global online communities.

Transparency has also improved, that is, by permitting and cultivating conversations between brands and consumers. Social media and fashion communities have opened the door to digital influencers (users with a strong digital following) who impact the adoption rate of fashion trends. The spread of trends through social media's reach and impressions has taken the digital word-of-mouth movement to a global level. The hierarchy of a trend is beginning to flatten out, and the trend spreads to the masses quicker than ever, unlike earlier when the pace of trend development followed a more traditional system.

Influential fashion bloggers can impact global communities consisting of millions of individuals. Some of the most notable bloggers include Style Bubble (London), Man Repeller (New York), Song of Style (Los Angeles), and The Blonde Salad (Milan). These influencers became the eyes and ears of their online community audience. "Fashion used to be very dictatorial," notes Constance White, eBay Style Director, but today, these influencers are "moving from the status of commentators to creators" and are viewed as taste-makers (Corcoran, 2006). Fashion bloggers have attained success by sharing and influencing from a new perspective of collective fashion. "The result is that consumers are becoming their own style curators, picking up ideas from online communities rather than just following the trend seen in a magazine," fashion photographer Yvan Rodic said of his street-style blog Face Hunter (Young, 2007).

The Business of Fashion (BofF)
Imran Amed, the founder & Editor-in-Chief

The Business of Fashion (BofF) was founded by Imran Amed. *The Business of Fashion* has gained a global following as an essential daily resource for fashion creatives, executives, and entrepreneurs in over 200 countries. It is frequently described as "indispensable," "required reading," and "an addiction." Founded in 2007 by Imran Amed, a fashion business advisor, writer and digital entrepreneur, *The Business of Fashion* began as a project of passion, aiming to fill the void for an informed, analytical and opinionated point of view on the fashion business. Today, the website has grown to leverage a network of savvy writers and fashion insiders in style capitals around the world, delivering fashion business intelligence on emerging designers, disruptive technologies, and global brands that are making their mark on the industry at a time of unprecedented change. **The following are his thoughts on digital storytelling, written specifically for this book:**

What is your advice on the art of storytelling in the digital landscape? How does the next generation of fashion journalist capture the attention of the highly connected consumers?

"Storytelling has always been a key part of connecting with fashion consumers. Even with the digital revolution, this has not changed. What's different is how these stories are told and how they are delivered. Today, instead of storytelling in PR or advertising with the goal of driving consumers to physical stores, fashion stories are told in a more fragmented way across a growing number of digital and physical touch points.

What's more, brands don't need to rely solely on other media to deliver their messages. Rather they can cultivate direct relationships with consumers via email, social media, and CRM to track and engage their fans across the customer journey.

The other major change is that this conversation happens in real-time, 24 hours a day. It's an ongoing dialogue and conversation that never ends! It's a story that begins but never ends, and brands have to continue to retell and reimagine their story in new, exciting ways that keep consumers surprised."

STYLE SHARING COMMUNITIES; USER-GENERATED CONTENT (UGC)

Online fashion communities have grown to be one of the most powerful collective voices on the Internet. Social websites host fashion-minded groups with strong, average-order-value (AOV) per session, which drives sales through social sharing and social shopping. UGC enables fashion enthusiasts to pool their inspirations and fuel purchases as new users join with comments or social shopping links. Within the creative community, UGC is one of the most valuable currencies today, ensuring authenticity of shared material within the connected community.

Crowd-Sourcing Fashion Communities

Fashion communities are **crowd-sourced** websites, allowing individuals with a common passion to share content and insights within the group. Users collect and share ideas involving inspiring lifestyle images and organize them based on communal preferences. Their communal activities include sharing personal outfit posts, styling tips, shopping links, online scrapbooking, and bookmarking, which are different means to gather and crowd-source common interests in order to create a common space. Members of style communities also consult each other as community-based fashion experts and receive scores (likes or hearts) based on their popularity and rankings (as seen in Polyvore). Consumers who traditionally follow fashion interpretations in magazines can now consult the opinions of others as well as share their own. Platforms that enable UGC disrupt and democratize the fashion industry by creating trend boards, pinning photos from websites, and editing/publishing content. Along with hosting these actions of engagement, websites simultaneously monetize information data collected from consumers' likes or dislikes and brand content. Polyvore (est. 2006), Lookbook.nu (est. 2008), and Pinterest (est. 2010) are some of the most significant online fashion-focused style communities today.

" SOCIAL MEDIA HAS ALSO CREATED A PLATFORM FOR LESSER KNOWN DESIGNERS TO BREAK INTO THE FASHION WORLD, WHICH HAS DISRUPTED THE TRADITIONAL TOP-DOWN MODEL OF DESIGNER TO MEDIA TO CONSUMER, AND MADE FASHION MORE DEMOCRATIC AND TRENDS LESS RIGID. ON THE MINUS SIDE, I DON'T ALWAYS THINK THE DIALOGUE AND ENGAGEMENT ON SOCIAL MEDIA ABOUT FASHION IS THAT CONSTRUCTIVE. SOMETIMES LOOKS ARE DISMISSED WITHOUT KNOWING THE STORY BEHIND THEM OR WORK THAT WENT INTO THEM, IN AN EFFORT TO BOIL A COMMENT DOWN TO 140 CHARACTERS OR A QUICK, DIGESTIBLE QUIP OR IMAGE. AND THE WAY CLOTHING AND APPEARANCE ARE CRITIQUED CAN BE SO HARSH, IT ALMOST REACHES THE LEVEL OF HATE SPEECH."
BOOTH MOORE, SENIOR EDITOR, FASHION
HOLLYWOOD REPORTER/PRET-A-REPORTER

Fashion Communities

Style-sharing communities for fashion enthusiasts allow these individuals to search fashion trends, looks, and inspirations globally by viewing style portfolios created through UGC. Communities can also filter through style-sharers that best match the users' style preferences. This "strength in numbers" enables these communities to influence the diffusion of innovation of fashion trends from one market to another. The community looks to others within itself to study and then incorporate their styles into their own wardrobe. The traditional method of trends being spread from one consumer to another has been disrupted; today, a global market is readily accessible for inspiration. This transnational community has no borders and enables users to share their styles to connect with like-minded individuals on social community platforms. On an average day, a member from a small town in California can discover trends from online communities in Ukraine or Barbados. Examples of social-sharing fashion communities are Lookbook.nu and Chictopia, as mentioned earlier.

LOOKBOOK.NU

Lookbook.nu stretches its global reach from North America to Southeast Asia and was one of the first personal style communities to contribute to crowdsourcing styles and looks from around the world. Founded in 2008 and driven by global user-generated outfit posts, this community supports itself by members uploading looks of the day and having their peers rank them to affirm or dispute trend-forwardness. Lookbook. nu allows consumers a glimpse into a larger market of style enthusiasts who are sharing their own unique takes on fashion. This personal style-sharing collective allows trendsetters and tastemakers to influence and inspire each other with their mined updates of latest looks and street fashion. Lookbook.nu statistics state that their audience is 80 percent female, between the ages of 18 and 34, with 50 percent of them running their own blog or personal website (Lookbook.nu/Advertise); As of today, Lookbook.nu has over three million unique visitors per month with seventy-five million page views per month.

1.21

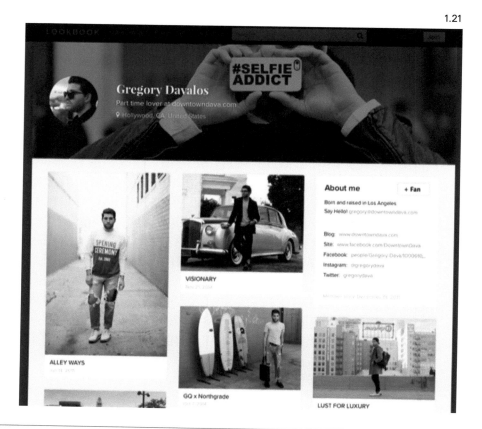

1.21
Gregory Dava of Downtown Dava blog,
GQ Influencer, Lookbook.nu

1.22a

1.22 a
Combination
of fashion and
technology, and a
4-D fashion show
in New York City's
Central Park for
the Spring 2015
collection from Polo
Ralph Lauren at New
York Fashion Week.

1.22b

1.22b
Givenchy Spring/
Summer 2016
collection runway
show opens the
door to the limited
200 seats for the
public. This changes
runway from the
private event for
buyers and press, to
more of a form of
entertainment to the
public.

INTERVIEW:
Rachel Arthur, Founder of Fashion and Mash

Rachel Arthur is an award-winning business journalist specializing in fashion and digital communications. She contributes to titles, including *Forbes, The International New York Times, The Daily Telegraph, Wired*, and *The Business of Fashion*, as well as her own tech-focused news site, Fashion & Mash. She also acts as a consultant on digital strategy and innovation to leading retail and luxury brands, and a mentor to start-ups on the likes of John Lewis' JLAB accelerator program. She regularly speaks on such subjects at conferences around the world, including SXSW, CES, Web Summit, and the Cannes Lions International Festival of Creativity. Rachel was previously based in New York as a senior editor for leading online fashion trade publication and trend forecaster WGSN, where she managed global coverage of the industry from a communications, branding, and technology standpoint.

The power of fashion communities (Pinterest, Polyvore, fashion blogger's communities, etc.) both enable and disrupt the fashion industry. How do you think the fashion industry can learn to unite better with these communities and utilize social media to share their stories?

RA: I think these communities have made a huge difference to the way "we" consume fashion today. This spans from such networks, to blogs, to of course the very existence of social media at large. Today, 81 percent of consumers trust the opinions and recommendations of our peers (including family, friends, and other influencers) over that of brands. It is a bit of a no brainer really, but it just means that we are much more likely to pay attention and accept the thoughts of others than what we are being supposedly preached at by corporations. I think, for brands, this has two implications: 1. That they have to focus on a content strategy that is very in-keeping with the way the internet exists. By that, I mean talking about what they love and not just what they sell. We refer to that as the 80/20 rule—80 percent of the time on other content, 20 percent of the time on product. It varies per channel (Instagram, for instance, focuses more heavily on products if it beautifully curated), but generally speaking it is a good agenda to set. It also means tone of voice to suit the digital generation, that is, more relaxed and informal than, perhaps, would be expected on websites, email marketing, or in-store material. And, the adoption of things like emojis, memes, slang, etc,, as we have seen so many brands do. It just has to be in a really authentic way for it to actually resonate and not seem too try-hard. Some of the best examples of brands doing this are indeed the new generation of brands themselves. Reformation, Everlane, Chubbies are some of the best in my opinion.

The other thing is working with influencers that have the sort of sway in these communities that matter. Brands today are spending big budgets on ambassadors who have significantly more power than traditional media collectively has in terms of numbers of followers and levels of engagement. Instagram is hugely impactful in this space, with multiple influencers (social media celebrities, models, and, of course, the expanded remit of the blogger), who all fit into this space. It is an absolutely necessary move for brands today, but one that takes really considered research and understanding on what the objective is in order to move into it. The influencers' space is a real "wild west" at the moment between who drives social likes and who drives actual conversions.

In what ways has social media democratized the fashion industry and where do you see the fashion industry heading?

Social media has democratized fashion enormously, evolving it from an industry that was once only accessible to the wealthy, to an industry where every consumer, no matter their age, size, salary, social class, or race has a right to entry. The anonymity it affords in so many ways is exactly what has enabled this sort of democratization. Nowadays, consumers expect to be able to have a dialogue with the brands they aspire to, without being judged for whether they are going to actually buy something. In fact, of course, most of the time, they do not. More than anything else, engagement today is about aspiration. But it is also about dialogue; the landscape has shifted from being about brands talking at consumers, to brands talking to them, and increasingly, to brands listening to them. Where once there was apprehension around joining social channels on that very basis, the savvy brands realized that conversations were happening anyway about them online, and that it was necessary to be a part of that discussion in order to help shape what it looked like.

Increasingly we are also seeing this start to impact product offerings. Today's most established digital brands (Burberry and Calvin Klein as inevitable examples, but also the likes of Chanel, Marc Jacobs, and even Oscar de la Renta) are successfully fuelling the appetite for digital content, by feeding these consumers (digital millennials) with the products they CAN afford, namely, beauty, fragrance, and small accessories. We've seen the return of big license deals in-house and the launch of multiple new lines as a result.

> *"Growth these days is, after all, largely coming from digital for such businesses. According to McKinsey, e-commerce will be worth $70bn or 18% of total luxury sales by 2020 (up from just 5% in 2014), and the world's third largest luxury market after China and the US," states Arthur in a* Forbes *article (Arthur 2015a).*

In terms of what is next, we are really seeing brands focus on a much more sophisticated approach to their social media strategy: concentrating on influencers, but more importantly their community of ambassadors and loyal consumers that can help build and share the brand for them. The input of data, more integrated campaigns and a significant uptick in paid media/social budget is helping to make this happen.

Long term, I am also expecting there to be some further categorization of the fashion industry as a result of digital/social media. See this piece regarding the future of fashion weeks:

> Arthur referring to an article she wrote for *Forbes* magazine investigates the changing landscape of runway. *"Caroline Homlish, a New York-based digital brand strategist who recently launched her own agency following senior digital positions at Chanel and Alexander McQueen, agrees communications around collections becomes all the more simplified, not to mention amplified, with a single release date. "Right now as a marketer, we have to come up with a whole set of content around the show, then make decisions about what to hold back and release later. We almost have to do two waves of communications, but the second wave is so much later the challenge has been around how to make it exciting. And you can't really." "If you're going to do something for the public, you need to help them craft the message, and you need to give them tools to tell the story you want told," she says. "That's a scary prospect for a lot of brands." (Arthur 2015a)*

There will need to be some breakdown between what is a "true" luxury brand, what is a "contemporary" luxury brand, what even is a "mass luxury" brand. I imagine that at some point, this will shift what fashion weeks look like, so, we have something along the lines of couture, ready-to-wear, and in-season consumer-facing collections.

THE FUTURE OF RUNWAY

Fashion shows are now being shared with a global reach across social networks and the Internet through live-stream videos, virtual reality, interactive social media, and real-time shoppability with "See Now, Buy Now." The original intent of runway presentations was to introduce the season's collection exclusively to the fashion press and retail buyers. While these motivations remain, the intended audiences of such fashion shows now include a broader public demographic, a facet that its current description "fashion entertainment" adheres to.

Live-streaming

Live-streaming video has positively altered the Fashion Week landscape by unveiling the presentations of designers to a larger audience. Originally restricted to press and major buyers, fashion shows have assumed the new role of fashion entertainment. Who better to pioneer this new approach of sharing creative vision and performance-driven extravaganza than Alexander McQueen? His theatrical and artistic slant keeps audiences riveted, yet uncomfortable at the same time, constantly capturing and sharing particular moments in time through his visionary designs. The exposure offered by live-streaming technology was important to the designer who did not always appreciate how traditional interpreters judged his collections. McQueen embraced the idea that his shows were not just a platform to sell his goods, but a stage to display his imagination (Knight, 2010).

Live-streamed collections permit viewers to experience the enthralling mood of shows through music, motion designs, and intricate set designs. It also empowers design houses to maintain control of their content and share it, on their terms, to a global audience. By embracing live-streaming and online style communities, brands invite their audiences to collaborate and become part of the modern fashion movement. These forms of digital engagement capture fashion-forward consumers en masse, hardly a bad marketing strategy. On a global scale the fashion weeks in 2015 had the most accessed live-streaming collections ever experienced by a global audience. While we had seen this tested in past seasons, the 2016 shows committed to this disrupted shift to provide consumers with the power to purchase runway merchandise without delay off the runway with "See Now, Buy Now" and "The Next Season Now" push by retailers. Brands today are becoming aware they need to capitalize on the consumer buzz on social media from the fashion shows with the ability to purchase the styles after the shows. Today's distribution channels have dramatically shifted, answering demand by instantaneously selling items through live-streaming events. This section covers the specific movements that made it the new normal.

" **YOU'VE GOT TO KNOW THE RULES TO BREAK THEM. THAT'S WHAT I'M HERE FOR, TO DEMOLISH THE RULES BUT TO KEEP THE TRADITION."**
ALEXANDER MCQUEEN (O'CONNOR, 2011)

1.23
Fashion entertainment and art installation seen at the Alexander McQueen Spring 1999 runway show at London Fashion Week.

1.24
While other designers were strategically placing celebrities in the front row of their shows, Valentino took the fashion world by surprise. Ben Stiller and Owen Wilson stunned the fashion industry crowd at the 2015 Fall/Winter Valentino show by making an appearance on the runway. The entire moment was covered on Snapchat and Instagram by onlookers and the Valentino social media team. The two celebrities were also in character as Derek and Hansel to promote their upcoming film *Zoolander 2*.

1.24

How Real-Time Runways are
Altering the Diffusion of Innovation

The democratization of a new frontier for fashion week has moved to live streams, immersive virtual reality (VR) fashion shows, 4D shows, 360° videos, street fashion trends (outdoor runway) and the abundance of bloggers and vloggers. The new normality of real-time fashion shows are more B2C-oriented (rather, B2R: business to real-people) than B2B-oriented. Displaying designer collections to the public has shifted the fashion narrative from editors to consumers in multiple ways, through the visibility of shows on mobile devices, public digital displays, and broadcasted events. Riccardo Tisci, creative director for Givenchy, opens his show for the public to attend his Spring/Summer 2016 women's collections in New York on September 11. Tisci invites 1,200 non-industry guests who have no fame tied to their name. These guests include 280 students and faculty from local fashion schools. The rest of the 800+ guests will receive their tickets online through Givenchy's collaboration with the city of New York called the "public-audience project." Times are changing in the business of runway promotion and while in 2010, the fashion elite who typically attend the show had to get used to sharing the front row with bloggers, now they have to share it with real-people. Modern shows are based on *Social Entertainment*, *Runway to Commerce*, and *Runway Social Media Engagement*.

" VALENTINO'S SHOW, WITH ITS SURPRISE INSTA-BAIT APPEARANCE BY HANSEL MCDONALD AND DEREK ZOOLANDER (A.K.A. OWEN WILSON AND BEN STILLER, WHO WILL REPRISE THEIR MALE-MODEL ROLES IN THE COMING *ZOOLANDER 2*), WAS THE MOST-TWEETED PARIS FASHION WEEK SHOW, WITH TWEETS PEAKING AT 740 A MINUTE."
THE *NEW YORK TIMES* ("HOW KANYE WEST," 2015)

Ken Downing, senior vice president, fashion director of Neiman Marcus, said, "I am an enormous proponent of relooking and recalibrating how we use the fashion show that has become a mega-marketing" event (*Women's Wear Daily* 2015). "The history of fashion shows was to show the buyers and the press the message of the season. But technology has utterly changed everything in our industry. That customer continues to follow Instagram and Twitter and watches the live-stream of fashion shows. When they are seeing clothes, they are less aware of seasons. What they are seeing, they want," he said (*Women's Wear Daily* 2015).

Valentino

The 2015 Fall/Winter Valentino presentation in Paris exemplified the notion that front-row audiences now consist of more than the fashion elite, and the fashion industry is aware of it. Two days before the show, Valentino announced that the brand would be shared on Snapchat through a live stream. Instead of primarily focusing on Valentino's craft, the audience was stunned by the presentation of actors Ben Stiller and Owen Wilson as Derek Zoolander and Hansel McDonald (characters from the film Zoolander) walking down the runway. This performance may have garnered mixed reviews, but it clearly highlighted the rapid change in the nature of fashion shows, as brands continue to court a larger social media presence.

1.25
Dolce & Gabbana embraced the story of the runway collection by having their models take selfies as they walked down in the runway.

1.26
Tokyo Girls Collection

1.26

RUNWAYS OF THE FUTURE:
Setting the Global Stage for Fashion Week

CONTRIBUTING WRITER - KEITH NISHIDA

Runway shows, a fast-evolving marketing platform, and the role it will play in maintaining the complex balance of retailer/consumer demand, is indicative of how brands will now have to foster a stronger and lasting relationship with its consumers, built upon what can be called the "trivergence of retail": entertainment, convenience, and information (Smulders, 2015). How well brands activate the creative configuration of 1) entertainment value 2) convenience in bringing runway to commerce, and 3) information worthy of social media engagement to its future marketing strategy, especially involving fashion week activities and runway shows, will be key to yielding higher return-on-investment for brands stakeholders. Below are examples of brands that have successfully integrated runway shows and fashion week activities with the trivergence of retail.

RUNWAY AS ENTERTAINMENT

Modern-day runway shows have become a marketing activity beyond its basic function of promoting latest collections to media editors and tastemakers; runway shows have now become a spectacle for entertainment worthy of an Instagram post or ten. Ralph Lauren made a splash during its Spring 2015 collection debut during Fashion Week with an innovative 4D presentation, projected against a screen of water. "[H]olographs of models sporting the new spring collection walked on water in the futuristic runway experience. The water-screen projection used four-story tall holographic effects, which showcased models walking through iconic New York City backdrops ranging from The Brooklyn Bridge to the High Line" (Fisher, 2014). It was a futuristic show worthy of getting the waterworks going.

The Victoria's Secret Fashion Show may well be considered the epitome of runway as entertainment. The show was catalytic in fashion brands embracing a true multi-channel multi-media marketing campaign. Victoria's Secret was not the first apparel brand to launch its new media department. However, in 1999, advertisement for its first web-cast fashion show was credited to be the first "dot-com" commercial in Super Bowl XXXIII (American football game).

This cross-promotion garnered one million website hits in half an hour (Durbin, 2002). The first large-scale real-time streaming video presentation of the annual fashion show that same year made fashion history when an overwhelming demand during the show crashed the company website and network throughout the United States.

RUNWAY-TO-COMMERCE (R2C)

Accessibility to live-streaming fashion shows and instantaneous social media feeds available from influencers and show attendees have created a sense of normalcy for modern-day consumers to expect a much shorter turn-around time for products to reach their doorsteps. The disruption of the fashion cycle, combined with heightened consumer expectation for convenience, consequently pressured brands to further integrate an efficient implementation of cross-platform promotional marketing with sales functions. Tokyo Girls Collection, a fashion event in Japan, solved the age-old conundrum of designers showing merchandising ahead of the intended season. During the live runway event, attendees clamored to their smartphones as they instantaneously bought items through the event's digital shop. One must be present at the event to buy the merchandise, affording attendees exclusive access to next seasons' fashions, otherwise unavailable until it hit retailers (Sidell, 2011).

Burberry hosted a runway show viewing party at its global boutiques where guests were equipped with iPads; they were encouraged to select/pre-order items as the clothes and accessories came down the runway. The added benefit of preordering items from the collection (and shipped before they hit retail stores) gave the customer a sense of exclusivity. Jenny Dyson, a creative director, noted that "Burberry's live streaming of its catwalk shows, plus inviting customers to buy directly off the screen, is a clever digital trick to democratize the brand experience without compromising on its brand vision/luxury status."(Barbat, 2013) Burberry's Autumn 2013 runway show was the first livestream on Twitter with "Made to Order" function, where customers were able to view the personalization process as they made purchases on their smartphones.

Topshop similarly enabled its livestream fashion show viewers to shop in real-time by clicking on the looks, ordering clothes/accessories/makeup gracing the catwalk, browsing color options, switching through music options,

downloading the show soundtrack from iTunes, and sharing screenshots through Facebook. Justin Cooke, Chief Marketing Officer of Topshop, called it a "social entertainment and commerce rolled into one." (Indvik, 2012). These R2C systems successfully combined a sense of urgency to purchase and accessibility to show content, otherwise privy only to industry professionals.

SHOPPABLE RUNWAY ON SOCIAL MEDIA

Twitter introduced a "Buy" button, which allows followers to purchase products directly through its platform; this made mobile shopping convenient, allowing brands to expand efforts to convert social media followers into customers (Jain, 2014). During the 2014 London Fashion Week, Burberry integrated the "Buy Now" button feature (Burrows, 2014). This enabled Burberry followers to react immediately to latest fashion products featured down the runway. Lindsay Nuttall, Chief Digital Officer of BBH, an advertising agency, and former global head of strategy & communication of ASOS, a British fashion store, offers this perspective: "Linking everything to mobile means awareness and engagement is never more than one swipe away from converting to purchase, right there and then, wherever they are," (Arthur, 2015b). It transformed the means of consumers gaining exclusive access to items otherwise unattainable via traditional retailing, and furthermore, solidified the future of online retailing bridging the runway to commerce.

Topshop partnered with Twitter during the London Fashion Week, generating real-time data collected from the #LFW hashtag. Wordclouds with shoppable products were generated from tweet results on billboards, six of which were within a ten-minute walking distance from a Topshop store. Additionally, tweets to @Topshop using a highlighted trend (i.e., #pleats or #colourblocking), received a curated shopping list in response. Sheena Sauvaire, Topshop Global Marketing & Communications Director notes "through Twitter's listening power, we can allow [consumers] to shop the trends [and give] them insight and access into runway shows…this will be a first example of real-time shoppable billboards." (Arthur, 2015b) Shoppable "See Now, Buy Now" and sharable social media outlets provide a competitive advantage to converting fashion week activities on/off the runway from purchase intent to transaction.

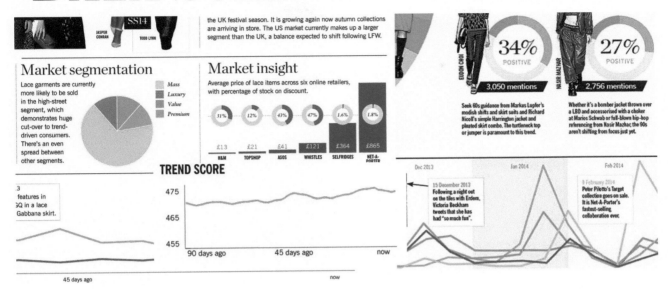

DATA SCIENCE + FASHION

Market segmentation

Lace garments are currently more likely to be sold in the high-street segment, which demonstrates huge cut-over to trend-driven consumers. There's an even spread between other segments.

Mass
Luxury
Value
Premium

Market insight

Average price of lace items across six online retailers, with percentage of stock on discount.

the UK festival season. It is growing again now autumn collections are arriving in store. The US market currently makes up a larger segment than the UK, a balance expected to shift following LFW.

31%	12%	43%	47%	1.6%	1.8%
£13	£21	£41	£121	£364	£865
H&M	TOPSHOP	ASOS	WHISTLES	SELFRIDGES	NET-A-PORTER

TREND SCORE

.3 features in GQ in a lace Gabbana skirt.

475
465
455

90 days ago   45 days ago   now

45 days ago   now

34% POSITIVE — 3,050 mentions

Seek 60s guidance from Markus Lupfer's modish shifts and skirt suits and Richard Nicoll's simple Harrington jacket and pleated skirt combo. The turtleneck top or jumper is paramount to this trend.

27% POSITIVE — 2,756 mentions

Whether it's a bomber jacket thrown over a LBD and accessorised with a choker at Marios Schwab or full-blown hip-hop referencing from Nasir Mazhar, the 90s aren't shifting from focus just yet.

Dec 2013   Jan 2014   Feb 2014

15 December 2013
Following a night out on the tiles with Erdem, Victoria Beckham tweets that she has had "so much fun".

8 February 2014
Peter Pilotto's Target collection goes on sale. It is Net-A-Porter's fastest-selling collaboration ever.

RUNWAY TO SOCIAL MEDIA ENGAGEMENT

Designer Rebecca Minkoff took to Instagram prior to the fashion week to solicit follower's feedback, inviting her users to help pick a look to grace the catwalk. Instagram followers responded to the call-to-action, casting their vote on which styled look from her Spring collection lives to make its debut on the runway (and which to be eliminated from the show).

During the London Fashion Week, Topshop approached five influential Instagrammers to generate original content throughout the week, to which the images appeared both on its Topshop.com e-commerce site as well as on a screened-installation at their flagship Oxford Circus store window (Arthur, 2014). The window display called-to-action the passerby fans, "Be Part of the Topshop social catwalk with Instagram and Facebook"; consumers were encouraged to tag their posts with #topshopwindow, which were then added to the digitally-curated installation. The brand achieved a multi-platform initiative of fashion promotion (both digital and physical), with a seamless integration of Fashion Week happenings to social and retail engagement.

1.27
Fashion Data + Analytics EDITED.com providing insight to the fashion industry leaders.
(More insight from Edited in chapter 6.)

In conclusion, runway shows have transformed into a promotional platform beyond its historic significance of serving merely the industry professionals. The future of fashion week and its runway shows has and will continue to be a critical component for many brands' marketing strategy, as a proven-effective promotional platform for consumer engagement on and off social media.

Keith Nishida is an Assistant Professor of Fashion Marketing in the School of Business at Woodbury University. His research touches on how the industry and its various stakeholders communicate fashion through various media channels.
@FashionMarketing

CONFIRMATION OF A TREND THROUGH ONLINE ENGAGEMENT

Trend confirmation from consumers and the fashion industry are now focused on measuring the social engagement of user-generated content. The measurability of social confirmation through online engagement creates interest in trends as a form of acceptance. High engagement and shares increase the value of the trend and its viral effect to spread rapidly throughout the Internet. Consumers are now following the progression of a fashion trend's social acceptance stats through content shared from sites like Polyvore, who tweet out what is trending on their site through #PolyData. In chapter 6, we will take a closer look at the fashion data company, EDITED.com. Through a one-on-one interview with their lead analyst, we are able to see how the company is providing the fashion industry with insightful innovated data that is contextualized to be actionable.

Confirmation of Fashion Trends by Polyvore Data Tweets

#PolyData provides the Polyvore user with unique insights of what is trending through consumer data such as likes, shares, and use of items available on the website. Polyvore's data intelligence is then shared in a fashion story format through additional social media outlets such as Twitter and Instagram.

" SOCIAL MEDIA HAS BECOME THE BIGGEST TRANSFORMATION THAT WE HAVE SEEN IN THE FASHION INDUSTRY, SINCE I CAN REMEMBER. I THINK THE INTRODUCTION OF SEE NOW, BUY NOW IN FASHION WEEK WILL CONTINUE TO DISRUPT THE INDUSTRY . . . THE WHOLE FASHION SYSTEM HAS BEEN TURNED UPSIDE DOWN BECAUSE OF SOCIAL MEDIA. THE DIRECTION OF FASHION IS NOW IN THE POWER OF THE CONSUMER."
ALEX BADIA, *WWD* STYLE DIRECTOR

1.28

While the fashion industry prepares for seasonless and "See Now, Buy Now" movement, retailers will be looking at runway for a measureable way for social confirmation of a trend. One way will be utilizing the highest-viewed shows on Vogue.com through consumer engagement and confirmation from social media: Adidas Originals X Kanye West Yeezy Season 1 4,578,461 page views (shown in figure); Chanel 3,405,945 page views; Dolce & Gabbana 2,905,544 page views; Valentino 2,547,711 page views; Saint Laurent 2,244,004 page views; Gucci 2,2102,173 page views; Louis Vuitton 2,0225,937 page views (http://www.vogue.com/13288496/most-viewed-collections-fall-2015-runway/). Chanel loses their position from the top viewed show from the year before. Vogue website runway show reviews featured the most-viewed events and their respective readers' comments.

Social Media Influence on The Fashion System; Runway to Commerce

1.29

GATEKEEPERS' CONTENT	MEDIUM	CONSUMER CONFIRMATION	ACTION
Runway Collections	**Live Streamed Directly to Consumers**	**Social Conversation About Trends** **Measurable Social Confirmation Through Levels of Engagement** *(Style.com/Vogue.com ranking the shows that have been viewed the most and showcasing them)*	**Buy It Now – Commerce "Fashion On Demand"** • *Through Brand (Buy Now Button – Burberry Shoppable Runway)* • *Social App (LikeToKnow.it)*
Pre-Viewing Collection *(Fittings, Sneakpeaks before the show)*	**Shared on Social Networks** *(Blogs, social media outlets)*	**Shareability and Reposting of Trends Confirm Further Acceptance or Rejection of Trends** *(Polyvore/Pinterest)*	**Retailers Find Similar Trends from Runway They Have In Stock To Push Consumers To Purchase Now** *(TopShop #LFW Twitter Campaign)*
Outfit Posts from Influencers *(Street Fashion; Guest of the show)*	**Magazines** *(Online)*	*Note: The fashion industry collects consumer data from engagement online to monitor consumers activity around trends (in chapter 6 will review)*	**Runway Collection at Retail Immediately "See Now, Buy Now" or delivered traditionally five to six months later** *(In Season or a Season Ahead)*
Runway Behind the Scenes			

1.29
The process of fashion trends moving from runway or influencers through the social system.

Social Confirmation of a Fashion Trend

Style.com is primarily a B2C publication targeted at fashion-conscious consumers, but the fashion industry should also take note of this published data as a valuable indicator of consumer interest. Style.com confirms what is currently trending on their website to their audience by posting the rankings of what shows were viewed the most on their website, tallying page views whilst also sharing their readers' comments about these shows. This functions as a reader's social confirmation of a particular fashion trend that is derived from number of views. This measureable action from the audience now influences consumers' acceptance of a trend. Before this type of social measurement, online consumers relied on the fashion editors' selections of which designers they considered the ones to watch. Now, this democratic way is based solely on the audience engagement. In chapter 6, we will review how the fashion industry is also using this insight for everything from marketing to merchandising.

Another example of how consumers (and the fashion industry) are able to confirm a trend through social confirmation of community engagement is during fashion weeks. This includes the endless content from street fashion, runway fashion, pre-launches (first exposure to looks behind the scene) and the buildup to the entire event that takes place twice a year, globally (not including the additional seasons). Online social communities, fashion bloggers, fashion editors, designers, and industry experts all add to the online conversations and value through social engagement. Figure 1.29 breaks down how fashion innovation that starts at the runway or street fashion level moves through the social system of fashion in the digital age of social media:

1. Gatekeepers: ultimately control what content the consumers view and are exposed to
2. Medium: the channel of communication that delivers the content (e.g., photos, videos) to consumers
3. Confirmation: engagement measureable through acceptance and denial (e.g., negative comments)
4. Action: the process or movement of purchase (ultimate support)

"I BELIEVE IN 'SEE NOW, BUY NOW'–WE HAVE TO STAY CONNECTED AND GO FASTER,"
~ OLIVEIER ROUSTEING CREATIVE DIRECTOR OF BALMAIN (VOGUE UK, 2016)

EXERCISES

Critical Thinking: How does the "diffusion of innovation" continue to change and alter the fashion industry with the help of social media? Track a trend from the runway to the consumer and follow the path of influence.

Practical Application: Examine bloggers' profiles, comparing blogs from different markets and communities. How do they impact fashion system from sharing content? Review a set of bloggers by market segment (e.g., luxury menswear) and measure their level of engagement received during a fashion week they attended and the trends they promoted.

Business Activity: Review a digital (social media) breakthrough or disruption of technology that is influencing the way brand marketers share content. Look to the "Technology Corner" for insightful up-to-the-minute content.

Journal Article Recommendation to Review:
Pierre-Yann Dolbec, Eileen Fischer
- Refashioning a Field?
Connected Consumers and Institutional Dynamics in Markets. *Journal of Consumer Research*.
Link: http://jcr.oxfordjournals.org/content/41/6/1447

Infographic: Create an infographic timeline of runway fashion adoption to entertainment, e-commerce or consumer engagement.

Technology Corner
- Discover the world of fashion forecasting through a fashion forecasting service such as WGSN.com and EDITED.com.
- News and updates from the tech world can also be viewed at BusinessofFashion.com, Drapersonline.com and WWD.com.

REFERENCES

Abnett, K. (2015), "Do Fashion Trends Still Exist?," *The Business of Fashion*, January 9. Available online: http://www.businessoffashion.com/articles/intelligence/fashion-trends-still-exist

Arthur, R. (2013), "S/S 14 Fashion Weeks—Digital Strategies," *WGSN*, October 14. Available online: https://www.wgsn.com/en/micro/2013/uploads/reports/S_S14fw_socialmedia.html

Arthur, R. (2015a). "Digital Has Irrevocably Transformed Fashion Weeks, Is It Finally Time To Change The Model?," *Forbes*, December 18. Available online: http://www.forbes.com/sites/rachelarthur/2015/12/18/digital-has-irrevocably-transformed-fashion-weeks-is-it-finally-time-to-embrace-and-change/#6e4c2c442666

Arthur, R. (2015b), "British Brands Enabling Fans to Shop Real-Time #LFW Trends by Leveraging Outdoor Advertising," *Forbes*, February 17. Available online: http://www.forbes.com/sites/rachelarthur/2015/02/17/british-brands-enabling-fans-to-shop-real-time-lfw-trends-by-leveraging-outdoor-advertising/

Axelrod, N. (2008), "The Changing Face of WWD," *Women's Wear Daily*, July 31. Available online: http://wwd.com/fashion-news/fashion-features/then-and-now-1693430/

Barbat, F. (2013), "A Digitized Burberry Personalizes Pieces Straight Off the Runway," *Branding Magazine*, July 31. Available online: http://www.brandingmagazine.com/2013/02/20/burberry-smart-personalisation/

Blumer, H. (1969), "Fashion: From class differentiation to collective selection," *The Sociological Quarterly*, 10 (3): 275-291.

Boyd, S. (2014), "RewardStyle and LIKEtoKNOWit founder Amber Venz Box is changing the retail industry," *Forbes*, September 30. Available online: http://www.forbes.com/sites/sboyd/2014/09/30/rewardstyle-and-liketoknowit-founder-amber-venz-box-is-changing-the-retailing-industr/#72eea1646ff7

Burcz, C. (2012), "The Most Important Moments In Fashion Blogging History," *Independent Fashion Bloggers*, July 12. Available online: http://heartifb.com/2012/07/12/the-most-important-moments-in-fashion-blogging-history/

Burrows, V. (2015), "Fashion Tech That's Made It-The Top 4," Bodi.me, October 3. Available online: http://fashion.bodi.me/fashion-tech-made-it-top-4/

Chapman, C. (2011), "A Brief History of Blogging," *Webdesigner Depot*, March 14. Available online: http://www.webdesignerdepot.com/2011/03/a-brief-history-of-blogging/

Corcoran, K. (2006), "The Blogs That Took Over the Tents," *Women's Wear Daily*, February 6. Available online: http://wwd.com/fashion-news/fashion-features/the-blogs-that-took-over-the-tents-547153/

Durbin, T. (2002), "Victoria's Secret," *Glassmeyer/McNamee Center for Digital Strategies, Tuck School of Business at Dartmouth*. Case study #6-0014.

Feitelberg, R. and Karimzadeh, M. (2009), "CFDA's Forum Debates the Fashion System," *Women's Wear Daily*, July 29. Available online: http://wwd.com/fashion-news/fashion-features/debating-the-fashion-system-2224363/

Fisher, L. A. (2014), "Polo Ralph Lauren takes fashion week to the future," *Harper's Bazaar*, September 9. Available online: http://www.harpersbazaar.com/fashion/fashion-week/a3490/polo-ralph-lauren-4d-fashion-show-spring-2015/

Garage Magazine (2012). *Take My Picture* (documentary). 2:27. Available online: https://vimeo.com/61348049

Gibbs, S. (2013), "Edited aims to spot the trends the fashion world doesn't,' *The Guardian*, September 13. Available online: http://www.theguardian.com/technology/2013/sep/13/editd-fashion-trends-big-data

Gladwell, M. (1997), "The Coolhunt," *The New Yorker*, March 17, 78.

Hamedy, S. (2014), "TV ratings: CBS wins night with Victoria's Secret Fashion Show.," *Los Angeles Times*, December 10. Available online: http://www.latimes.com/entertainment/envelope/cotown/la-et-ct-tv-ratings-cbs-victorias-secret-fashion-show-nbc-the-voice-20141210-story.html

Schneier, M. (2015), "How Kanye West Dominated Fashion Month (No Surprise, It Involved Social Media)," *The New York Times*, March 25. Available online: http://www.nytimes.com/2015/03/26/fashion/how-kanye-west-dominated-fashion-month-no-surprise-it-involved-social-media.html

Indvik, L. (2012), "Topshop to debut interactive , shoppable livestream during London Fashion Week," *Mashable*, September 12. Available online: http://mashable.com/2012/09/12/topshop-to-debut-interactive-shoppable-livestream-during-london-fashion-week/#xJY_SXdTvGqW

Jain, T. (2014), "Testing a way for you to make purchases on Twitter," *Twitter Blog*, September 8. Available online: https://blog.twitter.com/2014/testing-a-way-for-you-to-make-purchases-on-twitter

Kaplan, A.M. and Michael, H. (2010), "Users of the world, unite! The challenges and opportunities of social media," *Business Horizons* 53 (1): 61. doi:10.1016/j.bushor.2009.09.003

Knight, N. (2010, January 1), *Plato's Atlantis* [Video file]. Available online: http://showstudio.com/project/platos_atlantis/interview

Menkes, S. (2013), "Sign of the Times: The Circus of Fashion," *The New York Times*, February 10. Available online: http://www.nytimes.com/2013/02/10/t-magazine/the-circus-of-fashion.html

Menkes, S. (2013), "Sign of the Times: The New Speed of Fashion," *The New York Times*, August 23. Available online: http://www.nytimes.com/2013/08/23/t-magazine/the-new-speed-of-fashion.html

Noyes, K. (2014), "What's on trend this season for the fashion industry? Big data," *Fortune*, September 22. Available online: http://fortune.com/2014/09/22/fashion-industry-big-data-analytics/

O'Connor, M. (2011), "Alexander McQueen: Savage Beauty," *Little Lime Dress*, July 26. Available online: http://www.littlelimedress.com/blog/tabid/129/entryid/164/default.aspx

Oliver W. and Lau, S. (2012), "*Style Feed: The World's Top Fashion Blogs*," Munich: Prestel.

Rogers, E. (1995), *Diffusion of Innovations* (4th ed.). New York, NY: Free Press.

Ryan, T. (2012), "Let Me Shop What I Like," *PSFK*, July 14. Available online: http://www.psfk.com/2012/07/auto-curated-shopping-retail-trend.html

Seidler, B. (2013), "I.T.'S in the Bag," *The New York Times*, February 18. Available online: http://www.nytimes.com/2013/02/19/fashion/at-burberry-its-in-the-bag.html?_r=1

Shoemaker, P., and Vos, T. (2009), *Gatekeeping Theory*. New York: Taylor & Francis.

Sidell, M. W. (2011), "Japan's fashion spectacular," *The Daily Beast*, September 3. Available online: http://www.thedailybeast.com/articles/2011/09/03/tokyo-girls-collection-s-japanese-fashion-spectacular.html

Solway, D. (2012, November). The Original. *W Magazine*. Available online: http://www.wmagazine.com/fashion/2012/11/anna-piaggi-fashion-editor

Smulders, T. (2015), "10 new trends in fashion retail," *Mobile Commerce Daily*, October 6. Available online: http://www.mobilecommercedaily.com/10-new-trends-in-fashion-retail

Vinken, B. (2005), *Fashion Zeitgeist: Trends & Cycles in the Fashion System*. Oxford: Berg.

Women's Wear Daily (2015), *NYFW Going Consumers? CFDA Studies Ideas*, December 14. Available online: http://wwd.com/fashion-news/designer-luxury/cfda-boston-consulting-fashion-shows-consumer-10297602/

Xavier, J. (2014), "How tech startups are taking the fashion runway by storm," *Upstart Business Journal*, March 22. Available online: http://upstart.bizjournals.com/companies/startups/2014/03/22/how-tech-startups-are-remaking-fashion.html?page=all

Young, A. (2007), "Face Hunter hits the streets for fashion," *The New York Times*, October 7. Available online: http://www.nytimes.com/2007/10/07/style/07iht-rface.1.7782112.html

Zarella, D. (2010), *The Social Media Marketing Book*. Sebastopol: O'Reilly Media, Inc.

2.1
Hyper-connected consumers within the digital landscape. (Adapted from http://www.supplychain247.com/images/article/Custora_E-commerce_Pulse_Mobile_Report_cover.jpg)

02

PART 1
THE DIGITAL LANDSCAPE TRANSFORMS THE FASHION INDUSTRY

INTRODUCTION TO THE DIGITAL LANDSCAPE

Chapter Objectives
- Understand the social spaces of the digital landscape
- Explore the power of social media networks
- Obtain a global perspective on social media
- Investigate laws and regulations that govern social media
- Discover the ethical pitfalls of social media marketing

INTRODUCTION

The evolution of the Internet over the past two decades has paved the way for social media networks to capitalize on today's hyper-connected world. Social media is all about capturing and sharing the in-the-moment updates, and delivering the message of "real time" (live stories). Digital innovation continues to influence the expectations of marketers, managers, and consumers alike. In the previous chapter, we explored how the digital landscape disrupted the traditional fashion industry and forged new perspectives and protocols for the world of fashion.

In this chapter, we will take a closer look at social networks and explore the connections that they form with consumers. We will also survey new technologically driven experiences that continuously challenge the status quo as business as usual in the fashion industry. Daily technological advances are created in order to meet the ever-changing needs of consumers, as well as manipulate their engagement within their social environment. Social media, websites, and e-mail unite different channels of communication while new mobile devices enhance the availability of information. The goal of this chapter is to gain a better understanding of the shifting digital landscape of social networks, the laws and regulations that govern them, and the ethical risks that lurk within this fluctuating environment.

THE ENVIRONMENT IN DIGITAL SPACE

How do social networks continuously transform the way consumers interact with one another? Social networks have shifted the consumer's role from that of a mere observer to that of an active participant, all through the immediate social sharing of content and commentary in communities spanning the digital realm. These networks provide a social platform for like-minded individuals to congregate and create communities in the virtual world. They diversify consumers' perceptions, alter how relationships are shared (e.g., relationship status posts), and negate the "business as usual" mantra that dominated the fashion industry for decades. Through virtual relationships, brands are able to acquire consumer advocates for their products or services. For instance, impromptu shares from a social network audience empower brands to maintain an authentic voice by building upon the brand-consumer relationship. Over time, these users also develop filter systems to block unwelcome conversations. Social networks never sleep, and bristle with real-time global feeds to generate endless dialogue. This eternal wakefulness satisfies, and encourages, the users' constant need to seek what is novel, trending, and relevant to their peers.   A well-strategized digital presence for a brand online also increases their offline engagement.

" SOCIAL MEDIA HAS STARTED A REVOLUTION IN HOW PEOPLE CONNECT, LEARN AND COMMUNICATE, AND ITS EFFECTS CANNOT BE UNDONE."
BRAIN SOLIS, DIGITAL ANALYST, ANTHROPOLOGIST, AND FUTURIST
(BX WORLDWIDE SPEAKERS + ENTERTAINMENT, 2015)

The Fundamentals of Social Media

2.2

Social media networks such as Facebook, Twitter, Instagram, and YouTube have impacted the social behavior of consumers, altering the way they communicate, share, and network. While social media adoption continues to spread through generations, marketers have had to adjust their digital methods of influencing their consumers. The next generation of fashion marketers must adapt to an unprecedented level of brand-to-consumer relations; the interconnected consumers of today require authentic and dynamic engagement.

In order to remain "social" with social media, marketers came to realize that they must utilize a genuine voice when engaging with their audiences. This was quickly embraced, as avid social media users filtered out any brand that adopted a "sales-first" approach. Despite opening new channels to brands' target audiences, social media has also created the challenge of maintaining an acceptable level of discretion in a traditionally secretive industry. Consumer engagement dictates that conversations will swirl around brands with or without these brands' participation or approval. Online conversations are global in scope, often drawing millions of people to interact and draw polarizing opinions about a brand's identity.

The fashion industry will continue to be impacted (or disrupted) by the emergence of digital influencers and online communication such as mobile apps, image recognition, and live-video streaming. Relatively speaking, we have only just begun exploring the digital age of mobile and online technology. The social media landscape has evolved to encompass daily content consumption, the instantaneity of real-time information, and the "shareability" of interest within social communities. This movement has ushered in the era of the hyper-connected consumer, an entity that immediately demands for products seen on digital feeds. In chapter 3, we will assess hyper-connected consumers and their collective impact on the fashion industry. This transformation of adoption has forced the fashion cycle to speed up, as the global alliance of trends (seamless open-source distribution online) and the revolution of user-generated content have easily surpassed brand-owned content.

2.2
Online communication influences entire industries. (Adapted from http://www.barrydalton.com/wp-content/uploads/2013/08/Social-Media-Insights.jpg)

2.3

KENDALL JENNER

64%
AUDIENCE ON
Instagram

ENGAGEMENTS
PER POST
1,286,661

**POSTS IN THE
LAST 30 DAYS
35
FOLLOWERS
50,988,061**

79,060,157

TOTAL FOLLOWERS

1

**CURRENT D'MARIE
MODEL RANK**

LAST 30 DAYS
TOTAL SOCIAL POSTS:
185
TOTAL SOCIAL ENGAGEMENTS:
56,425,098

facebook.
👍 **12,024,842**

ENGAGEMENTS
PER POST
130,852.2

🐦 **16,047,254**
TWITTER FOLLOWERS

AVG. RETWEETS
5,603.7
🐦🐦🐦🐦🐦

D'MARiE
DATA PROVIDED BY
8-Mar-2016

2.3
Influencer Score Card—An
infograph of the data for a
custom measureable chart
(sample with Kendall Jenner)

Before reviewing the methods involved in developing a brand's digital strategy (which will be covered in chapter 5), it is necessary to first understand the key objectives in selecting the right social media platform. Brands need to explore the collection of online social conversations and find the ones that best complement their respective identities. They must participate in the right conversation on the appropriate social platform in order to capture the attention of their intended target audience. In order to remain relevant to their online audiences, brands must continuously find new ways to create dialogues with current or prospective customers. For instance, brands demonstrate their reliability and authenticity to social media communities by highlighting images/messages of consumers using their products (user-generated content). It is important to understand the value and adoption of user-generated content (UGC)—text and images originating from consumers (users) shared in blogs, wikis, discussion forums, posts, chats, tweets, podcasts, pins, and other digital images. User-generated content creates a new hybrid of online social community that freely discusses the affirmation or nullification of a brand or product. MySpace pioneered this UGC-based conversation as early as 2005 with the "scan," a community that shared original and repurposed content among friends and followers. Despite MySpace's emphasis on music, it paved the way for future online communities to collectively take interest in a variety of other topics.

The social transmission of content across social network channels (e.g., Twitter, Instagram) drives the process of communication. These encounters are measured by the user's reach and impressions garnered online. A social media user's impressions are typically derived from interactions and exposure to content or community engagement within the network. Impressions are created when shared content is exposed to users in a particular social media platform. Shared content is exposed not only to the users' followers but potentially to the list of followers of each individual, subsequently creating impressions (Dunham, 2014). This occurs when a follower opts to receive another person's status updates (text, images, videos). Social presence is the foundation of a user's existence in social media networks. Users increase their social presence or social position through the amount of activity, content, and engagement spread throughout their networks. Hence, the reach (size of the community) of a social media user is based on the total audience that user has on any given platform, for example, "likes" on a brand's Facebook page (Dunham, 2014).

2.4 # DEMATERIALIZATION:
Using less to produce more

The Smartphone: Dematerialization

Among the first smartphones to be launched, was the iPhone in the year 2007, which has sold 42 million units since launch. The smartphone has been recognized as one of the most important inventions of all time, alongside the light bulb, the tire, and the car engine. The smartphone gives consumers the power of information right in the palm of their hands, and it continues to change the way consumers communicate and connect.

The devices aid the hyper-connected consumers of today in their daily routines. The smartphone has replaced material gadgets and items that we used to depend on, such as a camera with film, a music player, television, flash light, fax machine, printed newspaper, and the list goes on and on. "Dematerialization," or using less material gadgets, but relying on the smartphone is changing the way consumers depend on their electronic smart device.

2.4
Dematerialization Infograph

Engagement

Dialogs between brands and consumers' are the fundamentals of social media. Brands are continuously measuring the strength of these dialogs and the overall engagement of their followers. Engagement (intensity of feeling) on social media is derived from interactions that occur within online communities. While some forms of engagement are more passive than others, their fundamental goals are to generate traction and drive return on investment (ROI). Engagement through social channels can be measured based on the different levels of audience participation. The following are some general categories of user participation with social media channels of brands:

1) Active participation (content creation)
2) Moderate involvement (liking, sharing, commenting, click-through action—by clicking through a hypertext link the user is connected to a particular website or "call to action")
3) Follows but merely observes with no actions (lurkers); invisible but measurable

Social media networks depend on community engagement to expand the reach of their current audiences and encourage powerful word-of-mouth marketing. Engagement is also measured by the speed of response from a brand's audience. Online engagement creates buzz throughout the network, thus encouraging further migration of shared content (Lowery, 2015). This direct communication through social network channels creates an online narrative that can be read or can generate a shareable movement of online content (Hartshorn, 2010). The strength of social engagement through social media networks encourages and develops brand trust, credibility, and overall authenticity. In chapter 6, we will evaluate engagement facets from measurability to conversation.

2.5

2.6

2.6
A selfie posted on Twitter by Ellen DeGeneres during the Oscars 2014 became the most re-tweeted photo that year. This was re-tweeted over three million times.

Capturing the attention of social media enthusiasts is challenging for marketers. They must ensure that engagements can be translated into measurable outcomes such as conversion by sales or brand awareness levels. In *What Social Media Analytics Can't Tell You*, Alexandra Samuel and Andrew Reid clarified how engagement is measured in today's world. They studied the variations of social media users while also examining "how their behaviors differ and what's missing from social listening" (Samuel). In this case, social listening refers to the assessment and monitoring of what is currently being said about a brand by users of social media networks. Such listening of a select group creates a "skewed perception" of the social audience as well as of the followers as a whole (Lowery, 2015).

2.5
Marketers do their best to capture and engage the attention of social media enthusiasts. Social media community managers work to create an authentic conversation to ensure strong engagement with social media audience.

" SOCIAL MEDIA HAS ALSO CREATED A PLATFORM FOR LESSER KNOWN DESIGNERS TO BREAK INTO THE FASHION WORLD, WHICH HAS DISRUPTED THE TRADITIONAL TOP-DOWN MODEL OF DESIGNER TO MEDIA TO CONSUMER, AND MADE FASHION MORE DEMOCRATIC AND TRENDS LESS RIGID. ON THE MINUS SIDE, I DON'T ALWAYS THINK THE DIALOGUE AND ENGAGEMENT ON SOCIAL MEDIA ABOUT FASHION IS THAT CONSTRUCTIVE. SOMETIMES LOOKS ARE DISMISSED WITHOUT KNOWING THE STORY BEHIND THEM OR WORK THAT WENT INTO THEM, IN AN EFFORT TO BOIL A COMMENT DOWN TO 140 CHARACTERS OR A QUICK, DIGESTIBLE QUIP OR IMAGE. AND THE WAY CLOTHING AND APPEARANCE ARE CRITIQUED CAN BE SO HARSH, IT ALMOST REACHES THE LEVEL OF HATE SPEECH. "
BOOTH MOORE, FASHION SENIOR EDITOR
HOLLYWOOD REPORTER/PRET-A-REPORTER

SOCIAL EXPLORATION

The power of social listening enables brands to acquire insight about their online audiences through behavior monitoring. Still, there are concerns about social media participation due to the prospect of providing a public platform for customers to air negative opinions about these brands. These online conversations will occur naturally, with or without the brand's acknowledgement or permission. While brands rely on social media to spread word-of-mouth (WOM), it also needs to plan for the moderation of both positive and negative online conversations.

Monitoring the Social Landscape

The traditional method of creating a strong analysis of a social media audience is to create a Digital SWOT Analysis (Fig. 2.7) that evaluates the strengths, weaknesses, opportunities, and threats of consumer engagement. Brands have learned not to carelessly shift between social media networks—they must first investigate the reach of each platform by listening, monitoring, and comparing. The key is to find where the brand's target market swarms, and then create a relationship within that platform. While brands may learn where their target markets congregate online, they must approach with caution, and not immerse themselves, without first understanding the nuances of a particular community. Brands need to understand the social community of the platform before they make their entrance. Remember, it is highly noticeable to community members when a brand jumps into their social feed merely to push products without caring enough to join the conversation.

Digital SWOT Analysis

2.7

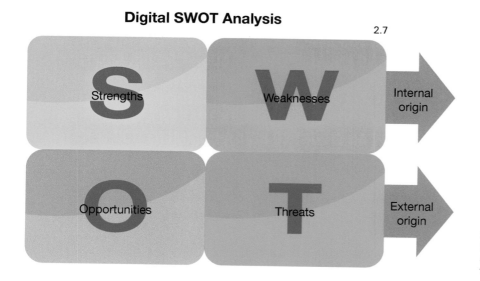

2.7
Digital SWOT Analysis. (http://www.professional academy.com/blogs-and-advice/marketing-theories---swot-analysis)

Digital SWOT Analysis

The following is a sample of how to create a Digital SWOT Analysis:

Introduction
Write a brief overview about the brand, its background, beginnings, and how the brand uses social media throughout its strategies.

Strengths
Strong movement and impact through social media or digital engagement online.

What are the company's strengths relating to their social media? How is the company successfully using social media outreach platforms relating to their marketing strategies, positioning, and planning?

Weaknesses
Reviewing the social presence within the brand's online community, and their relevancy. What are the brand's weaknesses or what are they lacking in social media? Where can they benefit from using social media platforms for their campaigns?

Opportunities
New areas of social spaces that could lead to strong brand awareness or social connection with target market. What are opportunities that the company can use from social media to gain more consumer awareness and interaction? Where can they beat their opponent in a sense of gaining more feedback from consumers through their social media?

Threats
Social space that is harmful to a brand or is not addressing concerns from the consumer about the brand. Where are other companies excelling, that this company is lacking, in social media? How can this company become aware and change its current ways to become more social media friendly?

Successful Campaign
What was a successful campaign that this company activated through social media? What was a competitor's campaign that was competitive or relative to this campaign? What were the results of this campaign?

Campaign Improvements through Social Media. Where could this campaign be improved through social media?

- Overview of Company Results and Awareness.
- Finalizing overview of the brand, their results within social media awareness, and how they will move towards a social media future.
- Results will enable a brand to develop the right content and messaging to build a strong social media out reach program.

CASE STUDY:
Social Engagement Disruption

One event that dominated the 2015 fashion season was Kanye West's presentation of his season 1 collaboration collection with Adidas X Yeezy collection from season 1 in New York Fashion Week, which broke records and made the world stand up and take notice. The show garnered over 162 million viewers (sourced from select key influencers in attendance) in mere minutes, simply through social media feeds. In addition to West's massive base of social supporters, the combined support of pop culture icons such as Justin Bieber, The Kardashians (including the Jenner sisters), Beyoncé, and Jay-Z fueled the rapper's exposure. This group of social media elite contributed to the large amount of social influence, which turned the Kanye X Adidas show into a social media phenomenon. Kanye West's runway show was live-streamed in 42 theaters across the globe and activated a frenzy of social media engagement spurring millions of hashtags and tweets worldwide (Ellison, 2015; Bain, 2015).

2.8
Adidas Originals X Kanye West
Yeezy Season 1; February 2015
New York Fashion Week

2.8

Ambient Awareness

"Social media networks provide real-time updates on what others are doing and experiencing at that moment in time. This, in turn, gives the online social community the experience of omnipresent knowledge, which increases the online viewer's interest about the real-time posts" (Thompson, 2008). Social scientists define this form of incessant online contact as ambient awareness. This reflects that being physically close to someone, you can pick up cues of their mood through body language (Kaplan and Haenlein, 2010). "Due to ambient awareness, applications such as Twitter result in relatively high levels of social presence, defined as the acoustic, visual, and physical contact that can be achieved between two individuals and media richness, defined as the amount of information that can be transmitted in a given interval. This is why micro-blogs should be considered the middle ground between traditional blogs and social networking sites within the general classification of social media" (Kaplan & Haenlein, 2010).

THE SOCIAL STRUCTURE

Social currency is acquired from value, insights, and data that result from the collective interaction across social networks and digital communities. It has value to others in social networks, whether it is curated information, opinions, or visual content. This true currency enables social media users to be recognized as impactful on the social communities around them.

Social Currency

According to tech journal *Tech Crunch*, "Social currency refers to the idea that every person has an online identity formed through participation in social networks, websites, digital communities, and online transactions. Our everyday activities—web searches, status updates, likes, tweets, and comments—they all leave a trail of data behind, which we tend to see as ephemeral or throwaway" (Barnikel, 2012). Users leave this trail of data by sharing what they experience, participate in, or feel at a particular moment with their followers in a given network. These users become social network enthusiasts who consistently spread fresh, relevant content. This form of social sharing influences users to believe that posts are specifically created for them. Further, this engagement creates a "trending" effect in social space. Trending topics are useful tools that inspire consumers to participate in social messages or campaigns, thus springing useful future content for brands. We will dig deeper into trending topics and search engine optimization (SEO) in chapter 6.

" SO TO GET PEOPLE TALKING, COMPANIES AND ORGANIZATIONS NEED TO MINT SOCIAL CURRENCY. GIVE PEOPLE A WAY TO MAKE THEMSELVES LOOK GOOD WHILE PROMOTING THEIR PRODUCTS AND IDEAS ALONG THE WAY. THERE ARE THREE WAYS TO DO THAT: 1) FIND INNER REMARKABILITY 2) LEVERAGE GAME MECHANICS 3) MAKE PEOPLE FEEL LIKE INSIDERS"
JONAH BERGER, CONTAGIOUS: WHY THINGS CATCH ON (BERGER, 2013)

CASE STUDY:
Leveraging Social Currency

Social currency can possess monetary value based on the content's worth and the user's reach. Marc Jacobs put this theory to the test in 2014 when he created a unique popup store called Tweet Shop, which launched during the 2014 Fashion Week in both New York and London. Tweet Shop did not accept traditional payment methods; instead, it accepted only hashtags as a form of social currency. This was an innovative participation campaign designed to stimulate interactions between the brand and its consumers. Followers were asked to create a chain of images pertaining to the launch of Jacob's new line of MJ Daisy fragrances (Daisy, Daisy Eau so Fresh, Daisy Dream). The form of payment was to simply post the hashtag #MJJDaisyChain on any social media platform. The images posted included artful bottle images, the popup shop, and the overall theme of creatively displayed daisies. This form of social currency would buy the MJ fan a free fragrance roller/spray and a daisy-shaped pin with the MJ fragrance lathered onto it; the more creative posts gave customers the chance to obtain perfume jewelry lines or a MJ handbag.

Ultimately, the campaign enhanced the bond between the brand and its direct fans.

2.9

2.9
Marc Jacobs POP UP TWEET SHOP

"THE DAISY BRAND HAS BUILT UP A PRETTY CONSIDERABLE FOLLOWING IN THE SOCIAL CHANNELS. WE LOOK AT THE TWEET SHOP AS A GIFT BACK TO MARC FANS AND DAISY FANS —THANKING THEM FOR ENGAGING WITH US."
LORI SINGER, GROUP VICE PRESIDENT OF GLOBAL MARKETING FOR COTY PRESTIGE. (COTY PRESTIGE IS MARC JACOBS'S FRAGRANCE LICENSOR) (TRUONG)

CASE STUDY:
Beyoncé Breaking the Rules and Harnessing Social Currency

Influence turns into currency when the user possesses something of interest to others. With 35 million followers on Instagram and 53 million Facebook fans, it makes sense for an artist like Beyoncé to talk directly to audiences through her most highly engaged social networks. In December 2014, Beyoncé's new album, *Platinum Edition*, was not released using a traditional marketing strategy. In an industry-shaking move, she leveraged her social currency by invoking word-of-mouth (WOM) to launch the album directly to her fans. She made her original announcement via Instagram with a short video clip and an update titled "Surprise" (Bullas, 2014). Beyoncé successfully utilized her social currency to convert fans into buyers, replacing a traditional multimillion-dollar marketing campaign with an immediate social post directed to her social communities. This personal and customized announcement gave fans an insider exclusive, making them the first individuals to become aware of the launch. The exclusive message created strong demand for her album, causing ripples across social media platforms filled with consumers wanting to purchase it immediately. The album sold 828,773 copies in three days and Twitter reported 1.2 million tweets in 12 hours. It was the largest single sales week in the history of Apple iTunes.

Capitalizing on the power of social media has allowed influencers with premium social currency to have a direct link to their "superfans" by creating strong positioning for direct marketing. Over time, an active social media fan feels a stronger sense of connection with his or her online "friend" (the influencer), more than simply following a fan website or a micro-blog fan club.

Social Proof

Social proof is validation or justification of the power of social influence (Hallen, 2014). The following sections discuss the five types of social proof.

EXPERT OR AUTHORITY SOCIAL PROOF

Have an influencer—who is regarded as an expert—endorse your products. This can be a designer, stylist, fashion blogger, or anyone else who is considered an expert. The behavioral science behind it is viewed as the "halo effect"—a cognitive bias in which the consumer trusts someone's opinion (Cherry, n.d.).

CELEBRITY SOCIAL PROOF

Have someone of recognized status such as in the entertainment industry confirm the value of a product or service. Behavioral science applies the theory of extended self in the digital world (Belk, 2014). The extended self is made up of the self (me) and the possessions (mine). It suggests that intentionally or unintentionally, we view our possessions as a reflection of ourselves. Thus, consumers look for products to signify group membership and mark their position in society.

In 2014 the fashion community embraced the viral phenomenon called the #ALSIceBucketChallenge to help spread awareness of Amyotrophic Lateral Sclerosis disease. Users on social media channels would hoist buckets filled with ice-cold water over their heads while simultaneously donating to the charity and encouraging others to do the same (Fig. 2.10). The ALS Association (ALSA) challenge raised $115 million. Thanks to the money collected globally from the challenge, researchers discovered a gene that contributed to the disease.

USER SOCIAL PROOF

Social proof is confirmation from current users of a product or service through testimonials or online sharing.

The behavioral science of social proof involves recognizing a point of view that we can relate to as if the person is "one of us" and, in turn, creates consumer trust (Widrich, 2012).

Strong reviews help differentiate a particular product from others, for example, the in-store floor activations promoting shoes from US retailer Nordstrom. Customers showed off their purchases while inside the store, then shared it with their social circles (Fig. 4.10). Drybar, a socially driven hair salon, utilized social media to activate a strong social presence and word-of-mouth, encouraging

2.10

2.10
Tim Gunn and Heidi Klum
taking part in Project Runway,
Mercedes-Benz Fashion
Week, Spring 2015. This was
also when Project Runway
showed their support for
#ALSIceBucketChallenge

"bragging rights" for customers to share the times they frequented the salon. The rather ingenious twist of this approach was that a customer had to be "in the know" to understand where this image was from, thus creating exclusivity, which is a critical component of today's fashion world. In both Nordstrom and Drybar cases, customers not only promoted these locations but also showed off their purchases as a form of self-identification.

CROWD SOCIAL PROOF

This social proof shows that acceptance of something from a large number of individuals, or members of a community, confirms an individual's acceptance. The behavioral science dictates that individuals do not want to feel socially unworthy by not purchasing or participating in what others do, a critical part of the "Fear Of Missing Out" (FOMO) phenomenon.

Bridging the gap between online and offline shopping or crowd-sourced proof of popularity (social confirmation), retailers are beginning to incorporate branded social proof with Pinterest, intergrating in-store "Popular on Pinterest" tags on items and in-store customer experience at US retailers such as Target and Nordstrom. This in-store social

confirmation provides a great strategy to support and blur the lines between the brick and mortar and online social communities. For example, Nordstrom's strong Pinterest presence (over 4 million followers) enables it to display the popularity of trending items online in order to encourage crowd social proof. This is done either in-store or on a featured page on the retailers' websites.

FRIENDS' SOCIAL PROOF

This is the confirmation from trusted friends and social network communities.

The behavioral science behind this concept is that people tend to emulate the people they follow and surround themselves with.

CASE STUDY:
Retailers Utilizing "Crowd Social Proof"

C&A in Brazil wanted to give their women shoppers a social confirmation from their community to make a purchase. This would, according to the retailer, solve the insecurity they have about their purchases. C&A wanted to create a social shopping experience that offers validation on purchases from their social media community on Facebook. C&A's collection would be shared on Facebook and would give their community a chance to select the items they "LIKE." While the Facebook community was selecting "LIKE," they were being calculated and displayed on a screen that was embedded on the hangers that coincide with the garment online. Shoppers could see from the hangers what was being liked and not liked on the Internet. C&A married social shopping with Facebook interface with brick-and-mortar digital displays to create crowd source social confirmation.

According to the C&A website (Fashionlike, 2012) More than 9,800,000 consumers were impacted; C&A received 1,000 new fans per hour; more than 1,700 posts were shared; part of the collection sold out in one day; and it resulted in more than 6,200 opinions in the first few hours of going live.

For example, a sponsored advertisement on Facebook showing friends who have "liked" a brand indicates social proof and confirmation that this brand is accepted by a user's social circle. "Depending on the topic, subject matter, or atmosphere, people congregate to join others with similar experiences and backgrounds. Conversations are at the core of social networking and through them, relationships are developed." (Hartshorn, 2010)

Gamification

Welcome to the sport of social gamification in social media—the need consumers feel to be first, to achieve something of honor, and to show others how well they are doing along the journey. Gamification boosts the competitive edge of the "sonic youth generation" who stay connected through their mobile devices. This competitive strategy uses the idea of gamer obsession and converts it to brand marketing through social media interactive campaigns. In a non-gamer context, gamification describes the elements of gaming, including strategy and competition, that offer awards to consumers. This marketing strategy enables a less interactive situation to prompt users to become more participatory (Eridon, 2012).

Augmented Gamification

Pokémon GO is a location-based augmented reality mobile application game that launched in 2016, creating the world's largest scavenger hunt. It enabled players to use their smartphones to find characters in different locations. Retailers are driving higher foot traffic by luring Pokémon GO players to share screenshots of character in stores. Rebecca Minkoff NYC retail store offered 15% discount to customers who showed the salesperson the character they found in the store and tagged with @rebeccaminkoff. Sensor Tower Store Intelligence data estimated there was over 75 million downloads with 21 million daily active users and $160 million in worldwide net revenue on App Store and Google Play.

2.11

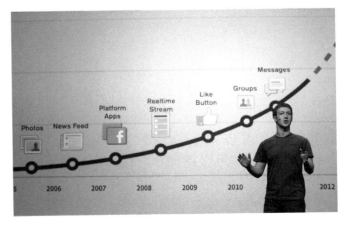

2.11
Facebook CEO Mark Zuckerberg delivers a keynote address during the Facebook f8 conference sharing how they plan on connecting the FB community through realtime stream, groups, and messaging.

CASE STUDY:
Urban Chase Turns To Gamification

The H&M Loves Music collection reaches out to their youth audience by collaborating with party organizer Boiler Room and created an "urban chase" by hiding tickets in stores in Warsaw and Krakow to sold out Boiler Room parties (Digital Training Academy, 2014). The clues to find the tickets were exclusively released as hints on Snapchat, which marked the first Poland Snapchat gamification (urban chase) campaign.

1) The Challenge: find the tickets
2) Social Experience: utilize the social media app Snapchat to help locate tickets in the H&M stores
3) Results of Digital Campaign: H&M gained 943 followers on Snapchat, 3.8 million unique users were reached with only 200 participants in the scavenger hunt "urban chase" (Digital Training Academy, 2014).

Social Media's Tipping Point

The overload of digital native consumption has created a digital tipping point phenomenon. In *The Tipping Point*, author Malcolm Gladwell analyzes the epidemical spread of thoughts, products, fashion trends, and latest social media platforms (Gladwell, 2002). The relentless surge of social content is very real. In 2016, there will be an estimated 2.13 billion social network users around the globe, up from 1.4 billion in 2012 ("Number of social," 2015). There is an average of 7.4 social communication applications on each smartphone today. Users between the ages of 15-19 spend at least three hours a day, on average, using social media, while 20-29 year olds spend about two ("Social Media Addiction," 2015). The frequency and intensity of such use involves viewing digital content: television, movies, social media, Internet, and games.

This social epidemic may be exponentially growing, but one thing holds true—social media expands its reach with each new channel introduced to the landscape. Currently, there are over 300 million active Instagram users with 70 million photos shared daily and 1 million active Snapchat users with 10 billion daily videos viewed (Brookman, 2015). In chapter 3, we will investigate the consequences of this social epidemic, including obsessive-compulsive behavior and consumers' changing definition of their respective social presences.

The advent of the immensely powerful smartphone is a key contributor to this epidemic, causing mobile phones and mobile applications to support social networks

" [IN] 2015, THE DATA INDICATES THAT AMERICANS WILL CONSUME MEDIA FOR MORE THAN 1.7 TRILLION HOURS, AN AVERAGE OF APPROXIMATELY 15.5 HOURS PER PERSON PER DAY. THE AMOUNT OF MEDIA DELIVERED WILL EXCEED 8.75 ZETTABYTES ANNUALLY–9 DVDS WORTH–OF DATA SENT TO THE AVERAGE CONSUMER ON AN AVERAGE DAY."
JAMES E. SHORT, USC MARSHALL SCHOOL OF BUSINESS ("US CTM RELEASES," 2013)

CASE STUDY:
Jimmy Choo #CatchAChoo, Launching Trainers with a Scavenger Hunt

In 2010, Jimmy Choo took on gamification with their location-based Catch-A-Choo (#CatchAChoo) Foursquare campaign. Nothing brings out the competitive nature of women like a free pair of shoes, especially those carrying the prestige of the Jimmy Choo brand. A real-time treasure hunt was launched in London with women running across the city to win the ultimate pair of newly released Jimmy Choo trainers. The digital agency, Matt Rhodes and FreshNetworks, reached out and engaged with existing Jimmy Choo advocates and influential fashion bloggers to spread awareness about the trainer hunt and to increase online coverage of the company's new trainer range.

The "Trainer Hunt" check-ins were announced on Facebook and Twitter to loyal fans and followers of the brand's social channels. This hunt had Jimmy Choo fans searching across the city at over one hundred upscale London locations. Some of the trendier spots included Lounge Lover, The Hummingbird Bakery, and the members-only Mortons. Scavengers had to locate a representative carrying Jimmy Choo trainers, approach them and say "I've been following you" in order to receive their pair of Jimmy Choo sneakers.

Digital agencies, Matt Rhodes and FreshNetworks, were hired to raise awareness and create buzz around the launch of the new Jimmy Choo trainer collection. According to Jo Stratmann, marketing manager at FreshNetworks social media agency, Jimmy Choo wanted to use social media to start a conversation about the new trainer collection. The campaign resulted in significant online buzz/coverage about the new trainer collection. It got people talking about the new trainer range, online and offline, and encouraged interaction with the Jimmy Choo brand. It increased: offline press coverage about the new trainer range; online positive sentiment and mentions; and sales from the new trainer range.

Four thousand individuals participated in the Jimmy Choo trainer hunt on Foursquare, Twitter, and Facebook in just under three weeks. The competition details were viewed on Facebook 285,000 times, and 250 different blogs covered the Jimmy Choo trainer hunt. Moreover, daily trainer sales in-store went up 33 percent after *The Evening Standar*d covered The Jimmy Choo trainer hunt, and positive mentions of the brand increased by almost 40 percent as a result of the campaign (measurements taken from April 19 to May 6, 2010).

> " THE JIMMY CHOO TRAINER HUNT, CATCHACHOO, HAS BEEN A REAL SUCCESS IN TERMS OF ACHIEVING OUR KEY OBJECTIVES FOR THE CAMPAIGN. THE CAMPAIGN NOT ONLY GENERATED SUCCESSFULLY TRADITIONAL OFFLINE MEDIA COVERAGE, IT ALSO SPREAD THE ONLINE WORD-OF-MOUTH ABOUT OUR NEW JIMMY CHOO TRAINER COLLECTION. WE HAVE BEEN PLEASED AT HOW IT HAS INCREASED THE LEVEL OF INTERACTION WITH OUR BRAND, AND WITH TRAINER SALES IN-STORE INCREASING AS A DIRECT RESULT OF THE CAMPAIGN, WE ARE VERY PLEASED THAT FRESHNETWORKS' STRATEGIC APPROACH HAS HELPED GENERATE REAL ROI."
> JOSHUA SCHULMAN, CEO OF JIMMY CHOO (STRATMANN)

without cessation. By the end of 2014, "half of the world's population had at least one mobile subscription, totaling over 3.6 billion unique mobile subscribers. By 2020, around three-fifths of the global population will have a mobile subscription, with close to one billion new subscribers added over the period" (Groupe Speciale, 2015). Two billion smartphone users today have the privilege of convenient, easy mobile access to their social communities at all times.

Dr. Larry Rosen, a professor in the area of psychology of technology, gave a lecture on "The Distracted Mind" and shared some levels of time of penetration rate in which technology reaches 50 million people (Wisdom 2.0, 2014):

Radio .... took 38 years
Telephone .... took 75 years
Television .... took 13 years
Cell phone .... took 12 years
World Wide Web .... took 4 years

Blogs .... took 3 years
MySpace .... took 2.5 years
Facebook .... took 2 years
YouTube .... took 1 year
Angry Birds .... took 35 days

Emoji

In 2015, for the first time, Oxford Dictionaries selected a pictograph as the "word" of the year. The emoji, called the "Face with Tears of Joy," was the best word that reflected "the ethos, mood, and preoccupations of 2015." According to the data collected by Oxford New Monitor corpus, the emoji best reflected the ethos, mood, and preoccupations of 2015 (Oxford Dictionaries, 2015)

2.12
Emojis allow for the sharing of thoughts and emotions without the use of words.

2.12

| | | A文 English | Not logged in | Talk | Contributions | Create account | Log in |

WIKIMEDIA COMMONS

Gallery Discussion | View Edit History | Search

Emoji

From Wikimedia Commons, the free media repository

English: Ideograms or smileys used in Japanese electronic messages and webpages

Source of information: Unicode, visited on 10/28/2015

Main page
Welcome
Community portal
Village pump
Help center

Language select
English
Select

Participate
Upload file
Recent changes
Latest files
Random file
Contact us

Print/export
Create a book
Download as PDF
Printable version

In other projects

Count ◆	Code ◆	Browser ◆	Noto Color Emoji ◆	Twitter Emoji ◆	Emoji One ◆	Firefox OS Emoji ◆	Phantom Open Emoji ◆	Name ◆	Version ◆	Default ◆	Annotations ◆
1	U+1F600							grinning face	V6.1*	emoji	face, grin, person
2	U+1F601							grinning face with smiling eyes	V6.0	emoji	eye, face, grin, person, smile
3	U+1F602							face with tears of joy	V6.0	emoji	face, joy, person, tear
4	U+1F603							smiling face with open	V6.0	emoji	face, mouth, open, person,

SOCIAL MEDIA NETWORKS

The social shifts that are felt with online communication are continuously changing as the need for consumers to engage with snack-size communication of threads. In order for brands to communicate digitally with their audiences, they must first recognize the method of communication within each social media channel. While the shift in available applications is ever-changing, it is important to understand what a brand's audience seeks in terms of daily social network insight.

Social Media Channels

Trial and error has shown marketers that not all social media channels are ideal for every brand. Also, it is not necessary for a brand to utilize all available social media channels going forward. The process of selection is key, when determining a brand's appropriate social platform. A brand's end goal is of paramount concern. Brand marketers and social media strategists constantly advise brands to select the social media channels that best connect with their targeted audience and properly engage within these chosen platforms. The social media landscape continues to grow in order to meet the needs of ever-changing digital natives that speak the language of "virtual social communities."

"Googling" has become an ingrained element of the modern world. New behavioral patterns have reinforced the consumer's reliance on the Internet as an accepted source of knowledge, and a primary driver of economic behavior. Social networks have dominated the lives of today's consumer market—they are usually the first and last applications used by these hyper-connected individuals on a typical day. The word "social" refers to the primary human need for connection and comfortable sharing of thoughts with others (Safko, 2010). Additionally, the word "media," in this context, refers to the digital technology channels that make conversations and connections possible (Didelot, 2013). Through social networks, marketers can directly start a dialogue with their target audience, and cultivate a social presence for their brands. These networks allow brands to spread information, create buzz, and generate momentum. For instance, social networks have used leisure activities (e.g., music festivals) to position brands as authentic lifestyle options for consumers. In chapter 5, we will review how brands curate and share content with their community while assessing the platforms that work best for them.

The social media landscape, therefore, includes networks that enable sharing, discussing, networking (community), and publishing. The following infographic is a social media comparison by Leverage New Age Media (Fig. 2.14) that breaks down some of the social outlets to demonstrate the advantage of each of the channels and how they are utilized.

2.13

2.13
Commuters from decades past receiving the latest news updates from their newspapers, similar to commuters today looking down at their smartphones to remain connected with news and popular culture.

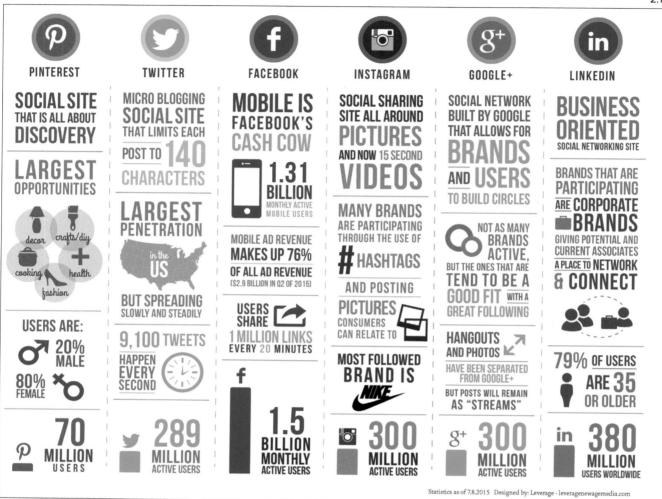

2.14

PINTEREST

SOCIAL SITE THAT IS ALL ABOUT **DISCOVERY**

LARGEST OPPORTUNITIES

decor   crafts/diy

cooking   +   health

fashion

USERS ARE:

20% MALE

80% FEMALE

70 MILLION USERS

TWITTER

MICRO BLOGGING **SOCIAL SITE** THAT LIMITS EACH POST TO **140** CHARACTERS

LARGEST PENETRATION

in the US

BUT SPREADING SLOWLY AND STEADILY

9,100 TWEETS HAPPEN EVERY SECOND

289 MILLION ACTIVE USERS

FACEBOOK

MOBILE IS FACEBOOK'S **CASH COW**

1.31 BILLION MONTHLY ACTIVE MOBILE USERS

MOBILE AD REVENUE **MAKES UP 76%** OF ALL AD REVENUE ($2.9 BILLION IN Q2 OF 2015)

USERS SHARE **1 MILLION LINKS** EVERY 20 MINUTES

1.5 BILLION MONTHLY ACTIVE USERS

INSTAGRAM

SOCIAL SHARING SITE ALL AROUND PICTURES AND NOW 15 SECOND **VIDEOS**

MANY BRANDS ARE PARTICIPATING THROUGH THE USE OF **# HASHTAGS**

AND POSTING **PICTURES** CONSUMERS CAN RELATE TO

MOST FOLLOWED BRAND IS *NIKE*

300 MILLION ACTIVE USERS

GOOGLE+

SOCIAL NETWORK BUILT BY GOOGLE THAT ALLOWS FOR **BRANDS** AND **USERS** TO BUILD CIRCLES

NOT AS MANY **BRANDS** ACTIVE, BUT THE ONES THAT ARE **TEND TO BE A GOOD FIT** WITH A GREAT FOLLOWING

HANGOUTS AND PHOTOS HAVE BEEN SEPARATED FROM GOOGLE+ BUT POSTS WILL REMAIN AS "STREAMS"

300 MILLION ACTIVE USERS

LINKEDIN

BUSINESS ORIENTED SOCIAL NETWORKING SITE

BRANDS THAT ARE PARTICIPATING ARE **CORPORATE BRANDS** GIVING POTENTIAL AND CURRENT ASSOCIATES A PLACE TO **NETWORK & CONNECT**

79% OF USERS ARE **35** OR OLDER

380 MILLION USERS WORLDWIDE

Statistics as of 7.8.2015   Designed by: Leverage - leveragenewagemedia.com

2.14
Social Media Comparison infographic by
Leverage New Age Media

Due to the rampant creation of online social spaces, it is important to understand the four overreaching categories required to develop social media engagement and campaigns, and understand social media landscape: Bookmarking (Social Curation); Media Sharing ("Lights, Camera, Action"); Micro-blogging (Bite Size Information); Timed/Expiring ("Now You See It, Now You Don't").

SOCIAL BOOKMARKING

Bookmarking allows individuals to save content and links within a community, a process akin to marking one's favorite passage in a book. Social bookmarking enables the user to take advantage of the Internet's vast array of content and share these with a like-minded collection of their peers. Individuals are able to search, curate, and share content within their respective social communities. Examples include Pinterest, Polyvore, Storify, Flipbook, and StumbleUpon

Polyvore

One of the first websites that enabled users to create innovative trend boards was Polyvore. Launched in 2007, this platform enabled users without a graphic design background to compose digital storyboards and organize endless online content. These trend boards also functioned as an e-commerce site, allowing consumers to generate their own voice, style, and trends, thus influencing the purchases of others. The "shopability" of the website directly impacts brands through consumer-driven commerce. In addition to user-generated content, Polyvore is a haven for a global community of stylists that offer tips, predict trends, and provides industry insight. The ingenuity of this website is that it creates an online shopping boutique that is individually tailored for every user. Hence, this form of retail sales driving differentiates Polyvore's business model from those of other social media platforms such as Facebook and Twitter.

Polyvore also offers consumer-generated boards and sets (trendboard collages) that foster a sense of belonging and achievement. This bond with the crowd-sourced content community helps increase the loyalty of users toward that particular website.

MEDIA SHARING

Media sharing platforms can transform users into digital media broadcasters, allowing individuals to create, share, and preview content. Brands have seized the opportunity to develop custom content for media sharing platforms; this content is shareable through photographs, videos, charts, artwork, and sketches. Examples include YouTube, Vimeo, and Flicker.

Media Sharing: The Haul Video

A haul video is similar to a video diary that enables one to share with their audience recent purchases (beauty and fashion being the most popular). The video begins with the host typically sitting in their bedroom, pulling each item out of the shopping bag and sharing details about the purchase such as price and location where it was purchased. In 2009 haul videos became a game changer capturing the attention of the teen market while today this is the norm for millennials and Gen-Z to watch their favorite Vloggers (video bloggers) share their shopping purchases.

Bethany Mota, an 18-year-old YouTube "haul" superstar, became a powerful personal brand through her videos, which shared fashion and beauty purchases. Mota has around ten million YouTube subscribers and 900 million views, more than Vogue, ASOS, and Lady Gaga's channels combined. Mota's massive YouTube following, coupled with her six million Instagram and three million Twitter followers, makes her a powerful digital influencer. The sheer strength of their followings has helped these influencers reach celebrity-like status and private product launches.

MICRO-BLOGGING

Micro-blogging platforms invite users to post brief updates of digital content (links, text, image, GIFs, video) through social sharing networks. They are the "group of Internet-based applications that build on the ideological foundations of Web 2.0, and that allow the creation and exchange of user-generated content" (Kaplan and Haenlein, 2011). Micro-blogs are different from conventional blogs as they generate smaller amounts of content (information) pushed through social networks. Micro-blogging can serve as a narrative medium by providing an instant stream of shareable consciousness; it also encourages spontaneity because it captures real-time moments. While consumers share, marketers subsequently monitor posts to track and mine data about the online movements and engagement of users. Despite the availability of other platforms, micro-blogs play a leading role in social and professional networking. Examples of micro-blogs include Tumblr, Facebook, LinkedIn, Instagram, Twitter, Vine, Weibo (China)

Microblogging:
Michael Kors' First Sponsored Content on Instagram

The fashion industry is an image-based business, making Instagram a powerful platform for fashion brands to operate in. According to Lisa Pomerantz, Senior Vice President of global communications and marketing at Michael Kors, "We go where our fans go, and we believe that more and more consumers are spending their time on Instagram for both inspiration and product discovery. We're successful on Instagram. The ads allow us to target a "like" audience outside of the women who are already familiar with Michael Kors." (Strugatz, 2014).

" LIKE INSTAGRAM ITSELF, FASHION IS DRIVEN BY VISUALS. IT IS A MEDIUM THAT PUSHES BOUNDARIES, AND IS FAMOUS FOR DEDICATING PAINSTAKING EFFORT TO THE DESIGNS THEY SHOWCASE AND TO HOW THEY ARE PRESENTED TO THE LARGER WORLD. BRINGING EVERY NEW COLLECTION TO LIFE—THE RUNWAY PRESENTATIONS, PRINT CAMPAIGNS, TELEVISION ADS—IS AS MUCH A PART OF THE CREATIVE PROCESS AS THE COLOR, MATERIAL, AND CRAFTSMANSHIP OF THE CLOTHING AND ACCESSORIES"
KEVIN SYSTROM, CO-FOUNDER AND CEO OF INSTAGRAM (FIFE, 2015)

2.15
Eva Chen (@evachen212), former Editor in Chief of *Lucky* magazine, surprised the fashion world with her surprise announcement on her Instagram feed. She shared that she would now be the head of fashion partnerships at Instagram. Chen will lead the company and their fashion initiative to work with designers, stylists, and models and assist them in telling their stories on the social media platform.

2.16

#INSTAPURGE 2014 // TOP 100 ACCOUNTS

◉ Followers Yesterday ○ Followers Today ○ Followers Lost ○ Percent

Followers Yesterday

instagram justinbieber kimkardashian beyonce arianagrande selenagomez kendalljenner taylorswift khloekardashian kyliejenner
badgalriri mileycyrus neymarjr kourtneykardash nickiminaj katyperry cristiano kevinhart4real harrystyles natgeo ddlovato nike
caradelevingne niallhoran leomessi 9gag kingjames jlo theellenshow onedirection nashgrier champagnepapi chrisbrownofficial
justintimberlake letthelordbewithyou therock vanessahudgens thenewclassic danbilzerian jamesrodriguez10 kinggoldchains
austinmahone itsashbenzo camerondallas shakira brumarquezine davidluiz_4 forever21 lucyhale realmadrid camposwell
mirandakerr fcbarcelona snookinic jenselter shaym krisjenner ladygaga mistercap zendaya nailsartvidss hm iamdiddy
channingtatum ciara floydmayweather angelcandices bethanynoelm bestvines akon jessicaalba nba pharrell anselelgort
snoopdogg easymoneysniper garethbale11 louist91 iansomerhalder elliegoulding ninadobrev zacefron nature britneyspears
laurenconrad adrianalima ritaora 50cent bellathorne fakeliampayne sarcasm_only gopro barackobama adidasoriginals
brunomars sleepinthegardn chiragchirag78 louisvuitton zozeebo nailsvideos

Biggest Loser (%)	Smallest Loser (%)	Avg Lost	Avg % Lost
chiragchirag78	nailsvideos	671,789	7.6653%

Rank ⬥	Username ⬥	Followers Yesterday ⬥	Followers Today ⬥	Followers Lost ⬥	Percent Lost ⬥
1	instagram	64,131,228	45,251,017	18,880,211	29.4400%
2	justinbieber	23,817,614	20,279,386	3,538,228	14.8555%
3	kimkardashian	23,519,002	22,218,039	1,300,963	5.5315%
4	beyonce	22,207,790	21,375,819	831,971	3.7463%
5	arianagrande	21,748,827	20,219,621	1,529,206	7.0312%
6	selenagomez	19,572,601	18,456,569	1,116,032	5.7020%
7	kendalljenner	17,048,332	16,141,435	906,897	5.3196%
8	taylorswift	16,540,314	15,814,935	725,379	4.3855%
9	khloekardashian	15,929,263	15,180,994	748,269	4.6974%
10	kyliejenner	15,651,311	14,824,782	826,529	5.2809%
11	badgalriri	14,454,434	13,294,570	1,159,864	8.0243%
12	mileycyrus	14,143,315	13,431,417	711,898	5.0335%
13	neymarjr	13,272,600	12,974,188	298,412	2.2483%
14	kourtneykardash	13,119,514	12,499,231	620,283	4.7279%
15	nickiminaj	12,439,081	11,953,782	485,299	3.9014%
16	katyperry	11,108,224	10,817,654	290,570	2.6158%
17	cristiano	10,263,581	9,965,591	297,990	2.9034%
18	kevinhart4real	10,224,161	9,630,725	593,436	5.8043%
19	harrystyles	10,195,045	9,375,270	819,775	8.0409%
20	natgeo	9,980,528	9,751,562	228,966	2.2941%

2.16
In December 2014, Instagram did some spring cleaning with a systematic deletion of fake accounts on their platform, which was referred to as their "Instapurge." While fake followers can be bought, this was Instagram's first attempt to rid their platform of false members. Shortly after Instagram cleaned their platform of spam accounts, users felt the effect of the cleanup, referring to it as "#InstaPlurge. Zach Allia created an interactive donut chart of the top 100 accounts that lost followers. To experience the research in an interactive platform called Infogram, go to the following website: www.64px.com/instagram/.

2.17
Instaplurge cleaned the Instagram landscape to leave room for the true followers and create a more authentic community.

INTERVIEW: Aliza Licht, Founder and President of Leave Your Mark (voice behind DKNY PR GIRL®) alizalicht.com

Aliza Licht is a fashion industry veteran and the founder and president of Leave Your Mark, LLC. She currently works as a strategic consultant to businesses at the intersection of fashion and technology. Licht was formerly the long-time Senior Vice President of Global Communications for Donna Karan International and the voice of DKNY PR Girl®, an award winning Twitter personality that she created. Licht has been widely credited as a social media pioneer in the fashion industry, building a dynamic and organic Twitter community of over half a million followers for DKNY from 2009 to 2015. The person behind DKNY PR Girl's true identity was kept anonymous for two years, until October 2011, when Licht revealed herself. Her story was chronicled by The *New York Times* in "PR Girl Revealed as PR Executive."

How did you get your start as the personality for the most powerful Twitter handles in fashion history?

AL: When we embarked on social media in 2009, we were one of the only fashion brands in the space. We knew Facebook was going to boast the brand voices for Donna Karan New York and DKNY respectively, but Twitter, as we understood it, was more of a conversation. Deciding who would be the voice was uncertain, but we were sure that we didn't want to dupe people into thinking it was Donna Karan herself, because that would have been disingenuous. I instinctively felt that public relations was the perfect lens to socially filter the world of Donna Karan through—between fashion shows, celebrity dressing, and everything in between, we had a ton of content to draw from. At the time, I was obsessed with *Gossip Girl* and I immediately thought, "What if we take the idea of an anonymous blogger like *Gossip Girl* and make her a publicist?" DKNY PR GIRL was the perfect answer—a seamless combination of PR person and *Gossip Girl* all rolled into one persona. No one had to know who she was as she would be represented by a fashion sketch. So that's how I began.

The more people started interacting with the @dkny handle, the more passionate I got about it. It also grew harder not be the person who's actually behind the @dkny handle. That's where it began to get tricky because in 2009, there weren't other fashion brands on Twitter. DKNY was really the first, or at least one of the first, to actively use the social platform.

As brands started to recognize that there was this new social platform that people were doing to promote their brand, they began to watch me closer. When we went to industry events, people would begin to be curious as to who was doing the tweeting and even though it wasn't meant to be my life at that time, it was still kind of a secret because we didn't want people to know.

I started to feel schizophrenic about, sort of, making up things DKNY Girl was doing, versus what I was really doing, and that's when I had an internal discussion and said, "[T]his is getting really hard." There is a lot of engagement, which is great, but I can't pretend to be in one place when I am actually somewhere else.

At a certain point, we made a decision that I would basically tweet my life in my job and outside my job anonymously, and that's what it was until 2011 when there were a lot of different factors that contributed to the reveal. One of which, people were obsessed with figuring out who it was and it became very difficult to keep it a secret. Two, we thought that possibly we could leverage what we are doing in social media from more of an industry standpoint. Because at that time, all those social media conferences were popping up, and we were always declining them because DKNY PR Girl couldn't go speak openly in public because no one can know who she is. In 2011, we did the reveal and the rest is, kind of, history.

Why do you think DKNY PR Girl connected so quickly and with such a large audience?

I began doing this with no training, and I think there are several reasons this was so successful.

One, I was constantly on it. No one checks anything as much as I checked that timeline: 24/7, for real. I used to tweet or respond up to 100 times a day to the point where it was too much, and you got a lot of "unfollows." It depended on what was happening: Was it award season? Was it fashion week? Was I live-tweeting commentary on something? It varied, but I was full-on addicted and I loved it. It didn't feel like a job.

Because I let people into a real human personality and curated the world of Donna Karan through my own case and my own filters, it gave people a more real sense of a brand through a more relatable way. It was an authentic and credible voice where people trusted me even though they didn't know me.

What are some of the things you learned as a fashion brand on social media?

I think the biggest thing is how much social media is really a customer service vehicle— you really are the front line for the brand. It became my function to basically take issues to internal customer service people and say "okay, drop what you're doing, this is the priority because someone has tweeted this." And making customer service realize what it means when someone tweets something and how problematic that can be from a viral standpoint.

What are the changes you see in the fashion industry when it comes to the speed of content that has to be delivered to the customers?

First of all, forget about the speed. The creation of the content is the biggest challenge that every brand has now, starting with budgets. Brands are basically their own publishing houses now, and it's a huge burden. [In] how many different ways can you shoot a product? How much you need to feed these platforms, how you have to change content depending on what platform you're dealing with, and having the foresight to know what you are going to talk about two months from now—these are some of the biggest issues.

If your strategy is not showing behind the scenes, you are going to have to have a content strategy—and that's a big, expensive job. You have to have an art director, people who have vision to think about how something should be shot, what should be shot, what's interesting, what's right for what platform . . . it's endless.

INTERVIEW:
Aliza Licht

Can you tell us about brand tonality in social media?

The tone for the DKNY PR GIRL was your best girlfriend: she's friendly, she's witty, she's sometimes sarcastic, and she's polished. That tone would fall into that filter and honestly, it is just how I speak and how I write. Because I was doing me, it was very easy to know how to speak. From a brand point of view, I was always really careful because I can have a very sharp sense of humor; I wanted to make sure people knew when I was being sarcastic, and that there would be no miscommunication because that could be detrimental to the brand.

Can you tell about your POV of brand storytelling in the digital landscape?

I think every brand has its own DNA and its own filter and brand code. Repetition and utilization of the brand codes creates this thread that connects pieces to create a visual identity that people associate with a certain brand. To me, the best ad campaigns are the ones where if someone took off the brand name, you would still know exactly what ad that is for.

When you are talking about telling a brand's story, you are talking about making the consumer understand heritage and history, why things are a certain way, why something is so expensive, and the craftsmanship that goes into something so that they can feel a sense of affinity to the brand.

2.18

2.18
Aliza Licht is the Founder and President of Leave Your Mark, LLC, Author of *Leave Your Mark*, a five-time Fashion 2.0 award winner, and Tedx Times Square speaker.

> " BECAUSE I HAVE BEEN A "PR GIRL" AT DONNA KARAN FOR FIFTEEN YEARS, I DIDN'T HAVE TO CREATE A PERSONALITY THAT LIVED AND BREATHED THE BRANDS, BECAUSE I ALREADY DID. ULTIMATELY, BY BEING MYSELF, I CREATED DKNY PR GIRL. FROM A MANAGEMENT STANDPOINT, WE KNEW THAT IT WAS IMPORTANT THAT ONE, SEASONED PERSON MANAGE THE HANDLE."
> ALIZA LICHT (LICHT, 2013)

CASE STUDY:
Expiring Digital Content: Snapchat

Bobby Murphy, Evan Spiegel, and Reggie Brown created the social media platform Snapchat with the ghost logo (named Ghostface Chillah) in 2011. Originally called "Picaboo," Spiegal wanted to make communication enjoyable and lively again; he felt that current social media platforms did not enable his friends to reveal their "weirdness," and he wanted to create limited-life social content that could be shared ("Snapchat Case Study," 2014). Snapchat has close to 100 million active Snapchatters daily (D'Onfro, 2015). While the platform initially enabled the user to hold onto social content for only one to ten seconds, it now has a share feature curated with a 24-hour "story" of activity. Snapchat's interface is intentionally simple in order to make it accessible to all users.

According to influence marketing agency Instabrand, they see Snapchat and other disappearing content application becoming the most sought-after social marketing channel in the social landscape. Marketers are reportedly spending $750,000 a day to run Snapchat advertisements, along with hiring teams to run the content (Instabrand, 2015). Instabrand points out that while the cost is high and the traditional metrics used to measure effectiveness of a campaign do not apply to disappearing content, the truth is that content shared on Snapchat gets 100 percent engagement (Instabrand, 2015). While other social media is streamed through threads of conversation, Snapchat provides more person-to-person engagement with the content taking up the full screen. The best part for marketers is they do not have to remind their audience to quickly view the campaign before it ends because the user knows that there is a limited window to see the content.

2.19

2.19
Many big names use Snapchat campaigns to promote. For example, Amazon decided to capitalize on a Snapchat campaign before it ends because the user knows there is a limited window to see the content. Amazon customers ordered more than five toys per second on their mobile devices between Black Friday and Christmas. This promotion is easily replicated and can be utilized by almost any brand, especially if that brand wishes to increase sales through mobile devices.

EXPIRING DIGITAL CONTENT

Sometimes referred to as "self-destructing" or "secret" application, this type of platform operates through exclusivity and hidden online enclaves. The youth market and its constant need to facilitate through social networks gave rise to expiring digital content. The urgency of looking at content before it expires is enticing enough to gain the attention of others. Call it FOMO of content before it disappears. Today's hyper-connected world of digital natives requires up-to-the-moment social feeds with little need for long-lasting content. Gen Z (born between 1995 and 2012) and Millennials (born between

1986 and 1994) look for social media platforms that fall under-the-radar: networks that are unknown to parents, bosses, and anyone considered to be authority figures. Another reason the youth market turns to these expiring digital content platforms, such as Snapchat, is that the content is primarily unedited self expressions. Users of Snapchat, an application for expiring photos/videos, view eight billion videos a day as a new form of entertainment. These images are less staged, filtered, or curated, leaving the content left to be more organic and shared in a more casual manner. Other examples include Instagram Stories, Burn Note, Whisper, and Yik Yak.

CASE STUDY:
Snapchat Takes On the Luxury Market

BY JANELLE MOLIN

When luxury first began to adopt Snapchat it was not welcomed by all but the truth was that those who did not welcome it weren't on social media platforms in the first place. With the goal of increasing the luxury sector's marketing mix whilst targeting the next generation of luxury consumers, fashion brands such as Valentino, Dior, and Louis Vuitton joined the highly engaged Snapchat community. Despite seemingly only catering to the youth market, Snapchat has now branched towards the exclusive luxury market segment. What makes this shift so interesting is that it's created a type of secret online society that intrigues the new *low-touch* luxury market. Low touch describes consumers who are well informed and require little education about the brands they heavily invest in. Crowd-curated content was Snapchat's major 2014 update to its "My Story" feature. The update, dubbed "Our Story," is a compilation of user-generated content from events such as concerts, sporting events, and luxury fashion shows. Utilizing geo-filters (overlays for Snaps), in 2015 the high-end brands and events first began to get involved in Snapchat's "Our Story" including:

1. Valentino
2. Dior Resort
3. Louie Vuitton Resort
4. Burberry
5. Stella McCartney
6. 2015 Fashion Week
7. MET Ball in NYC

Luxury brands are now dipping into new ways of reaching their audiences by showcasing clips and snapshots from their respective runway shows. Luxury's standard relationship with its audience is to remain aloof and mysterious, drawing in people via curiosity and the interest in elite status. While a Snapchat story that reveals the exact opposite with "all access" availability. However, if executed properly, brands can boost engagement for new and exiting users (Fiegerman, 2014).

Content curation is paradoxical because it intensifies consumer desire but also keeps luxury out of reach. Companies that utilize Snapchat's Live Story have full control of the published content for the world to see. However, the risk of losing exclusivity increases in tandem with the popularity of the Live Story. Live Story advertisements have the potential to increase revenue but may also lead to consumer confusion and diminished brand reputation. Nevertheless, strategies that have showcased exclusive, behind-the-scenes content have been successful so far.

Janelle Molin is a market researcher who is driven to redefine the area of users experience in the digital marketing sector of social media and user-generated content. Molin recognizes the value in social media platforms that give the audience an unrefined, behind the scenes glimpse to captivate their interest.

LEGALLY SPEAKING IN A SOCIAL MEDIA SPACE

Social media laws and regulations vary across the world and, therefore, it is crucial to know a country's legal standards and guidelines before launching any campaign or collaboration. While laws are created to protect online intellectual content, they are also set up to ensure content authenticity when bloggers promote products online. While social media has given consumers freedom of speech, there are still regulations in place that oversee ethical conduct on the Internet.

Copyright/Content Regulations

Since the launch of Facebook in 2004, social media has rapidly climbed the charts of Internet popularity and is now the most popular online activity nationwide (Carpenter, 2013). That being said, many social media users are unaware of the specific laws and regulations governing shared content. While users of these platforms are aware of the basic stipulations regarding legal and ethical usage, significant gray areas do exist. The waters of social media ethics and regulations are murky and seemingly bottomless; however, islands of usage restriction and ethical standards are slowly forming to provide a safer mooring for users.

Fair Use Restrictions

The issues of fair use and copyright constantly arise in the world of social media. Tumblr encompasses mostly reposted content, rather than original photos, which users share repeatedly across their individual pages for personal inspiration and entertainment. Likewise, Pinterest embraces the same concept as Tumblr, allowing users to "pin" republished images from various websites and other pinners for noncommercial purposes; users rarely upload their own original content. Because the nature of both sites is considered noncommercial, it would be difficult to prove that either platform reduces the value or position of the image/product within its market. In fact, republishing images could generate more traffic for the original content, thus increasing the object's marketplace status, while also serving as free advertising.

But social media platforms face a unique challenge regarding the third copyright standard—scrutinizing the amount of the work used—because in most cases, distinct images, rather than articles or books, are being republished, which generally need to be seen in their visual entirety. Nevertheless, as long as users do not take credit for the original content, platforms like Tumblr and Pinterest should find themselves clear of most copyright lawsuits. It is important to point out that each case is dependent on the country in which the case is reviewed. A case that skirts infringement upon fair use laws in the United States may not be lawful in other countries.

Twitter has often been investigated for copyright infringements due to the popularity of "retweeting" content posted by other users. When an individual retweets, he or she provides a link to the original author's post, thus crediting the author. Twitter provides an important disclosure within their Terms of Service highlighting this activity, stating that once a user uploads content in any form, the site retains "a worldwide, non-exclusive, royalty-free license (with the right to sublicense) to use, copy, reproduce, process, adapt, modify, publish, transmit, display and distribute such content in any and all media or distribution methods (now known or later developed)." By highlighting its right to reproduce content and to require that retweets link to the original source, Twitter appears to have a strong claim for fair use. Because of social media's relatively new presence in the digital world, definitive copyright rulings have not yet crystallized. However, specific legal boundaries and precedents will eventually develop once the legal consequences of technological innovations are better understood.

Users of sites such as Twitter should keep in mind that regulations are not uniform on a global scale. Many countries have far stricter regulations on content creation and sharing compared to the United States. The law often finds the content creator responsible not only for adhering to policies in the country in which the post was created, but also in the countries in which the post is viewed. This indicates the law's quivering stance on governing social media platforms. Social media regulations remain in a budding phase, eventually developing as more cases within the digital world emerge. Issues of copyright infringement, ethical standards, and content conflicts will prompt legal authorities to ultimately establish a definite set of terms that will distinguish right from wrong in the "share everything as if it was yours" environment.

CASE STUDY: The Applicability of US Federal Trade Commission (FTC) Law to Online Advertising

BY ALEX HAMILTON

As advertisers and marketers began to use social media to push products and services through digital influencers, the Federal Trade Commission (FTC) noted the need for rules on endorsements in advertising. In December 2009, it formally released its "Guides Concerning the Use of Endorsements in Advertising" (Caruso, 2011). In 2010, the organization made public its first investigation into a company's relationship with bloggers, and continuing investigations into the relationship between marketers and their online communities. Up until this point, brands did not think twice about getting a blogger to wear their clothes without revealing that those garments had been gifted in return for publicity on a blogger's platforms. The incident that caught the attention of the FTC was when Loft, a division of Ann Taylor, offered an "Exclusive Blogger Preview" of their Summer 2010 collection. Ann Taylor gave bloggers, who posted about the event, an opportunity to be entered into a "mystery gift-card drawing" to win $50 to $500 (Indvik, 2010). "We were concerned that bloggers who attended a preview on January 26, 2010 failed to disclose that they received gifts for posting blog content about that event," Mary Engle, the FTC's associate director of advertising practices, wrote in a letter dated April 20 to Ann Taylor's legal representation (Indvik, 2010).

A major concern at the time was that the FTC decided not to take any action on this matter. Ann Taylor's legal team argued that this was the first blogger event of its kind, only a handful of bloggers posted images, and several gifts were disclosed (Zmuda, 2010). Another key element that protected the retailer was that Ann Taylor's Loft division adopted a written policy regarding all promotional blogger collaborations within one month after the launch of the campaign. The takeaway of this situation is that any product or service being endorsed via social media can trigger an FTC action letter; therefore, it is in the best interest of companies to disclose all information to the FTC. The FTC Act's prohibition on "unfair or deceptive acts or practices" broadly covers advertising claims, marketing and promotional activities, and sales practices in general. The Act is not limited to any particular medium. Accordingly, the Commission's role in protecting consumers from unfair or deceptive acts or practices encompasses advertising, marketing, and online sales, as well as the same activities in print, television, telephone, and radio (FTC, 2013).

Alex Hamilton's research focuses on the laws and regulations in the digital landscape. Her interests are in the ever-growing study of developing regulations to help mitigate issues regarding social media and other newly developed Web networking platforms. Rooted in her personal interests of social good, ethics, and equality, Hamilton began in-depth research of the laws governing online advertising, specifically relating to the world of social media, and curated a study examining the various lawsuits that have arisen, the findings that resulted from them, and the infinite future of social media law.

UNITING THE WORLD

Due to the exponential increase in social media users, the degrees of separation between people have become narrower, effectively "shrinking" the world even further. To "follow" an individual's social network grants access to a new system of virtual friends. Users connect the dots and come to know a broad, intertwined collection of people occupying online communities.

How many friends does one have in an online social community? Pew Research Center showed that among adult Facebook users, "the average (mean) number of friends is 338 and the median (midpoint) number of friends is 200" (Duggan et al., 2015). As networks grow and special interest communities flourish, the degree of separation between consumers decreases.

Degrees of Separation

In the 1960s, social psychologist Stanley Milgram's famous "small-world experiment" (Six Degrees of Separation Theory) argued that the structure of a physical community (not a virtual one) connects two people by a surprisingly small number of intermediate connections (Backstrom, 2011). But the world of digital connection through social media differs radically. Professor Steven Strogatz of Cornell University analyzed how a population of dissimilar individuals can suddenly synchronize in an online environment (Woozeer, 2011). The world is becoming a smaller place; and commonality can be tracked through social platforms that suggest new friends, people to date, products to like, and places to travel to. In 2011, Facebook founder Mark Zuckerberg announced that the online world is now connected by only 3.74 degrees of separation (Parker, 2011). This statement was based on findings from a study conducted by Facebook and Università degli Studi di Milano. Their research created the first "world-scale social-network graph-distance computation" and found that the average degree of separation between any two people on the entire Facebook network is 3.74, while 99.6 percent of all pairs of possible Facebook users are connected within 5 degrees of separation. The study revealed that the digital world is much smaller than we believed, and even smaller than the "six degrees of separation" theory that characterizes physical communities.

Global Perspective of Social Media Marketing

Not every country interprets social media the same way. In order to grasp the potential of global marketing through social networking channels, businesses must first understand the social media landscape (including the most favorable consumer platforms) of each target country. Globally recognized brands such as Christian Dior (Russia), Marc Jacobs (Japan), and Vogue (France) have developed country-sensitive social media platforms, including country-specific content.

On the plus side, transnational social media alleviates many traditional communication barriers to international reach of brands, if they set the stage of communication to match the message to the receiver. Here are three guidelines when venturing into the global world of social media marketing:

1. Generate a narrative with a global perspective to deliver the right message and to communicate between the brand and the target market.
2. Have a country-specific social platform: Identify the local social media channels that best reach the brand's target market, if they currently exist.
3. Localize Reach: Social media campaigns have a geo-location value when they are based on local current events or key influencers.

"Each country's landscape has different country specific factors, such as culture, economy, government regulations and infrastructure that reflect the user base. Since social media is truly global, it is vital to determine segments between countries based on country specific factors to the efficiency of social media marketing. There seems to be a lack of research into how companies can create truly global communities [on social media] where participation is not hindered by language use" (Singh et al., 2012).

INTERVIEW: Leila Samii, Ph.D., Aurora University
Global Research on Connecting Through Social Media

Leila Samii is an Assistant Professor at Aurora University in the Masters of Digital Marketing and Analytics Program and adjuncts in Harvard University, Division of Continuing Education. Samii holds a Ph.D. in international business with a specialization in marketing, specifically social media marketing. Since 2009, Samii has been researching, implementing, and teaching social media strategy. Her research focuses on global social media marketing, investigating the link between brand image and social media from a global context. Samii's extensive knowledge on earned media has facilitated the development of various frameworks focusing on cost effective strategies for social media in the global marketplace.

Can you tell us about country-specific factors and social technographic profiles?

LS: Based on my training in international business and my passion for social media, my approach to social media marketing has always been from a global perspective. I noticed early on the impact that social media can have across borders. Therefore, when analyzing social media, I focus on its global reach and the truly global platform that it is.

When comparing social media to international business theories, the patterns were clear for analyzing global strategic social media marketing. Extended from international business research, for a brand to be successful, they should research the political, economic, social, and technological aspects of a country. The political assessment is important for a brand because the country's openness to freely post on the Internet, or the freedom of the Internet, will vary (Freedom of net). Therefore, it may be difficult for a brand to easily reach social media users in countries with low freedom of the net compared to those with high freedom of the net. Moreover, technology of the country can reveal the opportunities a brand has on social media in terms of quality. For instance, the Internet infrastructure will play a large part in the speed of a message and the richness and type of content from the brand to the consumer.

The country-specific factors are coupled with the social technographic profiles to create overall global market segments. The social technographic profiles are determined by the Groundswell tool (Li and Bernoff, 2010). Demographics of age, gender, and country are input in the Groundswell tool, which generates an index of overall level of engagement among users on social media. The Groundswell tool reveals six levels of engagement from the most engaged users on social media, the "creators," to the least engaged users on social media, the "inactives." Each country varies on all six factors of the Groundswell tool based on age and gender. The social technographic (characteristics and behavior) profiles based on country, age and gender supplemented with the PEST (Political, Economic, Socio-Cultural, and Technological) factors were used in my research to develop global market segments.

Can you tell us about global market segments on social media?

Global market segments on social media explain the difference between looking primarily at your social media from a country-to-country perspective and more so from segmenting your audience based on similarities of country specific factors. The message you communicate on social media should be positioned from the perspective of the country-specific factors and social technographic profiles on channels that the segment is on. For example, girls aged 6 to 35 from all cultures and countries are obsessed with Hello Kitty (Sanrio, 2015). Would it be useful for Sanrio, the parent company of Hello Kitty, to take a country-by-country approach to pushing out messages on social media? The answer is no. Sanrio would lose efficiency by customizing social media channels and posts to each of the 70 countries they sell Hello Kitty products in (Fitzgerald, 2014). Therefore, to increase efficiency on social media, Sanrio should look to the global market segments to determine overall positioning statements for specific segments.

Can you give us a breakdown of what brands should look for when expanding their social media reach by country-specific social media platform?

Interestingly, the same social media principles apply to brands from a one-country approach or a multi-country approach. Successful brands will be strategic and use what I call the R.E.A.L.L.Y. framework. The R.E.A.L.L.Y. framework stands for Research, Engage, Analyze, Listen, Leverage, and You (be yourself) on social media. A brand that wants to expand their social media strategy in other countries should start by researching and listening to the target audience, competitors, and influencers of the country they want to reach and engage with on social media. The research and listening data should then be analyzed to better understand the community they are looking to expand into. Only when a brand recognizes the norms of the community through their research and listening, should they start engaging with the social media audience. Similar to entering any societal culture or micro-culture, it is vital to learn the interaction style and the language of group. The same is true on social media. For the success of a brand, minimizing community cultural blunders is a must!

INTERVIEW: Misha Janette on the Impact of Fashion Blogging and Social Media in Japan   TokyoFashionDiaries.com

Misha Janette moved to Tokyo in 2004 to study at the prestigious Bunka Fashion College, which counts Yohji Yamamoto and Kenzo Takada as graduates. In 2014, Janette was named as one of Business of Fashion's "500 people shaping the global industry" for Japan, alongside Comme des Garçon's Kawakubo Rei and Junya Watanabe. As a fashion director, she is known for merging fashion with art for incredibly fantastical images and she has been tapped to style for Desigual for their New York Fashion Week runway show. She recently designed the costumes for Tokyo's newest attraction, The Kawaii Monster Cafe in Harajuku.

As a fashion journalist, Janette writes for respected publications and has been lead fashion writer at *The Japan Times* for eight years. In an effort to spread more information on the Japanese fashion scene, she started the bilingual fashion blog "Tokyo Fashion Diaries." She hosts several TV shows on Japanese television, is a guest lecturer at fashion schools and universities around Japan, and is the only foreign member on the advisory board for the Japanese government's "Cool Japan" initiative, meant to promote Japanese culture abroad.

How have you seen the fashion industry change since social media and fashion blogging have taken on a role as normal modes of communication?

MJ: I started out as a fashion journalist with *The Japan Times* newspaper and I still am a journalist there, before I became a blogger myself.

I have seen the fashion industry change. People say it is more democratic—it goes back and forth because some bloggers are not exactly democratic anymore, it's definitely more of a business. We have seen it go from bloggers shaking up the industry, to blogging becoming its own industry. Fashion editors are bloggers and bloggers are fashion editors.

How has the social media landscape changed how fashion is shared in Japan?

Japan has always had what we would consider a quote-on-quote blogger because we had Dokusha Moderu (reader model). Dokusha Moderu are basically normal girls who read magazines and have a cute style. The magazine will pick them up and feature them in the magazine, which will feature them a Dokusha Modueru. When they are featured in the magazine they are expected to do their own make-up, prepare their own outfits. These girls would also write for the magazine's blog and be featured in the magazine as well. A lot of these popular bloggers girls are also with an agency and the agency is taking their pictures for them. It's a little different from a blogger in the west.

There are very few girls like me who have their own website name and are doing their own thing, completely independent of a magazine. I am asked regularly by brands what magazine I blog under. I tell them "I am completely independent and I do not blog for a magazine."

2.20

2.20
Misha Janette

2.21

2.21
TokyoFashionDiaries.com

How has fashion blogging changed for you in the last two years? As a major Japanese fashion influencer what expectation have you found necessary to keep a global audience?

I was reading an article where a columnist was saying that nothing interesting has come out of Japan since Comme Des Garçons or Yohji Yamamoto. The columnist said that we keep expecting something to happen, and what is going on in the streets is not interesting, finally stating that nothing is going to happen in Japan.

I remember saying to myself, "Wait a minute! There are some really cool underground things going on but you guys (outside of Japan) just don't know about because it is not written about in English." And this is the moment I decided to start a blog. While I really just wanted to write my blog in English, it was a Japanese fashion editor who asked me to write it in Japanese as well. This way, they could see what I thought was interesting, coming up from the streets. Those kids who had smaller independent brands would come up to me directly and show me their designs. And so, that was kind of an access that the magazine editors didn't have. So I did it bilingually and share with a global audience some of the creative designs coming from Japan.

Do you customize your content for your Japanese and western audience?

Customize my content…My English captions are witty, sarcastic, and funny, while the Japanese content is very kind, not harsh, or not trying to be witty at all. It's just not a part of the Japanese culture to be self-degrading or self-deprecating. I change the wording in my blog between the two languages.

If I am too positive, in English, it comes off as fake, while in Japanese that's just how it is—you only talk about the positive. Of course I try to talk about the negative, that's kind of my "thing," that is what I am known for; but at the same time, it is done in a kind of tiptoeing way. That is because the Japanese culture and language are quite different. In the west, the saying "any publicity is good publicity" doesn't really apply to Japan. You don't want to be scandalous, you don't want to be shocking—you want to be smart about it.

Can you share with us some brands that you see best share their stories through social media in Japan?

The Dokusha Moderu (local models) who become popular in the magazines, and have their followers online, end up starting brands. The natural progression is for a girl, who is Dokusha Moderu in the magazine, and then becomes popular on social media applications like WEAR, a Japanese social media app.

The girl most followed on WEAR becomes a producer of a brand or a creative director of a brand. Every day, they show outfits they are wearing; in the end, it's not them supporting other brands but their own brand. You kind of grow up with them and see how they change their style. It is so common for these girls to have their own brands.

EXERCISES

Critical Thinking:
Evaluate how social proof is relevant to a brand that is determining whether a campaign (namely, social media) has been a success or not. How do these brands collect social proof? Refer to advertising news websites and also the Tech Corner section for insightful sources.

Practical Application:
Create a social currency plan of action or campaign for a brand of your choice. Refer to the Marc Jacobs Tweet Pop Up Shop as an example. Select one of the five forms of social proof to focus on.

Value of Social Media Platform:
Select a social media channel and generate quantifiable breakdown of the platform from reach to engagement. Share examples of the strengths and weaknesses of the platform and find examples of well-used campaigns to support.

Business Activity:
Create a case study of a new mobile application or social network that is currently impacting the fashion industry. Review digital industry press to locate the new applications.

Generate an updated social media and languages chart listing five social media channels used in countries outside of your country.

Infographic:
Create a dematerialization infographic for today's smartphone or the current social media landscape of types of social media.

Laws and Regulations:
Review new laws in the digital space and compare how these will impact the marketplace. Resource sites: thefashionlaw.com; SocialMediaLawBulletin.com

Technology Corner:
Review the technology-driven news and insight to locate new trends in the digital landscape. Suggested sources: Tech New World, PSFK, TechCrunch, Mashable, L2 Think.

REFERENCES

Backstrom, L. (2011), "Anatomy of Facebook," *Facebook*, November 21. Available online: https://www.facebook.com/notes/facebook-data-team/anatomy-of-facebook/10150388519243859?tag=mncol;txt

Bain, M. (2015), "Kanye's upset victory over Chanel shows personalities trump brands," *Quartz*, March 22. Available online: http://qz.com/367075/kanye-fashion-month-victory-over-chanel-shows-personalities-trump-brands/

Barnikel, M. (2012), "How Social Currency Is Driving Identity, Trust, and New Industries," *TechCrunch*, April 15. Available online: http://techcrunch.com/2012/04/15/how-social-currency-is-driving-identity-trust-and-new-industries/

Beck, M. (2015), "Did Lord & Taylor's Instagram Influencer Campaign Cross The Line?," *Marketing Land*. Available online: http://marketingland.com/did-lord-taylors-instagram-influencer-campaign-cross-the-line-123961

Belk, R. (2013), "Extended Self in a Digital World," *Journal of Consumer Research*, 40 (3): 477-500.

Berger, J. (2013), *Contagious: Why Things Catch On*, 1st ed., New York: Simon & Schuster.

Brookman, F. (2015), "Kathy O'Brien: The Transformation of Marketing in a Digital World," *Women's Wear Daily*, February 27. Available online: http://wwd.com/beauty-industry-news/marketing-trends/kathy-obrien-the-transformation-of-marketing-in-a-digital-world-8238439/

Bullas, J. (n.d.), "Is this the Social Media Marketing Tipping Point?" *Jeffbullas.com*, Available online: http://www.jeffbullas.com/2014/02/03/is-this-the-social-media-marketing-tipping-point/

BX Worldwide Speakers + Entertainment. (2015), "Brian Solis: Futurist, Anthropologist, Digital Analyst, Keynote Speaker" [Video file], April 7. Available online: https://www.youtube.com/watch?v=41_RHAtHdlc

Carpenter, C. C. (2013), "Copyright Infringement and the Second Generation of Social Media: Why Pinterest Users Should Be Protected from Copyright Infringement by the Fair Use Defense," *Journal of Internet Law*, 16 (7): 1-21. Available online: http://ezproxy.woodbury.edu:880/login?url=http://search.proquest.com/docview/1267792849?accountid=25364

Caruso, P. (2011), "Avoiding the Pitfalls of Social Media Marketing," *Law360*, December 1. Available online: http://www.law360.com/articles/288714/avoiding-the-pitfalls-of-social-media-marketing

Cherry, K. (n.d.), "What Is the Halo Effect?," *About.com*. Available online: https://www.verywell.com/what-is-the-halo-effect-2795906

Community Standards. (n.d.), *Facebook*. Available online: https://www.facebook.com/communitystandards

Didelot, P. (2013), "The History of Social Media. When Did It Really Begin? You May Be Surprised," *The Inquisitr*. Available online: http://www.inquisitr.com/830664/the-history-of-social-media-when-did-it-really-begin-you-may-be-surprised-infographic/#OPJ2cxPzSxFauPyE.99

Digital Training Academy (2012), "Snapchat case study: H & M runs mobile treasure hunt for a party invites." Available online: http://www.digitaltrainingacademy.com/casestudies/2015/01/snapchat_case_study_hm_runs_mobile_treasure_hunt_for_party_invites.ph

D'Onfro, J. (2015), "Snapchat now has nearly 100 million daily users," *Business Insider*, May 26. Available online: http://www.businessinsider.com/snapchat-daily-active-users-2015-5

Duggan, M., Ellison, N., Lampe, C., Lenhart, A., Madden, M., Rainie, L., and Smith, A. (2015), "Social Media Update 2014: While Facebook remains the most popular site, other platforms see higher rates of growth," Washington, D.C.: Pew Research Center.

Dunham, K. (2014, May), "The Beginner's Guide to Social Media Metrics: Reach and Exposure," *HootSuite.com*. Available online: http://blog.hootsuite.com/beginners-guide-to-social-media-metrics-reach-exposure/

Eridon, C. (2012), "10 Genius Ideas That Changed Marketing Forever," Hubspot.com, October 9. Available online: http://blog.hubspot.com/blog/tabid/6307/bid/33689/10-Genius-Ideas-That-Changed-Marketing-Forever.aspx

Fashionlike—C&A. (2012). http://results.epica-awards.com/2012/42-04028-INT.html

Federal Trade Commission, (2013, March), "How to Make Effective Disclosures in Digital Advertising."

Available online: https://www.ftc. gov/sites/default/files/attachments/ press-releases/ftc-staff-revises-online-advertising-disclosure-guide lines/130312dotcomdisclosures.pdf

Fiegerman, S. (2014), "Snapchat's not-so-secret weapon: Live events," *Mashable*, November 5. Available online: http://mashable. com/2014/11/05/snapchat-live-events/

Fife, E. (2015), "Exclusive: Kevin Systrom on Fashion and Instagram," *CFDA.com*, April 8. Available online: http://cfda.com/ blog/exclusive-kevin-systrom-on-fashion-and-instagram

Gladwell, M. (2002), *The Tipping Point: How Little Things Can Make a Big Difference*, Boston: Back Bay Books.

Griner, D. (2015), "Lord & Taylor Got 50 Instagrammers to Wear the Same Dress, Which Promptly Sold Out," *Adweek*, March 31. Available online: http://www.adweek.com/ news/advertising-branding/lord-taylor-got-50-instagrammers-wear-same-dress-which-promptly-sold-out-163791

Groupe Speciale Mobile Association (2015), "The Mobile Economy," March 31. Available online: http:// gsmamobileeconomy.com/global/ GSMA_Global_Mobile_Economy_ Report_2015.pdf

Hallen, E. (2014), "The Science of Social Proof: 5 Types and the Psychology Behind Each," *BufferApp.com*, May 1. Available online: https://blog.bufferapp.com/ the-ultimate-guide-to-social-proof

Hartshorn, S. (2010), "5 Differences Between Social Media and Social Networking," *SocialMediaToday*, May 4. Available online: http:// www.socialmediatoday.com/ content/5-differences-between-social-media-and-social-networking

Hawkins, S. (2011), "Copyright Fair Use and How It Works for Online Images," *Social Media Examiner*, November 23. Available online: http://www. socialmediaexaminer.com/ copyright-fair-use-and-how-it-works-for-online-images/

Hutchinson, A. (2015), "Everyone's Talking About Snapchat—and There's Good Reason Why," *Social Media Today*, May 30. Available online: http:// www.socialmediatoday. com/social-networks/ adhutchinson/2015-05-30/ everyones-talking-about-snapchat-and-theres-good-reason-why

Indvik, L. (2010), "No Fines Levied in FTC's First Blogger-Advertiser Investigation," *Mashable*, April 30. Available online: http://mashable. com/2010/04/30/ann-taylor-ftc-investigation/

Instabrand (2015), "Why Brands Should Embrace Disappearing Content and Have Fun with It," *Instabrand (blog)*, October 24. Available online: https://instabrand.com/ industry/2015/10/24/why-brands-should-embrace-disappearing-content-and-have-fun-with-it

Kaplan, A. M., and Haenlein, M. (2010), "Users of the World, unite! The challenges and opportunities of Social Media," *Business Horizons*, 53 (1): 59-68. doi:10.1016/j.bushor.2009.09.003

Kaplan, A., and Haenlein, M. (2011), "The early bird catches the news: Nine things you should know about micro-blogging," *Business Horizons*, 54: 105-113. doi:10.1016/j.bushor.2010.09.004

Licht, A. (2013), "Twitter is My First Love," *Twitter (blog)*, September 4. Available online: https://blog.twitter.com/2013/donna-karan-internationals-svp-of-global-communications-aliza-licht-twitter-is-my-first-love

Loatman, M. (2014), "Court: Former Employee Didn't Own 6 Million Likes on Facebook Page," *Bloomberg BNA*, August 29. Available online: http:// www.bna.com/court-former-employee-b17179894293/

Lowery, K. (2015), "Your Invisible Audience: A Q&A with Social Media Expert Alexandra Samuel," *SailThru.com*, April 16. Available online: http://www.sailthru.com/ marketing-blog/invisible-audience-qa-social-media-expert-alexandra-samuel/

Lunden, I. (2015), "6.1B Smartphone Users Globally by 2020, Overtaking Basic Fixed Phone Subscriptions," *TechCrunch*, June 2. Available online: http:// techcrunch.com/2015/06/02/6-1b-smartphone-users-globally-by-2020-overtaking-basic-fixed-phone-subscriptions/#.7o9qrmf:RPIH

Number of social network users worldwide from 2010-2018. (n.d.). Available online: http://www. statista.com/statistics/278414/ number-of-worldwide-social-network-users/

Parker, M. (2011), "Facebook's 3.74 degrees of separation is a world away from being significant," *The Guardian*, November 23. Available online: http://www.theguardian. com/commentisfree/2011/nov/23/ facebook-degrees-of-separation

Oxford Dictionary (2015), "Oxford Dictionaries Word of The Year," November 16. Available online: http://blog.oxforddictionaries. com/2015/11/word-of-the-year-2015-emoji/

Safko, L. (2010), "The Social Media Bible: Tactics, Tools, and Strategies for Business Success," Hoboken: Wiley.

Samuel, A., and Reid, A. (n.d.), "What Social Media Analytics Can't Tell You," VisionCritical. com. Available online: https:// www.visioncritical.com/resources/ socialcustomersreport/

Singh, N., Lehnert, K., and Bostick, K. (2012), "Global Social Media Usage: Insights into Reaching Consumers Worldwide," *Thunderbird International Business Review*, 54 (5): 683-700.

SnapChat Case Study (2014, January 25). Available online: https://www. nethosting.com/snapchat/

Social Media Addiction—Statistics and Trends, (2014, December 26). Available online: http://www. go-globe.com/blog/social-media-addiction/

Sorokina, O. (2015), "8 Types of Social Media and How Each Can Benefit Your Business," *HootSuite.com*, March 12. Available online: http:// blog.hootsuite.com/types-of-social-media/

Steele, D. (2012), "4 Tips For Gamifying Your Marketing Plan," *Mashable*, May 7. Available online: http://mashable.com/2012/05/07/ gamify-your-marketing-plan/

Stratmann, J. (n.d.), "Social Media Case Study: The Jimmy Choo Trainer Hunt," [Web log post]. Available online: http:// www.evancarmichael.com/ Marketing/5760/Social-media-case-study-The-Jimmy-Choo-Trainer-Hunt.html

Strugatz, R. (2014), "Fashion Brands Push Social Media Ads," *Women's Wear Daily*, October 13. Available online: http://wwd.com/business-news/advertising/fashion-brands-push-social-media-ads-7977246/

Terms of Use, Instagram. Available online: https://help.instagram. com/478745558852511

Thompson, C. (2008), "Brave New World of Digital Intimacy," *The New York Times*, September 5. Available online: http://www. nytimes.com/2008/09/07/ magazine/07awareness-t. html?pagewanted=all&_r=0

Top 6 social networks in Japan, (2013), *Digital Strategy Consulting*, June 2. Available online: http://www. digitalstrategyconsulting.com/ intelligence/2013/02/top_6_ social_networks_in_japan.php

Truong, A. (n.d.), "Tweet For Your Supper—and Handbag: Brands, Customers, and the New Social Currency," *Fast Company*. Available online: http://www. fastcompany.com/3026071/ tweet-for-your-supper-and-handbag-brands-customers-and-the-new-social-currency

Tupy, M. (2012), "Dematerialization (update)," *CATO Institute*, July 12. Available online: http://www. cato.org/blog/dematerialization-update

Twitter Terms of Service. (n.d.). Twitter. Available online: https:// twitter.com/tos?lang=en

"US CTM Releases Report on Americans' Media Consumption (2013)," *USC Marshall News*, October 29. Available online: http://www.marshall.usc.edu/ news/releases/2013/usc-ctm-releases-report-americans-media-consumption

Widrich, L. (2012), "The Science of Storytelling: What Listening to a Story Does to Our Brains," *BufferApp.com*, November 29. Available online: https://blog. bufferapp.com/science-of-storytelling-why-telling-a-story-is-the-most-powerful-way-to-activate-our-brains

Williams, J. (2014), "Retro Read: The Laws of Blogging," TheFashionLaw.com, September 5. Available online: http://www. thefashionlaw.com/the-fashion-law-1/the-laws-of-blogging

Wisdom 2.0 (2014), "Technology and the Brain, the Latest Research and Findings: Larry Rosen," March 2. Available online: https://www.youtube. com/watch?v=n0OqA0pmAag

Woozeer, A. (2010), "Six degrees of separation" [Video file]. Available online: https://vimeo. com/14196818

Zmuda, N. (2010), "Ann Taylor Investigation Shows FTC Keeping Close Eye on Blogging," *Advertising Age*, April 28. Available online: http://adage. com/article/news/ann-taylor-case-shows-ftc-keeping-close-eye-blogging/143567/

03

PART 1

**THE DIGITAL LANDSCAPE
TRANSFORMS THE
FASHION INDUSTRY**

THE RISE OF THE HYPER-CONNECTED CONSUMER

Chapter Objectives

- Understand the new hyper-connected consumer
- Assess how the Internet is becoming the consumer's external memory bank
- Investigate the psychological impacts caused by social media usage
- Identify new consumer expectations
- Explore the generational gaps in social media communications
- Recognize the overall online social experience of each generation

3.1
Consumers today are connected,
literally, to their phone.

INTRODUCTION

With over three billion Internet users and two billion social media users, it is no wonder that there is a shift in the behavior of consumers with the connected world around them (Kemp, 2015). Consumers continue to embrace these connections at accelerated rates through the adoption of mobile applications, social media communities, and the Internet itself. In this chapter, we will investigate these new connected consumers to see how they have adopted digital/social networks as part of their everyday normality. While digital landscapes were reviewed in previous chapters, we have not taken a look at consumer characteristics, requirements, and generations, which are critical factors in shaping how brands connect to these individuals. This chapter will introduce the learned consumer behavior traits that accompany this hyper-connected cultural shift, ranging from digital nesting to online social interactions.

As the digital landscape continues to flourish with participation, a new, more informed consumer has come to the fore, carrying a unique set of insights and expectations about products, pricing, and value. We will investigate how these new consumers conduct independent online research to expand their knowledge, and use social media to empower them to make better purchase decisions. This enhanced knowledge leads to more expectations, which, in turn, has changed the traditional retail business model into a more complex environment. Despite the influx of advanced social media tools, brands have been able to monitor the new consumer's learned behaviors and reposition themselves across the digital landscape. In order to make timely, appropriate adjustments, it is necessary for marketers, managers, and branding agents to understand these new behaviors as well as the differences between consumer generations (i.e., Gen Z vs. Baby Boomers). Brands continuously struggle to keep up with digitally driven cultural shifts, and develop new approaches to addressing consumer expectations. While there are more questions than answers on how to market to these new consumers efficiently, we must begin by examining the rise of the hyper-connected customer and the plethora of behaviors associated with the evolution of social media.

> " **SOCIAL MEDIA IS THE GREATEST SOCIAL EXPERIMENT IN THE HISTORY OF MANKIND. THIS EXPERIMENT WILL RESULT IN A PROFOUND SHIFT IN THE WAY PEOPLE SEE THEMSELVES AND THEIR PLACE IN THE WORLD."**
> PATRICK MULFORD, EXECUTIVE CREATIVE DIRECTOR FOR THE AUDIENCE

3.2a

3.2a
Taking the perfect selfie has become the pastime for a whole generation of social media users.

HYPER-CONNECTED CONSUMERS

Today's hyper-connected consumers continue to alter the landscape of the fashion industry, dramatically affecting elements such as fashion cycle speed and retail business models. In this section, we will examine their motivations, behaviors, and expectations. Learning social patterns (e.g., digital nesting) provides a solution for better understanding these new consumers. Cultural shifts have created a new normality, wherein people are perpetually connected to social media platforms and online communities. The formulation of marketing strategies must begin with understanding the characteristics of these new consumers.

3.2c

3.2b

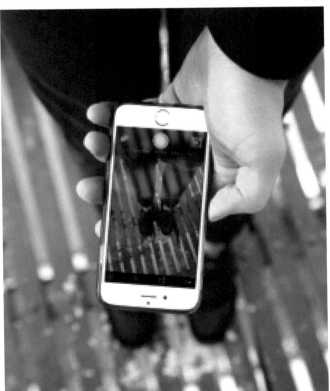

3.2b
Gregory Dava exploring—spanning all regions of the globe, hyper-connected consumers are transforming the world in dramatic ways.

3.c
No one seems to look up to see where they are going but remain focused on their mobile phone.

" THE INTERNET HAS BECOME THE ETERNAL HARD DRIVE FOR OUR MEMORIES, CHANGING HOW WE PERCEIVE AND REMEMBER THE WORLD AROUND US."
GARY VAYNERCHUK, VAYNER MEDIA

3.3

3.3
Consumers today consume and save their life experiences in the digital nest of social media spaces.

Digital Nesting

Hyper-connected consumers spend most of their day on their smartphones collecting, curating, quantifying, and filtering through their respective areas of interest. Posting, sharing, engaging on social media is so ubiquitous now, and people are so comfortable with their own "nests." Platforms such as Facebook allow users to curate their lives through a constant stream of images and social feeds. Armed with smartphones instead of conventional cameras, members of the social media generation capture memorable moments as they go, effectively jumpstarting the process of curation. The collection process continues as they search for platforms that will allow them to "pin" this content, preserving them for storage and sharing purposes. Curation enables consumers to express themselves in more meaningful ways—they take great pride in purposefully sharing what they think is funny, interesting, and acceptable to their peers. Mining (searching) has also increased as a result of more and more people using digital outlets to store their memories. Social community sites such as Facebook, Instagram, and Pinterest have made consumers more highly connected than before through the social aspect of collection. This shift in behavior is referred to as "Digital Nesting," which is quickly becoming the consumer's external memory bank. For example, while Gen Xers and Baby Boomers used photo albums to preserve their memories, today's generation depends on social media and Cloud storage to capture and share their most cherished moments. In 2011, Intel created "Museum of Me," a tool that collected a user's Facebook content and transformed it into a virtual museum experience. Digital nesting enables users to curate a comfort zone within their online social space, giving them a feeling similar to being at home (nest).

Posting, sharing, and engaging on social media is so ubiquitous now and people are so comfortable with their own "nests" that they do not seem to exaggerate much about themselves online anymore—it would be like lying to yourself in your own diary.

Psychological Impacts of Social Media

Social phobia can occur when traditional interactions (i.e., in person) are replaced by communication through devices. Modern society is attuned to communicating behind the safety of screens, resulting in ignored calls, late responses, and the use of inappropriate language. Social phobia is the strong fear of being judged or ridiculed by others. This fear causes anxiety amongst social media users in the form of online bullying, liking features, and/or read receipts. People may begin to experience social phobia if they receive nasty comments on an online post (Cavanaugh, 2012). Similarly, people develop post-posting depression when they post content and do not immediately receive "likes"—they then begin to question themselves and the content that they chose to share. Read receipts, used by both Apple and Snapchat, can create anxiety and insecurity because you can see when someone has read your message (and if the person chose to ignore you). These new features have impacted the manner in which consumers feel and operate within online social communities.

Extended Mind

Researchers from the department of psychology at the University of Waterloo in Ontario, Canada, found that those who think more intuitively rely on technology. A research study was published from the journal *Computers in Human Behavior* is titled "The Brain in Your Pocket: Evidence That Smartphones Are Used to Supplant Thinking" (Barr, Pennycook, Stolz and Fugelsang, 2015). "Humans are eager to avoid expending effort when problem-solving, and it seems likely that people will increasingly use their smartphones as an extended mind," states one of researchers Nathaniel Barr (IANS, 2015). "Our reliance on smartphones and other devices is likely to rise. It is important to understand how smartphones affect and relate to human psychology before these technologies are so fully ingrained that it is hard to recall what life was like without them," cautioned Barr (IANS, 2015).

" ... CELLPHONES ARE ALWAYS PRESENT AND RARELY TURNED OFF—AND THIS CONSTANT CONNECTIVITY CREATES NEW SOCIAL CHALLENGES. THIS "ALWAYS-ON" REALITY HAS DISRUPTED LONG-STANDING SOCIAL NORMS ABOUT WHEN IT IS APPROPRIATE FOR PEOPLE TO SHIFT THEIR ATTENTION AWAY FROM THEIR PHYSICAL CONVERSATIONS AND INTERACTIONS WITH OTHERS TOWARD DIGITAL ENCOUNTERS WITH PEOPLE AND INFORMATION THAT ARE ENABLED BY THEIR MOBILE PHONE."
(2015, RAINIE AND ZICKUHR)

The Emotional Journal of Social Media
Contributing Writer - Shani Yehezkel

Measuring Moods
Social media and technology have a great influence on our self-esteem and emotions. Emotional states are often contagious; interacting with a happy person is a friendly experience, while interacting with an unhappy person is usually a more unpleasant one. A person's mood is greatly influenced by the emotions of those around them. Data from a social network experiment suggests that moods can be transferred to others through networks via emotional contagion (Guillory, Hancock and Kramer, 2014). People often express their opinions and feelings on Facebook, which is then seen by their friends on the "News Feed." An algorithm based on relevance and engagement determines what posts, photos, stories, and activities a user will see on their "News Feed" (Guillory, Hancock & Kramer, 2014).

Fear of Missing Out (FOMO)
Social media has changed our relationship with the world. Today, we are a click away from finding out exactly where our friends are and what they are doing at any time of the day. Features such as Facebook "check-ins" and constant social feeds have given us the ability to become cognizant of other people's activities and whereabouts. Each upload and share develops our "digital self" as we create a trail of personalized content about ourselves. The Fear of Missing Out (FOMO) is the reason that most people check their phones moments before going to sleep and immediately after waking up and. Many theories claim that FOMO stems from seeing your peers engage in positive activities on social media, making you compare their lives to yours. "FOMO can cause anxiety, stress and, in more extreme cases, even depression" (Catanese, 2013). However, this can also become favorable if motivated toward a positive change.

Joy of Missing Out (JOMO)
Not all consumers are susceptible to FOMO; in fact, many individuals become empowered by social media instead of being alienated on these platforms. Blogger Anil Dash conceptualized the Joy of Missing Out (JOMO)—a means by which users can disconnect from the pressures of social media and appreciate their detachment from online communities (Castillo, 2014). By not focusing on the activities of others, one can discover and embrace solitude within the digital realm, thus leading to a host of positive outcomes.

Shani Yehezkel's emphasis of study is on social media and how it relates to marketing practices. Yehezkel delved into researching the positive and negative effects of social media and its influence on a user's psychological process. Her research concluded in findings of social media disorders: narcissism, obsessive compulsive disorder, social phobias, fear of missing out, and joy of missing out. Well-versed in the world of social media, activate participation in social media platforms inspired her research and findings. Since then, Shani has furthered her research to discover how social media impacts ethical practices in marketing and public relations.

Interview with Author of *iDisorder: Understanding Our Obsession with Technology and Overcoming Its Hold on Us*, Dr. Larry Rosen

Dr. Larry Rosen is professor and past chair of the department of psychology at California State University, Dominguez Hills. He is a research psychologist with specialties in multitasking, social networking, generational differences, parenting, child and adolescent development, and educational psychology, and is recognized as an international expert in the "Psychology of Technology."

Tell us about the "look at me" culture.

LR: This culture has to do with connection to technology rather than an age group. Underlying issues have to do with values and views of communication and technology. Younger generations prefer to connect differently than previous generations. They are "connecting," rather than "communicating" (talking, face to face, etc). They want to have flexibility to communicate any place, anytime, and with anyone. There is also the "Rule of three: if there are three people taking part in a conversation, then you can go look at your phone." They value the ability to connect with anyone at any time. It is not a deep connection, but it is still a connection.

How do you define or differentiate between communication and connection?

The model is called the "5 C's of Communication":

CONNECT:
This starts with finding a way to connect, whether it is texting, phone call, face-to-face, email, etc. If you cannot connect, you cannot communicate effectively.

CONTENT:
You have to have some sort of message that you want to transmit or convey.

CONTEXT:
Meaning must be established—one person is sending their message in one context and the other person is receiving it in another context.

CONGRUENCY:

The content and context have to match. This is why texting is hard: the two people's contexts are different.

COMPLETION:

New forms of communication do not ever get completed. Most of the communication falls apart under "connection" because some people try to text when it is not appropriate, and context is totally screwed up because you have no idea about the context of the person receiving your message. Completion can happen very easily face-to-face or on the phone, but most young people refuse to do the completion step when texting. With texting, people withhold most cues and there is confusing context. You have to interpret emojis, you have to interpret feelings from words and the presentation of these words, and you make assumptions.

We are in an era of connection, not communication, even when we are together, because we are so into what is in our phone that we neglect the people we are with. Everybody has a second screen. No one does just one thing anymore. They try to juggle multiple things and none of those things happen to be your relationships, and they tend to take backstage to your screens.

Tell us more about "Multitasking" and "Attention Spans" within the context of social media.

Research shows that our attention span is 2-5 minutes at most, and even before we switch our focus from one thing to another, we are already anticipating the switch, so, we are spending less time doing what we think we are doing because part of that time is our preparation for the switch.

What are your thoughts on "Fear of Missing Out" (FOMO)?

Social Media is a perfect environment for FOMO because we have hundreds of people potentially commenting on things that we feel are important to us. If you set alerts for every time you get a comment or notification, your phone is beeping all day long, and you constantly feel a pull to check. This pull plays a major role in our self-esteem and self-perception.

There is an urgency to be noticed and be seen. Social media is "one to many," not just one-to-one such as texting or calling.

It is a place where we display ourselves because we know that there will be a host of people reading what we say. They will make assumptions about us, so we act accordingly and rarely post things that will make us look bad, unhappy, or imperfect. We want the world to see us in a particular way. As Carl Rogers says, "We want to present our ideal self."

How would you describe or define social phobia?

An ex-editor for *The New York Times* once wrote that young people do not ever look you in the eye, and this is concerning because part of communicating is from the face. Some people have been raised communicating primarily from a distance without having to look people in the eye and so they do not understand the pragmatics of communication. That is going to be seen more even now. A lot of kids have developed social phobia because they do not want to have face-to-face communication and even when they are together, they are on their phones, or looking down, or looking away. People's faces can be saying something completely different than how they are saying things or what they are saying. People would rather see life through a 2x2-inch lens than actually looking face to face. They are constantly taking pictures. Selfies have become the most important thing in the world to kids and they say "pics or it didn't happen."

Social Communities

Connectivity to online communities is now the norm for over three billion people, and will reach over six billion individuals by 2022 ("Global Theme"). Prior to this movement, the consumer's voice was only heard through filtered channels controlled by select gatekeepers (editors, news media, television networks, etc.). One of the most powerful movements in social media today is the rise of connected communities. Today, the consumer's voice is collectively expressed through online social communities and heard by millions around the globe. Whether through an entrepreneur social community, such as Poshmark. com, or a community powered by social curation, such as Polyvore.com, the collective power of communities drive the fashion industry nowadays.

The rise of connected consumers has resulted in a sharp uptick in brand expectations. These new audiences hold strong opinions that are derived from knowledge acquired through online communities. Community-driven behaviors are prevalent across the digital space, which naturally imposes new standards and expectations for brands and retailers alike. Today's consumers desire acknowledgement and want to be viewed by their brands as loyal patrons instead of ordinary supporters. This section will explore how social communities enable brands to improve experiences for their customers.

Society's acceptance of social media culture has united people around the world in a manner never seen before. The idea of connecting through the Internet was groundbreaking; however, it was the advent of social media that truly altered the way consumers engaged with brands and with each other. Social media transformed the very nature of engagement by allowing consumers to build their respective online communities without borders. Users who have never met conglomerate in the digital world and build communities based on common interests or shared causes. With digital spaces no longer limited by demographics, online communities have prospered, propelling content and information as the new forms of commerce. "Googling" and "friending" are part of the modern lexicon, successfully transitioning from pop-culture verbs to an authentic way of life.

Social feeds can also be used as avenues for online social bragging—users often choose to share content that reflects how they want to be seen by others. Today's "look at me" generation was born out of the ability to share content with others and add intrinsic value to each new post and connection. This shared content may come in the form of images, videos, links, and text that are designed to give followers the idea that the user is intelligent (e.g., book recommendations, informative articles), exciting (e.g., social life, travel, entertainment), compassionate (e.g., charitable cause link) or attractive (e.g., selfies).

Netnography, or online ethnography, is a marketing research technique that is a rich source of consumer insight (behaviors) of individuals on the Internet. This term was developed by Robert Kozinets and originates from "inter[net] and "ethnography." He first introduced this with his article on virtual communities (Kozinets, 2002)

3.4
"Selfie" by j.Pierce @iamjpierce

The "Look at Me" Culture

The "Look at Me" culture is the growing movement that is embraced by today's digitally connected society. You are what you share. . . . While many do not agree with this type of sharing, this is an important cultural shift that marketers and managers must understand in order to make better decisions. Social media's meteoric rise has allowed consumers to create an environment that features moment-to-moment feeds and expansive sharing with online communities. Social networks themselves were designed as a medium for individuals to share information about themselves with others within a social network (Gonzales and Hancock, 2011). This "look at me" momentum is derived from the consumers' need to position their personal brand in a favorable light. This philosophy involves posting and sharing content (images, videos) that represents an idealized version of oneself, which helps promote and increase social engagement levels. However, maintaining this online presence also requires a great deal of effort, involving countless hours of creation and curation.

This shift in the social media "self" has created the societal phenomenon known as the "selfie." One's online self-image plays a cognitive role in altering one's emotional equilibrium—this is derived from feelings of acceptance or rejection formed within the digital landscape. While each post is viewed, measured, and judged by one's social community, what cogitation takes place in the development of the "self image?" How much "judging" is actually taking place when one has so much control over the community they select for themselves on social media? For instance, we can "like" a post very easily, but where is the "dislike" button? Where is the "discuss/debate" button?

" ...THROUGH INTERACTION WITH THE SOCIAL MEDIUM, THE REAL AND IDEAL SELVES INTERSECT; AND THE IDEAL SELF IS AT LEAST PARTIALLY ACTUALIZED. IN ESSENCE, OUR ONLINE SELVES REPRESENT OUR IDEALS AND ELIMINATE MANY OF OUR OTHER REAL COMPONENTS."
R. KAY GREEN, PRESIDENT OF RKG MARKETING SOLUTIONS
GREEN, 2013)

3.5
The selfie social movement

3.5

According to renowned humanistic psychologist Carl Rogers, personalities are composed of one's "real self" and "ideal self" (McLeod, 2014). The virtual world gives brands and consumers the ability to predetermine the "self" that they want represented throughout the social media space (social communities). One method is remaining authentic with the "real self," which is further humanized by attributes and character traits that are uniquely one's own. The other approach is creating the "ideal self," which is developed by environmental and societal approval, sometimes resulting in a more unachievable level of acceptance.

As previously discussed, social media enables users to create, edit, and curate various forms of content. This material is shared across social spaces, making it something relatable (real self) and/or something envied (ideal self). The desire to be envied from a societal and environmental standpoint on social media is motivated by competition, success, and social status (Green, 2013). Thus, interacting with someone who portrays desirable qualities (e.g., attractiveness, intelligence, humor) reflects something favored or desired by the engaging user.

Consumers receive reassurance through "likes," "favorites," "retweets," and favorable comments—this confirms that an acceptable decision was made in sharing one's content. Without this reassurance, consumers tend to reflect critically upon ways to gain acceptance and approval from their social community. Due to constant interaction and feedback, consumers are now modifying their real and ideal selves to match the acceptable norms of their online communities. For instance, some Gen Z consumers tend to remove any content that may cause them to be labeled as "oversharers."

Selfie

A selfie is a photograph that one takes of oneself with a smartphone or any camera-like equipment. In the twenty-first century, this tradition was shared through social media. The term had acquired enough of an impact to be declared "word of the year" in 2013 by the *Oxford English Dictionary*.

CASE STUDY:
Selfies Create Sale Conversions by EDITED

EDITED provides real-time analytics that help retailers determine the right products at the right time by monitoring online social interactions of consumers. EDITED shares a clear example of how social confirmation of curated content dictates the innovation of trends in the market and translates to sales.

"The celebrity who posts the highest number of Instagram selfies is Kylie Jenner, who has over 32 million Instagram followers. Scroll through her latest offering, and sure enough, the littlest Kardashian(ish) does not feature many accessories in her snaps. There are the occasional pair of sunnies, but more prominent are crop tops, full-length all-in-ones, anything tightly

fitted and white in shade, topped off with the latest hair color she's endorsing. But what stands out most is the 18-year-old's swimwear-exhibitioning prowess. She has posted 26 swimwear pics this summer alone. You can't blame her. 'Tis the season for it after all. And lo and behold, retail matches up. There's been a 39 percent increase in new arrivals of all in ones, and a 27 percent increase in arrivals of swimwear at our selfie-serving retailers. Better still, it seems like selfie gen are influenced—full priced sell outs of swimwear grew by 238 percent this July compared to last and 197 percent growth in all in ones selling out. Selfie takers are getting bolder: go forth and pose. Just please, keep it classy gang" (Smith, 2015).

3.6

The Kylie Effect: Selfie Influenced Sell Outs In the Last 6 Weeks EDITED

Based on the number of products sold out at fast-fashion retailers since July 1, 2015

Black swimwear · White all in ones · Ripped denim · Grey crop tops · Slogan tees

Images from @kyliejenner / Instagram.

3.6
The Kylie Jenner
Effect

EVOLUTION OF SOCIAL BEHAVIOR ON SOCIAL MEDIA

The shift in collective social behavior within social media gives a glimpse of upcoming trends and areas of interest. During the early days of social media, the fundamental idea was to form as many connections possible (i.e., to "friend everyone") through a loose selection process. This process focused on what the user looked like to others, rather than the intrinsic value of what they wanted or needed. There was also the pressure of possessing a large number of followers and becoming part of a larger social circle of acceptance.

"Look at me, I'm just like you"

The content shared in a "look at me" context is shifting from showing off to "look at me, I'm just like you." Today, consumers are beginning to create their own filtering systems that reduce the number of those they follow; instead, they curate their social space around people, brands, and companies that they are more invested in. These filtered networks are now becoming more focused on entities that make people feel good about themselves. It also enables a user's social space to become more refined and personalized.

Unedited sharing

This is of particular interest to social media users who are looking to relieve the pressure of posting heavily curated or edited content. This is ideal for users who focus on positioning their images on social feeds by using an abundance of self-enhancing image filters.

Brands are also pressured to provide real-time content and pre-set editorial pieces without losing the tone of authenticity in their posts. Evan Spiegel created Snapchat because he wanted to promote reactionary (as opposed to planned) posts in order to "put the fun back in social media." Platforms like Snapchat feature a lack of permanence (i.e., expiring images and videos) in order to limit editing and promote real-time content. This is a highly refreshing move meant to stimulate spontaneity and inventiveness throughout the social media landscape. This form of unedited sharing has already been used in behind-the-scenes content at luxury runway shows (e.g., Christian Dior).

Protection behind the Safe Zone of Social Media

The ability to hide behind the medium of social media has created an equal playing field online. Social media has the power to boost users' confidence when they are supported by the majority; these platforms can also attract large global movements with the power of a single post. However, the world of social media is not restricted to the norms of real, non-virtual communities. Not all are brave enough to share their real names for fear of repercussion; therefore, many consumers typically use false user handles to become incognito and protect themselves behind the "safe zone" of social media. Introverts now tend to share their opinions openly on online platforms through the use of avatars (an image that represents a user). Thus, social media empowers users to speak their minds because of this assumed sense of security. The anonymity of the Internet virtually gives the idea that the consumer will not be held accountable for the things consumers say or do on the Internet. Unacceptable actions and behaviors offline now approach the idea of acceptance in an online setting.

Eight seconds

Consumers are now limited to 140 characters to express their thoughts with others or even turn to emojis to communicate. Today, the average person's attention span is eight seconds, where a goldfish can hold it for nine seconds, representing a four-second drop in just thirteen years. Social media platforms such as Vine and Instagram have capitalized on this alarming trend by offering limited-time content.

While Gen Z's attention span has greatly diminished, research shows that this generation has evolved to the "eight-second filter" to help them process information (Finch, n.d.). The underlying idea is that the consumer's attention span is greatly diminished by the time a brand is able to capture their attention. Attention is a limited reservoir; resources divided between tasks take away from the effectiveness of completing each one individually. Hence, members of Gen Z absorb excessive amounts of small, "snack-sized" media and communicate with short, temporary content of their own. Seventeen percent of website page views last less than four seconds and 4 percent last more than ten minutes ("Attention Span Statistics," 2015).

The average time a single video is watched online is two minutes and forty-two seconds. Despite the short attention span, it is key to capture your audience's attention. According to Wistia, a video hosting and analytic provider, a shorter clip will encourage an audience to watch the entire video, thus increasing reception and engagement levels. Here are more interesting findings from Wistia Video Analytics (Ruedlinger, 2012):

- 50 percent more people will complete a one minute video than a two minute video.

- After a certain point, the engagement will balance out so a four to five minute video has the same engagement as a five to ten minute video.

"**SHORT VISUAL CONTENT WILL DOMINATE THE DIGITAL SPACE. THE COMPANIES AND BRANDS THAT WILL WIN GOING FORWARD WILL BE THE ONES WHO FIND A WAY TO BRIDGE THE GAP BETWEEN THE AUDIENCE'S SHORT ATTENTION SPAN AND THE RIGHT SHORT FORM CONTENT.**"
CORBETT GUEST, CEO AND PRESIDENT OF IMAGINUITY INTERACTIVE (MARTIN, 2015)

Social Media Looking Glass Self

The sharing of personal content on social media has reached unprecedented levels—online social communities provide an open platform that welcomes all to pass judgment, which, in turn, influences the way consumers and brands are viewed by others. The "Looking Glass Self," a psychological concept created by sociologist Charles Horton Cooley, can be applied to this new self-concept of social experience. This theory relates to how a person grows to understand and form the self (or his/her self-concept), reflecting upon his or her interpersonal interactions and understanding of how others perceive him or her to be (Buschini, 2014).

The three primary factors of the Looking Glass Self:

1. We imagine how we must appear to others. Each post placed on social media offers one's extended-self to be approved or criticized through engagement in positive (e.g., "like") or negative (e.g., "unfollow") ways.

2. We imagine and react to what we feel others judgment about our appearance will be. Users who post on social media long for social acceptance through different forms of approval.

3. Consumers base their social self-concept largely on how they think others see them, not how they actually see them (and correlations between the two are not very high). The extended-self that is projected onto social media will affect the nature and manner in which text, images, and videos are posted.

The "New" Factor

Consumers have always been interested in "the next new thing," but today, it appears that some things are perceived to be old before they are given a chance to demonstrate their true value. As previously discussed, modern consumers have short attention spans and do not feel the need to wait, demanding instant gratification with the click of a mouse or a tap on their smartphones. Informational delays have now been replaced with instant indulgence due to the hyper-connected nature of individuals around the globe. The availability of real-time content and exposure to novel trends fuel the consumer's urgency for immediate claim of ownership or possession of something new. Nevertheless, despite this dramatic shift, the fashion industry still adheres to traditional seasons when scheduling fashion (five to six months before shipment).

Before introducing the "Fashion on Demand" customer in chapter 5, we will need to carefully examine the consumer's need for "new" and "hot" items and how social media has enabled this behavioral pattern. People are now able to search for products online at rapid speeds, resulting in immediate satisfaction. Coupled with their shortening attention spans, brands are now tasked to develop real-time products and share these with contextual value. Consumers who feel that the content is not current or relevant will move to the next brand at a moment's notice.

The constant stream of "new" can pressure users to post something before others do; it can also influence them to post content that is relevant to trending online conversations.

In today's information age society, even the youngest social media users feel the pressure to upload content in order to receive acceptance from their fellow community members. The information age provides a constant feed of visual splendor that benefits both brands and consumers. However, it requires that content providers be adaptable to new movements in order to leverage the brand's relevance on social media.

Four Contributors to the "New" Factor

1. The Information Era: Content consumption is stimulated by the global connectivity of social media. This content is filtered expeditiously and is quickly spread throughout social sharing communities, fueling consumers' pursuit for the idea of "new."

2. The Accessibility of the Mobile Phone: The world is more connected than ever before, thanks to the seven billion mobile phone subscriptions worldwide, representing 95.5 percent of the total population ("Global Mobile Statistics," 2014).

3. The Influence of Others: Consumers can spend hours reviewing social media updates from friends and family, browsing for the latest news, and monitoring influencers online. This visual consumption translates into consumers who desire and demand the newest products or services.

4. On Demand: The digitally proficient social-media user has outgrown the mere "liking" of content that they viewed on social networks. They now demand and expect to be able to locate or purchase items at their own convenience.

Consumers' Expectations

Marketers are focused on utilizing social media tools that will navigate consumers to their moment of intent, which is when their customers are ready to move forward from their decision process and take action. In order to successfully move consumers to this space, brands must engage their customers while meeting their expectations. A consumer's expectations about a brand, product, and service can change rapidly, and these depend on factors such as speed, delivery methods, and customization abilities. The psychological effect, called "the expectation factor," notes that people enter specific situations expecting to receive a specific something in return. So, how have the expectations of consumers changed? Their perceived control over their purchase power comes from knowledge acquired through Internet searches, brand websites, and social media insights. This control needs to be represented with each step that consumers make, whether they walk into a retail space or search a company's website.

MANAGING NEW CONSUMER EXPECTATIONS

Nothing should be forced onto consumers—those who feel pressured by a brand's actions can simply leave a store, exit a website, conduct another search, or stop following a social feed. Consumers are in charge of their own actions but are willing to engage with traditional sales tactics. When managing these expectations, it is imperative to remember that consumers have little patience and can instantly evaluate a brand's level of engagement. Through the power of the collective voice of social media, customers feel a stronger need to be heard and given a chance to voice their opinions more then ever before. Fashion powerhouses like Kate Spade, Topshop, Urban Outfitters, and ASOS have successfully provided a better online environment and user experience for their consumers. Customers want to be valued, rewarded, and given creative input through their social media conversation from the brands. In Chapter 6 will will review profiling digital personas to better understand the brand's online audience. The following are some of the actions taken to manage new consumer expectations:

- Customer service is being enhanced to better connect with the on-line audience's requests and expectations. New divisions of customer service and community managers that are focused on social media distribution channels, are opening to provide better response coupled with a more authentic level of engagement.

- Brands provide digital outlets that are easy to use and are responsive to the needs and expectations of the consumers, thus creating a strong user experience.

- Brands maintain transparency with their customers while remaining true to their respective manifestos.

- Brands are finding new ways to enable customers to feel valued, get rewarded, and given creative input.

" CUSTOMERS WANT EVERYTHING. THEY WANT THE ADVANTAGES OF DIGITAL, SUCH AS BROAD SELECTION, RICH PRODUCT INFORMATION, AND CUSTOMER REVIEWS AND TIPS. THEY WANT THE ADVANTAGES OF PHYSICAL STORES, SUCH AS PERSONAL SERVICE, THE ABILITY TO TOUCH PRODUCTS, AND SHOPPING AS AN EVENT AND AN EXPERIENCE."
DARRELL RIGBY, HEAD OF GLOBAL RETAIL PRACTICE FOR BAIN (SOSA, 2015)

3.7

UNDERSTANDING, APPROACHING, AND ENGAGING WITH NEW CUSTOMERS VIA SOCIAL MEDIA

Social media has democratized the brand-to-consumer path, providing a direct link for both parties. However, brands are still corporate entities and must approach their customers with care and sensitivity. A brand's reputation comes under intense scrutiny with each social media post, thus necessitating an increased level of regulation when engaging with consumers.

Before joining the conversation, it is crucial for brands to first observe and recognize the platforms inhabited by their target audiences. Understanding the social environment on these networks will enable them to gain the trust of consumers and maintain their loyalty. Brands are required to provide content that will best reach and connect their target audiences (i.e., generational cohort groups). Also, they must regularly test and monitor how their online audience reacts to the provided content in order to ensure desired engagement.

Social media's wealth of content and sourcing features have given new tools to consumers to search for the best deals on products, product reviews, and insight before making their purchases. These informed consumers have higher expectations from the brands, but also for themselves with their purchase decisions. It is important to understand how social media is impacting the lives of consumers: why they constantly want to know about the latest technological advances, and what their influencers are posting on multiple social feeds. As consumers attempt to "Keep Up with the Joneses," the effects of social media have taken this pressure to unprecedented levels. Consumers are striving to keep up with all of their

3.7
Communication no longer follows the traditional linear connection, but has multi-connections when communicating to others utilizing social media.

digital social spaces and connections, resulting in various compulsive behaviors. A study by Pew Research Center, titled *Social Media and the Cost of Caring*, reveals that the social use of digital technology increases awareness of stressful events in the lives of others (Hampton et al., 2015). The hyper-connected consumers of today are now even more affected by the pressure of trying to keep up with others on social media platforms. This rise in social awareness can vary, ranging from positive messaging to the constant comparison between users and their peers.

NETIQUETTE

"Netiquette" is the rules of etiquette that govern communication on the Internet. It determines what is socially accepted in a digital situation between social media users.

3.8

3.8
Chiara Ferragni wearing the
Apple watch seen in the streets
of Manhattan during New York
Fashion Week. The introduction
of wearable technology keeps
the consumer more connected
than ever.

" THE 'COST OF CARING' ASSOCIATED WITH
AWARENESS OF OTHER PEOPLE'S STRESSFUL
EVENTS MAY BE A NEGATIVE CONSEQUENCE OF
SOCIAL MEDIA USE BECAUSE SOCIAL MEDIA
MAY MAKE USERS MORE AWARE OF THE
STRUGGLES OF THOSE IN THEIR NETWORK."
PEW RESEARCH CENTER (HAMPTON ET AL., 2015)

Social media provides the connectivity that keeps consumers up-to-date with the topics they care about: movies, television, fashion, music, and everything else directed by their social feeds. However, it also offers users access to endless feeds of others' lives, possibly giving a glimpse into "things" they never knew they wanted (Dick, 2013). The prevailing concept of social media communities was that it welcomed all users and encouraged them to share their lives in a digital space, thus functioning as a type of self-extension.

The active social media user may feel pressured to post content that outshines his or her last post. Social media users have continued to admit that they post updates in order to portray their ideal selves to others. While this may seem harmless, keeping up this portrayed image can build and develop stress levels (Dick, 2013).

As high as 51 percent of US adults surveyed by Pew Research Center consider themselves addicted to their digital devices and find these as their primary source of connection to the world around them (Dick, 2013). These consumers are constantly in the hunt for the latest tech gear, referring to popular sites such as Mashable, Gizmodo, Dogg, and TechCrunch for insight. Some also go as far as becoming involved in beta testing prototyypes, and joining the tech movement through crowdfunding sites such as Kickstarter. Alas, we should note here that the use and adoption of digital devices differ between major age groups and generational cohorts.

GENERATION GAP THROUGH THE DIGITAL LANDSCAPE

Different generations turn to social media for different reasons, thus marketers need to understand how to approach each generation with an honest voice. The generational gap enables room for error on the level of social media use—but each generation wants to be addressed through social media as the message is directly targeted to "them" as valued consumers, not merely as valued standard customers. In many ways, social media demands that brands refer to traditional roles of customer service and understand the importance of customer relations.

Same Behavior, Different Aptitudes

Each generation uses social media in a way they value it for improving their overall social experience. Consumers belonging to various cohort groups have the ability to use social media tools to make their daily routines easier: one cohort group may regularly use the Starbucks mobile application to purchasing convenience, while another group may utilize a beauty enhancer filter on their "selfie" images. Therefore, the adoption of social media networks within each cohort group tends to have similar behaviors with different aptitudes—most cohort groups communicate via social media but the manner in which they communicate varies.

When marketing on social media, brands must understand that different generations use social media in different ways, with different methods, expectations, and desired outcomes. One method is not more viable than the others, but all enable the user to live more efficiently through the convenience of social media.

To market to new consumers, it is important to understand how they perceive value and how their expectations have changed. Who is the "new socially connected consumer" of the information age, and how do marketers and social media community mangers begin to provide meaningful content to this individual? When referring to the "new socially connected consumer," we include all individuals that use technology (Internet, mobile apps, social media) to assist them in their daily lives and improve their ability to retrieve information. Brands that market in this highly connected climate must use a personal approach, giving off the impression that each conversation is authentic and directed toward each individual consumer.

Relatable content or shared past experiences with like-minded individuals can band them together and create a community through the empowerment of social connection (Muniz and O'Guinn, 2001). Communicating through social media networks allows each cohort group to have a very specific area of influence by actively engaging with their online community. These communities (or cohorts) are referenced by a variety of titles depending on the source. In this book, we will take a closer look at four key generations: Gen Z or Generation C for Connected (1995-2012); iGeneration or Millennials (1986-1994), Gen X (1965-1985) and Baby Boomers (1946-1964) (Nisen, 2013).

Pre-millennium (2000) consumers did not share content as freely as they do today. Before the advent of Facebook (2006), most individuals were generally uninterested in learning about the daily, mundane acts shared by their peers online. Today, the sharing of content by millennial consumers such as meal photos and spontaneous "selfies" has become accepted as common social behavior. There used to be more of a selection process in how consumers shared what they know, whereas now the filters have been lifted as each generation grows into the digitally connected world.

The sphere of social media's influence is not limited only to Millennials. Do not rule out the Baby Boomers who are using social networks to meet their own needs—from planning a cruise to crowdsourcing websites, monitoring health care updates through Twitter, and sharing images of their grandchildren. Whether referring to younger siblings, friends, or parents/grandparents, the common driver of sharing is forming connections with others while telling the world that "I am here, this is happening in my life."

Generational Adoption of Social Media and the Digital Space

While some generations do tend to favor one platform over another, the truth is that preferences change in tandem with their needs. Facebook, a social media network that originally catered to Millennials has now become a platform favored by Gen X and Baby Boomers. The reasons for this change and loss of interest in the platform can be viewed from many perspectives, but the prevailing notion is that these "older" generational cohorts began flocking to Facebook because of sharing and audience engagement.

Millennials began sharing their Facebook content without the fear of parents (or other figures of authority) seeing their posts. The "cool" factor of Facebook has rapidly begun to disappear, as parents, aunts and uncles, and other older family members, are all joining the Facebook platform. "Teenagers are migrating from Facebook as their parents are now sending them friend requests. Researching the Facebook use of 16-18 year olds in eight EU countries, the Global Social Media Impact Study found that as parents and older users saturate Facebook, its younger users are shifting to alternative platforms" (Kiss, 2013). The generational gap between users of social media will continue to narrow as time progresses. While younger generations generally adopt technology faster, "older" cohorts have reduced adoption cycle times by familiarizing themselves with digital tools. It is quite amusing to remember that there was a time when the Internet was such a strange (and scary) concept to most, back when it was called "cyberspace."

3.9

3.9
Different generations have
different attitudes towards the
social media movement.

As social media continues to evolve, so does the adoption of use by each generation. The guidelines for how brands communicate with their online communities change as consumer interests fluctuate and competing content fills the social channels. The online competition for consumers' attention is strong, leaving little room for mistakes in transparent social spaces. No two brands can approach their audience the same way without having a unique attribute or informative insight that can enable a stronger connection with the consumer.

When taking a closer look at different generations, it is also necessary to recognize the overall online social experience of each. Through social media distribution channels, brands are now using selective content to leave a strong and lasting social imprint with their audiences of all generations. The goal is for online consumers to react to this carefully selected content through sharing, liking, or possibly converting their reaction to purchases and brand exposure. Each generation utilizes social networks differently, but they all continue to build their relationships by listening, participating, and communicating directly with their brands of interest. In order to know what they value, let us take a closer look at consumers who use digital channels to purchase or obtain information about certain brands, products, or services.

Consumers in different generational cohorts react uniquely to social platforms as well as influence the adoption of social media culture as a whole. It is not only the generations accustomed to this disruptive technology that are challenging the status quo; a new type of consumer has risen, one that is connected to a wealth of linked information from the Internet and social media networks. When using social media to connect with different generations, it is important to note that consumers within each group have different emotional needs and interests, which influence their impulse to engage online ("Social Psychology," 2013).

GENERATION Z: 1995–2012

Digital is in Gen Z's DNA, as they are the most dependent and emotionally connected to digital devices and content. While they are dependent on digital devices and content for daily activities, they are also a generation of net natives who are beginning to flee the social space for privacy. This generation grew up with iPads and was educated through open-platform communities and find it second nature to produce basic in-game coding on games such as Mindcraft. They are value-conscious and possess a secure level of confidence, not entitlement as generations before, and are viewed as the crowdsourcing generation with unprecedented visions of the world (Kingston, 2014). While they regard material items as signifiers of their success, they believe that they need to work hard to acquire the level of materials they have (Dua, 2015). Gen Z is a DIY generation that creates and cultivates their ideal social environments without the help of others.

Media company MTV has given this generation the name of "The Founders." They came up with this name by asking over a thousand kids who were born after December 2000 what their own generation should be called, names included the Navigators, the Regenerators, the Builders, the Bridge Generation and the final name given was the Founders. "They have this self-awareness that systems have been broken," MTV President Sean Atkings told *TIME* ahead of the announcement. "But they can't be the generation that says we'll break it even more." (Sanburn, 2015)

Gen Z's Focus on Social Media

Gen Z's active online participation through social platforms speeds up the pace of cultural changes due to technological advances (Rodriguez, 2015). Cultural changes speed up the daily accumulation and consumption of information. This cultural shift also influences the rapid changes in the fashion cycle with real-time content and social connections; Gen Z is not accustomed to waiting for information such as monthly magazine subscriptions. Members of this generation also have key influencers who they value and monitor online. They strive to be unique individuals with the way they dress and the message they set with each outfit, or extended self, through a social media post (Rodriguez, 2015).

3.10

3.10
Generation Z or also referred to
as Generations Founders.

3.11

Starting as early as the age of three, this generation begins their online activities through gaming community platforms. Members of this generation search for acceptance and popularity (fame) through online recognition such as being retweeted by a brand or celebrity. They believe in social communities and are comfortable with their like-minded peers even if they have never met.

Trust begins with peer endorsements and product recommendations that are actively used by their community (Singh, n.d.). Gen Z approves of advertisements and likes those that are humorous, inspiring, and have music they can relate to (Dua, 2015). This group may speak in cute stickers (Japanese inspired), emoticons, and emojis as a common form of communication.

Similar to the Millennials, Gen Z inherited the concept of storytelling with interest in narratives and realistic plots. Real people who share experiences and endorse brands/products further help the belief process of this generation (Dua, 2015). Listening, learning, and consumer-generated content drives the connection between Gen Z and brands. They do not want to feel that the merchandise is being pushed to them in their private digital space. They have a set of influencers that are very specific. YouTube episodes that specialize in a task or interest, such as gaming, DIY box opening (watching an influence opening a product of interest), science, technology (coding), and beauty tutorials, are often referred to. Interactive social media content that embrace creative outlets continue to flourish for this next generation of tech-savvy individuals. Social media applications that focus on creating and sharing content flourish across social media mobile applications that are available for Gen Z. One media application created in 2014 and focusing on a video community that made an impact in 19 countries was Musical.ly. According to the company, every day, millions contribute, share, and discover videos that fill the social media channel through singing, dancing, and lip-sycing to their favorite pop-culture music or famous pop-culture monologues.

3.11
Gen Z takes to community sharing playful lip syncs of popular music through their mobile application Musical.ly.

CASE STUDY:
Tavi Gevinson—Giving a Voice to The Next Generation

3.12

3.12
In 2009, Tavi Gevinson, a 13-year-old fashion blogger from Oak Park, Illinois, took the fashion world by storm with her blog, Style Rookie.

Tavi Gevinson's strong voice was heard by a generation directly through the narratives created on her blog. Gevinson became popular online despite not being conventionally famous (i.e., being in a band or on a popular TV show). Tavi was the first influencer of her generation to become part of today's online influencers and gatekeepers. She embraced the world of social media, making it her platform to share her thoughts and beliefs with anyone who would listen.

Gevinson's blog, Style Rookie, quickly found a loyal community at the time when the blogosphere was just becoming normalized into social settings. She began her journey as a fashion blogger with a voice that reflected an entire generation of teenage girls, otherwise known as Gen Z. Her narrative approach in the blogosphere enabled her to facilitate with her community and captivate her audience with an authentic voice. Gavinson's objective was not to fit in; instead, she wanted to show others that it was okay to stand out and be comfortable with the uniqueness of oneself. This was merely the beginning of how a young girl from Oak Park, Illinois, created an organic, authentic social presence that became contiguous for a whole generation. The teens to twenty-somethings, who at the time were the primary active users on social

media, consumed her social feeds as quickly as she could create them. Her fashion blog provided her with an elevated platform to share content without the fear of being judged or ridiculed by her peers. Considered by many in the fashion industry as "the voice of her generation," Gevinson sternly declines this praise, instead claiming that she is merely one voice within a tremendously impactful generation.

The fashion industry took notice of Tavi and at the tender age of 12, she was introduced to fashion icons such as Miuccia Prada, Karl Lagerfeld, and Anna Wintour, which transformed Gevinson into an influencer herself due to her social presence (Wiseman, 2012). Today, Gevinson continues to have a strong voice that is actively shared throughout social networks and the digital native generation. When *i-D Magazine* asked Gevinson what makes her generation so unique, she stated, "We have incredible access to information, we don't have such a huge generation gap with people older than us, and we have been given tools that we are better versed in than our seniors, which is both exciting and dangerous" (Kinsella, 2015). Gevinson, who goes by the name "Tavi" to her audience, has paved the way for others to continue empowering this generation.

3.13

" …BY UNPICKING THE AWKWARDNESS OF FEMALE ADOLESCENCE AND PROVIDING A PLACE TO TALK ABOUT IT, [ROOKIE HAS] HELPED FEMINISM BECOME ALMOST FASHIONABLE. "
EVA WISEMAN, THE OBSERVER ("TAVI GEVINSON," 2014)

3.13
Millennial blogger spokesperson and editor-in-chief of "Rookie" magazine (pop culture magazine), Tavi Gevinson, 17, reads to audience who embraces her every word.

Gen Z Takes to YouTube

The entertainment industry has now recognized YouTube as Gen Z's hub. While traditional television shows remain valued through streaming portals (e.g., Netflix, Hulu), this generation is rapidly moving away from conventional television programming. Traditional and community-based networks (such as YouTube) enable viewers to actively participate through social media, and both platforms are aware that the shift is moving toward content viewing on personal tablets (iPads). This is where the social change has begun with Gen Z consumers, who have turned to user-generated content and shared experiences from peers on social video channels. They are no longer reliant on broadcast networks, instead favoring content created on YouTube channels.

Gen Z favors original "webisode" series offered on YouTube channels—these shows are created by their generational peers and offer relatable content and "real-life" experiences. These "just like me" shows give the viewer a glimpse into the lives of YouTuber users in a reality-DIY format. Insights may include personal stories about their friends, family, and pets, fashion critiques, room décor ideas, and humor. Gaming is big for Gen Z with Mindcraft gamers such as British YouTube personality, Daniel Middleton or better known to his followers as The Diamond Cart/DanTDM. On YouTube

he has 12 million subscribers, eight billion views and estimated to be making over 20k a day. This generation is no longer reliant on traditional television shows but is drawn toward user-generated content that boosts their level of engagement.

The YouTube format involves small bits of content presented with a focus on ordinary teenager situations. Through this connection with famous YouTube users, members of Gen Z also become exposed to product placements and brand endorsements that are integrated into a show's script. Brian Robbins, a longtime TV and film producer, capitalized on this trend and launched a teen curated YouTube channel in 2012 called Awesomeness TV. Robbins has built 86,000 kid-created channels within a multichannel network that has three million subscribers, 762 million views, and 65 million monthly visitors (Stanley, 2014). The shows feature topics such as teen advice, celebrity gossip, pop culture, comedy specials, and beauty specials.

YOUTUBE CHANNELS FOR PRE-TEEN AND TEEN GIRLS

There is a full range of Gen Z channels to choose from, but two that have been extremely successful are Seven Super Girls and Meg DeAngelit. These two channels of highly engaging viewers tally over six million subscribers.

Another famous YouTube star is Meg DeAngelis (MayBaby), who has over five million subscribers and 460 million views on her channel. Her strength lies in her authenticity and her ability to connect with young, like-minded girls. What began as a simple outlet for her cheerleading experiences has now expanded into a clothing line and a multi-channel deal with Awesomeness TV.

3.14

3.14
Internet personalities Tyler Oakley (eight million YouTube Subscribers) and Bethany Mota (ten million YouTube Subscribers) accepting their Teen Choice Awards for Web Star in the male and female category.

3.15

3.16

3.15
Gen Z are highly loyal to their YouTube celebrities, lining up at any chance to meet them in person and watching their video on repeat. YouTube personality/actor Joey Graceffa has a highly engaging 6 million YouTube subscribers and over one billion views.

3.16
The Beckerman sisters; fashion bloggers who embrace the movement of free-spirited designers, such as Moschino, under the supervision of Jeremy Scott.

" KIDS NOW DO NOT PLOP IN FRONT OF THE TV AND WAIT FOR THEIR FAVORITE SHOWS TO COME ON. THEY HAVE AN ENORMOUS APPETITE AND THE TIME AND TECHNOLOGY TO CONSUME A LOT OF CONTENT. MORE AND MORE, KIDS TURN TO YOUTUBE TO FIND AND CULTIVATE THEIR OWN STARS."
BRIAN ROBBINS, FOUNDER OF AWESOMENESSTV
(STANLEY, 2014)

MILLENNIALS/GEN Y: 1986–1994

Brands, retailers and marketers continue to explore ways to cultivate relationships with the Millennials, a generation that displays fascinating and complex behaviors. Fellow Millennials include: Rihanna ('88), Justin Bieber ('94), Harry Styles ('94), founder of Snapchat—Evan Speiegel ('90). Millennials spend an estimated $200 billion a year, which gives them the upper hand when it comes to controlling their market segment of consumer goods ("Millennials and Boomers," 2015). In 2015, the Millennials finally outnumbered the Baby Boomers with a population of 75.3 million and by 2050, it is projected that their population will reach 79.2 million (Fry, 2015). They forge connections and become loyal to brands on social media, but only after receiving content that is lifestyle-driven as opposed to product-driven. Marketers continue to connect with this cohort group on social networks through one-on-one conversations, keeping in mind that this generation is not very trusting of conventional sales approaches.

Millennials' Focus on Social Media

The Millennials are the first generation of consumers that blurred the line between online and offline domains. To them, the "real world" exists online. In order to best connect with this generation, it is necessary to identify their ever-changing social habits and brand expectations. Millennials voice strong opinions online and search for acknowledgement through social media communities. They are quickly growing up and brands are fiercely competing for their loyalty at this new (and profitable) stage of their lives. The needs and usage patterns of Millennials evolve as they transition into new roles such as college students, business owners, and parents.

> " BLOGS ARE MEANT TO BE AUTHENTIC AND MANY OF THEM ARE RUN BY A SINGLE INDIVIDUAL. MILLENNIALS CONNECT BEST WITH PEOPLE OVER LOGOS. "
> FORBES MAGAZINE (SCHAWBEL, 2015)

Millenials are active in cause marketing and social good campaigns, such as TOMS, One for One Promise, and Marks & Spencer's Shwop (shop + swap = shwop) program. This generation grew up during the sustainable movement and is focused on making a difference in the world by being socially responsible ("Elite Daily Millennial," 2015). In Chapter 4 we will look closer at Millennials movement in social good. They respond well to native advertisements as opposed to traditional banner advertisements with a strong click-through rate (Hoelzel, 2015). Native advertisements appear in the same format as the content audience on platforms such as Instagram and Facebook. This type of advertisement carries less disruption compared to traditional advertisements (e.g., banners). Millennials openly express complaints on social media about school, relationships, and other concerns for all to read (Loechner, 2014). They expect brands to react and respond immediately to their needs.

This group values authenticity more than content shared. 43 percent of Millennials rank authenticity over content when consuming news they filter through on social media (Schawbel, 2015).

They need to trust a company or news site before spending time to read (Schawbel, 2015). This is one reason fashion bloggers help brands gain authentic trust when they promote those brands through their blogs or tweet support for those brands. In Chapter 5 we will explore influence marketing and the impact on brand's social engagement.

The Millennials are one of the most ethnically diverse generations and have a global family base (Loechner, 2014). Through applications such as WeChat and WhatsApp, they seamlessly connect globally with feeds of images, text, video, and voice memos.

Experience-driven campaigns receive a strong reaction from Millennials since they favor truth and real-life involvement/participation (Qader and Omar, 2013). This generation bases their decisions through social confirmation on social media; the number of likes, shares, or mentions confirms authentic and adoptable movement.

3.17

3.18

3.17
Airbnb's social media accounts connect the modern consumer for on-demand traveling.

3.18
Sharing economy encourages website-founded businesses to expand into brick-and-mortar locations. Businesses that began online are now beginning to move into physical stores such as Amazon, Warby Parker, Rent the Runway and Nasty Gal.

They expect to be offered special deals, previews, and behind-the-scene content for following a brand; they are not opposed to advertisement when they are relevant to their own interests. Individuals in this group are highly visual shoppers and want to have many options when viewing products. Brands should think of gamifying their next campaign to capture the attention of this generation. As mentioned in Chapter 2, gamification—competitive behavior associated with being the first to check into a location, such as a restaurant or sharing an image of an exclusive location, continues through geo-location available on most mobile applications. Millennials consider themselves as influencers and the center of self-created digital networks. They believe that advertising is not authentic and untrustworthy (Schawbel, 2015).

Sharing Economy: Generation of Sharing

"To care is to share" is the Millennial philosophy wherein ownership is less important than having something for a purpose. Social sharing to crowd sourcing is part of the sustainable way of thinking: re-purpose, re-use, and return as part of a community. This sharing economy is powered by social communities and include companies such as Uber, Rent-the-Runway (borrowing a dress), Airbnb (borrowing a home), and Poshmark (shopping for previously worn attire in other people's closets).

AIRBNB

Millennials are constantly in pursuit of something new and witnessing what the rest of the world has to offer. Traditional hotels and hostels are quickly being replaced by crowdsourced homes and living spaces from community-based companies like Airbnb (Fig. 3.17). Millennials want to travel affordably, thus giving rise to this movement of shareable housing. Through mobile apps that allow you to review, book, and pay, community-based excursions have forever altered the way Millennials travel.

BAG BORROW OR STEAL AND RENT THE RUNWAY

The sharing economy flourishes with the idea of part time ownership. The possibility of borrowing a dress or bag that would normally be unaffordable has drawn Millennials to this form of shared shopping. Two leaders of this business model are Bag Borrow or Steal and Rent the Runway (3.18). These companies enable shoppers to select items that they can borrow for a short period of time at a fraction of their retail cost. Both also offer social media apps that assist customers in planning their respective outfits for important events.

**"TO COMMUNICATE WITH A MILLENNIAL AUDIENCE, YOU NEED AN EMPLOYEE BASE THAT SPEAKS THEIR LANGUAGE—THROUGH DIGITAL AND SOCIAL MEDIA.
-THAT'S THEIR MOTHER TONGUE."**
BURBERRY'S CEO AT THE TIME ANGELA AHRENDTS (LEAHEY, 2012)

3.19a

3.19b

3.19a
The Prince and Princess of Wales return to Buckingham Palace by carriage after their wedding, 29th July 1981.

3.19b
American singer Madonna in New York, 1984.

3.19c
MTV launches in 1981 and brings music television to consumers. This changes the music industry and introduces the world to television personalities called "video jockeys" or VJs.

3.19c

GENERATION X: 1965–1985

Gen X, Net Generation and sometimes called the MTV generation, is referred to as such because of the creation of music television and its dedicated channel in 1981. Fellow Gen Xers include founder of Facebook, Mark Zuckerberg ('84), Co-founder of Instagram, Keven Systrom, Beyoncé ('81), Kim Kardashian ('80), David Beckman ('75), Kate Moss ('74), Gwen Stefani ('69), and founder of Net-a-Porter, Natalie Massenet ('65). They are also considered to be the generational middle child since they are situated between the two largest cohort groups: Millennials and Baby Boomers. This was the first generation to grow up with more than three television stations and personal computers that made the Internet a part of their daily routines. Gen X also called Net Generation experienced the beginning of the consumer-driven digital age through the commercial launch of the Internet or better known as Cyberspace in the early 1990s and the beginning of email companies such as AOL.

While this generation was not the first to embrace social media, Gen X members believe that they were the first to compare these platforms to traditional methods of the past. Messaging was originally conducted through pagers/beepers (a small gadget that delivered short one-way messages) or answering machines on home phones. Gen X members enjoy reflection, often waxing nostalgic about people, products, music, and movies that they grew up with. Social media has capitalized on this nostalgia by engaging with Gen X through memories of yesteryear. The nostalgia movement generates positive emotions and is of great interest to both brands and consumers, especially to those belonging to Gen X and Baby Boomers. Facebook took advantage of this desire to search for long lost classmates, boyfriends, and girlfriends by offering the opportunity to re-connect with virtually anyone on the planet.

3.20
In the 1980s, teens passed their messages to class mates through handwritten letters folded to hide from others while in class.

" **THEY KNOW WHAT THEY WANT AND WHAT THEY LIKE AND, MOST IMPORTANTLY, WHO THEY ARE. RECOGNIZING THIS CREATES AN OPPORTUNITY FOR MARKETERS TO APPEAL TO THIS POPULATION WITH A GENUINE AND REALISTIC CAMPAIGN THAT GEN XERS CAN IDENTIFY WITH."**
EVP, ADVERTISING EFFECTIVENESS ANALYTICS FOR NIELSEN (BLAIR)

Gen X's Focus on Social Media

Gen X-ers are the most likely to consume and share information about new technologies. They utilize social media to gain insight about world news and politics, and they respond to the use of hashtags, participate online as they watch their favorite shows, and engage in conversations about politics through hashtag filtering systems. Members of this group look for inspirational, positive, and empowering messages online while functioning as advocates for brands that they can engage (Loechner, 2014). They will be first to join a mobile application movement if it makes their lives easier, and use apps like Airbnb, Uber, and Spotify (Loechner, 2014).

One key factor that sets Gen X-ers apart from other generations is their view of the past—nostalgic moments and life before social media are treasured. They also have trust in brand loyalty—Gen X follows brands and engages with them. Content marketing campaigns directed at this generation should stress the value of a product or service. Do not make grand offers or claims, because Generation X is the "Show Me" generation; they believe in actions over words (Chandler, n.d.).

For this generation, e-mail is not dead. Gen X has grown accustomed to e-mails as well filtering systems that allow them to receive content they value. E-mail campaigns show strong conversation rates when targeting this generation. Gen X and Baby Boomers both actively engage, but make sure not to inundate them with an abundance of meaningless communications. Members of this group will not necessarily be the first to try the latest social media tools, but they will slowly migrate toward them if they display longevity. Gen X is comfortable making purchases online—they were the first generation to adapt to paying their bills online.

PINTEREST

The need to collect, organize, and share the endless content available on Pinterest has captured the attention of Gen X women (with men catching up from a global standpoint), involving projects such as DIY hairstyles to redesigning living spaces. While there are more then 14 millions items are pinned a day on Pinterest this is a strong platform to drive brand awareness to Gen X.

MOTIVATION THROUGH COMMUNITY-SUPPORTED WORKOUTS AND HEALTH MONITORS

Gen X welcomes online community drive groups in the area of health and fitness from companies such as Fitbit® and Strava. Strava is an online community that allows people around the world to connect through workout goals and routines. The GPS, through an approved device, records activities and can share the data against friends and others in your community ("Strava Challenges, n.d."). Members of Strava participate in "Strava Challenges" to receive badges of success and connect with like-minded individuals. Rewards offered on Strava are an important element to the community supported workouts that motivates Gen X users.

3.21

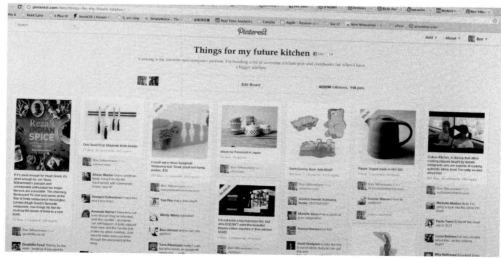

3.21
Pinterest boards to help design the perfect kitchen though a pinning system and utilizing the database of endless opitions.

3.22a

The NikeFuel band enables users to track their workout/ fitness activities and synchronize the data directly to Nike's mobile apps. These motion-tracking devices work in tandem with the mobile app, monitoring the fitness regime of users and establishing fitness goals for them. Gen X has embraced this movement through Nike+ Friends, a program that allows users to share their fitness progress with other people.

ADAPTING ONLINE CONTENT TO OFFLINE

Gen Xers want tangible products but with images being saved in the cloud or on a social media platform there is a need for printable products. My Social Book enables Facebook users to print and collect their social wall posts into a hardbound book. Another unique way of transferring digital content to off-line mediums was pioneered by ArcLight Cinemas. The company's marketing team printed images of Instagram social feeds and created a twelve-foot wall post, displaying these throughout their theaters.

3.22b

3.22a
ArcLight Cinemas wall lobby display of printed Instagram posts of users sharing their movie experiences

3.22b
My Social Book allows Facebook users to print and collect their social wall posts into a hardbound book.

3.23

3.23
The Baby Boomers are more active and
youthful in spirit then their parents at this age.

" THE ONLINE CHANNEL HAS CONTINUED
TO GROW SIGNIFICANTLY. IT'S GROWING
IN TERMS OF THE WAY THE BOOMER IS
ADAPTING TO TECHNOLOGY, WHETHER IT'S
SOCIAL MEDIA OR MOBILE TECHNOLOGY."
CHRIS GAYTON, J. JILL'S VICE PRESIDENT OF BRAND MARKETING

BABY BOOMERS: 1946–1964

Baby Boomers were one of the largest generations reaching their peak in 1999 at 78.8 million (Fry, 2015). Baby Boomers include Tom Ford ('61), Marc Jacobs ('63), founder of Microsoft—Bill Gates ('55), founder of Apple—Steve Jobs ('55). According to Forrester Research, they account for about $230 billion of consumer-packaged purchases and outspend young adults online 2 to 1 on a per-capita basis (Lockwood and Conti, 2014). Companies would be wise to utilize social media platforms to connect with this highly profitable "gray market." One in every five Twitter users are over the age of fifty and 53 percent of 65-year-olds are on the Internet (Barakat, 2014). Technology is of great importance to Baby Boomers—a Nielsen study revealed that this generation accounted for 40 percent of Apple's sales. As a response, Apple has created programs tailored to the needs of this generation. Peter Hubbell, Founder and CEO of BoomAgers, praises the company: "They totally get it. It's a brilliant Boomer concept. Instead of saying, 'You old people don't understand technology and we can help,' it's 'come add to your genius abilities.'" (Lockwood and Conti, 2014).

Before marketing to this generation, it is critical to deviate from age segmentation—dress them by style, not age. Boomers are living longer and more active lives, looking to purchase apparel to reflect this movement. They view themselves as exuberant spirits who are wiser than their younger selves. With approximately forty-one million female Baby Boomers in the US alone, it has become apparent that brands are just beginning to learn how to market to this generation within a hyper-connected environment.

Baby Boomers Focus on Social Media

Baby Boomers are active Internet and social media users and spend close to 27 hours a week on-line. They are in search of straight forward answers and officiate solutions. According to a US Government Consumer Expenditure Survey, women over age fifty spend $21 billion on apparel alone (Lockwood and Conti, 2014). Baby boomers have very specific purposes for using social media; they do not use these platforms to kill time or simply hang out with their peers. They may still prefer older mobile phones (e.g., flip phones) over modern smartphones. However, they are still able to view websites through their computers and/or tablets, and brands must set their user experiences accordingly.

Baby Boomers are partial to popular brands and frequently participate with brand advertisements on social media platforms (Loechner, 2014). They seek value through free recipes, healthy living, vacation escapes, and discount coupons. They are more likely to conduct price comparisons online in order to extract maximum value from their purchases. Before pushing them to follow, like, or share branded content, be sure to give them a viable reason to participate. Relevant content and language is the key when marketing to this generation. They should be interested in the marketed content in order to elicit a response. Informative and insightful content is key to Baby Boomers. While other generations may have spent more of their lives on digital platforms, this generation needs to have purpose when connecting with brands on social media networks. This generation seeks monetized value through coupons or informative insight that will educate them on products and services. Top insights searched on social media include health information and travel options.

3.24

3.24
Model Linda Rodin expressing
her style as she approaches
70 years old. She is also actively
on Instagram with over 100k
engaging followers.

Even more so than other generations, there is heavy focus on nostalgic memories shared on Facebook with this group. Facebook is their friend. They are fiercely loyal to the first platform that gave them the opportunity to connect with old and new friends. This generation favors ease of use, recommending microsites to others that enable them to stay connected.

Trust is the key when connecting with Baby Boomers. Build trust through online engagement by answering questions, providing options, and responding quickly to any concerns on questions. Make sure to back up any offered benefits with data or results. Keep social media simple and visually based, and provide easily accessible links and tabs that lead to cross-promotional features.

Don't Exclude—Include the Baby Boomers

Expressing the reality of generations adapting to various selected lifestyles will benefit a brand's authentic presence, especially if the brand is targeting Baby Boomers. When reaching out to multiple generations, it is important to represent all generations in a campaign without exclusion. J. Crew has successfully responded to this challenge with its "Style at Every Age" program that allows users to shop for age-appropriate clothing online. Users can select clothes that appeal to every age; these looks are displayed on models in their twenties, thirties, forties, and fifty-plus. This feature integrates all generations by providing a positive message of inclusion, giving each generation a chance to shine with styled looks that appeal to each group's needs. The movement online is to focus on the persona of the online user and create more of an inter-generational conversation.

" STYLE IS NOT A MATTER OF AGE ANYMORE. YES, THERE MAY BE SOME CONSERVATIVE, RATIONAL CONSUMERS IN THE 50-PLUS AGE GROUP, BUT THEY WERE LIKE THAT BEFORE. SIMILARLY, A WOMAN WHO FAVORED A FANCY STYLE OF DRESS IN HER 30S IS NOT LIKELY TO WANT TO DRESS DOWN AT 50. YOU HAVE TO SEGMENT TARGET GROUPS BY TYPES AND PREFERENCES. IT'S A QUESTION OF STYLE IN THE FIRST PLACE."
JÜRGEN DAX, DIRECTOR OF THE GERMAN APPAREL RETAILERS ASSOCIATION (DRIER AND STONE, 2014)

3.25
Fashion icon Iris Apfel (365
Instagram followers) attends
Mercedes-Benz Fashion Week
in New York. In August 2016,
Macy's (US retailer) created
Iris emojis for mobile phone
keyboards.

EXERCISES

Critical Thinking: Determine where you see the future of the "selfie trend" leading. Do you think it is growing or dying with the new generational marks? Do you actively participate in the selfie trend? Do you think brands can benefit from using the selfie trend to better engage consumers?

Practical Application: Evaluate how one brand ambassador, social media guru, or major influencer of your industry of interest connects and even upsells a brand to their followers. Then, propose a new influencer you think would identify well/correctly with the brand and their target cohort market/group. Examine how fashion brands reach out to generations through social media. Share examples of the process that turns consumers into brand marketers.

Business Activity: Create a digital marketing pitch or promotion material that focuses primarily on one cohort/generational group. Make sure that your plan has not been executed before by this brand and that it reaches your group through their major social media outlets. Make sure you choose social media outlets on which they actively participate. Afterwards, review the plan and evaluate how its strengths and weaknesses will be impactful on the brand's community. How will both the brand and group benefit from this pitch? Review the most recent research about the generational gap or new consumers' expectations from social media to support the pitch.

Infographics: Create an infograph based on data-driven social science research on a selected generation (Gen Z to Baby Boomer) and their social media personas and social media activity (look to the technology corner below for sources).

Technology corner: Investigate current cohort trends by reviewing websites that focus on data-driven social science research such as Pew Research Center, Forrester Research, Nielsen, and Ipsos.

REFERENCES

Antonios, J. (2010), "The Social Media Hierarchy of Needs," *JohnAntonios.com*, February 6. Available online: http://johnantonios.com/2010/02/06/the-social-media-hierarchy-of-needs/

Attention Span Statistics (2015, April 2), In Statistic Brain Research Institute. Available online: http://www.statisticbrain.com/attention-span-statistics/

Barakat, C. (2014), "How the Older Generation is Embracing Social Media," *Adweek*, May 16. Available online: http://www.adweek.com/socialtimes/older-generation-social-media-use-infographic/149574

Barr, N., Pennycook, G. Stolz, J.A., and Fugelsang, J.A. (2015, July), "The Brain in Your Pocket: Evidence That Smartphones Are Used to Supplant Thinking," *Computers in Human Behavior*, 473-480. Available online: http://www.sciencedirect.com/science/article/pii/S0747563215001272

Blair, T. (2012), "Marketing to Generation X," *TerrenceBlair.com*, December 10. Available online: http://www.terrenceblair.com/blog/advertising-to-generation-x/

Buschini, L. (2014). "I'm A Fun Person: How Social Media Has Made Us Obsessed With Our Online Selves," September 23. Available online: http://isys6621.com/2014/09/23/im-a-fun-person-how-social-media-has-made-us-obsessed-with-our-online-selves/

Castillo, S. (2014), "JOMO: 8 Ways to Embrace the Joy of Missing Out,' *Greatist.com*, June 8. Available online: http://greatist.com/grow/benefits-of-missing-out

Catanese, N. (2013), "FOMO Is Real—Here's What You Need To Know," *Refinery29.com*, May 23. Available online: http://www.refinery29.com/fomo#slide

Cavanaugh, M. and Faryon, J. (2012), "iDisorder: Does Technology Feed Psychological Disorders?," *KPBS News*, March 28. Available online: http://www.kpbs.org/news/2012/mar/28/psychological-disorders-and-technologyu/

Chandler, T. (n.d.), "How to Tailor Your Content Marketing Strategy for Different Generations," *Yahoo! Small Business*. Available online: https://smallbusiness.yahoo.com/advisor/tailor-content-marketing-strategy-different-generations-210059440.html

De Clerck, J.P. (2015), "Why We Are All Digital Customers," *Social Media Today*, April 19. Available online: http://www.socialmediatoday.com/social-business/2015-04-19/why-we-are-all-digital-customers

Dick, J. (2013), "Why Do Social Networks Increase Stress?," *Huffington Post*, July 12. Available online: http://www.huffingtonpost.com/john-dick/social-networks-and-stress_b_3534170.html

Drier, M. and Stone, S. (2014), "The German 50+ Customer," *Women's Wear Daily*, August 25. Available online: http://wwd.com/business-news/marketing-consumer-behavior/the-german-50-customer-7846915/

Dua, T. (2015), "Four things brands need to know about Gen Z," *Digiday*, April 9. Available online: http://digiday.com/brands/four-things-brands-need-know-gen-z/

Elite Daily Millennial Consumer Study (2015), *Elite Daily*, January 19. Available online: http://elitedaily.com/news/business/elite-daily-millennial-consumer-survey-2015/

Finch, J. (2015), "What Is Generation Z, And What Does It Want?," *Fast Company*, May 4. Available online: http://www.fastcoexist.com/3045317/what-is-generation-z-and-what-does-it-want

Fitzgerald, S. (2013), "New Reality Show @SummerBreak Will Unfold on Social Media," *Mashable*, June 14. Available online: http://mashable.com/2013/06/14/summer-break-reality-show-social-media/

Fry, R. (2015), "This year, Millennials will overtake Baby Boomers," *Pew Research Center*, January 16. Available online: http://www.pewresearch.org/fact-tank/2015/01/16/this-year-millennials-will-overtake-baby-boomers/

Global Mobile Statistics 2014 Part A: Mobile subscribers, handset market share; mobile operators. *mobiForge*. (2014, May 16). Available online: https://mobiforge.com/research-analysis/global-mobile-statistics-2014-part-a-mobile-subscribers-handset-market-share-mobile-operators

Gonzales, A. and Hancock, J. (2011), "Mirror, Mirror on my Facebook Wall: Effects of Exposure to Facebook on Self-Esteem," *Cyberpsychology, Behavior, and Social Networking*, 14 (1-2): 79-83. doi: 10.1089/cyber.2009.0411

Green, R.K. (2013), "The Social Media Effect: Are You Really Who You Portray Online?," *Huffington Post*, August 7. Available online: http://www.huffingtonpost.com/r-kay-green/the-social-media-effect-a_b_3721029.html

Guillory, J., Hancock, J. and Kramer, A. (June 2014), Experimental evidence of massive-scale emotional contagion through social networks. *PNAS*, 111 (24): 8788-8790. doi: 10.1073/pnas.1320040111. Available online: http://www.pnas.org/content/111/24/8788.full

Hampton, K., Rainie, L., Lu, W., Shin, I. and Purcell, K. (2015), *Social Media and the Cost of Caring*, Washington, D.C.: Pew Research Center.

Hoelzel, M. (2015), "Spending on native advertising is soaring as marketers and digital media publishers realize the benefits," *Business Insider*, May 20. Available online: http://www.businessinsider.com/spending-on-native-ads-will-soar-as-publishers-and-advertisers-take-notice-2014-11

IANS (2015), "Are smartphones becoming an extended mind?," *The Express Tribune*, March 7. Available online: http://tribune.com.pk/story/849483/are-smartphones-becoming-an-extended-mind/

Kemp, S. (2015), "Digital, Social & Mobile Worldwide in 2015," *WeareSocial.net*, January 21. Available online: http://wearesocial.net/blog/2015/01/digital-social-mobile-worldwide-2015/

Kingston, A. (2014), "Get ready for Generation Z," *Macleans*, July 15. Available online: http://www.macleans.ca/society/life/get-ready-for-generation-z/

Kinsella, F. (2015), "Tavi Gevinson is the Icon for an Activist Generation," *i-D Magazine*, April 8. Available online: https://i-d.vice.com/en_gb/article/tavi-gevinson-el-icono-de-una-nueva-generacion

Kiss, J. (2013), "Teenagers migrate from Facebook as parents send them friend requests," *The Guardian*, December 27. Available online: http://www.theguardian.com/technology/2013/dec/27/facebook-dead-and-buried-to-teens-research-finds

Kozinets, R.V. (2009), "Netnography: Doing Ethnographic Research Online—Info, Free Book Chapters, and More." Available online: http://kozinets.net/archives/357

Leahey, C. (2012), "Angela Ahrendts: The secrets behind Burberry's growth," *Fortune*, June 19. Available online: http://fortune.com/2012/06/19/angela-ahrendts-the-secrets-behind-burberrys-growth/

Lockwood, L., and Conti, S. (2014), "Special Report: Boomers, the Neglected Market," *Women's Wear Daily*, August 25. Available online: http://wwd.com/business-news/business-features/the-neglected-market-boomers-7846913/

Loechner, J. (2014), "Generational Social Media Behaviors," *MediaPost*, June 30. Available online: http://www.mediapost.com/publications/article/228996/generational-social-media-behaviors.html

Martin, E.J. (2015), "The State of Social Media 2015," *EContent*, February 23. Available online: http://www.econtentmag.com/Articles/Editorial/Feature/The-State-of-Social-Media-2015-101713.htm

McLeod, S. (2014), "Carl Rogers," *Simply Psychology*, Available online: http://www.simplypsychology.org/carl-rogers.html

StudioD (2015), "Millennials and boomers are onto your tricks and other key facts about the generations," *Digiday*, June 22. Available online: http://digiday.com/sponsored/demandtt-005-787-266-mobile-millennials-skeptical-xers-and-boomers-wholl-tell-you-to-get-lost-a-marketers-guide-to-the-generations/

Morgensen, D. (2015, May), "I-Want-To-Do Moments: From Home to Beauty," *ThinkWithGoogle.com*. Available online: https://think.storage.googleapis.com/docs/i-want-to-do-micro-moments.pdf

Muniz, A.M. and O'Guinn, T.C. (2001), "Brand Community," *Journal of Consumer Research*, 27 (4): 412-432.

Nisen, M. (2013), "How To Know If You're Too Old To Call Yourself A Millennial," *Business Insider*, May 25. Available online: http://www.businessinsider.com/definition-of-generational-cohorts-2013-5

Qader, I.K., and Omar, A.B. (2013), "The Evolution of Experiential Marketing: Effects of Brand Experience among the Millennial Generation," *International Journal of Academic Research in Business and Social Sciences*, 3 (7): 331-340.

Rodriguez, A. (2015), "Stung by Millennial Misses, Brands Retool for Gen Z," *Advertising Age*, May 19. Available online: http://adage.com/article/cmo-strategy/informed-millennial-misses-brands-retool-gen-z/298641/

Ruedlinger, B. (2012), "Does Length Matter?," *Wistia*, May 7. Available online: http://wistia.com/blog/does-length-matter-it-does-for-video-2k12-edition

Sanburn, J. (2015), "Here's What MTV Is Calling the Generation After Millennials," *Time*, December 1. Available online: http://time.com/4130679/millennials-mtv-generation/)

Schawbel, D. (2015), "10 New Findings About The Millennial Consumer," *Forbes*, January 20. Available online: http://www.forbes.com/sites/danschawbel/2015/01/20/10-new-findings-about-the-millennial-consumer/

Selfie [Def. 1]. (n.d.). In Oxford Dictionaries. Retrieved September 3, 2015, from http://www.oxforddictionaries.com/us/definition/american_english/selfie

Singh, S. (n.d.), "Generation Z: Rules to Reach the Multinational Consumer," *Sapient*. Available online: http://www.sapient.com/content/dam/sapient/sapientnitro/pdfs/insights/TR1_GenZ.pdf

Smith, K. (2015), "Me, Myself and My Selfies: A Look At How Selfie Culture is Impacting Retail," *Editd.com*, August 19. Available online: https://editd.com/blog/2015/08/me-myself-and-my-selfies-a-look-at-how-selfie-culture-is-impacting-retail

Social Psychology and Marketing Tactics [Web log post]. (2013, August 15). Available online: https://scripted.com/social-media-2/social-psychology-and-marketing/

Sosa, E. (2015), "The Rise of the Connected Consumer and What it Means for the Retail Industry," *Huffington Post*, March 17. Available online: http://www.huffingtonpost.com/ernesto-sosa/the-rise-of-the-connected-consumer-_b_6852276.html

Stanley, T.L. (2014), "Meet 12 of the Biggest Young Stars on YouTube: The sensations behind AwesomenessTV's 65 million monthly visitors," *Adweek*, March 9. Available online: http://www.adweek.com/news/television/meet-12-biggest-kids-stars-youtube-156180

Strava Challenges. (n.d.), *Strava*. Available online: https://www.strava.com/challenges

Tavi Gevenson: A teen just trying to figure it out [Web log post]. (2014, March 28). Available online: http://selfhelpguidesonline.com/03/tavi-gevinson-a-teen-just-trying-to-figure-it-out/

Taylor, P., Doherty, C., Parker, K. and Krishnamurthy, V. (2014), *Millennials in Adulthood: Detached from Institutions, Networked with Friends*, Washington, D.C.: Pew Research Center

Wiseman, E. (2012), "Tavi Gevinson: the fashion blogger becoming the voice of a generation," *The Guardian*, December 8. Available online: http://www.theguardian.com/fashion/2012/dec/09/tavi-gevinson-fashion-blogger

04

PART 2
**THE BUSINESS OF
MARKETING FASHION**

DIGITAL STORYTELLING

Chapter Objectives
- Understand the role of storytelling in marketing
- Analyze the social connection of stories to brands
- Discover the contextual relevance of curated content
- Understand the integration of social stories
- Learn the principles of digital curation
- Investigate the science behind stories
- Explore the social good's new digital space

4.1
The convergence culture of today continues to search for immersive stories that are told through the digital landscape, while advances in the way stories are told in social media and how they are told continue to transform as platforms change.

INTRODUCTION

In order for a brand to efficiently engage with their audience on social media they must be able to curate, share and convey their story. To show measureable results in real-time social space, marketers (social media strategists) must first develop and convey a strong media story about a brand. Storytelling is critical; it enables the consumer to experience different elements of that brand. In this chapter, we will explore a changing of the narrative, from brands being the storytellers to consumers becoming story givers by advocating for a brand. The principal idea behind good storytelling is to satisfy the curiosity of the brand's target audience while simultaneously maintaining their interest throughout the story. We will also take a closer look at the persuasive power of storytelling as brands drive loyal customers to forge a personal connection between the brand's story and its audience. Online audiences seek out noteworthy, entertaining stories that will resonate with them and generate value for their conversations with members of their respective social circles.

The age-old craft of storytelling conveys a message, persuades the reader, and creates a bond between the narrator and the reader through relatable content and the context of shared experiences. Storytelling is one of the most effective and oldest ways of passing knowledge from one human being to another. Each story can teach, provide insight, connect individuals, and generate new experiences through the narrative approach of audience communication.

With all of today's online clutter coupled with an overwhelming abundance of information, marketers face the challenge of capturing and retaining customers' attention. As such, marketers must add a human component to their stories in order to resonate with their target audiences. We will take a closer look at how brand stories spread through social communities and how a unity is formed from social engagement.

Throughout this chapter, we will examine the power of digital storytelling through social networks, and how it creates a new level of shared experience for a wider audience through this digital experience. As loyal customers, consumers first search for relevancy and authenticity when engaging with their favored brands.

We will also evaluate the favorable rise of "social good" brands (sustainable, socially responsible, philanthropic, etc.) utilizing these new platforms to create positive brand awareness and stronger word-of-mouth. The democracy of social media sharing through digital media empowers new up and coming brands—no matter their size—to share their stories on an equal playing field with larger, more established brands.

" THERE'S ALWAYS ROOM FOR A STORY THAT CAN TRANSPORT PEOPLE TO ANOTHER PLACE"
J.K. ROWLING, AUTHOR OF *HARRY POTTER* FANTASY SERIES

STORYTELLING IN MARKETING

Storytelling is a vital tool for content marketing that allows brands to take consumers on a journey that will relay insights and forge stronger connections. Telling a brand's story requires more than laying images together and posting them throughout multiple social media feeds. It requires carefully placed images, words, and videos in a sequence that best tells a story, giving the consumer the feeling of self-discovery and intriguing them to follow or engage with that story. Stories can be told through carefully curated content to show the brands' personality and expertise.

Role of Storytelling

When activating storytelling as a part of the marketing strategy, it is important to capture the audience's attention long enough to pique their interest in connecting with the brand's story. Some brands focus on their already established customer relationship management (CRM) data to better connect with existing customers, with storytelling used to attract potential customers. Through technology's ever-evolving effect on social communications, brands use a collaborative (two-way) method in communicating directly with consumers through a storytelling narrative that personifies those brands and creates new, emotion-based connections. There are many approaches in delivering a brand's story; it involves carefully planned sequences and positioning to capture attention and direct the consumer to the call-to-action within the story. This persuasive communication through storytelling helps develop the ideal framework and tactics behind developing a strong message. In this book's context, the role of storytelling is to deliver a message that elicits a personal connection that motivates and persuades the audience.

In the digital landscape, brands continue to weave the story with their branded content. The story then enables the movement of the content, making it more visible and easier to find for others on social networks. As stories spread, increase in consumer engagement follows. Measurable action is derived when the reader actively participates through association of shared experiences, encouragement, and knowledge. The process of sharing a story with a targeted audience can stimulate the process of understanding the brand's message. The measurable value is how the story will influence the reader and how well it will be remembered. A story's structure allows the reader to experience a journey through written or visual

4.2
Social Storytelling: The future of immersive storytelling is happening with virtual reality (VR). TOMS flagship store in California offers customers a chance to take a immersive experience through VR and travel to Peru. Blake Mycoskie, founder of TOMS shoes, says the number one request people have is they want to go on a "giving trip." Now with Samsung's Gear VR virtual reality goggles customers can be part of the story and accompany Blake to Peru and experience giving a new pair of TOMS shoes to kids in need.

content, thus generating suspense, curiosity, and intrigue. Plots deliver messages with compelling content that encourage the reader to form a connection with the story. With the use of persuasive power words and images, the narrative helps the reader learn the importance of the symbolic potential of language. A story's context guides consumers, enabling them to use their own experiences to react to emotional triggers in the story. Stories create curiosity, spur innovation, and drive the reader to take action. When shared appropriately, stories have the power to resonate with consumers, leaving a lasting impression of the emotional connection. While there are many ways to share and deliver a story, the primary function is to provide context for audiences in order to stimulate engagement and conversations that generate an experience for the consumer.

Anatomy of Storytelling

Sharing a brand's message through story requires marketers to examine the following in order to create a clear, impactful story: emotional connection, clear narrative, humanizing, and medium of distribution.

Emotional Connection of Storytelling with the Audience:

What is the emotional connection to the audience?

What is gained from the story? entertainment, curiosity, believability, or experience?

Narrator of the Story
Who is telling the story to the audience?

From what point-of-view is the story told? Brand, Consumer, or Third Party?

Humanizing the Brand through Story
Is there a likeable character the audience wants to engage with?

Is there a relatable connection to bond the relationship? A Trustworthy, Transparent, Authentic, Unique Voice?

Medium of Distribution
How will the story be delivered to the audience? Visual (photograph, image, video, gif, chart, infograph), Text, Multi-Social Media Platforms? Delivery content multi-times a day in different platforms?

What expectations will the audience have from the selected medium?

Crafting the Perfect Story

CONTRIBUTING WRITER LESLIE K. SIMMONS

Digital storytelling is a relatively new phenomenon thanks to social media, but the use of visual imagery to tell a story is not. Mankind has used spoken and written words paired with visuals for thousands of years, since our early human ancestors painted parietal art, commonly known as "cave paintings." We are a visual society, so, it is important to craft a well-thought-out digital story into your marketing plan. But where do you start? The answer is simple: it starts with the idea. After that, it is a matter of identifying everything needed to turn that idea into a story. To tell a story, you need to put on your journalist hat and think about what the takeaway will be for your audience.

Every day, journalists around the world create stories for public consumption. So, how do they do it? The first thing they do is gather facts. Then, by using the Five Ws (and sometimes H), they plug those facts into a story outline:

Who? What? Where? When? Why? And sometimes, How?

Who: This can either be the subject of your story or from the marketing POV, your target audience.

" STORYTELLING IS THE MOST POWERFUL WAY TO PUT IDEAS INTO THE WORLD TODAY."
ROBERT MCKEE, AUTHOR OF *STORY: STYLE, STRUCTURE, SUBSTANCE, AND THE PRINCIPLES OF SCREENWRITING*

What: This can be what the product is, or it can be what message you are trying to convey to your audience.

Where: Is there a place where this product is mostly used? Or could be paired to create a visual impact on your audience? Snow-capped mountains? Sandy beaches? Industrial downtown spaces?

When: With most marketing campaigns, "when" is NOW. Look at the question of when as the action you want your audience to take, for example buying a product. When should they buy the product?

Why: All successful marketing campaigns provide a reason for the consumer/audience to want their product or service. Why should anybody care about what you are trying to sell or what message you're trying to convey? This might be the hardest of the Ws to figure out—but it is also where your creativity comes into play. "Why" shapes your story.

How: If your marketing campaign is happening around an event, then "how" should be added to the story plan. "How" can also take a creative side—such as telling the story of a product and how it is made. How can also be your plan of action of how you are going to tell your story—video? Interviews? Dialogue? Photos?

Once you answer these simple questions, you have your story outline and a place to begin. That's it. It seems simple because it is simple, which brings us to another acronym to remember when crafting a digital story: K.I.S.S. Some define it as "Keep It Simple Stupid," or, the nicer version "Keep It Super Simple." In both cases, simplicity is the goal.

Leslie K. Simmons is working in the communications and marketing industry on major national and international campaigns for union and progressive organizations. She has won awards from the Los Angeles Press Club, Public Relations Society of America, and PR Week.

4.3

4.3
Collections of stories enrich the heart and expand the mind.

Storytelling Marketing Funnel

In order to share the digital experience of brands through their compelling social stories, marketers effectively need to take new and existing customers through a journey across emotional tied touch points. The story revolves around the essence of the brand's perceived values and the very heart of what makes up the brand to their audience. Storytelling as a sequencing technique is beginning to break away from the traditional method of advertising, which involves a single message with a direct call-to-action approach. A brand that operates in social marketing (sharing, comments, networks, blogging, click-throughs) must create a narrative to continuously drive social conversations and integrate the brand's story. Brand storytelling with the traditional purchase journey,

or the AIDA (Awareness/Interest/Desire/Action) funnel (Fig. 4.4), utilizes social sharing on social media networks to spread awareness faster. The story can filter through a non-linear social media passage on multi-screens and mediums to share "one story." The same story is shared in social media but through different media, depending on the social media platform it is viewed on. Rethinking the Marketing Funnel (Fig. 4.5) reflects both old and new attributes that drive the customer's journey through to purchase. This funnel explores the path through all five psychological stages including; awareness, consideration, preference, action, loyalty and advocacy. This can work especially well for lesser-known brands that aspire to cultivate stronger reputations going forward.

4.4

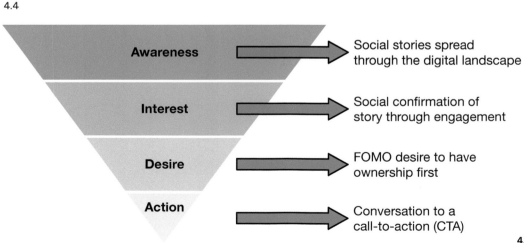

Awareness → Social stories spread through the digital landscape

Interest → Social confirmation of story through engagement

Desire → FOMO desire to have ownership first

Action → Conversation to a call-to-action (CTA)

4.4
AIDA Funnel: the brand's story journey through the traditional purchasing funnel.

4.5

Rethinking the Marketing Funnel

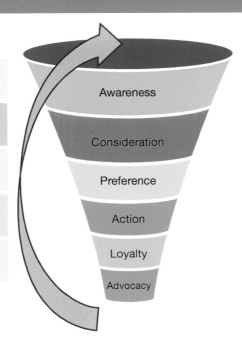

OLD: Broadcast

TV, radio, out-of-door

Direct mail, brochure

Product test, comparison

In-store purchase

Reward points

NEW: Customer networks

Search, buzz, blogs

Online research, user reviews

Social networks, YouTube, local search

Group discounts, purchase on-line/in-store/mobile

"Friending" (FB, twitter, email), customized up-selling

Reviews, links, "likes," social buzz

Awareness

Consideration

Preference

Action

Loyalty

Advocacy

4.5
From "The Network is Your Customer," by David Rogers (Yale University Press, 2011) www.davidrogers.biz

CASE STUDY:
Storytelling Marketing Funnel–Chanel

Branded story content (images, videos, quotes, guests) shared during fashion week is an element of storytelling funnel that provides context for the collections that are being launched. Runway photos, which are seemingly controlled by the press, and the influencers in the front-row snapping images from the best seats in the house. Images are then fed across social media channels through live stories, photographs, and video taken by the new group of gatekeepers; they filter and share these images in real-time with their respective social media communities. Brands utilize this as a way to increase awareness, generate interest, and potentially incite action from consumers. Images shared by a single gatekeeper have the potential to reach millions of impressions with one post. Top fashion brands now depend on the real-time distribution of branded story content to support each season's collection. We have used Chanel's ready-to-wear collection show in Paris to better illustrate how the storytelling marketing channel works. The story was released through a careful distribution of accessible content to gatekeepers, who then provided real-time content distribution through their respective social media communities.

> " I DON'T SEE WHY EVERY HUMAN BEING IS NOT ON THE SAME LEVEL."
> KARL LAGERFELD (BANKS, 2014)

STAGE ONE: AWARENESS

= Searchable Social Stories that are Relevant to Current Popular Trends
= Advertising, Popup Windows, Live Stream Virtual Reality 360 Experience, Announcements on Social Channels

Fashion forward consumers are aware that Chanel shows their prêt-à-porter (ready-to-wear) collection twice a year during Paris Fashion Week. Over the years, Chanel's shows have grown to be one of the most anticipated shows (events) of the season, owing to their graceful, yet innovatively themed, collections. Consumers now can gain front-row and behind-the-scenes access of the brand's collections from live-streams or social media posts from influential gatekeepers. Gatekeeper distribution also allows Chanel to remain in control of any content, and the timing of its release to the public.

STAGE TWO: INTEREST

= Diffusion of innovation brings consumers closer to gatekeepers and trend leaders. They remain connected, bringing the gatekeepers and leaders of the trend closer to the consumers, who are connected through social/digital media with gatekeepers maintaining active feeds of content.
= Spark curiosity by telling different, compelling stories instead of rehashing previous content.
= Share interesting, memorable quotes and images in the story to boost interest.

Karl Lagerfeld, the head designer and creative director of the fashion house Chanel, spearheaded the birth of a new popular feminist movement during their Spring/Summer 2015 collection shown at Paris Fashion Week. Models armed with placards took to a street-themed runway to create a faux-feminist protest existing patriarchal conditions while demanding society to raise the bar on women's equality. Feminism and women's equality are topics of high interest, effectively making the show a social story with high impression potential across social media spaces.

STAGE THREE: DESIRE

= The act of participation from consumers raises brand awareness while driving engagement and social confirmation of acceptance.
= Fear of Missing Out (FOMO) influences consumer's anticipation of missing out. The story gains relevance and desire for the next stage of "action" through social media.

Viewer engagement was amplified by peer-to-peer influencers sharing user-generated content relating to the message of women's equality showcased at the show. Images, videos, and graphics were quickly spread through word-of-mouth (WOM) across social media platforms. After the show, Karl Lagerfeld spoke about the show's intentions: "I don't see why every human being is not on the same level," said Lagerfeld (Banks, 2014). This captivating story coupled with the powerful visual content of models marching down the street scene drove consumers to the next stage of "action."

STAGE FOUR: ACTION IN A NON-LINEAR FORM

= This shift in action within the funnel is derived from the user's desire to spread the story on various platforms, such as posting the content on Facebook or pinning an image on Pinterest.
= The story enables consumers to reach the next stage of purchase or intent to purchase. This also utilizes the ability to spread the message across the digital landscape.

The power of social stories lies in its potential to become personal to audiences. Readers can quickly identify with a story's context, influencing them to share, purchase, or support the brand. Chanel captured attention of audiences early in the marketing funnel journey and tapped into one of the most effective ways of spreading positive WOM. The show was ranked #1 on Style.com in terms of viewership, placing the collection at the pinnacle of that year's fashion week season, with Chanel receiving 3,954,241 page views. While the shared content is geared more toward brand loyalists, the authenticity of the story allows it to reach larger audiences across the digital landscape.

> **" WE ARE ALL STORYTELLERS. WE ALL LIVE IN A NETWORK OF STORIES. THERE ISN'T A STRONGER CONNECTION BETWEEN PEOPLE THAN STORYTELLING."**
> JIMMY NEIL SMITH, DIRECTOR OF THE INTERNATIONAL STORYTELLING CENTER

Sequenced Approach to Digital Marketing

Adaptly (social media advertising technology company), Facebook (social networking service), and Refinery29 (independent style website) got together to conduct research on how effective advertisements are in a sequence approach. Facebook titled their research "The Power of Storytelling: Taking a Sequenced Approach to Digital Marketing." The study was conducted in order to take a closer look at the power of storytelling across digital channels and investigate other ways to improve the creative diagnostics and sequencing of campaigns.

Despite hyper-connected consumers possessing the compulsive need to "buy it now," marketing strategists believe that this behavior stimulates interest in the sequence frequency of digital brand storytelling. Brands share their stories through social media feeds, while limiting its call-to-action (CTA). This is done to provoke an immediate response without needing the story to reach its optimal position. The project also took a closer look at the effectiveness of delivery strategies throughout digital mediums, generating insight into funnel-based storytelling, and how it assists marketers in the pacing and frequency of their storytelling processes. The information in the following box was derived from the particular Facebook IQ study "The Power of Storytelling: Taking a Sequenced Approach to Digital Marketing."

The Funnel Approach to Storytelling (Facebook IQ study)

Phase 1: Meet The Brand (Facebook IQ, 2015)
Educate the consumer on the brand to share their values without any push or CTA. This is the beginning of the story to draw in the customers or potential customers.

Phase 2: The Teaser (Facebook IQ, 2015)
Now that the introductions are made, the next phase is to share what the brand can do for the consumer. The story continues to share more insight to draw new value that can be seen within the visual content being shared.

Phase 3: The Hook (Facebook IQ, 2015)
This is the final stage in the funnel to clearly demonstrate to the customer the call-to-action to the story or sequence they had followed.

" BY TELLING THE REFINERY29 STORY DURING THE ACQUISITION PROCESS, AND BUILDING AWARENESS AND CONSIDERATION BEFORE DRIVING TO CONVERSION, WE WERE ABLE TO INCREASE OUR RETURN-ON-INVESTMENT AND ULTIMATELY ACQUIRE A MORE INFORMED AND QUALIFIED SUBSCRIBER."
MELISSA GOIDEL, CHIEF REVENUE OFFICER OF REFINERY29 (FACEBOOK IQ, 2015)

INTERVIEW:
Raman Kia, Founder/CEO RJK Project

Raman Kia was the former Executive Director of Digital Strategy for Condé Nast Media Group. Kia was also the founder Condé Nast Social Media Task Force Team, a multi-divisional team comprised of senior executives focused on enhancing the organizations social media business. Today Kia is the Founder and CEO of RJK Project, an elite trust network of brand strategists and marketers. Brands serviced include Ann Inc., Bergdorf Goodman, Capital One, Global Brands Group, J Brand, John Hardy, Kate Spade New York, and Vince.

How do you define storytelling from a digital publishing point-of-view?

RK: I would not redefine storytelling from a digital publishing point-of-view. Let me expand. A story is something one entity tells another. It can be about the self (the narrator), another person, or a thing. And, all good stories follow a particular structure, which includes the introduction, the layers of complexity, the climax, and ultimately, the resolution. In this sense, the definition of storytelling has not changed much over time.

What has changed is the medium by which stories have been distributed. From the cave wall to print, radio, the screen, and now digital, these are all canvases for the story.

When it comes to digital I think there are two key points for consideration:

1. You must understand the mechanics of digital distribution.

   By that I mean it is important to fully understand the framework of each channel as a native tool. What works on one digital channel does not guarantee success on another. Trains, planes, and automobiles are all vehicles but just because you know how to drive a car, it does not mean you know how to fly a plane.

2. Digital allows one to go beyond the story.

   As I mentioned, a story is something one entity tells another, and it comes with a particular structure, which typically has a beginning and an end. Digital, social media in particular, allows going beyond the story and creating a narrative. A narrative is essentially a story that cannot reach its conclusion without the participation of others.

How do you think consumer's expectations have changed the way brands produce content?

Since content is something that is created, I want to answer this question by first considering what separates the great creations from the bad ones. The truth behind the greatest creations, whether content or product, is that they do the best job of serving a particular purpose. That purpose may not always be utility; it could be entertainment, information, inspiration, or aspiration.

Over time, technological innovations have created paradigm shifts in the cost, speed, and personalization of content creation, distribution, and consumption. As the demand for content has increased, the cost of creating and distributing it accurately has diminished, and brands have seized the opportunity by becoming content makers. To begin with, this was mostly done quite reflexively, rather than reflectively, and a lot of content was created for the sake of having created content. It is easy to see why this would have been the case too. There are a great number of levers that brands can pull to increase the reach and distribution of their content. However, only truly purposeful content has inherent spread built in it. The more inherent the spread, the less the cost of distribution. What technological innovations have not done, therefore, is eradicate the need for content to be purposeful. Today, product creators are understanding this better than ever before and being much more reflective in creating purpose-driven content.

Storytelling in the Digital Landscape

When developing a marketing strategy around storytelling, you must first listen to your audience to understand their needs, desires, and beliefs. This type of qualitative research gives the brand a better way to gauge how to become part of the conversation, helping them set measurable goals for the campaign. It is important for marketers to have a clear understanding of how a brand's story will be delivered as well as the potential results that will be obtained from its execution.

Here are some areas to focus on when using a social story strategy to deliver a strong marketing message:

• Know the brand's audience; listen to the audience first
• Develop the framework (storyboard) with a clear, structured message. Have a beginning, middle, and an end.
• Connect the trigger points to the emotional bond of the audience
• Create an authentic narrative to personalize the story
• Establish a consistent message through all social channels (touch points)
• Develop contextual relevancy to consumers; connectivity
• Create empowerment through inspiration and gain knowledge
• Promote the shareability of user-generated content
• Drive engagement through story

Despite the focus of brands on distributing their curated stories to influencers, they are looking for ways to drive social conversations through their own digital landscapes. The two-way relationship denotes that the customer, when relating context to content, is the story's main character, while the brand is the supporting character that enables the customer to find solutions and inspirations (De Clerck, n.d.).

Brand Social Connection through Story

The empowerment of the information age and the shareability of socialization have caused society to consume stories with increased expectations. Brands, which focused only on providing individualized context, have now shifted their attention to the overall experiences of users. These experiences are driven by shared stories and connections that are dispersed across multiple social media channels. Stories are inherently social, and social media is predicated on creating, developing, and retaining connections. The combination of these two elements motivates consumers to pursue the content across digital platforms, while potentially creating strong emotional connections between themselves and the brand. The narrative captivates the reader's attention, influencing him or her to recall old experiences and familiar events. Consumers then attempt to decode the story's meaning while tying it to existing memories. While they search for these memories in the brain, it activates the insula, which connects experiences with emotions such as happiness, joy, sadness, and disgust (Widrich, 2012).

Maya Angelou, renowned poet and civil rights activist, once said, "People will forget what you said, people will forget what you did, but people will never forget how you made them feel." Angelou's words give credence to the merits of effective storytelling that is built on the creation of emotional connections. Thus, marketers today have taken advantage of the power of stories, combined with the scope of social media—social media's reach allows brands to foster customer loyalty and evoke consumer advocacy across various channels.

> **" GREAT STORIES SUCCEED BECAUSE THEY ARE ABLE TO CAPTURE THE IMAGINATION OF LARGE OR IMPORTANT AUDIENCES.... GREAT STORIES ARE TRUSTED."**
> SETH GODIN (GODIN, 2006)

Both factors ensure the strong delivery of impactful stories directly to the brands' target audiences. Successful storytelling involves the process of developing relationships through the creation of connections. Stories can add to the value of consumer experience, build trust, and deepen the connection between brand and consumer. Brands can capitalize on this to communicate a deeper emotional connection within the story, and systematically share this is with an array of communities.

Thanks to social media, stories do not remain stagnant on a website's home page (Pre-Web 2.0) anymore; instead, they actively thrive and disperse across different networks. This is the primary difference between traditional "sales" style marketing and contemporary, emotion-based storytelling. Brands may also maintain their stories on their respective blogs for consumers to keep returning to that brand's website. Today's brands that lead within the market in community engagement have learned how to communicate their stories on multiple channels, thus making communities function as the voice of the brand (e.g., lifestyle blogs, influencers, community-driven topics). Through co-creation, brand-loyal consumers can evaluate the quality together, through communal consumption (Kozinets, 1999). The community relates to the emotional connection by sharing and exposing their personal experiences (personally invested) through story giving and through the social exchange theory of innovation (Füller, 2010). This requires that the brand raise awareness for the sharing of its story and surround itself with a community that unites around the message. Sharing an impactful, resonating story requires brands to deliver their message with a consistent, authentic voice through multi-channel touch points.

The consistency in a brand's story (message) maintains interest of consumers, and strengthens their long-term involvement. For instance, The Brooklyn Circus's unique method of narrative sharing has made the brand stand out among its competition. The menswear and lifestyle company, based on the vision of founder Ouigi Theodore, has successfully engaged with its community of loyal followers for the past ten years. The Brooklyn Circus is more than just menswear connoisseurs—all of the content they produce adhere to the brand's story and philosophy, which captures the authentic voice of American history.

The impact of their marketing methods relies on the company's commitment to emotional storytelling and impactful presentation. Visit the website to see more of their story; thebkcircus.com.

Some brands share stories based on their positive reputation and acquired credibility. Consumers learn brand insights from these stories, resulting in the formation of connections (positive or negative) between companies and their customers. Content creators have various approaches in formulating digital strategy—a brand's message may be built on emotional associations and delivered through visual consumption.

Visual marketing involves the careful positioning and sequencing of a visual narrative with the goal of pushing a brand's context toward its audience. This can be accomplished by streamlining contextualized content, thus delivering a narrative that flows through multiple channels and connecting with audiences through different touch points. Visual marketing is the placement and sharing of relatable images and objects in the hopes of forming a connection with the viewer. These images must be distributed in the right social feeds at opportune moments—doing so will increase the likelihood that the audience forms a connection with the content. Relevance goes hand in hand with visual context; the wrong timing of delivery may give the impression that a product/service is being pushed onto consumers.

" **EVERYTHING WE MAKE HAS A STORY, FROM THE CONSTRUCTION OF OUR VARSITY JACKETS TO THE LOOMS WHERE OUR DENIM IS WOVEN, AND WE TAKE THESE ELEMENTS INTO CONSIDERATION WHEN WE CULTIVATE OUR BRAND. WE ARE HERE TO TELL THE STORY OF STYLE THROUGHOUT AMERICAN HISTORY AND TO EMPHASIZE THE POWER OF PRESENTATION. WE WANT TO CHANGE THE WAY AMERICANS DRESS, ONE ICONIC SILHOUETTE AT A TIME THROUGH THE 100-YEAR PLAN."**
THE BROOKLYN CIRCUS ("BEHIND THE BRAND")

INTERVIEW: Bumpy Pitch Co-founder Ben Hooper
by Farah Chajin

One organic business model that embodies the power of social, authentic storytelling is California-based Bumpy Pitch ("bumpy soccer field"). Founded in 2004 by childhood friends Ben Hooper and Brian Dunseth, Bumpy Pitch is a soccer apparel and lifestyle company that has capitalized on today's booming soccer craze in the United States (BumbyPitch.com).

Bumpy Pitch harnessed the power of social media in order to share their story and increase awareness for the then-burgeoning soccer culture movement in the United States. Their products and promotional content all tie in with the story that the creators wanted to share with their communities.

Each graphic that Bumpy Pitch has developed for their products tells a story that ties in with a nostalgic memory or an important moment in the sport's history, thus developing the brand's credibility in the eyes of soccer aficionados who comprise the company's primary target audience.

How did Bumpy Pitch build a community blog to start a business?

BH: Bumpy Pitch was where everything started. In the beginning, we would tell everyone that it was inspired by the lifestyle and culture of the sport. People told us we were crazy. Retailers laughed at us and said they would never sell a soccer product that was not performance-based. It was hard to try to tell people what the lifestyle of the sport was. So we started the online magazine *The Original Winger* solely as a way to showcase the lifestyle and culture that we preached. Having a blog was a much better platform for us than trying to spread our message one person at a time.

What were the key elements to developing Bumpy Pitch in order to be supported by the online audience (community)?

I think being honest in our storytelling and messaging was really important. Niche audiences are hypersensitive to things. They can smell people (or brands) trying to do things for the wrong reasons. The American soccer community is, or has been, pretty insular and guarded. We are a part of this community and can sense when people are being authentic. When we started telling stories and positioning the brand, we were doing it from a very pure place. Nobody could question our love for the sport. Our credentials as former professional players were there. We talked about our love for the sport and backed it up with real stories that illustrated that love. I think the community recognized that.

Also, we have always spoken to people from a place where we are all equal. We are a part of the soccer community. We want the sport to succeed here in the US as much as every other soccer fan. So, we were very inclusive in our messaging. We always talked about "us." "Us" is all of us soccer fans. It is our community. We never said what we were specifically trying to do, only that we were a part of a community that is doing amazing things, and that we are lucky to be a part of such a rich and passionate community.

Farah Chajin is a marketing professional, with years of experience in design, production, and merchandising. Chajin is a multi-media content producer and social media developer for Sears and Kmart US. She generates brand awareness by activating cross-promotional campaigns across multiple digital platforms. Chajin manages the distribution of branded content and supports customer experience through multi-channel engagement.

4.6a

Bumpy Pitch - Made in Los Angeles

Manufacturing apparel in the US is not the easiest or most inexpensive way to go. But it's important to us and it is something that we have been able to maintain over the

4.6a
Bumpy Pitch's blog shares stories about the company and its love for soccer

4.6b
The distinct shows of soccer players on the field at a night game inspired Bumpy Pitch's T-shirt screen. The brand maintains the integrity of the soccer lifestyle through their social feeds and designs.

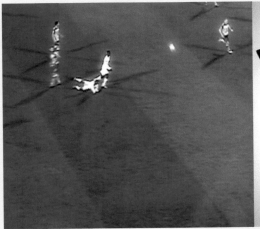

4.6b

4.7

4.7
Hermés shares their skilled craftsmen through social media posts on Instagram and Facebook. This photo demonstrates one of the textile craft specialist at Hermés at the engraving stage as they prepare a scarf.

" STYLE IS INFORMED BY A MOMENT IN TIME, AND CONTEXT IS CAPTURED BY PRESENTATION."
THE BROOKLYN CIRCUS ("BEHIND THE BRAND")

Identifying the Brand's Voice within a Story

The transparency of the digital age requires brands to cultivate greater trust and create lasting relationships with their customers. Conveying an authentic story requires a consistent and purposeful brand voice that projects its unique style and personality, thus allowing it to be recognized by its audience. A brand's integrity can be highlighted by a powerful story delivered with a personalized approach because consumers use these stories to perceive the credibility of a company's message. Also, a story's reach is determined by how effectively it is delivered and how interesting it is in the eyes of its audience.

Brands utilize stories as a persuasive tool to bridge the gap between themselves and their patrons. Hence, the most effective storytellers are those that incorporate their customers into the overall story, which then leads to the creation of a more lasting, meaningful relationship. A story's details and emotions enable marketers to trigger cues that will enhance memory retention in audiences. Storytelling facilitates an emotional bond attached to the brand through a cognitive process that recalls pre-existent brand knowledge. These stories can reveal a brand's unique history or a symbolic event that forms the connection with their audiences. Stories naturally vary by brand—while some may focus on heritage and traditional craftsmanship like Hermés, other companies, like Nike, concentrate on lifestyle, and base their stories on athletics, well-being, and fitness. These brands are successful storytellers because their messages are consistent and filtered through multi-channel social media feeds.

Stories are important facets of a brand's voice; using them effectively creates a sense of familiarity and builds trust throughout the community. This trust is a form of social currency and can reap monetary gains for brands that harness it correctly. The value of storytelling has grown due to the emergence of social media platforms that enable brands to connect with wider, highly targeted groups of consumers. Ana Maria Escobar, Oroton's (Australian luxury brand) creative director, sums it up perfectly: "You can't design a bag anymore and just leave it there for people to buy it. You need to create a dream around it. You need to create a story around it. You need to place that bag where it's supposed to go or where it's supposed to live" (Huntington, 2014). Authentic stories can dramatically increase a brand's visibility and forge connections with multiple networks of like-minded individuals.

4.8
Nike shares images in their digital communities that unite their audience through fitness, sports and well-being. Sharing images such as the US Women's Soccer Team made their US followers stand up and cheer at the FIFA Women's World Cup Canada 2015.

Consumers today actively share their own stories in bite-sized feeds throughout the day. Researchers who focus on the process of story have determined that personal stories and gossip make up 65 percent of our conversations (Hsu, 2008). Social media networks thrive on actively observing the trending topics, stories, and conversations that are broadcasted as meta-narratives (a story interpreted about a story) within their platforms. Doing so activates new insights because it creates new conversations and expands the original storyline.

Social media analytics make it possible for marketers to monitor what users personally share on their personal feeds. In chapter 6, we will examine how marketers collect this data and pinpoint certain types of behavior in order to better connect with consumers. "Shared movement" on social media involves consumers participating in a common story with other users. Factors such as social confirmation and FOMO exhibit the power of collective thought across digital platforms. Many consumers are influenced by trending topics because of a fear of being left out. Citizen storytelling occurs as more and more people begin to share a story, thus making them active participants in the process.

CASE STUDY:
Brand Voice Through Second Voice: Barbie® Takes on Social Media

Mattel, Inc. is an American multinational toy manufacturing company whose highly recognized fashion doll, Barbie® (launched in 1959) takes on social media. Her global audience stretches over 150 countries. While Barbie is traditionally marketed for kids and parents, in the digital landscape, Mattel has taken on two separate social media personas on two separate Instagram accounts. "We talked a lot about having a second voice out in social media to speak directly to an audience that's interested in art, culture, and fashion," stated Kim Culmone, Barbie's Vice President of Design (Rubin, 2015). On Instagram @Barbie focuses on kids and parents, and then a second voice on the @BarbieStyle account focuses on the fashion-minded twenty-something audience. "We thought it was a strong enough part of who we are that it deserved its own specific feed. @BarbieStyle is a curated, very specific story about Barbie's role in pop culture today" (Rubin, 2015). @BarbieStyle has 1.5 million followers with the average post receiving 39,000 "likes" and 300 engaging comments. The content would share the story of her very fashionable life as she attends cultural art events such as Art Basel and fashion weeks (month) from New York Fashion Week to Milan Fashion Week. "There are moments in Barbie's world where she is a fantastical princess or a mermaid or whatever—this is not the place for that. This is firmly rooted in reality," says Barbie's director of design, Robert Best. "Now, that reality can sometimes be over the top, like staying in the Bristol in Paris or going to the Golden Globes, but that's what makes it fun and exciting. People love the glamour quotient. Whatever it is, it's gotta be glamorous" (Rubin, 2015).

4.9

4.9
The twenty-something
@BarbieStyle audience.

CASE STUDY:
Brand Voice through a Social Story: #LikeAGirl Campaign

Social networks and word-of-mouth have helped brands offer their stories to wider, more targeted audiences. The most effective stories are able to entertain, educate, or inspire such as the "Like A Girl" campaign that spread the message of non-conformance to stereotypes. Procter & Gamble's "Like A Girl" campaign for its Always (feminine hygiene) brand was designed to educate, entertain, and inspire. It relayed an authentic message of female empowerment that impacted women and young girls. The story was highly effective and continues to gain popularity with new videos being released long after its launch. Its videos reached 39 million views in less than three months with countless impressions garnered through females who shared the story online.

The "Like A Girl" campaign was directed by award-winning director Lauren Greenfield who viewed the project as a social experiment in order to determine what "run like a girl" meant to teenagers, both male and female. "In my work as a documentarian, I have witnessed a confidence crisis among girls and the negative impact of stereotypes first-hand," said Greenfield. "When the words 'like a girl' are used to mean something bad, it is profoundly disempowering. I am proud to partner with Always to shed light on how this simple phrase can have a significant and long-lasting impact on girls and women. I am excited to be a part of the movement to redefine 'like a girl' into a positive affirmation" (Always, 2014).

The story was powerful, authentic, and was able to connect with women around the world. Female empowerment was an effective narrative that resonated with females of all backgrounds, spreading quickly through multiple social media platforms through the hashtag #LikeAGirl (153 million mentions on Instagram alone). This campaign stimulated a global conversation about the lack of confidence felt by women due to negative experiences and stereotypes. It quickly went viral, spreading the message that "women can do anything and should not be limited by society."

4.10

4.10
The "Like a Girl" campaign gave strength to women young and old, sending out the message that they could do and be anything.

INTERVIEW: Cindy Whitehead, Founder of Girl Is NOT a 4 Letter Word

Cindy Whitehead conquered the male dominated profession of professional vert skateboarding in the 1970s, and quickly became one of the top ranked professional female vert skateboarders in the US for pool riding and half-pipe. In 2016 she was inducted onto the IASC Skateboarding Hall of Fame. Whitehead has gone on to coin the term "Sports Stylist®," working as a fashion stylist for the past 25 years, specializing in sports, with companies like Gatorade, Nike, the NBA, and athletes such as Tiger Woods, Michelle Kwan, Kobe Bryant, Bethany Hamilton, Maria Sharapova, and Mia Hamm.

In 2013, Whitehead created a brand called "Girl is NOT a 4 Letter Word," and came out with a collaboration skateboard in partnership with Dwindle Inc. (the largest company in professional skateboarding) by designing a skateboard aimed at the female market. With every collaboration, the GN4LW brand gives back to women in action sports, and Cindy recently signed an additional two-year deal for her skateboard line and an additional collaboration with a XS Helmets that was launched in January 2015.

How has social media helped you reach the next generation of girls in sports?

CW: Social media has allowed girls in every sport to be seen/heard easily and at a rapid pace. We no longer have to wait for magazines that cover each sport to decide if they want to feature women. Girls are out there posting what they are doing, what their friends are doing, and reposting content they love about girls they know only through social media. We are able to see girls from all over the world excelling in sport and now know about homegrown events, contests, clubs, groups, trips videos and more. The more girls see other girls playing any sport, the more these girls realize that "I can do it too." It has also allowed girls to take it one step further and bring back the old school Zine, promote their YouTube channels and even start their own online magazines as they have a built in following from their social media pages.

4.11a
Cindy Whitehead, skateboard Hall of Fame honoree, created a brand called "Girl is NOT a 4 Letter Word"—GN4LW.

How have these Gen Z girls utilized social media to advance them in their career?

By putting out content that they shoot or film themselves with iPhones and GoPro's, and using apps like SnapChat, Periscope, Instagram, FB, and Twitter, girls can now share anything they want, anytime they want. They can cultivate their online image and show the sponsors that they excel at what they do, and that "followers" love what they post. Sponsors in turn definitely look at social media numbers when sponsoring a girl. We look at how many followers they have, what the interaction rate is on each post, which is extremely important as there are companies that let you "buy" followers. Even newer is the fact that you can also buy "likes" and "comments," but if a sponsor looks at some of those interactions and they keep coming from accounts with zero posts or followers and no profile info/pic, we know these are not organic interactions. So, it is always best to build up your following slowly and organically. We also like when girls not only post about their sport but also show are a little bit of their down time as well; the post can even be a healthy breakfast you made, your dog, a vacation you took, you and your friends hanging out. We also notice that girls even reach out to us for sponsorship via social media, always a great way to connect, but do not forget to follow it up with an email, your biography, and some pictures. Another way girls are advancing their career in sport via social media is posting photographs and comments immediately after an event—an action shot, podium shot, etc.—and sharing the news. Tagging the sponsors and thanking them is a great way to show sponsors you appreciate what they are doing for you. When a sponsor posts about you, leaving a fun message back is appropriate as well. The head of the The Ladies Professional Golf Association had a very good quote that I love: "When you are on the podium, make sure you thank not only your sponsors but whoever's name is on that check you just won." Good Advice!

4.11b
Cindy Whitehead skating on her collaborative long board with Dusters California. The collection of boards support "Long Boarding for Peace," which acknowledges as well as encourages ALL female skaters. (GirlIsNotA4LetterWord.com).

Any story you would like to share about girls in sports and social media is welcomed.

Yes—we had a very big incident with skater and surfer girls on Instagram earlier this year—their accounts were being deleted at a rapid rate and there was no communication as to why. I wrote a couple of articles about it on our website/blog and then posted on all our social media sites with that URL. It was picked up by some big athletes who shared the posts, giving the cause more traction, and all but one of the accounts was reinstated. That is the power of social media—your reach can be huge and your cause can gain fast-paced traction in a very short amount of time for very little output financially.

VISUAL CONSUMPTION OF CONTENT

A picture can be worth a thousand words, but in the context of social media, it could potentially be worth millions of impressions (views). Social media embraces the visual-centered approach to marketing and increasing the brands overall awareness in the digital landscape. The way stories are delivered has undergone a renaissance over the past decade—this is due to the widespread adoption of social connectivity and an increased migration toward visual content consumption. This voracious consumption of information has transformed the very nature of society, forcing marketers to reposition their brands accordingly.

Attraction to this type of content is a key driver of consumer engagement—users engage with visual content 180 percent more than text, and their browsing times are 100 percent more on websites with videos (Walter & Gioglio, 2014). The human brain transmits 90 percent of information visually, and processes 60,000 times faster in visual form than in text. Consumers are no longer reliant on traditional media's use of long narratives to distribute stories, instead seeking accessible, bite-sized content.

Visual Culture

Facebook is a prime example of how to effectively use visual content to spread stories and forge connections with its users. Photos, videos, images, emoticons, and status updates provide a glance into what is popular or trending around the world. These visuals also increase brand awareness, drive demand, and streamline their on-line presence. According to Simple Measure, a social analytics firm, the introduction of Facebook timelines for brands resulted in a spike of visual content engagement by as much as 65 percent.

The amount of information being shared through social networks can be somewhat overwhelming to consumers who like to filter through content before sharing. Across the space of digital media, visual consumption is now the leading method of introducing new information to users.

Content moves through social media rapidly and has a very short lifespan. Therefore, it is necessary to quickly capture the consumer's attention upon first contact. Visual consumption has reached an all-time high owing to the vast amount of content available through websites, social networks, and search engines. In 2015, more digital photographs were taken than ever before. Thirty billion photos were shared on Instagram alone, with an average of seventy million uploaded per day. Due to the congestion caused by endless online content, consumers have begun to filter out within seconds what interests them or not. In order to visualize how the future of Internet marketing will change, it is important to first understand how visual content circulates across various platforms.

Visual storytelling is the core of the success for the fashion industry, beauty industry, interior design and other visual spaces. Business of Fashion editor Lauren Sherman discovers that brands fight to tell their story during "fashion month" and beyond. Sherman states, "Brands have become savvier about how they leverage the app to impress and engage followers—especially during "fashion month," when the stakes are higher than ever. Indeed, last season, from February 12, 2015 to March 12, 2015, fashion week-related images attracted over 140 million likes and comments, according to Instagram." (Sherman, 2015).

CASE STUDY:
The Burberry Dream Team: Digital Storytelling

Burberry is a strong example of a luxury brand that merged offline with online in order to increase brand advocacy for spreading visual content that increases connectivity with the audience. While the UK-based company has always maintained a strong heritage label, they had begun to stray with heavy licensing that threatened to destroy the brand's unique strengths (Ahrendts, 2013). This "Burberry Dream Team" was composed of Christopher Bailey, current Creative Chief and President of Burberry, and Angela Ahrendts, former Burberry CEO and now Senior Vice President of Apple's retail division. "Our instincts confirmed, we clearly saw the way forward: We would reinforce our heritage, our Britishness, by emphasizing and growing our core luxury products, innovating them and keeping them at the heart of everything we did," stated Ahrendts in *Harvard Business Review* (Ahrendts, 2013). With innovative storytelling and developing a meaningful visual experience through digital spaces, Burberry took on the future of retail head on.

Their vision and leadership transformed Burberry into a social media powerhouse, as they utilized visual storytelling to its fullest capacity throughout their digital landscape and within their retail space. Moreover, they managed to build customer communities through omni-channel experiences and embracing user-generated content. The first fully digital luxury company that their customers took on a journey with their multichannel approach to provide a seamless experience from mobile, desktop to their bricks and mortar retail locations. (Omnichannel, 2015). The imagery that they used showcased more than branded merchandise; it explored the evolution of the brand's heritage and lifestyle. The team hired a cultural anthropologist to study the company's story ensure that they told an authentic Burberry story. Bailey always envisioned Burberry to be something significantly more than a luxury name—he strove to become a pioneer in content generation and consumer experience development.

According to Angela Ahrendts, "Great brands and great businesses have to be great storytellers too. We have to tell authentic stories, emotive, compelling stories. I think even more so because we are non-fiction and we are building a lifelong relationship with people, and every great relationship has to be built on trust. It is a big, great story, celebrating 150 years' anniversary

4.12
4.12
The Burberry Dream Team, composed of Christopher Bailey and Angela Ahrendts, drove digital marketing through innovative customer experiences.

when I started. In one of our very first group meetings, Christopher and I stood up in front all the associates in the UK, and in that very first presentation, we told the team that the amazing novel had been written about the company. So, we actually brought in a cultural anthropologist to study the company in order to be sure that he understood the story. We said that we should capture this story for the last five years so that we can pass it on to the next generation, enabling them to understand how we built this amazing culture, how we have turned or transformed the brand around, and that we were looking to write some really exciting chapters" (Future of Storytelling, 2013).

TRENDING SOCIAL STORIES OF THE #HASHTAG

The impact of trending social media moments—measured by hashtags—is a cultural phenomenon that influences both active and passive consumers within digital spaces. Marketers rely on these trends to obtain measurable insight about the needs and preferences of their respective target audiences.

These moments also expose online groups to ideas, topics, and perspectives, thus functioning as a communal platform where like-minded individuals can connect. As trends begin to unfold, every post, share, comment, or like moves social stories toward a "tipping point," a concept illustrated by Malcolm Gladwell and reviewed in chapter 2. This point is reached when information spreads across media channels like a virus. Gladwell remarks: "The Tipping Point is that magic moment when an idea, trend, or social behavior crosses a threshold, tips, and spreads like wildfire" (Gladwell, 2000). Hashtags (#) spread ideas, expose topics to wider audiences, and help unravel larger brand stories.

A trending social story gains momentum on social media because of two major principles: content and distribution (Rampton, 2014). Storytelling is predicated on content—users choose to share topics that reflect a common interest with other members of their respective online communities. Like-minded individuals then distribute this content throughout their social media networks in order to intensify the impact of these moments. Trends usually form stories around areas of interest such as sports, fashion, entertainment, and politics. From a global standpoint, trending moments are necessary tools in spreading information to modern, hyper-connected consumers.

4.13

4.13
Social trending hashtags takes tangible content and transforms it to digital conversations without borders. Image: American author #JackLondon #typewriter.

4.14a

4.14b
Teana Nails (@TeanaNails)
gains thousands of "likes" by
sharing her hashtags and directly
reaching her audience. #Nails has
over 43 million posts.

4.14b

4.14a
US retailer Nordstrom has used
a floor installation to encourage
consumers to take shareable
shoe selfies, which help spread
the word-of-mouth from within
their community. The hashtag
also enables the brand to monitor
the conversation in real time.

" WHAT'S REMARKABLE ABOUT INSTAGRAM IS
THAT IT'S A PROGRESSIVE PLATFORM ABLE TO
CAPTURE THESE REAL MOMENTS, PUSHING
THE LIMITS, ALLOWING UNIQUE EXPERIENCES
TO BE SHARED ACROSS A BROADER
CHANNEL, EVEN OUTSIDE OF FASHION. IT'S
ALIGNED WITH OUR ETHOS AND SPIRIT IN ITS
CREATIVE AND INCLUSIVE APPROACH."
HUMBERTO LEON, OPENING CEREMONY CO-FOUNDER AND
CREATIVE DIRECTOR (SHERMAN, 2015)

CASE STUDY:
#LoveWins–The Rainbow Movement Goes Viral

2015 was a momentous year for LGBT community with the US Supreme Court's legalization of same-sex marriage. As a response, President Obama took to social media to spread the message "Love Wins," combined with an image of a rainbow-colored heart. While not everyone agreed with the court's decision, many displayed their overwhelming support online through hashtags, images, and videos.

Facebook gave users the option to place a rainbow filter over their profile pictures in order to show support for same-sex marriage (facebook.com/celebratepride). Twenty-six million users, including Facebook CEO Mark

Zuckerberg, added the rainbow to their profile photos. This sparked a chain reaction, causing rainbow images to trend globally across different social media platforms. Corporate entities also got into the act, temporarily changing their official logos to rainbow-colored ones. Marriage equality was a powerful, emotional social story that resonated with millions around the world. Fueled by social media sharing, it rapidly gained momentum because of increased online visibility. What started as a chain of tweets from the President transformed into a movement wherein consumers, brands, and communities actively participated in a collaborative story.

4.15

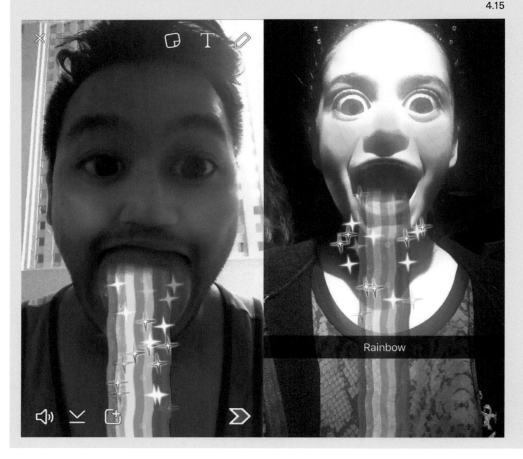

4.15
Snapchat provided playful filters allowing users to share experiences. The rainbows here were used to celebrate Pride Week.

CASE STUDY:
#TheDress—Is It White and Gold or Blue and Black?

A single dress and a debate over the color of the dress trended globally for thirty-six hours with over 16 million people sharing the story within five hours of its release. Ireland native Caitlin McNeill started this phenomenon by posting an image of a dress on Tumblr and asking her followers whether the dress was "white and gold" or "blue and black." The post prompted frenzied discussions about the actual color of the dress, with users fiercely taking sides on a trending debate that dominated the Internet for a period of time. High profile celebrities such as Lady Gaga and Taylor Swift also weighed in on the debate, effectively maintaining the story's relevance as more and more individuals scrambled to have their say on the topic. #TheDress created a divide amongst social media users—some believed that the dress was white and gold while others believed that it was blue and black. Users voiced their opinion with hashtags like #TeamWhiteGoldDress and #TeamBlackBlueDress.

Functioning as more than an ordinary trending topic, #TheDress drove online engagement to unprecedented levels because it required users to actively share their thoughts on the subject. The controversy over the actual color of the dress drove communal contribution, making the story one of the most notable social media trends in recent history. Within a three-day period, the original Tumblr post garnered twenty-one million views with the hashtag #TheDress mentioned over 600,000 times (Spargo, 2015). British retailer Roman Originals claimed that sales of this particular dress soared by 347 percent just days after the trending topic began spreading online (Petroff, 2015).

4.16

4.16
Trendmap provides real-time social media feeds. #TheDress was a powerful social story that quickly went viral around the world.

Infographic = Information + Graphics

Infographics are a key marketing tool for the visual consumer. It is a way of sharing information in a manner other than traditional flow charts or data bullet points that can seem inaccessible for modern users.

4.17

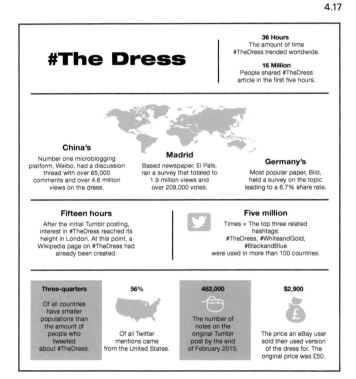

4.17
#TheDress infograph (Adapted from infograph by Wendy Bendoni)

THE SCIENCE OF STORIES: NEUROLOGICAL RESPONSE TO STORIES

Humans are hard-wired to process the narrative of stories through cause and effect. The thought process begins by searching for something that was previously felt or experienced. The familiar situation then sparks a new thought process, generating new memories and experiences about the story currently being absorbed. The cognitive effects of a story's narrative influence one's view on the story's impact. Modalities such as dialogue, narration, music, and visual effects all affect a user's experience with stories.

Ed Lantz, founding director of Immersive Media Entertainment, Research, Science & Arts (IMERSA), is internationally recognized as a leading authority in large-format digital cinema and immersive experiences. Lantz breaks down the neurological responses to stories into two categories: The Affective (feeling, moods, reactions, etc.) and The Cognitive (thoughts, beliefs, language, etc.) responses to the audience brain and nervous system (Lantz, 2011).

Neurological Response to Stories: The Affective

Energized, motivated = adrenaline
Curiosity, anticipation = endorphins, beta-endorphins
Chills, goosebumps = pilomotor reflex
Sense of accomplishment = norepinephrine, epinephrine
Humor, laughter, pleasure = dopamine
Happiness, satisfaction = serotonin
Relaxation = GABA, anadamide

Neurological Response to Stories: The Cognitive

Conceptualization
Problem Solving
Interpretations
Recognition, Remembering
Logical Connections
Learning, Skills, Technical Information
(Lantz, 2011)

THE SCIENCE OF ✿ STORYTELLING ✿

As more brands make the move towards content marketing, cutting through the noise is more vital than ever before. But our brains are built to connect with compelling stories.

IF

100,500
digital words are consumed by the average US citizen every day

92%
of consumers want brands to make ads that feel like a story

60X faster
rate at which the brain processes images in comparison to words

THEN

Keep it short (and have a great title to grab readers' attention).

Deliver content that is linear and expresses a clear narrative.

Show, don't tell. Use images for more compelling content.

HOW STORYTELLING AFFECTS THE BRAIN

NEURAL COUPLING
A story activates parts in the brain that allows the listener to turn the story in to their own ideas and experience thanks to a process called neural coupling.

MIRRORING
Listeners will not only experience the similar brain activity to each other, but also to the speaker.

DOPAMINE
The brain releases dopamine into the system when it experiences an emotionally-charged event, making it easier to remember and with greater accuracy.

CORTEX ACTIVITY
When processing facts, two areas of the brain are activated (Broca's and Wernicke's area). A well-told story can engage many additional areas, including the motor cortex, sensory cortex and frontal cortex.

THE ANATOMY OF USAGE FOR THE TOP CONTENT MARKETING TACTICS USED BY B2C BRANDS

SOCIAL MEDIA	OWNED ARTICLES	EMAIL	BLOGS	VIDEOS
88%	78%	76%	72%	72%

IN-PERSON EVENTS	3RD PARTY ARTICLES	MOBILE CONTENT	MICROSITES	CASE STUDIES
65%	61%	46%	43%	41%

A FORMULA FOR SMARTER CONTENT

QUALITY CONTENT + **DISTRIBUTION** + **RETARGETING** = **BETTER RESULTS**

QUALITY CONTENT
Quality is a balance between working with what you have and partnering with the right collaborators. 42% of B2C marketers start with existing assets/talent, using outsourced help for specialized skills like writing and design.

DISTRIBUTION
Next, you need to determine how and where you will get your content in front of the right eyes. Consider channel objectives, the personas addressed, key metrics for success and an overarching editorial calendar to help guide your plan.

RETARGETING
Retargeting is a paid search marketing strategy that allows you to message consumers who are already interested in your business. It can aid in increasing brand recognition and encouraging repeat site visits.

BETTER RESULTS
70% of consumers say content marketing makes them feel closer to the sponsoring company, which generates 3 times as many leads at 62% less than the cost of traditional marketing.

SOURCES:
New York Times, Your Brain on Fiction
Buffer.com, What Listening to a Story Does to Our Brains
Content Marketing Institute, B2C Content Marketing Benchmarks, Budgets and Trends 2014; N. America
http://socialmouths.com/blog/2013/07/15/how-to-help-your-content-rise-above-the-noise/
http://www.business2community.com/content-marketing/how-content-marketing-helps-demonstrate-thought-leadership-and-boosts-seo-0193245#!OGZnY

 one spot™

4.18
The Science of Storytelling infographic depicts the neurological response to stories (OneSpot.com / designed by Erica Boynton and Adam Weinroth).

STORYTELLING BECOMES STORYGIVING

In the digital landscape of marketing, the strategy of storytelling involves utilizing social network tools to better engage with a brand's community. The narrative tone of storytelling is derived from a brand's desire to educate consumers about their company. Brands use social media networks to contribute to the communal environment with engaging content that flows into the context of online conversations. Today, brands have learned that community collaboration is inherently more advantageous than traditional push-style tactics from a singular point of view.

Storygiving: Consumers Become Marketers

The overall narrative of marketing is quickly changing. Instead of companies merely telling their stories to audiences, consumers are now becoming active participants in the process by becoming advocates who share their personal brand stories. Storygiving enables consumers to tell their personal, unique stories about the brand. The movement of these stories is more engaging and compelling because it is driven by "real people" and shared with active audiences.

Mike Monello, CCO of Campfire, explains that storygiving allows participants to become the storytellers themselves. His rich experience in the film industry has taught Monello how to empower consumers to become word-of-mouth marketers. In fact, he was one of the producers for the 1999 indie hit *The Blair Witch Project*. The film's promotional approach revolutionized how entertainment properties are marketed online nowadays. Blairwitch.com was created in order to spread the idea that the movie was based on actual events. It also pioneered the "found footage" style of filmmaking and showed clips of the missing students on the website. Word-of-mouth grew, generating massive buzz for the film because of the controversial nature of its subject matter. Audiences wanted to know whether the footage was real or staged, making the low budget production one of the more surprising box office successes of 1999.

This approach was highly unorthodox at the time, especially in a pre-social media world. Due to its low budget, the film relied on people to become marketers and stimulate interest in the movie. This proved highly effective, as more and more people flocked to cinemas to see what all the hype was about. The more people talked about it, the more others wanted to see it. In a unique collaboration, viewers participated in a story of fear that revolved around discovering whether the Blair Witch footage was fiction or reality.

Storygiving allows consumers to enter a story's narrative by becoming active participants in the process of personal sharing. Customers who share their own stories lend credibility and authenticity to a brand's message while helping deliver the message in an organic way. Wojtek Szumowski, Executive Vice President of CP+B, states: "Today, people want to be in their own story, while brands keep telling their own stories through advertising masquerading as storytelling." The social phenomenon of sharing has dramatically altered the marketing landscape, enabling large audiences to capture personal moments and topics of interest and share it with their followers. Snapchat and Instagram Stories enable users to build their personal stories throughout the day while making it viewable in its entirety or in individual chapters. Each social share makes the consumer feel an emotional connection to their community and allows them to retain control of their personal narrative. Conversations then develop online as stories become viewed through different points of view.

Brands are afforded the opportunity to integrate user-generated content in its overall narrative and build upon its conversations with target audiences. Storygiving captures a moment in time that has not been shared in a common place and social media provides a platform for brands and communities to share their story. Brands attuned to their consumers have learned to provide curated content in order to facilitate a connection through storytelling.

INTERVIEW:
Marketing Storyteller, Mike Monello of Campfire Marketing Agency

Mike Monello is a pioneer in digital marketing and storytelling. He was one of the creators of the *Blair Witch Project*–a movie that forever changed how audiences engage with story, and how marketers approach the Internet. Monello founded Campfire in 2006 and leads the creative team, working with some of the world's biggest and most prestigious brands. Campfire shapes perceptions and enhances brand preference through social storytelling, digital content, and physical experiences. Still a staunch storyteller at heart, Monello is a charismatic and in-demand speaker, who is regularly asked to present at high-profile events such as Advertising Week, the Futures of Entertainment at M.I.T., SXSW, Digital Hollywood, and more.

How would you breakdown what storytelling is for a brand? How does trans-media storytelling differ?

MM: This is a tough question because "storytelling" has become an overused buzzword in marketing. Agencies and "gurus/consultants" have sold brands on the idea that they need to become storytellers, which has led brands to believe that they need to create gobs of content and "tell" their stories. The reality is that a brand is a combination of the story the brand tells and the experience that people have of every aspect of the brand. The story and the experience must be aligned. A brand can talk about "helping people" all day long, but it will not matter if the product and the behavior of the company do not live up to that promise.

Brands are no longer what they say they are; brands are what people say they are. So, storytelling for a brand is a combination of what they say about themselves, and how people experience every aspect of what the brand does. When those are deeply connected, you get strong brands like Apple and Nike. When they are broken, they come off like airline brands, where their marketing stands in direct contrast to the actual experience.

How did storytelling turn into story giving?

"Story giving" is not really a codified thing; it is more a creative approach to how we develop our ideas and experiences. It is really a phrase I use to get people to think about not just the story but how the story is experienced. "Don't just tell a story, give people a story to tell" puts people at the center, not the story or the brand. Stories are how we remember things, but experiences are how we acquire our most personal and meaningful stories.

What would be the best advice you can give to a brand trying to tell their story in the digital landscape?

My advice is quality over quantity. Brands today are so busy throwing out low-grade "content" for social feeds that they forget the only way to get authentic word-of-mouth is to be remarkable, and do remarkable things. Brands should figure out how to make everything they touch better by their presence, not worse. Brands should understand that sometimes, the most powerful thing they can do online is to connect like-minded people to each other, rather than trying to be at the center of attention.

Storytelling Brand Community

Brand-driven microsites (individual webpages) are exclusively hosted to enable storytelling communities to create and control a network based on the brand's commonality. A microsite is a dedicated platform that hosts community discussion and is a subset of a brand's main distribution channel (website). Microsites are beneficial because it creates spaces for like-minded consumers to connect with each other. One of its main advantages is that it offers a private community that is free from advertisements and other informational clutter. As brands seek to boost awareness, these microsites have become avenues for loyal customers to share their personal stories with other brand patrons. Traditional social networks are effective for certain digital strategies and impacts how a brand gains or maintains their social presence.

Burberry became a leading innovator in the fashion industry by continuously taking chances in its digital marketing approach. In many ways, the company has been responsible for making the digital environment a socially accepted platform for other luxury brands. In 2009, Burberry was one of the first luxury brands to invite consumers to become a part of its story with the creation of a microsite called "Art of the Trench." This platform featured photographs of consumers showing off their "relaxed moments" while dressed in classic Burberry trench coats. Scott Schuman, blogger for *The Sartorialist*, was the campaign photographer to initially launch the site.

As interest in the Art of the Trench microsite developed, the community members began acting as content curators by filtering photos submitted by other Burberry aficionados. A narrative quickly began to emerge, one that conveyed the heritage of Burberry from a consumer's point of view. The campaign proved to be successful from a metrics standpoint. Within the first year of its launch, the microsite received 7.5 million views from 150 countries, while surpassing Burberry's average conversion rates.

Creating and Developing the Community

Most brands have failed to replicate Burberry's levels of digital storytelling success. In this section, we will provide guidelines on how to develop a storytelling microsite that will create a space for user-generated content to flourish. Doing so will enable loyal customers to collaborate with social sharing communities online. Storytelling has now evolved toward experience-based narratives that require participation in a community format. Brands are currently stepping back and allowing their customers to share their stories via images, videos, and other forms of media. This changing of the narrative is an effective tool that helps users form communities inside a single location (microsite). Consumers who share their stories are rewarded with different types of value, such as being showcased on a brand's social media channel (fame through association). The following list will provide examples of how brands use story sharing to better connect with their customers:

1) The Approach/Setting Goals
2) Reaching The Brands Community
3) Common Thread Community
4) Motivation/Incentive to Co-Create

THE APPROACH/SETTING GOALS:

During the early stages of creating a storytelling platform (microsite), it is necessary for the brand to set measurable goals and determine how to approach its community (existing and prospective customers) and set measurable goals. Goals and measurable outcomes vary from brand to brand and should be as unique as the brand itself. Thus, it is important to begin with these factors in order to assess the best way to reach a company's target audiences. Built on a relationship marketing approach, the emphasis of microsite development builds brand awareness, increased satisfaction, and customer retention. When approaching a community, brands must first recognize what consumers want to share and how they want to share it. A brand must also know how to incorporate these social stories into its overarching message. Social stories are shared and understood by a community because of their unifying message.

To best address the collaboration between brand and consumer, it is important to ask the following questions:

- How does the brand's community relate to the brand itself?
- What value does the brand's story provide to the community?
- What are the measureable outcomes that will best support the brand's overall mission and message?

REACHING THE BRAND'S COMMUNITY

Brand microsites need to function as self-contained platforms unlike popular social media sites such as Facebook and Pinterest. The platform could run as a type of public forum that invites members to share their views on a variety of brand topics as part of the community. It also serves as a location for those with similar interests and lifestyles associated with the brand. Similarly, it is also important for community members to clearly signify their connections to the brand and why they chose to participate in a collaborative community.

- Developing a social sharing community based on user-generated content requires community participation.
- A relationship based on social sharing requires consumers to be engaged not only through story sharing but also by interacting with the community members.
- This community will focus on contributing to the brand's story. In place of customer product reviews, members will share images of themselves using the products.

A community is encouraged to maintain a social presence on the site and assist in the development of a brand's story. Consumers are not obligated to purchase anything to become a member of the community. However, brands are required to open multiple channels of communication between themselves and their customers.

CHOO247 Stylemakers

CHOO247 Stylemakers is the brainchild of digitally savvy brand Jimmy Choo. It is an interactive microsite designed to celebrate street fashion and invite the brand's fans to share their respective shoe styles in a community gallery. The community flourished because it touched upon consumers' desire to share their unique styles with other fashionistas around the globe.

CHOO247 website shares fashionable women in their Jimmy Choo shoes. http://us.jimmychoo.com/en/choo-world/stylemakers.html

COMMON THREAD COMMUNITY

Consumers engage best with a brand's story when they connect with it on a personal-relatable-emotional level. The process of storygiving relies on members uniting through brand characteristics (tangible and intangible elements of a brand), common interests, or shared points of view. Common interests, coupled with the prospect of social confirmation, encourage others to share stories and display measurable actions, such as liking, commenting, or re-posting. Shareable user-generated content is a powerful tool for brands. It is a form of social currency that adds validation to the microsite and increases the strength of an online community.

Consumer storytelling works because of the virtual co-creation platform that unites individuals with common interests (i.e., the brand) (Füller, 2010). Unlike brand reviews that focus on user concerns, the storygiving narrative is written as an "experience" shared by an author about a common thread. This experience is authentic and provides brand insights from a consumer's point of view. Moreover, these stories stem from a collective purpose (joint focus) and are curated in a community space. The act of authentic storytelling must proceed from the words of the community with no influence from the host or brand. Brands must be mindful of interfering with the development of the narrative in order to realize long-term gains.

MOTIVATION / INCENTIVE TO CO-CREATE

Brands have to decide whether to use intrinsic or extrinsic motivation when encouraging consumers to contribute to the community. Extrinsic motivation could come in the form of offering monetary value through prizes, while intrinsic motivation may be derived from an individual's desire to be part of the brand community (i.e., sense of belonging). Consumers obtain social currency from shared content or through association with the brand. They bond and develop groups around common interests and preferred traits. Not all audiences participate in the same way; therefore, it is also important to create a community platform wherein creators share and audiences observe.

The Story of Dance: i-D X DIESEL: Dancing in Jeans, A–Z of Dance

With the launch of DIESEL's Jogg collection, they signaled its intention to engage with a very specific community, one comprised of jean-loving consumers who were also interested in the art of dancing. The brand collaborated with *i-D* Magazine to launch a community microsite as well as dance documentary directed by Jacob Sutton. Driven by user-generated content, the site flourished and created an online community for dance lovers around the world.
The Dance of A-Z:
https://www.youtube.com/watch?v=UFZxK8edZWA

CASE STUDY:
Tiffany & Co, Incentive through Love: "What Makes Love True?"

Motivated by a desire to connect with a larger community of consumers, Tiffany & Co. launched True Love, a microsite conceived around the ideas of love, romance, and happy endings. "Tiffany has long been a major presence at engagements and weddings, and now we have built that presence online with love stories and a whole world of romantic possibilities," said Caroline Naggiar, CMO of Tiffany & Co. The company, which has 175 years of experience in touching the lives of couples, also launched a smartphone app in conjunction with the site in order to gain access to a wider audience. Both platforms were designed to allow community members to define their personal notions of true love and everlasting romance. The site asked users to share photos and videos of their romantic stories and allowed them to interact with those who shared the same interests.

Love Stories: This feature allows users to share photographs that will serve as a personal visual diary. It essentially empowers consumers to curate their unique love stories through the power of imagery and share them with other members of the community.

Love is Everywhere: With the help of geo-location, this feature enables True Love app users to tag locations on a virtual map. This serves as a tool for consumers to curate their romantic journeys and find commonalities between themselves and other community members. It also allows the user to place a heart with their initials on a desired map point. This heart may mark where a couple first kissed or where they got engaged.

The brand had to address the challenge of how to become available to users around the world while remaining uniquely exclusive to its valued customers. Segment exclusivity is a valued commodity in the luxury market. Thus, brands must maintain their positioning when utilizing user-generated content in its story. The advantage of being an established luxury brand, such as Tiffany & Co., is that community members feel privileged when asked to contribute to a brand's story. They take pride in being asked to share their personal stories and become featured on a successful brand's microsite.

4.19

4.19
Tiffany & Co. launches its "True Love in Pictures" project. When like is not enough Tiffany & Co. also introduces "LoveNotLike"

INTERVIEW:
Braden Harvey Sharing Stories of Good All Over The World

Branden Harvey story… "I started telling stories for my neighbors in Portland, Oregon, who are living life in a way that inspires me. I started telling stories for some of the biggest brands out there, helping them create compelling narratives. I started hopping on planes, trains, and rickshaws telling stories for people doing life-changing work around the world. My favorite photos that I have made are the ones that tell a story. My favorite projects that I have worked on have been about crafting a narrative. I believe stories hold immeasurable power to inspire, change, and encourage humanity. I love telling stories filled with hope, justice, love, and joy because I trust that those stories hold the power to change the world."
(BrandenHarvey.com)

How do you think storytelling in the medium of social media has helped you tell your authentic stories?

BH: One of the things I love most about telling stories through social media is how personal it is. Most of our time on social media is spent staying in communication with people we trust— whether those are our friends, family, or celebrities. When I am able to build trust with people who are following me, it gives me the opportunity to share stories through the personal lens of my own experience—as if they already know me. That same personal experience creates a one-on-one relationship with the people in my audience. Everyone can join in the conversation, and I can shift and morph my stories to fall more in line with the audience that I have come to know.

Can you tell us why Snapchat works to tell your engaging stories with your audience? #GoodIsWinning

Snapchat is an especially interesting platform because of just how personal it is. The app is poorly designed and glitchy, the effects are goofy, and you are always an arm's length away from the storyteller. Not to mention, the ephemerality of a story that disappears and does not last forever mirrors our reality—moments in real life do not truly last forever. All of this together makes stories told through Snapchat feel more like a conversation than a production. I have spent hours laboring on Instagram, blog posts and tweets before, making sure that the editing is just right and the words are exactly as I want them. But on Snapchat you shoot, and share live and in the moment, and when you watch other people's stories on Snapchat, you feel much more a part of the experience than when you read a tweet, or see a curated and edited Instagram.

For me, I love the simplicity. It is easy for me to create a story, but it challenges me creatively to actually create a unique and compelling story. I love that it gives me the opportunity to let my audience into the greater story of my life in a more authentic and personal way.

Your love of storytelling is somewhat contagious to all who see and experience your work in photography and social media. What do you think brands should look for when looking for someone like you to tell their story?

I will flip this question on its head and share what I look for when I partner with a brand to tell their story. I receive at least a dozen emails a week from brands wanting me to tell their story. Sometimes, they want me to create content that shares their story for use on their channels. Other times, they are asking me to share their story on my channels.

> **" MY FAVORITE PHOTOS I'VE MADE ARE THE ONES THAT TELL A STORY. MY FAVORITE PROJECTS I'VE WORKED ON HAVE BEEN ABOUT CRAFTING A NARRATIVE. I BELIEVE STORIES HOLD IMMEASURABLE POWER TO INSPIRE, CHANGE, AND ENCOURAGE HUMANITY. I LOVE TELLING STORIES FILLED WITH HOPE, JUSTICE, LOVE AND JOY BECAUSE I TRUST THAT THOSE STORIES HOLD THE POWER TO CHANGE THE WORLD."**
> BRANDEN HARVEY

4.20

4.20
Brandon Harvey sharing one amazing story at a time. Photography by Gregory Woodman. Hand-lettering by Judson Collier.

When it is the former, it is much easier for me to say yes. I really love any opportunity I get to tell someone's story, and if a brand is giving me the opportunity to do that, they already have a great understanding of how stories move the needle.

When it is the latter, though, there is a lot more to consider. I have built a trust with my audience and I never want to break that trust with them just to make a few bucks. I am constantly looking to partner with brands to tell stories that will add value to the lives of my audience and add value to the brand. While I get more than a dozen storytelling requests from brands every week, I say no to most of them because they are not a good fit. I exclusively say yes to opportunities that fall in line with what my audience and I are passionate about.

I specifically love telling stories of the good in the world—the pockets of hope and light and change in the midst of darkness and cynicism. I love telling the stories of lives changed, hearts softened, and people brought together. When a brand asks me to share a story that falls in line with these ideas, I will almost certainly say yes.

The best thing that a brand can do when they are looking for someone to tell their story is to find the thread that connects a storyteller's work. What are they passionate about? What does their audience respond to? How does my story align with these passions?

SOCIAL GOOD MARKETING:
PURPOSEFUL STORIES IN THE DIGITAL AGE

Social good (philanthropic cause/charitable actions) companies have successfully used the power of storytelling to reach wider audiences in the digital environment. Social marketing operates by sharing stories and utilizing the humanizing touch of social media networks (Lovejoy and Saxton, 2012). The concept of social marketing was first introduced in 1971 in order to describe the application of commercial marketing principles to health, social, and quality of life issues. This type of marketing sought "to influence social behaviors not to benefit the marketer, but to benefit the target audience and the general society" ("Bridging the Gap," 2010). Today, certain brands use social marketing to create a positive, lasting impact on its environment.

Effective storytelling occurs when brands are able to create emotional connections between the story and its audience. This connection is referred to as pathos (Aristotelian theory of audience persuasion), a quality that evokes empathy for the story being shared. A story that is delivered properly can trigger a host of emotional cues while stimulating an intrinsic need to contribute to the cause. Social marketing stories must not only be impactful but must also be able to show how the brand is actively making a positive contribution to others. This form of "social proof" can be shared through images, videos, infographs, and motivational anecdotes, with the ultimate goal of connecting a brand to its target audience.

Social media's role in spreading awareness about "social good" movements has not only helped existing nonprofit organizations but has also created viable platforms for new ones. The digital era of communications has helped these movements improve their community-building practices and thrive across social media networks and improve their community-building practices. Companies, such as Hatch, assist charitable businesses in developing online spaces while encouraging consumers to participate in these companies' agendas.

" ALONG THE WAY, WE COLLECT STORIES ABOUT THE PEOPLE AND PLACES WE VISIT, THE GOOD DEEDS WE OBSERVE, THE LIVES THAT WE SUSTAIN. THESE STORIES ARE THE POWERFUL PRODUCT OF OUR WORK"
HATCH FOR GOOD

CASE STUDY:
Social Good from Ford Motor Co.

What is the driver of the car missing when they are not liking an image on Instagram while they are driving down the road? The fear of missing out while driving is a problem, and Ford has taken on this problem with a campaign to reach drivers, or to reach consumers, to think about it twice before they go on social media while they are driving. The public service announcement went to state on Instagram, "Go further responsibly. Please, don't like and drive."

This post went up on Ford's global Instagram account, sharing the image with a heart covering up who is crossing the road. This is one powerful message for drivers who saw this message as they were "driving." AdWeek stated, "The campaign is almost perfect—a great concept that can target the user right at the crucial moment; memorable visuals; a nice use of the medium's imagery; and a strong copy line" (Nudd, 2015).

CASE STUDY:
The Giving Keys

It all began with one key. Founded in 2008 by singer Caitlin Crosby, The Giving Keys is a company that refashions old keys into jewelry and accessories engraved with inspiring words or messages. Recipients of these items are then encouraged to "pay it forward" and give their keys to those who may need it more in the future. The Giving Keys is a social good company that relies on storytelling to deliver its intended messages. What started as a single key with the word "LOVE" engraved on it has grown into a profitable business that has touched the lives of countless people in need. The Giving Keys envisioned the brand to spread messages of love, goodwill, and compassion and simply wanted to inspire, encourage, and empower other people with simple words and phrases. Crosby also wanted the company's customers to function as active participants in the brand's narrative. Thus, she also created a platform (website) that enabled consumers to share their stories and connect with other individuals in need of encouragement. The website functions as a #PayItForward hub where consumers can connect with other members of the community. Users share their stories and why they chose to have certain words or phrases engraved on their keys. Each key tells a unique story; seemingly innocuous words like "HOPE," "BRAVE," "COURAGE," "FEARLESS," "BELIEVE," all carry tremendous meaning for key owners.

The company employs individuals who are transitioning out of homelessness, signifying their deep commitment to social responsibility. The Giving Keys can now be found in over 1,200 retail locations worldwide.

INTERVIEW: Stewart Ramsey of Krochet Kids—Social Good; Stories with Purpose. by Bailey Hanson

Krochet Kids intl. began when three guys named Stewart, Kohl, and Travis transformed their love and talent for crochet into a difference-making venture. Today, it is a non-profit organization that empowers, mentors, and educates women by creating and selling apparel knit and crochet hats. These products are made in Uganda and Peru—each woman who creates the item signs the tag, giving each product a personalized touch. The company's founders believed that impact is measurable and improvable; thus, they utilize digital media to tell their story and connect with consumers and advocates.

How has social media helped you voice your story?

SR: Social Media has played an integral part in the dissemination of the KK intl. message. Initially, this was the only way we could engage with and grow a community beyond ourselves. Our brand launched online with literally zero budget. Social media outreach made it possible in a lot of ways. I can remember signing up for Twitter back in 2008 not knowing what the heck it was, or how to use it. I still do not know how to use it, but we hired someone who does. It has been fun to see how it has evolved so rapidly, and we try to take advantage of different platforms.

Despite its limitations, social media has been great in forming our voice in many ways as we are forced to share our story in concise and creative ways, whether it is character restrictions or posting photos. My favorite impact, which social media has had for KK intl., is leveraging the digital space for connecting with real people offline whom we might not have otherwise connected with if it was not for some small interaction on social media. Real, face-to-face human interaction and communication supersedes any other form we have and I am grateful that social media can act as a conduit or catalyst for real connection. It is amazing and astonishingly powerful.

How has social media influenced your engagement with consumers?

At KK intl., we do not refer to our advocates as "consumers." We tend to see them as very equal partners, where impact is achieved through voluntary exchange for mutual benefit. Viewing customers as partners directly influences how we use social media to engage with them. As a result, we have social media in place not only to act as our voice, but also for things like customer care or rallying points where we directly ask our "partners" to participate with the brand. A lot of energy is poured into organically connecting with our partners and advocates through social media. Thus, most of our digital campaigns and strategies are built specifically to leverage or grow these social channels.

What social media platform helps you best tell your story and connect with your community?

I would say that no form of social media could share our story like a person or our product can; in reality, it is the collective aggregate of all our digital properties that tell our story best. Specific platform effectiveness has changed over time in relation to the content. At one point, we asked our Facebook community to rally around a voting contest to help us win $500,000. At other times, we have shared messages of empowerment through

4.21a

STORIES OF CHANGE

a retail partner on Twitter. We have also seen amazing engagement with product photography on Pinterest. As of now, we are seeing extremely positive interaction that is creating content for Instagram. The reality is that each channel tends to have a specific audience that likes to be communicated with in a specific way. The stable constant has been changed.

How does the company reward or show gratitude to the community that supports the movement?

We thank them, both digitally and in real life. But we try our best to share the impact that purchases and donations have on the ladies in Uganda and Peru. We give our supporters the absolute best product that we can offer. We are completely transparent and genuine about how money is spent and how the women in our programs benefit from a product purchase or donation. We also try to flip the idea of gratitude on its head—we give our supporters the opportunity to write a digital thank you note on our website, which we then deliver to the women in our project locations as a form of encouragement. Again, using digital media to connect with folks in real ways!

What influenced you to begin sharing the story of these women across the digital world?

Speaking purely from a business aspect, social media is the only tool we have had in order to share our story with a broader community. Our primary motivation was making our audience realize that the women in Uganda and Peru are not really different than you and I. They are people that want and need things very similar to what you and I need (as opposed to how the developing world usually tends to be depicted). Additionally, any cultural differences are points of celebration and deserve recognition. We wanted to provide evidence regarding the work we were doing and our supporters' participation. Sharing the women's stories on social media gives further insight into who the ladies are and how their lives were changed by the efforts of the brand and our community.

What influenced you to use e-book to help others start their own non-profit?

Three things:

1. A lot of people helped us in our infancy, and they continue to advise us. We wanted to pass that knowledge along.
2. We wished we had a tool to expedite the process when we were just getting started. The e-book is a great tool for making an impact.
3. We have learned a lot over the last eight years, and we want people to be oriented toward having measurable and provable impact. This is especially true as more socially conscious brands and organizations are beginning to enter the digital space.

Bailey Hanson is a lifestyle blogger who strives to show readers that anyone can make a difference in the world and pass on the social good movement. While her professional interests are in the area of retail management, her personal interests are in the area of non-profits that are making a difference within a community.

4.21b

4.21a
Krochet Kids intl. empowers women in Uganda and Peru.

4.21b
Krochet Kids intl. recognizes the individuals who make their products and has all their products hand signed by the people who made them.

CASE STUDY: Fashion Revolution Day:
The Power of a Hashtag Telling a Story of Human Interest

In 2014, Fashion Revolution Day showed a new generation of activists how to use social media to disrupt the established order. The day was selected in remembrance of the factory/textile workers who lost their lives in the Rana Plaza (Dhaka, Bangladesh) complex disaster on April 24, 2013. Fashion Revolution Day turned to social media to create a movement and share a powerful and relevant story. Consumers took selfies of themselves with certain brand labels and used the hashtags #WhoMadeMyClothes and #FashRev. This form of "hashtag activism" was used to question manufacturing and employment practices used by brands today. Participants essentially become marketers for the #FashRev movement by using the social currency they have acquired within their personal digital space. They connect to the cause through the effects of brand integrity and sustainability. The Fashion Revolution encourages consumers to "be curious, find out, and do something" about the people who actually made the clothes you wear, from those who picked the cotton to those who sewed the garment. Fashion Revolution Day's goal is to spread awareness of the true cost of fashion and recognize the brands that are making a difference in alleviating the conditions of laborers from third-world countries. This is a collaborative movement that raises awareness by utilizing user-generated content and consumers' personal connections to their respective social communities.

4.22a

FASHION REVOLUTION

SHOW YOUR LABEL

ASK BRANDS WHO MADE MY CLOTHES?

BE CURIOUS FIND OUT DO SOMETHING

24.04.16

#WHOMADEMYCLOTHES? FASHIONREVOLUTION.ORG @FASH_REV

4.22a, b
Fashion Revolution Day—
Who Made My Clothes?

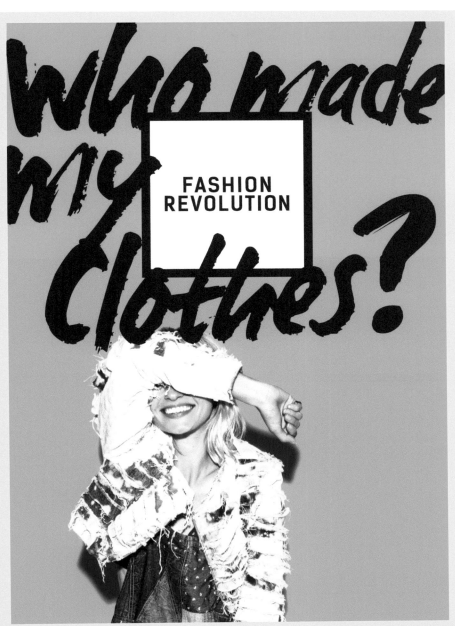

4.22b

" WE BELIEVE IN A FASHION INDUSTRY THAT VALUES PEOPLE,
THE ENVIRONMENT, CREATIVITY, AND PROFIT IN EQUAL
MEASURE. OUR MISSION IS TO BRING EVERYONE TOGETHER
TO MAKE THAT HAPPEN."
FASHION REVOLUTION, FASHIONREVOLUTION.ORG

EXERCISES

Critical Thinking: Develop a social media campaign based on a brand's story. Create a storyboard by laying out in images, short clip videos or text on how you will share a preselected brand's story. Show in your curated images how you will best convey the brands story through a social media campaign.

Practical Application: Evaluate a successful campaign that is centered on the principles of storytelling marketing funnel.

Business Activity: Create either a campaign or study focusing on the evolution of changing the narrative of a brand story from the brand to the audience. Within this campaign or study, develop a community around storygiving.

Refer to the case story of Tiffany & Co.'s True Love and Burberry's Art of The Trench community.

Keep in mind the importance of building the community through digital curation, and use these components when building the community.

Infographics: Create an infograph based on a social media measureable hashtag marketing campaign. Refer to the sample in the chapter about #LoveWins, #LikeAGirl or #FashRev.

Technology Corner: Review advertising news outlets such as Adweek.com to review how storytelling is being used through advertising and branding.

REFERENCES

Ahrendts, Angela (2013), Burberry's CEO on Turning an Aging British Icon into a Global Luxury Brand," *Harvard Business Review*, January-February. Available online: https://hbr.org/2013/01/burberrys-ceo-on-turning-an-aging-british-icon-into-a-global-luxury-brand

Always, (2014). Always #LikeAGirl [Video file], June 26. Retrieved from https://www.youtube.com/watch?v=XjJQBjWYDTs

Behind the Brand (n.d.), *The Brooklyn Circus*. Retrieved from http://thebkcircus.com/pages/behind-the-brand

Blanks, T. (2014), "Chanel Spring 2015 Ready-To-Wear Review," Vogue, September 30. Available online: http://www.vogue.com/fashion-shows/spring-2015-ready-to-wear/chanel

Sales and Marketing (2010), "Bridging the Gap: Measuring the Value of Social Marketing and Media," *Sales and Marketing*, July 31. Available online: https://salesandmarketing.com/article/bridging-gap-measuring-value-social-marketing-and-media

De Clerck, J.P. (n.d.), "Using storytelling to strengthen your brand," *I-Scoop*. Available online: http://www.i-scoop.eu/using-storytelling-strengthen-brand/

Facebook IQ. (2015, August), "The Power of Storytelling: Taking a Sequenced Approach to Digital Marketing." Available online: https://fbinsights.files.wordpress.com/2015/08/facebookiq_powerofstorytelling_august2015.pdf

Füller, J. (2010), "Consumer Empowerment through Internet-Based Co-creation," *Journal of Management Information Systems*, 26 (3): 71-102.

Future of Storytelling (2013), Authentic Branding for a Global Audience: Angela Ahrendts (Future of StoryTelling 2013) [Video File], September 16. Available online: https://www.youtube.com/watch?v=krQG2Hceov4

Getty Images (2014), Super Sensory, Getty Images, *Youtube*, July 9. Available online: https://www.youtube.com/watch?v=gNvQdFomjl4

Gladwell, M. (2000), *The Tipping Point: How Little Things Can Make a Difference*, Boston:Little, Brown.

Godin, S. (2006), "Ode: How to tell a great story," April 27 . Available online: http://sethgodin.typepad.com/seths_blog/2006/04/ode_how_to_tell.html

Graj, S. (2012), "Skill Set of a Brand Curator," *Forbes*, April 16. Available online: http://www.forbes.com/sites/simongraj/2012/04/16/skill-set-of-a-brand-curator/

Huntington, P. (2014), "Digital Strategy: Oroton," *FELLT*, August 4. Available online: http://fellt.com/industry/2014/08/digital-strategy-oroton

Hsu, J. (2008), "The Secrets of Storytelling: Why We Love a Good Yarn," *Scientific America*, August 4. Available online: http://www.scientificamerican.com/article/the-secrets-of-storytelling/

Kakroo, U. (2015), "5 Ways to Use Storytelling in Your Social Media Marketing," *Social Media Examiner*, October 26. Available online: http://www.socialmediaexaminer.com/5-ways-to-use-storytelling-in-your-social-media-marketing/

Kozinets, R. (1999), "E-Tribalized Marketing?: The Strategic Implications of Virtual Communities of Consumption," *European Management Journal*, 17 (3): 252-264.

Lantz, E. (2011), "Immersive Environments as Next-Generation Storytelling Platforms" [Lecture], April 16. Available online: http://www.xmedialab.com/presentations/xml_perth_2011_Lantz.pdf

Lovejoy, K. and Saxton, G.D. (2012), "Information, Community, and Action: How Nonprofit Organizations Use Social Media," *Journal of Computer-Mediated Communication*, 17 (3): 337-353.

Nudd, T. (2015), "Ford Is Using Instagram Perfectly for These 'Don't Like and Drive' Posts Getting to the heart of the matter," *Ad Week*, November 19. Available online: http://www.adweek.com/news/advertising-branding/ford-using-instagram-perfectly-these-dont-and-drive-posts-168223.

Petroff, A. (2015), "#TheDress goes viral: Sales soar 347%," *CNN Money*, February 27. Available online: http://money.cnn.com/2015/02/27/smallbusiness/the-dress-blue-black-gold-white

Rampton, J. (2014), "How To Get Your Hashtag Trending," *Forbes*, August 7. Available online: http://www.forbes.com/sites/johnrampton/2014/08/07/how-to-get-you-hashtag-trending/

Rogers, D.L. (2012), "The Network is Your Customer," August 7, Yale University Press.

Sherman, L. (2015), "Inside The Instagram Wars," *The Business of Fashion*, September 9. Available online: http://www.businessoffashion.com/articles/intelligence/fashion-instagram-brands-social-media-proenza-schouler-calvin-klein

Social Media Case Study: Burberry encourages customer participation with "Art of Trench" (n.d.). Available online: http://www.digitaltrainingacademy.com/casestudies/2013/07/social_media_case_study_burberry_encourages_customer_participation_with_art_of_trench.php

Spargo, C. (2015), "The optical illusion that's divided the internet: Celebrities join fierce debate over whether this frock is white and gold or blue and black... so which colours do you see?," *Daily Mail*, February 26. Available online: http://www.dailymail.co.uk/news/article-2971409/What-color-dress-White-gold-blue-black.html

Walter, E. and Gioglio, J. (2014), *The Power of Visual Storytelling: How to Use Visuals, Videos, and Social Media to Market Your Brand*, New York: McGraw-Hill Education.

What We Do. (n.d.). In *Hello Society*. Available online: https://hellosociety.com/whatwedo

Widrich, L. (2012), *"The Science of Storytelling: What Listening to a Story Does to Our Brains,"* *BufferApp.com*, November 29. Available online: https://blog.bufferapp.com/science-of-storytelling-why-telling-a-story-is-the-most-powerful-way-to-activate-our-brains.

05

PART 2
**THE BUSINESS OF
MARKETING FASHION**

STRATEGIC MARKETING IN THE DIGITAL AGE

Chapter Objectives

- Investigate social media marketing strategy
- Rethink the marketing funnel
- Look at influence marketing
- Find out about affiliate marketing
- Understand the importance of collaborations and digital experiences
- Explore the world of influence marketing
- Analyze the art of digital curation
- Explore the world of fashion on-demand

5.1
Connecting communities,
influencers and brands through
the digital landscape.

INTRODUCTION

In this chapter, we will take a closer look at social media marketing's role in integrated marketing communication strategies, social influence marketing, and affiliate alliances. Through interviews with digital and marketing industry leaders, we will learn the steps involved in the planning stages of a digital strategy and the growth of influencer power. We will also evaluate how brands and retailers approach strategy development, execution, and assessment of their marketing efforts across multiple channels and touch-points.

Digital strategists are required to possess a strong understanding of core marketing principles and technologies in order to assist them in their marketing decisions. Throughout this chapter, we will analyze the importance of influencer content marketing and affiliate programming within a brand's social media strategy. As we focus on digital curation and branded content distribution, we will highlight how retailers and brands are leveraging consumers' need for social proof and digitally activated experiences. In order to increase online awareness, brands and retailers are now incorporating performance-based programs and collaboration projects (both online and offline) to create digitally engaging customer experiences. Goals and outcomes vary, but the idea behind these collaborations is to tap into online social communities through the social currency of influencers and bloggers of measurable status.

Through digital curation, as well as user-generated content, stories can make it possible for brands to evolve from the traditional methods of telling stories to a more experience-based movement. The stories that brands tell in the digital landscape can form a deeper emotional connection and leverage the buying behavior of consumers. This chapter will show how brands can tell captivating stories that stand out among an endless feed of content that bombard consumers' attention. We will also examine the role of digital influencers in brand campaigns and affiliate programs endorsements. Traditional fashion bloggers are not the ones making waves in the industry; it is bloggers as brands who have real and considerable influence over users. Fashion bloggers leverage their user influence, forcing brands to form alliances with these influencers to stay on-trend and remain relevant to their target markets. Throughout this chapter, we will review how brands and retailers monetize these collaborations and share some benchmark collaborations.

In this chapter we will also take a closer look at the evolution of "fashion on demand" and the visual consumption of products online. While the normality of shopping on the go through mobile apps is a reality, the fashion industry is turning to companies such as Science Project to help them enhance user experiences.

" YOU NEED TO START BY DEFINING WHAT KIND OF EXPERIENCE YOU WANT TO CREATE FOR YOUR CONSUMERS, DECIDE WHICH SOCIAL CHANNELS WILL BEST PROVIDE THAT EXPERIENCE, AND THEN IDENTIFY HOW YOU CAN DELIVER VALUE TO THAT AUDIENCE, THROUGH THOSE CHANNELS. FROM THERE, YOU'LL HAVE A GOOD BACKBONE TO YOUR STRATEGY AND YOU'LL REALLY KNOW HOW TO FIND YOUR MARKET FIT."
CHELSEA MATTHEWS, FOUNDER AND CEO OF MATTE BLACK

SOCIAL MEDIA MARKETING STRATEGY

The role of the social media marketer today in the digital landscape is to effectively drive messaging across multichannel distribution while securely positioning the brand in the best setting in the digital space. The non-linear narratives that social media offers, drives content and social validation for the brand. While social media is the medium that consumers use today to connect to others, it is also the platform that has enabled brands and retailers to establish a voice and confirm their social presence.

Social Media Strategic Outline

The digital footprint (data trace of activity) that each brand leaves behind creates a curated story, which, through carefully planned strategies, impacts the brand's positions in the digital landscape. It is important to understand how to develop an effective social media marketing strategy through setting clear goals and measureable results. This is further explained by the following box.

Social Media Marketing Strategy

1 Start with Listening:
- Locate the platform of preference of new and prospective customers
- Determine where the conversation is taking place about the brand, product/service provided by the brand, and the related industry.
- Utilize social listening tools to ensure that there is less misalignment between the perceived and actual social audience of a brand.
- Locate and monitor influencers within the brand's market segment.
- Develop positioning of brand
- Celebrate and empower
- Monitor audience, customers, consumers, clients, friends, followers

2 Media Conversation and Rules of Engagement
- Openness
- Transparency
- Truthfulness/Integrity
- Authenticity
- Adding Value/Insight

3 Consistency in Content
- Keep the brand's message consistent across all social media touch points.
- Unify the digital experience through insightful and entertaining content.
- While remaining consistent, be sure to share content that is not simply copied and pasted throughout all social feeds. Utilize each social platform's individual strengths to spread the message.

4 The Persona
- Develop a brand "persona" that will function as the voice that relates target audiences back to the brand.
- The persona can be shared through text, images, photos, videos, and messages.

5 Development of Engaging Content
- Develop content that supports the brand message.
- Create shareable content that educates, motivates, improves, entertains, or is unexpected.
- Enable audiences to follow content as a narrative of the brand's story in order to connect with them.

6 Integrate Social Media Marketing
- Streamline integrated social media marketing, sales, and communications in order to develop a clear audience message.
- Personalize your connection with audiences through curated content.
- Utilize actionable customer data.

7 Measure and Adjust
- Test new media strategies and, along the way, learn what works for the brand.

8 The Power of Collaboration
- Forge partnerships and tie-ins to increase viral conversation.
- Use social influencers to help spread the message among their communities.

REAL-TIME MARKETING STRATEGIES

CONTRIBUTING WRITER TERI THOMPSON, PRESIDENT - ROCKY PEAK ENTERPRISES, LLC

There is much chatter about social media and a great deal of noise. The volume may often seem overwhelming in addition to the fear of not being able to control what people are saying about one's brand. "What if they say something bad about me?" "What if they criticize me?" The reality is that no one can control the social conversation spinning around the world. However, it is possible to manage the conversation by having a social media strategy. Traditionally, strategy is a specific direction and approach that an organization takes over the long term to meet the needs of the market and fulfill business expectations. A social media marketing strategy is the roadmap that enables the organization to concentrate specific resources on the greatest opportunities to increase sales and ratings, achieve a sustainable competitive advantage, or deliver value to its customers and other stakeholders. The timeline for a strategy can be weeks or can span months and years. Whatever plan or strategy is devised, social media needs to have a seat at the table from the outset. Rather than being an afterthought or ancillary marketing function, social media becomes the strategy "glue" that permeates, integrates, and holds together all other forms of media, when activated properly.

Building a Strategy Foundation

Whether the brand is a long-standing luxury fashion name from Milan or an aspiring breakthrough designer from the lofts of downtown Los Angeles, a plan or strategy is necessary to provide structure and sense to social media efforts. The benefit of having a plan or strategy is that it provides a visual roadmap that enables a brand to maximize time, personal energy, financial resources, and success.

A **consideration set** is the brand that a consumer or customer thinks about when considering a purchase. For instance, Hermés may come to mind when determining where to buy a luxury purse.

When the strategy is shared with everyone contributing to and involved with its implementation, stakeholders will then understand the "why" behind the plan, how their actions impact results, and a deadline that will focus their efforts and expected results. A strategy should also include regular monitoring and measurement to gauge your share of voice in the social conversation. "Share of Voice" was a media term that meant how much a brand was outspending the competition to have a presence or "voice" on TV, radio, or print. "Share of voice" is now the activity and volume of conversations taking place in social media.

Developing a Strategic Plan

It is said that a journey of a thousand miles starts with a single step. In social media marketing, that journey of a thousand miles starts by choosing the right shoes that will get you to your destination. In social media marketing, this requires answering hard questions to determine the end goal. For example, businesses often claim that they want to develop a strategy to increase sales. Upon deeper inspection and careful listening, it may be found that the problem may rest in terrible customer service due to personnel issues that need to be resolved first. This can be painful to a company that is in denial about their internal operations. Making the leap to social media to solve problems requires a clear and truthful state-of-business assessment before an effective strategy is implemented to gain successful results. A number of social media marketing strategies and best case studies are included throughout this book. Some questions that help identify goals and a subsequent strategy are the following:

- Does the brand need to increase sales?
  If so, by what percentage?
- Looking for investors? Why? How much control are you willing to relinquish?
- Is weakness due to low build awareness?
  If yes, how do we get in front of the ideal customer?
- How do we change brand perception or increase social presence?
- How can we be part of the consideration set?

It is possible that more than one factor listed here may be "pain points" for the brand. To further demonstrate this, we chose to "be part of the consideration set" from the selection above. This is for brands that are experiencing flat sales. Potential customers are not thinking about the brand to consider buying their products. The brand may need a "refresh strategy" that will stimulate active sharing and conversation about the brand. Answering one question leads to stating an objective.

Strategy Activation

When goals and objectives are defined, the result will most likely be increased sales without even needing to say it outright. Stating an objective and then placing a goal in the bulls-eye of the target will help guide the strategy or plan of successfully getting from A to B. A comprehensive social media marketing strategy has three components, as seen in the following box.

Strategy = Objective > Goal > Tactics

1 **Objective:** An objective is the big ask, the giant wish, the overall vision stated in one short sentence. For example, M.A.C. Cosmetics' objective is to offer high quality, innovative products that meet the needs of all races, ages, and gender.

2 **Goal:** A goal is a specific path to achieve the objective. For example, to address diverse consumer make-up needs that are not fulfilled by the competition and M.A.C. Cosmetics.

3 **Tactics:** Create global campaigns that propagate diversity and break down barriers for collective equality. Deliver trusted creativity through collaborations with the image-makers who stand for change. For instance, Viva Glam Lipstick raises funds for M.A.C.'s AIDS Fund for men, women, and children with HIV/AIDS. This is supported through advertising campaigns that feature A-list celebrities.

Winning chess players have strategies that allow them to outmaneuver their opponent before they even sit in front of the chessboard. Tactics are the moves and specific actions that will lead to the goal. In social media marketing strategy, this is often a comprehensive action list with many tentacles. For example, tactics can be broken down into phases to organize activities, manpower, and budget.

Tactics and its phases in social media marketing

Phase 1: Listening Campaign
- Target consumers—Based on consumer segmentation and targeting, identify the social sites where you suspect conversation is taking place about your brand or industry.
- Social Sites—Set up social sites with a consistent brand name and graphics across all channels.
- Research—conduct a listening campaign across social media to gauge sentiments about the brand. Determine the percentage of the conversation that is positive, neutral, mixed, or negative. Assess, which social sites have the most active conversations and which will be the best channels to establish engagement.
- Define existing content—Create fresh, engaging content that reflects the new brand image.
- Identify influencers—Influencers are people who have the power to persuade and change opinion and behavior. They can be famous people or among friends and family. During the research and listening process, identify those people who have large followings, are actively posting content, and appear open to interaction and sharing.

Phase 2: Engagement
- Influencer outreach—follow, friend, engage, and share content with them
- Blog updates—short daily posts to pull content for all other sites
- Meme and infograph creation—tell stories in graphics (a meme is an image, video, or text that is shared and replicated with similar versions of the original and spread through the Internet).
- Newsletter—include social site links; make them feel that that the engagement is especially for them in order to cultivate emotional investment.

Timing

Timing is crucial to social media strategy. It includes timing all social elements in conjunction with all related efforts from various departments including sales, public relations, press and publicity, and corporate communications. Within phases, tactics are placed on a calendar with the dates and times the messages are to be, along with associated text, links, and graphics. The calendar organizes the messages for timing with other possible marketing components (TV commercials, print ads, events). It is simplicity that allows it be presentable to senior executives for review and approval. Social media marketing strategies are often referred to as "real-time" marketing strategies. It is also referred to as "content marketing" due to photos, text, audio, and other media shared through social networks. In a perfect world, social media strategy should reflect the overarching brand strategy. The voice of the consumer is very powerful in our social media world, as the center of the marketing bulls-eye is no longer just a brand's identity. Instead, brands have had to move over and share the space with their consumers who now confirm, reaffirm, confront, or advocate their products and services.

Various Strategies

All of the strategies listed below are in addition to the ones mentioned earlier for brand building or perception shift. Each can have its own objective, goal, tactics, and timeline.

- **Research**—Doing nothing more than listening to the conversations taking place on social media about your brand or product.
- **Conversation**—Stepping into social platforms to start talking directly with and to key constituents.
- **Competitive**—Watch and track the competition with the use of free tools on open social sites.
- **Cost Reduction**—Use as an alternative to traditional communication methods.
- **Customer Service**—Improve how service, advice, and information are distributed and handled in a public forum so that more people have access to the most asked questions at the same time. This substantially reduces calls to service centers if thousands see the answer on Twitter or a video on YouTube.
- **Leadership**—Position the brand as a thought leader and industry innovator
- **Education**—Provide added value in a particular areas that are being underserved

The collective rush towards social media strategy often influences marketers to act hastily. Fear may set and impede the campaign if results are not up to par. The most successful efforts are planned, reviewed, and fully executed on a continuous basis. Monitoring conversation and applying the insights gathered are the building blocks for revising a particular strategy. It is also more affordable to change a graphic in a Facebook advertisement than to pull an advertisement from a major magazine or TV station. To ensure that your social media strategy will be successful, you must know who you are; commit; be courageous; and measure.

5.2

5.2
Various strategies require time to
review, test out and research.

Tips for a successful social media strategy:

Know who you are—Clearly and simply define the
brand. Do not overthink or complicate it.

Commit—If a social media agency is hired, be ready
and willing to participate in getting them what they
need. They cannot do their job without you.

Be courageous—Stay the course, especially during the
early stages when engagement may be low.

Measure—Make sure that the brand strategy is on the
right track, especially during a brand reputation crisis.

Measurement

Measuring strategy success and key performance indicators will depend on the original objective. Measure your current standing before the strategy is put into place. For example, if a goal is to increase sales, note the sales numbers before implementation and then track weekly, monthly, and quarterly sales, along with any changes that may have been done to the social media strategy itself.

Return on Investment (ROI) can be quantifiable through sales, increased donations, number of new volunteers, etc. ROI may also be qualitative, such as improved brand perception or more customer satisfaction stars on Yelp. The equation below is a standard ROI formula for actual dollar calculation—it is a useful tool when money has been invested and a return has been received. The following is an example of a real ROI social media campaign:

Return on Investment

Compare numbers against the costs for the campaign
(people, process, and technology)
= $44,000

Benefits or revenue from ticket sales:
= $2,600,000

The Return on Investment (ROI) is a staggering 5809%. This means that every $1 spent on marketing yielded a return of $58.09.

$$\text{ROI} = \frac{\$2,600,000 - \$44,000}{\$44,000} \times 100 = 5809\%$$

The Periodic T

An overview of the key elements of cont

1						
Cs Content strategy						

2	10				
Ar Article	**Sh** Slideshow				

Strategy **Plat**

Format **Met**

Content Type **Goa**

3	11
V Video	**Vi** Visualisation

4	12	18	21	25	30
Im Image	**Pr** Press release	**Ho** 'How-to' based	**Re** Reviews	**Qu** Question-based	**Ti** Tim

5	13	19	22	26	31
Ev Event	**Wb** Webinar	**Iv** Interviews	**As** Ask the experts	**Rs** Resources	**Li** Link

6	14	20	23	27	32
Gm Game	**Ap** App	**Qz** Quizzes	**Ex** Experiments	**Pd** Productivity	**Fi** Fur

7	15		24	28	33
To Tool	**Eb** Ebook		**De** Definitions	**Gl** Glossaries	**D** Dat

8	16			29	34
P Print	**So** Social			**Ga** Galleries	**M** Mi

9	17
El E-learning	**Em** Email

107	108	109
Fu Funny	**Sx** Sexy	**S** Sh

120	121	122
Sq Search queries	**Se** Search optimisation	**C** Co edi

Econsultancy
Achieve
Digital
Excellence™

5.3
The periodic table of content marketing by Econsultancy.

5.3

# of Content Marketing

A seven-step guide to success

1. Take some time to define a **strategy**.
2. Figure out the **formats** you plan on using.
3. Think about the **content types** that will appeal to your audience. Do your research. Brainstorm ideas. Create.
4. Share your content across the key content distribution / social **platforms**.
5. Track the key **metrics**, and map these to your **goals**.
6. Be aware of the main sharing **triggers**. Be sure to work the emotions.
7. Always **double check** your work.

Sharing Triggers

Checklist

68 **Pv** Page views	76 **Uv** Unique visitors	84 **Nv** New visitors	91 **Br** Bounce rate	99 **Tf** Traffic
69 **Nl** New leads	77 **Do** Downloads	85 **Cl** Cost per lead	92 **Kp** Key pages	100 **Le** Leads
70 **Bm** Brand metrics	78 **Rp** Reputation metrics	86 **Pm** PR metrics	93 **Dg** Demographic metrics	101 **Br** Branding

40 **Co** Compilations	45 **Ca** Case study	50 **St** Stats	55 **De** Debates	59 **We** Website	63 **Bl** Blogs	71 **Of** Offline media	79 **Mi** Microsite	87 **Am** Acquisition metrics	94 **Rm** Retention metrics	102 **Sa** Sales
41 **Ee** Event-based	46 **Rc** Research	51 **Tr** Trends	56 **Cm** Competitions	60 **Tw** Twitter	64 **Fa** Facebook	72 **Li** Linkedin	80 **Pi** Pinterest	88 **Is** Instagram	95 **Sc** Search metrics	103 **S** Search
42 **Bg** Beginner's guides	47 **In** Inspiration	52 **Op** Opinion	57 **Ch** Checklists	61 **Yo** YouTube	65 **Vm** Vimeo	73 **Gp** Google+	81 **Fo** Forums	89 **Tu** Tumblr	96 **Nm** New members	104 **Me** Members
43 **Sv** Surveys	48 **An** Analysis	53 **Fi** Fiction	58 **Gf** Gifs	62 **Re** Reddit	66 **Ig** Imgur	74 **Vn** Vine	82 **Sl** Slideshare	90 **Fl** Flickr	97 **Sm** Social metrics	105 **Sh** Shares
44 **Tm** Testimonials	49 **Dm** Demos	54 **Nj** Newsjacking			67 **Hn** Hacker News	75 **Ps** Partner sites	83 **Ad** Advertising		98 **Eg** Engagement metrics	106 **En** Engagement

111 **Un** Unbelievable	112 **Cv** Controversial	113 **Co** Cool	114 **Ig** Illuminating	115 **Rd** Random	116 **Zg** Zeitgeist	117 **Aw** Cute	118 **Up** Uplifting	119 **Di** Disgusting
124 **Hd** Headline optimisation	125 **Tv** Tone of voice	126 **Gd** Brand guidelines	127 **Pe** Plain English	128 **Do** Device optimisation	129 **Fc** Fact-checking	130 **Cd** Credit sources	131 **Ct** Calls to action	132 **Fd** Invite feedback

Devised & designed by Chris Lake (@lakey).

You may share it around, embed it on your website, print it out or tear it up, with appropriate credit.

Copyright Econsultancy Ltd.

Contributing Writer: Teri Thompson is an award-winning advertising and social media marketer, adjunct professor, and international speaker on social media for entertainment, business, non-profit, and government agencies. She has held production and executive marketing positions at ABC, CBS, NBC, and Fox SportsNet, where she promoted and launched networks, stars, and primetime series. Thompson has produced and directed campaigns for some of the world's leading brands, including McDonalds, Toyota USA, Coors, Dominos, Audi of America, Lionsgate Home Entertainment, and Victoria's Secret.

INTERVIEW:
Trina Albus, founder of Magenta Agency | @MagnetaAgency

Trina Albus is the founder of MAGENTA AGENCY, LLC, a beauty-focused social marketing agency whose client roster includes Kardashian Beauty, Dr. Brandt Skincare, *W* Magazine, GLAMGLOW, and Jouer Cosmetics. Before founding MAGENTA, Trina worked at PriceWaterhouseCoopers, Discovery Communications, Time Inc., and BeachMint. She balances her time running the agency and teaching social and digital marketing workshops and courses.

Can you tell us about Megenta Marketing?

TA: MAGENTA is an analytics-focused social marketing agency. We work with top beauty brands to optimize and manage their social media channels, and to stand out in an extremely competitive consumer marketplace. The social media content and campaigns we create drive measurable brand awareness, engagement, and sales. On behalf of our clients, we post regularly on Facebook, Instagram, Twitter, Pinterest, YouTube, Google+, and Snapchat, run monthly contests and giveaways, and run advertising campaigns to boost content, to reach and engage with the target customer, and to drive sales.

How does a brand determine the right social channels that will help them reach their overall goals?

MAGENTA works with brands to match their target customer bases to the best social media platforms. For example, if a brand sells anti-aging skincare to women in the 30s and 40s, then Snapchat is probably not the best place to focus. This could change, however, as Snapchat continues to grow and attract more brands and advertisers. The active demographic of Snapchat could shift to an older audience, and it is our job to notice that shift and adjust our clients' social strategy accordingly.

After we determine which social media platforms to use, we focus on client goals. If a brand is selling products both online and in stores (e.g., Sephora, Ulta), our social marketing goals are likely to be three-fold: drive brand awareness, drive sales online on e-commerce sites, as well as Sephora.com and Ulta.com, and drive foot traffic into Sephora and Ulta stores that lead to sales. We implement tracking links, conversion tracking pixels, and special promotions in order to determine the ROI of various campaigns so that we can quickly understand what is working and what is not, and shift our strategy accordingly. In the digital space, you have the opportunity to "fail fast" using all the available data. Do not be afraid to try new things; if they do not work, you can shift your focus to winning ideas and further optimizing and refining for better results over time.

When utilizing advertising on platforms such as Facebook, what are some basic guides to leveraging the "custom" audience and the "lookalike" audience? Can you briefly explain what a lookalike audience is?

Facebook and Instagram advertising allows you to leverage custom audiences for better targeting and improved campaign results. In many cases, retaining a loyal customer is much easier and more cost effective than acquiring a new customer. Facebook allows you to import a customer e-mail list, and then reach those customers via targeted advertisements on Facebook and Instagram. Alternatively, you can use that same email list to create a new group of potential customers, called a "lookalike audience." Facebook uses available data and its elaborate "interest graph" to identify new users, who are similar to your current customers, and who are likely to become your customers. Lookalike audiences offer a cost efficient way to quickly expand your customer base.

THE SOCIAL MEDIA TEAM

The purpose of a social media marketing team is to effectively utilize resources and generate brand content across social media channels in order to engage with the right audience. The team is made up of thought leaders operating in the digital social space who create, monitor, and implement a brand's overall strategy. Social media's ever changing landscape continues to alter how each company delegates their online marketing outreach programs and influencer interactions. The social media team must track and respond to engagement in order to affect real time improvements for the brand and its customers. When optimizing a campaign's reach, the team begins by establishing the audience's current expectations of the brand. This process of listening is critical for learning more about their community and its expectations.

Positions within social media marketing teams

Social media has changed the way our society socializes, networks, and communicates. The significant influence of social media platforms has imposed the need for brands and retailers to be more assertive and transparent when communicating with their audiences. Today, brand storytellers run the show—individuals who are data-driven thinkers with the ability to interpret, provide insights, and generate recommendations based on collected information.

Brands are now spending more time and money to craft original, engaging content and digital experiences for their audiences. The social media team incorporates the brand's message throughout its multichannel marketing strategies, thus ensuring the delivery of rich and compelling content. It is essential for strategists to possess strong analytical skills in order to understand their profits and losses and strive to meet or exceed their targeted revenue key performance indicators.

While not all social media marketing and content teams are the same, here are some of the positions industry experts have shared within the industry:

- **Social Media Director:** They approve content strategy, develop brand awareness, generate inbound traffic, and cultivate leads and sales for the company's brand.

- **Social Media Marketing Manager:** They approve content for all social media accounts that they administer. The position involves frequently posting updates on various platforms (Facebook, Twitter, LinkedIn, Google+, Instagram, Pinterest) and the use of social media analysis tools. Social media marketing managers are required to be aware of trending topics and know when it is right, or not, to post something related to real time marketing opportunities.

- **Social Media Copywriter:** They are essential in cultivating an online presence. They create unique, engaging, and factual online content that is distributed to a brand's community. Posts often include keyword links that take the reader to the specific company website.

- **Digital Marketing Coordinator:** This position supports the primary social media team in doing their jobs more effectively. Coordinator responsibilities may include ensuring the effectiveness of online presence discovery through profiles updates and linked touch points. These professionals assist with the daily management of search engine marketing campaigns including budget (advertising buys), keyword research, campaign creation, and campaign optimization. They also collaborate with the marketing team to manage daily campaigns on social media platforms. Digital marketing coordinators in the retail sector assist in tracking, approving affiliate management, and identifying new social community opportunities.

Measurement Value

A **key performance indicator** (KPI) permits businesses to utilize a metric to assess, evaluate, and decipher the factors that are key to the success of the organization.

• **Social Media Community Manager:** They are responsible for advocating to members of a brand's online audience. Using the brand's unique voice, they monitor community expectations and raise awareness for potential customers. They are required to interpret and evaluate weekly social media metrics and compile weekly or monthly social media reports. The position involves frequent social media post moderation on Facebook, Twitter, LinkedIn, Google+, Pinterest, etc. with the use of social media analysis tools (Patterson, 2014). Social media community managers also monitor social profiling and tagging on social media platforms such as Pinterest, Polyvore, and Wanelo.

• **Social Media Strategist:** They analyze large amounts of data in order to determine the best strategy to market products and connect with consumers. In order to do so, they are required to understand market trends. They are responsible for tracking all current social improvements and plan out future community engagements. Strategists manage the different areas of the creative team as they optimize images and videos across all allocated social platforms. They also create reports, share and update content, manage a company's web presence, and identify new communities for marketing efforts.

• **Account Manager:** The account manager acts as the liaison between brands and influencers by moderating and augmenting all forms of communications between both parties.

INFLUENCER MARKETING/ MARKETING AGENCIES

Collaborating with influencers to help promote products/ services on social media has been a part of digital marketing strategies since 2010. According to *Women's Wear Daily*, brands and retailers began incorporating collaboration strategies with bloggers to directly appeal to their customers. "They might invite a blogger to guest blog, sponsor a series of daily outfit posts featuring their product, create or request a video of the blogger talking about the brand or wearing the product or even ask the blogger to design for the brand." (Corcoran, 2010). This was the case when bloggers were just beginning to carve their own niche in the fashion industry and proving how effective they were as "citizen journalists." Back in 2010, blogger posts were more organic and highly engaging for audiences who had never experienced this form of communication. These influencers, gatekeepers, and tastemakers eventually contributed to the disruption that the industry is experiencing currently.

" **AN INFLUENCER OUTREACH PROGRAM IS QUICKLY BECOMING INDISPENSABLE TO THE MODERN DIGITAL MARKETING STRATEGY. INFLUENCERS ARE MORE VALUABLE TO BRANDS NOW THAN THEY HAVE EVER BEEN FOR THEIR ABILITY TO DELIVER ON SOCIAL CHATTER, EARNED MEDIA, AND ACTION."**
TESSA WEGERT, BUSINESS REPORTER FOR CLICKZ
(MORRISON, 2015)

CASE STUDY:
Kate Spade Camp #CampKateSpade

Planning an influencer event requires building a shareable experience that is fundamentally unique and demands to be shared. For instance, Kate Spade was able to create a special event that built considerable buzz around Hampton fashion and lifestyle. The brand invited fashion editors and bloggers to an exclusive weekend retreat to celebrate its new retail space in East Hampton. The weekend was packed with fun-filled activities such as yoga, paddle boarding, and wine tasting. Influencers then shared these experiences with their social communities through blogs and social media posts, thus promoting Kate Spade and delivering the brand's message to a wider audience. During the event, the brand received 8.3 million impressions across their social networks ("Kate Spade's Mary Beech"). ROI is off the charts!

Brand-influencer collaboration is a win-win situation for both parties, especially if the influencer's online community aligns with the brand's target audience. Brands need to do their own research to determine if the chosen influencer fits the same niche market and can become suitable brand ambassadors. Influencer-marketing agencies are valued today because they are able to match brands with the right influencers.

" INFLUENCERS ARE INDIVIDUALS WHO HAVE THE ABILITY TO INFLUENCE THE OPINIONS OR BUYING DECISIONS OF YOUR TARGET AUDIENCE. THEY MAY BE ANYONE–CELEBRITIES, JOURNALISTS, OR EVEN BLOGGERS. INFLUENCERS TYPICALLY HAVE A MASSIVE FOLLOWING ON SOCIAL MEDIA OR BLOGS. A REPORT REVEALS THAT 90 PERCENT OF CONSUMERS TRUST RECOMMENDATIONS, ESPECIALLY FROM INFLUENCERS. SO, WHEN AN INFLUENCER RECOMMENDS A PRODUCT OR A SERVICE, IT SEEMS MORE TRUSTWORTHY THAN ANY OTHER FORMS OF TRADITIONAL ADVERTISING."
ECONSULTANCY ("INFLUENCER MARKETING")

INTERVIEW:
Zoe Waldron, Social Media Strategist at HelloSociety

Zoe Waldron is the social media strategist at HelloSociety. She works with her team to optimize campaigns, track client advertisement performance, manage brand social media accounts, consult clients on their social goals, and write blog posts on strategy.

About HelloSociety

HelloSociety is a full-service, social media marketing agency that connects brands with the most-followed and talented creators across social media and the blogging world. We have been a leader in the influencer marketing space for four years, so, we have been around since the early stages. Our team connects top-followed influencers with like-minded brands to have them create customized content, share sponsored posts, write blog posts, attend events, and more. By working with these highly followed creators, brands are able to connect with thousands to millions of consumers in a unique and memorable way.

We have a team that is dedicated to influencers to ensure strong relationships with each of our clients. Communication lines are always open for campaign questions, idea suggestions, getting approvals, and more. Our sales team functions as the primary line of communication for brands we work with. We ensure that we understand exactly what their goals are and to convey the creators we think would be a best fit for them, what platforms make the most sense, and what kinds of content could perform best. Every HelloSociety team member has an extensive understanding of creative and logistics. As a team, we are able to provide brands with the perfect influencers to represent their brand with high-quality, customized, and creative content to help spread their message across social media. Influencer marketing is the future of marketing and advertising.

" YOUR CAMPAIGN IS MUCH MORE THAN PICTURES–IT'S A STORY."
HELLOSOCIETY

Can you tell us a little about your position at HelloSociety?

ZW: I am a strategist for a premier social media marketing agency in Los Angeles. HelloSociety was one of the first agencies to really dive into influencer marketing by putting Pinterest influencers on the map. I have always been passionate about advertising, and my love and extensive knowledgeable around Pinterest, Instagram, Vine, and photography has really helped solidify my role as a social media strategist. As new platforms are established and continue to grow, like Periscope, I will be there to learn, test, strategize, and assist brands with all their platform strategies in order to ensure that their online presence is as on point as possible.

My eye for content that will perform best on social media has been extremely useful for brands. When I speak to brands, I can usually start to piece together what they need to do in order to achieve their goals within their means. The first step when crafting together any social strategy is to identify the top one to three goals of each campaign. For instance, when I know that e-mail signups is one of their main goals, I'm able to piece together what exactly will help them get these signups, and what will not. It is a delicate formula and each brand is different, but there is nothing more rewarding than the moment you see the numbers surpass the goals set.

What does HelloSociety specialize in?

HelloSociety's specialty is creating custom content (photos and videos) for everything from fashion and food brands to home décor and movie companies. We focus mainly on visual platforms by developing campaign packages to help brands reach their goals. From custom Pinterest board curation and custom Pin creation to sponsored blog posts and sponsored YouTube videos, we make sure that our creators are loving the projects that they are working on and that brands are excited about the partnerships we are building.

The HelloSociety network is composed of some of the most talented creators on social media, a collective group of over 1,500+ influencers. These influencers span the globe, cover a wide variety of platforms and specialties, and have their own unique aesthetic, background, niche, and major audience. They all have one thing in common

5.4

5.4
HelloSociety Case Study with
Bright. Bazaar and client
"Ted Baker"

5.5
HelloSociety case study with
MOOREA SEAL and client
"The Gap"

5.5

though—they have each earned their large audiences through their amazing ability to create and curate beautiful, inspiring images across the Web.

How has influencer marketing positively impacted marketing?

Influencer marketing has created a whole new avenue for promotion that is performing extremely well at low costs for brands. Instead of spending a million on a magazine back cover or a major TV spot, brands are becoming more interested in less traditional ways to reach their target markets. By being able to spread a budget across several social media platforms and top-followed influencers, they can reach their target consumers at a fraction of the cost and connect with them at a more personal level.

How is influencer marketing changing the future of advertising and promotions?

Influencer marketing has changed the way brands can market themselves online. By reaching consumers through popular social accounts, these advertisements, even when disclosed as such, may be seen as more of an organic discovery. Influencer marketing has become the modern celebrity endorsement. However, it is more

effective because their messages have a more authentic feel compared to those of celebrities. As regular people, the influencers' followers can relate to them and aspire to be more like them.

I can see marketing dollars continue to increase for influencer marketing campaigns over the next ten years. As more and more new social platforms emerge and grow, the amount and variety of influencers will grow in conjunction with brand opportunities.

INTERVIEW:
Chelsea Matthews, Founder and CEO of MATTE BLACK

Chelsea Matthews is the founder of Matte Black, a culture marketing firm based in Los Angeles that believes in developing brand strategies, experiences, campaigns and content that creatively and strategically garner consumer engagement and evangelism. Some of their clients include OPI, Juice Served Here, Operation Smile, TOMS, L'Agence, Beyond Yoga, Solstice Sunglasses, WWDMAGIC, Goldfaden MD and many more. Matte Black is an inspired group of storytellers who create innovative content, seasonal campaigns, and strategies for lifestyle brands globally.

What makes MATTE BLACK a different type of marketing firm?

CM: We try to differentiate ourselves by being culture focused, which means that we are looking for those key moments, stories, and connection points between a brand and their consumer. Brands can create consumer culture in the same way that companies develop corporate culture. That culture can be created through digital assets, messaging, and visual content—all areas we hone in on with our clients. It is also important to understand your competition: what channels they are using what kind of content they post that gets high engagement, who their audience is, etc.

How important is experiential strategy in marketing? Who does it well?

It is imperative. Offline drives online, and we continuously see this with our clients. For example, we work with a local LA-based juice brand called Juice Served Here. In each of their locations, there is a small sign at the checkout that encourages customers to share a photo of their juice and tag the brand to get a free wellness shot. People literally share image after image each day to get their wheatgrass shot! Think about it: how do you connect with a brand that you have not had some sort of personal experience with? Typically, we talk and share about the experiences we have with people, places, and things. It is much harder to feel connected toward something if you do not have that "touch point."

What is influencer marketing?

Influencer marketing is essentially a form of native advertising. It leverages social influencers (bloggers, Instagrammers, Snapchatters, etc.) to talk on your behalf in a way that feels authentic and holistic to their community.

How do brands select a social influencer to represent their brand in social media?

Brands will look at the following elements:

Content: They look to see if it is relevant and stylistically on target for the brand.

Engagement: The amount of likes and comments they get on their posts. Ideally, this engagement is higher than 3 percent of their total following.

Followers: This is both the total amount of followers and who the followers seem to be. This can be done by scanning through a few of their followers to get a gauge of demographic, age, and content.

How has content marketing changed in social media in the last couple of years and where do you think it has headed?

It is changed dramatically. Just three years ago, social media marketing was more reliant on a brand's assets that were created on a larger level (think: lookbooks, campaign images, etc.); now, it happens in the moment. When I started MATTE BLACK, I recognized that Instagram was a fast-growing channel that would require our agency to be more nimble in creation of content. We then hired a photographer to shoot content on a weekly basis on behalf of our clients. This way, we did not compromise on quality, and were able to create more on-demand content on a weekly basis.

At this point, no campaign we that run is integrated with original content and imagery, and it is almost as if social content is trickling up (up to brand, campaign, and web imagery) rather than the other way round.

What does a social media strategist do?

A social strategist analyzes and ideates around the following on a consistent (typically quarterly) basis:

Social Framework: What networks to operate on and why, how each social channel will be utilized, and what the general look and feel will be.

Content: The framework for content categories, cadence of content and the outside-the-box ideas that will set a social feed apart from the rest.

Growth and Engagement: How will this community grow, both organically and through paid channels?

Paid Channels: Will the brand advertise, and if so, what will be the brand's game plan?

User Acquisition and Campaigns: What opportunities are there to develop and launch campaigns in an effort to drive users?

Can you tell why it is important for strategists to understand profits and losses in their marketing programs and strive to meet or exceed their targeted revenue key performance indicators?

Ultimately, it is important to ensure there is return on investment on any campaign you run, especially if you are allocating a budget against it (i.e., recoup your dollars where possible). However, there are circumstances where a hard ROI is not the main focus; for example, can you really quantify the value of a social community? Not really. Can you quantify a billboard? Tough. That said, key performance indicators that tie to a brand's profit and loss could be e-mail capture (the value of remarketing to an email list can be highly valuable), sales of a specific product, number of app downloads, or ticket purchases. The ability to quantify your success as a marketer will become one of your most valuable assets. We can all do "cool," but if it is not driving growth and revenue for a brand, it will ultimately not live on for long.

INTERVIEW:
Kyle Hjelmeseth, Affliliate and Blogger Marketing Tactics

Kyle Hjelmeseth is an authority in sales/influencer management, leadership development, and creative direction, with experience specifically tied to aspirational fashion brands, private education, and architecture. Hjelmeseth is the founder of God & Beauty, a content creation and influencer management agency. Formerly the director and chief strategist for rising star Chloe + Isabel, training and onboarding the eight thousand strong direct sales force.

Can you tell us how influencer agencies work with bloggers?

KH: Influencer agencies are akin to celebrity talent management, wherein a manager or agent represents the talent in all business dealings. Taken directly from one of the top digital agencies of the moment, an influencer/blogger agency negotiates lucrative contracts for their clients that can include global advertising campaigns and high-profile brand ambassadorship, or even national television deals and commercials, as well as helping to define a blogger's personal brand, shape public profiles, and expand influence beyond the blogosphere. There are a swarm of smaller, boutique agencies cropping up all around the larger agencies, taking on bloggers who might not have the large number of followers, which is something a big agency wants to focus their attention on.

There are many benefits for a blogger to have representation. Agencies provide general business advice and help bloggers shape their budding business. Sometimes, just having a manager respond to an e-mail lends a certain credibility that allows bloggers to book more work. If nothing else, having a manager gives the blogger more freedom to focus on the creative/fun side of blogging, hone their craft, and generate better content.

What is affiliate marketing and how does it work?

Think of affiliate marketing like getting paid every time you recommend a new coffee shop or cute boutique to your friend, and they go buy a cup of coffee or new dress based on your recommendation. You are now affiliated with the brand. Brands establish affiliate programs to incentivize people with influence to promote their products, and in-turn, earn a commission off of every sale that comes from someone they influenced to buy that product.

Affiliate marketing does not typically happen in your neighborhood though. In the real world, you might call it referral bonuses, but today, affiliate programs exist primarily online and reward influencers for the sales they generate. Influencer partners are provided with a unique URL and each sale that comes through that link is credited to the influencer. The influencer is thus incentivized to promote products on their blogs, websites, and social media accounts because they can earn commission for every person who purchases through the unique URL link.

The more clicks an influencer generates, the more likely that someone will end up purchasing the product that the influencer is promoting, resulting in more money going into the influencer's pocket.

What are the top affiliate programs that you know about?

Some of the affiliate marketing programs that stand out today are Share a Sale, Pepperjam, Amazon, Linkshare, Commission Junction, Reward Style, and LiketoKnow. it. Bloggers would load their posts with affiliate links from different sources to try to get paid for click-through from their followers. RewardStyle has some of the larger retailers that a blogger would want to work with on one platform, whereas older affiliate programs were disjointed and confusing to work with. For example, a blogger who wanted to post about Chanel or Christian Dior might have to sign up for two different affiliate programs, each with different rules, commission rates, and linking methodologies. RewardStyle brought brands under one umbrella, streamlined commissions paid to affiliates, and provided communities with education and resources to help affiliates earn more. RewardStyle one-upped the affiliate marketing industry again when it introduced LiketoKnow.it. It is a ground-breaking API (application programming interface) that ties affiliate links to Instagram posts, allowing followers of influencers to shop for the looks they see in Instagram images.

How have bloggers changed the affiliate game?

Bloggers are changing the affiliate game because they are starting to see themselves as content creators and influencers. As content creators, as a graphic designer or photographer would, influencers now want to be paid for the time and effort that goes into story creation to promote the brands that they work with. Bloggers have costs to doing business—the services of writers, photographers, graphics editors, and site hosts need to be covered.

How this changes the affiliate game is by having created a situation where influencers are no longer satisfied with posting on their blogs or social media accounts and hoping that a reader converts into a purchaser of those brands' products. The second part of the equation is the influence they have over their following, and realizing that influence is worth something. This has emboldened bloggers to say, "Pay me for my work!" Affiliate linking can be a nice addition to the compensation package, but if an influencer is going to create content and ask their followers to trust that they believe in product XYZ, they want to be paid for the time, effort, and influence, regardless of the outcome.

How does a brand know what blogger to match themselves with?

Brands should evaluate the blogger they align themselves with, and vice versa. For both, the brand and the blogger, the game is about finding a brand value match. Do the values, look, and feel of "X" brand match up with "Y" blogger? Bloggers need to pay careful attention to this alignment as well. If a brand becomes embroiled in controversy because the CEO said something inappropriate on social media, then a blogger aligned with the brand may stand to lose or alienate their following.

Evaluating a good brand-blogger fit mostly relies on two areas for information: the website and the social account. Based on a blogger's photography and writing, a brand can determine if he or she will be a good representative of the brand's values. Conversely, a blogger can tell from the brand's website and product line if the fit seems natural. Social accounts should always be checked, especially by the brand, to make sure that the blogger's voice on social media is not completely different from how they portray themselves through the blog.

INTERVIEW: Christopher Griffin, President of WWDMAGIC Fashion Industry Trade Shows

MAGIC is the global pillar of fashion tradeshows. Twice annually, 60,000+ industry insiders meet in Las Vegas, Nevada. Its comprehensive marketplace covers the top men's, women's, and children's apparel, accessories, footwear, and resources. With eighty-five years of experience and attendance from over 120 countries, MAGIC moves fashion forward globally. From the fabric to the finished product, the hottest brands to the top designers, and the tastemakers to the power buyers, if it is fashion, you will find it at MAGIC.

How has the disruption of social media changed the B2B marketplace?

CG: Trade shows have mostly been enhanced by social media, from fashion bloggers walking the show and posting in real-time what they like, to pre-show Instagram stories that followed brands as they prepared to come to Las Vegas. Social media also forced all trade shows to join in and be a part of the conversation, from Facebook to Twitter and Instagram, each show now communicates directly with their community—something that did not always happen in the past.

How does WWDMAGIC embrace fashion bloggers to help create more of a non-linear conversation with the buyers and exhibitors?

WWDMAGIC was the first to engage with fashion bloggers when they partnered with *Teen Vogue* Magazine to launch the "*Teen Vogue* Blogger Lounge" in 2011. Inviting 30 bloggers, including Jane Aldridge of Sea of Shoes and Erica Domesek of P.S. I Made This, we created a social media hub at a prime location where live streaming and interactive panels were held. Brands participated with products selected by the bloggers, and buyers participated via crowd sourcing—voting on their favorite styles. It was a huge success, sixty blog posts with 4 million impressions, 6,000 tweets, a Klout score of 57 (earned media) and grand total number of impressions—15.6 million (Klout. com uses social media analytics to rank their network of users according to their measureable online social influence, which creates earned media).

How has real-time content on social media changed the retailers' buying process?

Buyers certainly are able to follow and be aware of trends much faster than before—so yes, the selling cycle has been compressed. Digital platforms such as our ShopTheFloor® have created a year-round engagement between brands and buyers—allowing for line preview, networking, and appointment setting for the upcoming MAGIC, all before you ever leave your office. Ironically, all this exposure to online content seems to make people hungrier for face-to-face meetings and line review— buying apparel is still driven by the visceral experience of seeing, touching, and feeling the garment.

> **" THINK ABOUT THE LAST TIME YOU HEARD ABOUT A GREAT PRODUCT FROM A FRIEND. THE RECOMMENDATION PROBABLY DID NOT START WITH "BUY THIS NOW," BUT INSTEAD, WAS CONTEXTUALIZED WITH AN ANECDOTE ABOUT YOUR FRIEND'S EXPERIENCE WITH THAT PRODUCT."**
> JAMES MCDONALD, CONSULTANT FOR DIGITAL COMMUNICATIONS & ELEARNING SYSTEMS
> (MCDONALD, 2015)

5.6
British fashion blogger Susanna Lau sits in the front row and doubles as a reporter and blogger. Today these citizen journalists have grown to be editors in their own right and are the driving forces behind some of the most successful social media campaigns in both fashion and beauty communities.

" THOUGH TOP BLOGGERS ARE MAKING THEIR FORTUNES, THEY ARE NOT PASSING THEMSELVES OFF AS JOURNALISTS. INSTEAD, THEY ARE BRAND STARS WHOSE VOICES ARE SUBJECTIVE TO WHAT THEY LIKE OR DO NOT LIKE AT THE MOMENT—OFTEN TIMES DEPENDENT ON WHICH COMPANIES WILL PAY THEM THE MOST. NONE OF THE TOP BLOGGERS INTERVIEWED FOR THIS ARTICLE SAY THEY ADHERE TO A STRICT SET OF JOURNALISTIC CODES OR ETHICS."
JAMES NORD, CO-FOUNDER AND CEO, FOHR CARD

Social Metrics

Most leading networks work on cost per acquisition (CPA), which in the case of bloggers means they are paid a percentage of each sale they drive for their brand partner. These percentages vary by partner and network, but can be very lucrative for bloggers driving the right traffic for the right brands. Bloggers who collaborate directly with advertisers optimize the partnership with custom campaigns, increased commissions, and incentive to generate maximum exposure across all marketing channels, like social media (Weiss, 2015).

A **click-through rate (CTR)** is the relationship between impressions and clicks out of the number of times your advertisement or search result is shown to a visitor, and how often users click it and not ignore it. This metric is among some of the most important benchmarks of your toolset for online marketing (Oberoi, 2013).

THE ART OF THE PITCH: GETTING THE RIGHT INFLUENCER FOR THE BRAND

BY EMILY KOLBERG

Pitching an influencer for your product can be tricky territory. Sometimes influencers do "favors" for brands that they like (or for employees that they like). Because of the way that influencer marketing blew up, these social media masterminds are the ones who lay down the law. This is interesting to watch because influencer marketing was like hitting the jackpot when it first flew into the brand radar. It was a magical wonderland where one could get customer endorsement, product placement, and rave reviews in exchange for a product; most of the time, it was borrowed and returned product. This was incredible for brands and also incredible for those early influencers.

The Influencers of Today

Today, these influencers are not only given this product but also paid to talk about it. Many influencers insist that they would not ever post a product that they would not buy for themselves, or that they will give a 100 percent honest review whether their opinion is positive or negative. This is one of the biggest reasons why it is incredibly important for a brand to choose the right influencers to work with. Modern audiences are quickly catching on, and they follow these influencers so closely that they will know immediately if something feels even slightly off brand. They will most likely recognize insincerity in a post on social media before the influencer themselves may even recognize that insincerity. For the influencer/blogger, this is their job, occupation, paycheck, and image. Their livelihood counts on the content they produce and share. For a brand, this social content should be support to their brand identity—an extension of who they are by highlighting and connecting with "digital influencers" that align perfectly with their identity.

To choose the right influencer for a brand, you must first take a few minutes (or even hours and days) to self reflect. Look back on your brand, and ask—who are you? What do you stand for? Maybe you are a fashion company committed to supplying fast fashion to the trendiest teenage girls for a price that they can afford with a paycheck from their first job (and the occasional back-to-school binge with mom). An influencer like Danielle Bernstein, with 1.3 million followers, would not be the right fit for your brand. Although Danielle's reach is impressive and girls around the world follow her for fashion inspiration, Danielle wears Fendi instead of Forever 21. Someone like Larsen Thompson (@larsenthompson) may be a better fit for a fast fashion brand. She's young, energetic, colorful, and most importantly, relatable to the target audience.

Contributing Writer: Emily Kolberg is a "thought leader" in the digital and social space. Kolberg has created and implemented social strategies for multiple brands including WWDMAGIC (largest tradeshow in North America). Kolberg has developed influence programs and created all custom assets to share across social media as well as communicate directly with digital influencers to create compelling brand awareness and content. As the former Digital Media Coordinator for AG Jeans, she led creation and execution of social strategy across all social platforms for both AG and AG Green Label.

HIDDEN INFLUENCERS: COSTUME DESIGNERS

Costume designers are image-makers responsible for researching, planning, and executing the unique looks of our favorite movie and television actors. Until recently, costumers traditionally worked behind the scenes and were not considered to be influential by those working outside the entertainment industry. However, the advent of social media has lifted the curtain on this once-secret world and positioned costume designers as pivotal influencers today. Collaborations between retailers and costumers are more common today, and there are certain designers leading the way in these creative partnerships.

CASE STUDY:
Pretty Little Liars

ABC's highly watched drama-mystery television series, *Pretty Little Liars*, has been breaking records on social media due to their highly engaged audience. According to Nielsen Twitter TV, one of the show's episodes was the second most tweeted cable series episode on record, amassing over 1.6 million tweets, accounting for 50 percent of all Twitter TV activity for the day. The tweets were seen by a Twitter TV audience of 6.2 million unique users and generated over sixty-eight million Twitter TV impressions (Kissell, 2015). *Pretty Little Liars*'s Instagram account has over four million followers and their Snapchat account gained 400,000 followers within the first twenty-four hours by sharing an exclusive three-minute preview with their fans. Within two weeks, its Snapchat account gained an additional 100,000 followers. The show's target audience, Millennials and Gen Z, comprise the core of the digital generation. Thus, it is not surprising that PLL's loyal followers are actively engaging about the show across social media platforms.

As a response to this level of engagement, *Pretty Little Liars*'s costume designer Mandi Line partnered with retailer, Aeropostale to launch a collection inspired by the show. She also uses social media to connect with fans, providing them with style tips and advice on how to replicate the famous looks of Aria, Hanna, Emily, and Spencer. "I cannot tell you how many times I have Instagrammed or Tweeted a piece that I am going to use on one of the characters on the show, and fans of the show are just yearning for it," say Lane. "They want to know where to buy it right then! And sometimes, it is at a store they do not have or a price point that is just not affordable." (Talarico, 2014).

5.7

5.7
Mandi Line at the opening of the capsule "Pretty Little Liars" collection at Aeropostale

CASE STUDY: Costume-to-E-commerce
Arianne Phillips, Costume Designer

Costume designer Arianne Phillips has twenty-eight films and countless music videos under her belt, including *Walk the Line*, *3:10 to Yuma*, and *A Single Man*. She has also been Madonna's costumer for over nineteen years (responsible for numerous tours, including 2015's Rebel Heart).

Costume Designer E-Commerce Collaboration
Introducing the concept of costume-to-e-commerce, costume designer Arianne Phillips, director Matthew Vaughn, and the creative team at Mr. Porter (part of the luxury e-commerce website Net-a-Porter family) created the first shoppable movie collaboration based on 20th Century Fox's spy thriller *Kingsman: The Secret Service*. Phillips created character personas based on their costumes and Mr. Porter offered the collection on its website, one of the most recognized luxury e-commerce sites in the world. This collaboration

ushered in real-time movie shopping and successfully captured the attention of a worldwide audience.

Despite Phillips being the driving force behind the Kingsman collection, it was Matthew Vaughn, the film's director, who originally came up with the idea. He pitched the idea to Natalie Massenet, founder of luxury commerce website Net-a-Porter to create a collection that would be featured in the film and sold to consumers worldwide. The idea was to enable audiences to purchase the actual collection worn by actors in the film, not some watered-down version of these looks.

What makes this collaboration unique?
This collaboration featured a costume designer leading the way and working with the creative team of an e-commerce brand. The partnership also made history as a film director, costumer, and luxury retailer combined to develop a global fashion collection.

5.8
LACMA's Senior Curator, Sharon S. Takeda, introducing the Kingsman "Costume To Collection" conversation with award-winning Costume Designer Arianne Phillips-Hosted By Mr. Porter And LACMA Costume Council.

5.9
Actor Colin Firth attends the World
Premiere of *Kingsman: The Secret
Service* at the Odeon Leicester
Square in London, England.

Vaughn envisioned a collection that was more than a mere spinoff. He wished to invoke the creativity of British craftsmen and honor the timeless looks featured in the film. Phillips wanted to develop looks that would feel exclusive but be available for a large selection of consumers. Phillips sought to capture the traditional British gentleman's wardrobe by featuring a curated collection from the country's top craftsmen, including Bremont (timepieces), George Cleverley (footwear), Mackintosh (outerwear), and Turnbull & Asser (shirting) (Harilela, n.d). Phillips used the narrative aspect of costuming in bringing these looks to life. The sixty-piece menswear collection was not merely inspired by the movie—it also features the actual wardrobe used in the film, thus infusing the collection with quality and authenticity. She also had to ensure that the entire collection adhered to the heritage of genuine British style.

The Results

Mr. Porter calls *Kingsman* the e-commerce portal's most successful brand launch ever and says that the new collection is among the top five best-selling brands for spring/summer (Sheff, 2015). This unique collaboration broke new ground for costume designers, allowing them to align their industry with the future of fashion and gain recognition as influencers for consumers worldwide.

" THIS IS THE FIRST ONE THAT REALLY SPOKE TO ME—BECAUSE IT IS STRAIGHT STORY TELLING. THE COSTUMES HAD TO SERVE THE FILM FIRST, BUT ALSO WERE DESIGNED AS A COLLECTION WHILE WE WERE CREATING THEM. I'M HOPEFUL THIS WILL RESONATE ON A GLOBAL SCALE—THIS IS THE FIRST PROJECT AND COLLECTION OF ITS KIND. A LOT OF TIME MOVIE MERCHANDISING DOES NOT INVOLVE THE COSTUME DESIGNER, BUT THIS IS SO MUCH MORE THAN MOVIE MERCHANDISING."
ARIANNE PHILLIPS, COSTUME DESIGNER (GINSBERG, 2014)

CASE STUDY:
Authenticity of Modeling Consumers as Brand Influencers

#CastMeMarc was an open casting call inviting consumers to audition to become a Marc Jacobs model for the brand's 2014 Autumn/Winter campaign. The social content marketing strategy behind this campaign utilized user-generated content to increase the brand's social currency. Not only did this drive user-generated content, but it also increased brand presence across social networks. "David Sims portraits, Peter Miles layouts, the credibility of the cast, and the approach to casting the advertisements transmit a current social lifestyle that does not play into other clichés, and totally feels like our company—a cast of colorful and dynamic characters" (Karimzadeh, 2014)

#CastMeMarc was the first social media casting call campaign of its kind. The brand splashed the open call across its social channels, garnering significant levels of engagement from members of the digital native generation. Using the #CastMeMarc hashtag, contestants shared their unique looks and styles throughout social media in the hopes of becoming the new face of Marc Jacobs. The contest generated massive amounts of buzz because it gave everybody the opportunity to be featured in the brand's international advertising. By turning an ordinary, behind-the-scenes casting call into a meaningful campaign, Marc Jacobs successfully tapped into the hyper-connectivity of consumers today, resulting in increased publicity for the brand. Jacobs said, "We wanted the advertisements to shout with youth and energy…to be fresh and reclaim the spirit that the collection had when we first conceived of it—to be another collection, not a second line" (Karimzadeh, 2014).

2015's version of #CastMeMarc was one of the most talked about user-generated content campaigns since Burberry's Art of the Trench. The Instagram post read, "Want to be the face of Marc by Marc Jacobs FW15? Cast Me Marc is back! Tag a photo of you with your friends (we are looking for groups!) on Instagram or Twitter with #CastMeMarc for a chance to star in our #FW15 ad campaign. Start snapping."

Results:
The campaign's reach increased Marc Jacob's connection with its community, as geography was not a limiting factor for potential entrants. Over 70,000 entries were submitted from around the world; the thirty finalists included hopefuls from Russia, South Korea, and Australia (Tsjeng, 2014). The casting call announcement was made across all of the brand's social channels, earning 1.5 million likes on Facebook, 2.87 million followers on Twitter, and more than 12,000 on YouTube. Moreover, the campaign's visibility was boosted by search engine optimization as more and more users used the official hashtag across different platforms.

" WE WANTED THE ADVERTISEMENTS TO SHOUT WITH YOUTH AND ENERGY…"
MARC JACOBS (KARIMZADEH, 2014)

DIGITAL CURATION

The crowded social media space can be chaotic, driving consumers to look toward brands and platforms that are able to organize information in a concise, efficient manner. Thus, marketers continuously work on developing content that will attract and retain their target audiences. One way of doing so is through digital curation. Digital curation (sequenced, organized, disrupted) is the process of gathering, organizing, filtering, and categorizing products to create a coherent collection of content that will be presented to consumers through online channels. The process of content organized sequence allows consumers to visualize and locate the products and services they are looking for. While there are many ways of applying digital curation to create a consumer experience, it is important to focus our attention on how this technique is being applied. Simon Graj states, "The curator knows the brand connects with its target market, and the values that differentiate it as valuable" (Graj, 2012).

Types of digital curators

While there are many types of curation, all of them enable brands to strategically position themselves. Social media platforms assist in curating content that will allow users to enhance their experiences within the digital space. These platforms will be best served by encouraging their users to explore and discover stories that they might be interested in. Tools such as trending hashtags and "discover zones" assist users in locating topics of interest and help direct the flow of conversation and visual consumption. In chapter 6, we will discover how content filtration uses algorithms to understand the persona of a brand's audience. Instagram's blog does a great job of encouraging users to join in the conversation by reviewing the week's most talked about stories and topics.

There are three types of curators: (1) third party curators (such as ahalife), (2) brand content curators (such as those for brands like BCBG Max Azria), and (3) gatekeeper curators (such as influential fashion bloggers). Digital curation shares and distributes content across the necessary touch points in order to reach the desired audience. It also enables fashion marketers to differentiate their collections and connect with a wider base of users. Successful curation opens communication channels, stimulates customer interaction, and filters the available information for easier consumption.

THIRD PARTY CURATOR

A third party curator has an established reputation and will typically be mentioned by name or area of expertise to make the user aware of the curator's authority of selection. The curator's primary objective is to enable the community to connect with the curated content through exclusive insights. It is also responsible for "mining" through endless Internet content and providing a contextual point-of-view for users.

E-commerce sites are now incorporating digital third party curators with certain areas of expertise (e.g., food, fashion, lifestyle) to select specially curated products. Brands can now rely on influencers to filter content for their respective audiences. This type of collaborative curation is generally used when experts, opinion leaders, and influencers choose to contribute their knowledge to the e-commerce site.

> " THE INFLUENCERS AND BRANDS THAT MANAGE TO BRIDGE THE GAP BETWEEN THOSE ONLINE STORIES AND REAL-LIFE HAVE PROVEN TO BE THE MOST SUCCESSFUL IN LEVERAGING DIGITAL FOR BUSINESS PURPOSES. HOWEVER, THERE IS NO TEMPLATE FOR THIS—THE MORE DIRECTED AND DETAILED THOSE DIGITAL INITIATES ARE TO A SPECIFIC GROUP OF PEOPLE, THE MORE GENUINE THEY BECOME AND THEREFORE MORE EFFECTIVE IN THE END. SOCIAL MEDIA HAS AN INTERESTING WAY OF WIDENING THE REACH OF PEOPLE TO A GLOBAL AUDIENCE, BUT IT'S IMPORTANT TO REMEMBER THE BEST TACTICS ARE STILL THE ONES THAT TARGET A NICHE GROUP OF INDIVIDUALS."
> CUIT GONZALEZ, THE A-LIST, DIGITAL DIRECTOR FORMERLY THE BRAND ENGAGEMENT + SOCIAL MEDIA MANAGER AT BCBGMAXAZRIA & HERVE LEGER

BRAND CONTENT CURATOR

A brand content curator uses a digital platform to begin a conversation about a brand and the lifestyle it represents. Consumers today shun conventional "push" strategies that only focus on marketing the brand's product. Instead, they choose to engage with brands that converse with them by being authentic and transparent. Brand lifestyles are shared through curated posts/feeds on social media sites because doing so lends credence to a brand's integrity. Hence, the curator's job is to capture an audience while adhering to the brand's philosophy.

Expressing or advocating a certain lifestyle is critical in adding context to digital feeds. The curator's job is to pique the curiosity of consumers by creating a certain personality for the brand. The difference between digital curation and traditional marketing (e.g., magazine advertisements) is that curators use behind-the-scene images as a means of social currency, thus enabling audiences to feel a connection with the brand or its product.

GATEKEEPER CURATOR

Independent digital influencers such as YouTube "vloggers" are effective curators because of their loyal, highly engaged audiences that brands try to reach. The first wave of digital influencers was merely an outgrowth of independent citizen journalism; today, they are viewed by brands and marketers as vital components of digital strategies. These influencers mine through countless brands and differentiate products of particular value or interest while informing their audiences about a brand's authentic point of view. Digital curators share their own experiences when selecting, organizing, and categorizing. The gatekeeper's selection process represents the human component of curation because it gives a voice to the brand. Hence, marketers recognize that consumers relate more to the opinion of an independent blogger than the biased views of a brand.

5.10
HelloSociety's influencer network creates content that is made specifically for the platform it gets posted to. Add that to the fact that our influencers are showcasing everything in their own unique style—the very style that earned them an audience in the first place ("What We Do").

BEFORE

5.10

AFTER

A PAIR OF SHOES IS
INSTANTLY COOLER
AND MORE VISUALLY
APPEALING WHEN
TAKEN OUT OF THE
TYPICAL WHITE
BACKGROUND
CATALOGUE SHOT

FASHION ON-DEMAND WORLD

The way fashion is marketed and consumed is in the midst of a revolution. Consumers today are driven by the "on demand" culture with the power to demand twenty-four hours a day through online connectivity and empowerment of technology. The power of social media and new mobile technologies, and their effects on the fashion system are remarkable. The leverage marketers had on consumers is shifting the role on consumers expectations and traditional fashion theories are falling short in terms of addressing the way fashion trends disseminate in today's digital world.

In the Internet Age, instant interactions and transactions occur between marketers and consumers, with consumers displaying unprecedented behaviors and needing instant gratification. With all these changes taking hold, it is necessary to reconsider the longstanding theories of innovation diffusion, especially in the field of fashion marketing. A scan of top academic journals in the field of fashion marketing and management yield little recent research that addresses the role and impact of digital technology and social media on fashion. Thus, older theories must be revised in order to address how modern fashion is disseminated and distributed from designers to consumers.

Real-Time Commerce

We are now in the midst of the fashion industry's great disruption. New business models are being developed for hyper-connected consumers such as the introduction to See Now, Buy Now. Customers are demanding the latest fashion trends immediately. Brands and retailers providing content that was previously limited to a select few. Manish Chandra, founder and CEO of Poshmark, claims that "fashion is ripe for disruption [...] because a lot of the ways things are done now—fashion-of-the-week shows, buyers, very powerful editors in major fashion capitals— these were the ways that trends were distributed, and they were not very democratic. But the Internet democratizes everything." (Xavier, 2014). Social media has undeniably democratized the way fashion is previewed and trends are shared. Today's digital applications and the convenience of Internet access give customers the opportunity to discover and become interactive in the shopping process. (Weingarten and Brooks, 2013).

The fashion industry had to adjust to the new availability of real-time content, wherein consumers were now being exposed to styles and trends directly from the runway. Fashion marketers are scrambling to adapt to the next generation of digital nesters (people using digital channels on a regular basis) by coming up with trends that will withstand the quick cycle of real-time fashion content. In this more turbulent environment, trends are born and die with greater frequency while the media, influencers, and end consumers determine what is "in" or "out" of fashion (Abnet, 2015). Digital technology continues to shape consumer behavior, and the fashion industry is responding in different ways. The following are some examples of disruptive technologies that influence how fashion is disseminated to the masses:

COMMERCE ON SOCIAL MEDIA

Social media's emergence caused consumers to experience new forms of engagement with brands, products, and services they encountered online. This change is social media's version of the Home Shopping Network model. Shoppable social media such as LikeToKnow.It and Japan's WEAR API software applications are some prime examples of functions that allow customers to shop directly through social media platforms.

CROWDSOURCING FOR THE FASHION-CONSCIOUS CONSUMERS

Using their smartphones and tablets, social media users take screenshots or save images of items they desire. Consumers now trawl the digital space, and technological advances allow them to "walk into stores using their Instagram feeds" (Jones, 2014). An application called The Hunt enables users to "post "hunts," or pictures of unidentified clothing items from Tumblr, Pinterest, or the like that they want to track down (on The Hunt's site)" (Brooke, 2013).

IMAGE/SOUND RECOGNITION TECHNOLOGY

Image/sound recognition technology is changing the way consumers shop and interact on their mobile devices. This innovation utilizes visual and sound search databases to track brands or garments with similar features. Applications like Gandr allow consumers to track pieces of clothing seen in movies and television and purchase them with a simple click. The premise of applications like these is to make shopping a more streamlined process for customers (Fratti, 2014).

THE "BUY" BUTTON

The heightened demand to shop directly from social feeds has given rise to the creation of the "Buy Button." Popular sites such as Twitter, Facebook, and Pinterest have invested in this feature, which allows users to purchase items sold through these platforms. Mobile users of Facebook and Pinterest who see a product they like in a sponsored post can now use one click to purchase it without ever leaving the app (DeMers, 2015).

The Internet has democratized the fashion industry by disrupting the established process of fashion dissemination that trickled down from the privileged few who had access to runway shows to the masses who have real-time, instant access to the same content. There is no doubt that new commerce technologies have shifted the way consumers engage with brands, and vice versa. Modern fashion consumers are now exhibiting unique behavioral patterns, such as sharing, liking, commenting, and shopping all from the convenience of their personal devices. The fashion-on-demand era is truly upon us—content-hungry consumers spend hours scanning social platforms while having the power to immediately purchase the goods and services they desire.

INTERVIEW: Fashion On Demand
Damian F. Scoglio, Founder and CEO of Gandr

Gandr believes in a world where you can use your phone to shop and buy within the TV shows and content you are currently watching. No need to try to remember it, no need to search for it—with a touch of your Gandr app, you can purchase the products directly.

Can you tell us more about your company?

DS: Our company is trying to create an on-demand way for the average TV viewer to find something they are interested in, whether it be clothing, home goods, or some kind of item in the show. There are websites, but they cater to the very fashion-forward people who are so obsessed, but we are more for simple ones that do not have to be obsessed with the show. You could just be watching the show and you see something that catches your eye and with Gandr, your show can now be shoppable.

How does one use Gandr?

The user simply needs to download the Gandr app and sign in with Facebook or Twitter. When the user launches the app it says, "Touch to Gandr" and the user holds up their phone to the TV and touches the screen. Gandr will recognize what show the user is watching and what scene it is. It will show the user a screenshot of where they were in the show with the image tagged, in which they can touch different points to see where things are available to purchase.

So, for example, the television series *Pretty Little Liars*, the user is five minutes into the show and they see a shirt they like, the simply open the app, touch the screen and after a few seconds it will recognize that they are watching *Pretty Little Liars*. Gandr will select the scene they are in and it will show the user right there the still image on the scene and little tags will pop up like "touch here" for things available for purchase. The user then touches the shirt and then a little slide out panel comes out showing them the shirt and the ability to buy the shirt. You can tag it for later and it saves to your little tag area or you can buy it right there.

We enable the user to go directly to the website that carries the merchandise. Since the television shows are filmed in advance, most of the exact merchandise will no longer be available when the show airs. The Gandr app will show the original image but then it will also show the user a substitute item of what is that season's equivalent or a cheaper version. It is like comparable shopping.

How did you know that consumers would be ready for GANDR?

The way things have been evolving with technology lately, with on-demand consumerism such as Uber (car service on demand via mobile phone). This is the next step in the on-demand world. The whole point of TV advertising on commercial breaks is to advertise things that people will want to buy. This is connecting consumers instantly, in an unobtrusive advertising way. The whole point of advertisers paying for spots on television is because you have the "eyeballs" on the screen, so this is another innovative way around it.

First shoppable runway and now shoppable television?

If you were to go on Twitter feeds from a show, like *Pretty Little Liars* (3.1 million followers), you'll always see people commenting where to get this and that was seen on the show. People are always curious, no matter what the show is about, where to get something that someone is wearing. Even if it is not a show that is fashion centric, there will be some element of the products in the show consumers may have a connection with and want to purchase immediately. Our goal was basically "everything you see, you can get." We did not want to limit it to just a shirt or pants here and there, and that is how it is in the beginning with beta stuff but our goal basically was that you could shop an entire scene, from the clothes to the furniture.

What would you call this type of technology?

Whether it is audio or video recognition, the technology term is just Automatic Content Recognition (ACR). We are using audio recognition right now but that could always change. It is more universal than just video recognition because for people who are not using iPhones, the cameras will not pick up the exact same thing. So, audio has pretty much been stabilized across the board so that is why we went that route. We initially started with video recognition but found that it is not going to work universally yet; therefore, we just went with the audio in the end.

How does this influence advertising with television shopping on-demand?

Say there is a pair of jeans that is not available anywhere. Even though it is not available, we still save that data that there was an interest in that specific pair of jeans. That is all tallied up in stored data, anonymously, obviously, because we do not collect personal data but all that really matters is that "x" number of people are interested in that item. So, if it's a pair of Seven Jeans on *Pretty Little Liars* or ABC Family television, one can now can go to Seven Jeans and say we have this many people that are interested in your clothing, so, why don't you do an advertising campaign with us. We are kind of creating a relationship with the brand because we are showing them the targeted audience that are interesting in something that they might not have known about before. ABC Family benefits because now they are doing advertising with them.

Is this similar to forecasting information of what consumers are demanding?

One of our future steps is our analytical dashboard, and we have already designed it, but have not finished building it. This is what we would do for networks, where they can access the data to see what brands the viewers of their show are interested in. They can take that information and work with those brands to advertise or collaborate like the television show *Scandal* did with the retailer, The Limited, letting the networks know what their viewers are interested in. There are "x" number of clicks on a certain brand, which would give confirmation to the networks about the shows' audience. From a brand standpoint, even without having to work with networks, on their own, they could utilize this information and gear some of their advertising whether it be on social media or toward that show or demographic.

5.11a, b, c, d

5.11a, b, c, d
Gandr utilizes a social app on mobile optimization and enables television show viewers to shop as they watch their favorite television episode.

INTERVIEW: Cuit Gonzalez, Brand Engagement + Social Media Manager at BCBGMAXAZRIA & Herve Leger

Gonzalez led digital strategy efforts, social media content management and influencer relations for global fashion brands @BCBGMAXAZRIA and @HerveLeger. He helped in the development of the online communities and execution of the creative direction through innovative social media campaigns. He was instrumental in the execution of the first ready-to-shop runway show on Instagram during the SS2015 season at New York Fashion Week in partnership with rewardStyle and LIKEtoKNOW.it.

Can you share with us the process of how you brought social media to BCBG:

CG: Before social media, the fashion industry was always a B2B setting. Now, in this day and age, brands are able to connect directly with the consumer and engage with them openly. We have events, like fashion week that social media revolves around and its our opportunity to increase our following, engage with our consumers, and showcase the new collection through behind the scenes and exclusive access to different kinds of content (e.g. photos, video).

When I started at BCBG, they had an established presence and, like most brands, they knew they had to be on it and be digital but no one really understood what was correct because there was no plan or standard to follow. At this time, everything in the industry as a whole was new and exciting and you kind of figured it out as you went along. BCBG had a presence in the social media space but there was no particular strategy. When I came on board after spending some time having my own digital and PR business, I was honing in on the strategy part of digital. Strategy was a big part of what I brought to BCBG, and how I organized the platforms and the purposes.

In an ideal world, you want to communicate differently to the Facebook community than on Twitter and Instagram, more so, the way you speak to each community and what kind of content works with each platform. With all the content that a fashion brand produces, like editorials, look books, advertisement campaigns, catalogs, and things like that . . . there are enough platforms for you to find a purpose for each one. At the end of the day, you want

a consistent message across the board. So, if today I am visiting BCBG on Facebook, Instagram, and Twitter, I should have new content because that is what keeps the audience engaged. While Instagram is more behind the scenes and pretty photos, because it is a very visual platform, in Twitter it is short, witty, news-like, in the moment activities that get the most amount of engagement.

What do you do as the digital director at New York Fashion Week?

For fashion week in New York, each season, we try to do something we have not done, and it comes down to sitting down and figuring out what else is happening other than the fashion shows and how we might be able to collaborate with someone. Overall, there's an opportunity to do something we have not done before as a brand. It will depend on what we do, based on the season. We get to sit down and, maybe, have a budget in mind and figure out a fashion week strategy and kind of connect the dots. It usually starts with the target list of people we want to work with, then we reach out with invites to the show and take a more curated list of people, and we invite these people to come into the showroom and be dressed in our pieces. There is really a balance between PR, marketing, social and design and then, there is how are we going to capture the content this season: similar to or in a different way than we did last season.

Part of being online and having followers who want to engage with you is because of the story you are sharing with them. So, we capture the story along the way through photos and videos. I also think we prioritize, with all this content, how carefully to curate it because you have to even up that point where you are capturing the content. You have to think about what the message is and what each post is going to say individually and how it all comes together on a storyboard. This is where we share how the collection starts to come together, and where the inspiration comes from. We share peaks of what the design team is doing behind the scenes, and what color palettes or prints will be selected.

But you also have to think about how it is going to lay out on the Instagram "grid" or a Facebook album. How it works together—you start to put things into categories and the colors, moods, and vibes need to have a consistent voice but not look exactly the same. It is hard sometimes to do this for a brand when you have a team of different people taking different photos on different equipment with different lighting. So, we, as a brand, essentially developed our own filter so that everything works together within the same story, and it feels like one cohesive BCBG story.

How did BCBG come up with idea of creating the first shoppable runway collection from Instagram and LikeToKnow.it?

Amber Venz Box, president and co-founder of RewardStyle and LikeToKnow.It, texted me and said she had something that she want to share with me. We spoke immediately afterward and she told me about this new initiative that they were hoping to do and this was just a month before, so, it was a fairly quick turnaround. It had to do with their new company LikeToKnow.it, which enables users to potentially instantly shop straight from Instagram photos through an email service and applying that to an "in-the-moment," live, one-way e-commerce platform. I was ecstatic and as we continued to talk about it, we strategized a little more. I threw out some ideas on the branding side in terms of coming together and, of course, the relationship that we both had with key influencers that would help to get the message out. That is how we produced the first ever shoppable runway during fashion week.

5.12   5.12

Cuit Gonzalez @MrCuit prepping the social media on the runway floor.

The Process: We selected ten influencers and celebrity bloggers to launch this collaboration. We had to do some back-end tech things because when a collection is produced, it is never shot for e-commerce purposes so we essentially had to push up the production of the collection, which is always very tough because everyone is working and changing things up until the day before. But we had to be ready much sooner than that because we had to shoot the clothes. We needed to have something up so that we could set up the shop, which was very difficult because we had to work with the design team members, who were already on a tight schedule. We set up the e-commerce shop so that was all ready to go and loaded on the influencers' LikeToKnow.it account. The pre-selected bloggers took photographs during the live runway show and tagged them with the LikeToKnow.it handle on Instagram, which would feed out the linage of the product to their followers. It is common for fashion bloggers to share with their followers where to get the

product that they are wearing. Once the user "liked" the photo they would instantly get an email to their inbox giving them a link to an exclusive section of the BCBG website where they can buy a look from the runway.

At the end of the day, when you put these ten girls together, it was a small percentage of their combined power based on the followers that they had. It was again an opportunity to collaborate with the influencers to get the message out, not directly through BCBG. With the LikeToKnow.it platform, their incentive was that they earned a commission for every purchase that was made through that specific influencer. So, it is kind of a mutually beneficial collaboration, and that is why it is such a great thing because if you love the brand and we love the influencer, we can collaborate and then we know that because of them, there was a purchase made on our site and then, of course, we want to compensate them for that accordingly.

CASE STUDY:
COMICS-TO-COMMERCE: Phillip Lim

CONTRIBUTING WRITER—MAYA GOODING

Inspired by his fascination for graphic pop art, Phillip Lim released *Kill the Night*, an original comic book designed to showcase his latest looks to the brand's audience. Lim collaborated with writer John Onstrander (who authored *Suicide Squad*, *Grimjack*, and *Star Wars: Legacy*) and illustrator Jan Duursema (*Star Wars* comic book fame) to create the first fashion-specific comic book that mirrors the dark noir imagery of *Sin City* and *V for Vendetta*. The collector's item was a way for Lim to capture his vision within a tangible, consumable object, and go beyond the scope of clothing and accessories.

Though visually captivating on its own, the comic was designed to be used in conjunction with an app called Agent 3.1, which would create a holistic viewing experience for audiences. With a copy of the comic in hand, the viewer would activate the app by hovering over or scanning panels with their smartphone. When certain panels were in view, the viewer would "unlock" exclusive content—design inspiration, anecdotes from behind-the-scenes, peeks into Phillip's personal life (his dog Oliver makes a cameo), and shoppable items worn by characters in the comic book that link directly to the 3.1 Phillip Lim e-commerce site.

Maya Chu Gooding is Los Angeles-based within the fashion and art industries. She spent time working with the branding and social media departments at 3.1 Phillip Lim and the fashion department at W Magazine.

MOBILE INTERACTIVE SHOPPABLE STOREFRONTS: "FASHION-ON-THE-GO"

The Inspiration Shop allows customers to immediately purchase or "insta-buy" items from the convenience of their mobile devices and scannable QR codes on the window. eBay collaborated with interior designer Jonathan Adler to develop an innovative shopping experience that was designed to mimic the traditional storefront experience.

According to a national survey on shopping, commissioned by eBay, nearly half of shoppers want to make an immediate purchase when they find something they love (48 percent) and also enjoy browsing store windows for inspiration (46 percent). The majority cited frustration with traditional shopping experiences, particularly, long queues (57 percent), crowded stores (54 percent), pushy sales teams (52 percent), and lack of or limited inventory (65 percent) (eBay and Jonathan Adler, 2011).

Innovative Code System

QR (Quick Response Code) is a two-dimensional barcode. The bar code can be scanned with a mobile tagging application in a smartphone that enables the phone to link to a preset web page for other information.
("QR Code," n.d.)

" **CONSUMERS TODAY EXPECT TO SHOP HOW THEY WANT, WHEN THEY WANT AND MOBILE TECHNOLOGY IS BLURRING THE LINES BETWEEN ONLINE AND OFFLINE RETAIL TO MEET THIS DEMAND."**
RICHELLE PARHAM, CHIEF MARKETING OFFICER,
EBAY NORTH AMERICA ("EBAY AND JONATHAN ADLER," 2011)

5.13
eBay store front with QR codes enabling
insta-buying from window shoppers.

> **" WE'RE REDEFINING WHAT IT MEANS TO WINDOW SHOP. THERE'S NO INVENTORY AND NO [STORE ASSOCIATE]"**
> HEALEY CYPHER, HEAD OF RETAIL INNOVATION AT EBAY
> (INDVIK, 2013)

CASE STUDY:
Kate Spade Saturday shoppable window

Kate Spade and eBay collaborated to further evolve the modern shopping experience. Kate Spade Saturday launched digitally enhanced pop-up shops that catered to consumers' demand for flexibility and convenience. These twenty-four-hour interactive kiosks allowed shoppers to shop in a fun and creative way without having to visit an actual Kate Spade store. The featured items were deliverable within an hour and free of charge. Couriers also provided additional service by accepting payments and waiting for customers to try on the clothes they have ordered (Indvik, 2013). Approximately thirty items were displayed and made available to consumers through "brick-and-click."

INTERVIEW: Jeremy Bergstein, President of The Science Project

Jeremy Bergstein, president of the Science Project, has successfully led breakthrough efforts at the intersection of technology and fashion for the last 12 years. The Science Project is an agency reinvigorating the architecture of digital and shopping environments, bridging shopping from home, mobile, physical, and beyond. He works with a wide variety of clients including Perry Ellis, UNIQLO, Clinique, and Kate Spade New York. He has been featured in *PSFK*, *Women's Wear Daily*, and *The Wall Street Journal*, and the Theater of Retail was profiled on NPR (radio station) for its participation in NYC Holiday Magic.

How does your company continue to blur the lines between digital and physical?

Our digital experiences are receding further into the fabric and materiality of the physical by not being the story themselves and rather supporting natural human and brand interactions.

Can you share with your take on the customer journey (funnel) in today's retail space—enabling social stories?

My "take" on the modern customer journey revolves around "statefulness." What states they are in different locations, times of day, and places they are in their relationship with the brand. Devices and stories are built to prompt, create desire and emotional responses that push that customer along a journey towards an interaction.

How does it enrich the in-store experience and build upon relationship with the shopper? You mentioned how this helped to facilitate a new era of customer interaction driving reach, revenue, and transparency while delivering more valuable customers.

In an omni channel retailer's face, growing complexity as consumer touchpoints multiply, data collection demands increase, and the need to connect it all back to the in-store experience intensify. Most retailers simply do not have the tools or expertise to effectively create, deploy, and scale consistent and connected digital experiences across their entre retail enterprise. Retailers of all sizes share four main challenges:

- Connecting in-store and out-of-store activity for true channel synthesis
- Rapid, nimble testing and deployment of innovative enterprise solutions
- Future-proofing against new content, commerce, and data touchpoints
- Efficiently adding interactive square footage to every store

Can you explain to students how you have to prove to your clients about driving results (traffic, conversion rate, average order value)

Value and attribution in an omni-channel world is difficult. I would say don't get stuck in unusable data. Make sure to be creative, contextual, and relevant.

You mentioned that you work across the digital, mobile, and physical spaces to deliver a unified customer experience for brands. How does The Science Project go about understanding consumers?

We look to deeply understand the brand and what is different about it. We then use those key points to understand how we can create completely unique interactions between the brand and its customers.

How do you think the future of retail will change in the next five years?

Tactics must merge into strategy. Enterprise technology must advance.

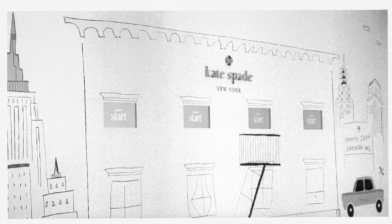

5.14a

5.14a, 5.14b
"Shoppable Barricades" for
curated window shopping for
Kate Spade. Video available at
vimeo.com/163610293

5.14c
The "Lady Gaga Constellation"
window display at Barney's
New York. Video available:
vemo.com/96643415

5.14b

5.14c

" OUR DIGITAL EXPERIENCES ARE
RECEDING FURTHER INTO THE
FABRIC AND MATERIALITY OF
THE PHYSICAL BY NOT BEING THE
STORY THEMSELVES BUT RATHER
SUPPORTING NATURAL HUMAN AND
BRAND INTERACTIONS."
JEREMY BERGSTEIN, THE SCIENCE PROJECT

EXERCISES

Critical Thinking:

(a) Determine the current expectations of consumers in relation to "fashion on demand" and the current social media applications that address these needs.

b) Social media brand and retail report card: Monitor two brands and two retailer's digital footprint. Review how well the brand(s) and retailer(s) are represented online through their social media channels, blogs, and websites. Do they have a consistent brand voice and messaging? Do they participate with influencers or affiliate programs? Do they have an independent blog for the brand or retailer creating a community such as Urban Outfitter's blog? To successfully market to the digital natives of today, a brand and retailer must have a strong presence online. Who is successfully connecting with their audience and who needs help in the area of online engagement? Understanding the evolving online landscape by looking at the successful digital marketing activation of the brands that you admire.

Practical Application:

Develop an influencer program for a pre-selected brand or retailer. Look to the Kate Spade Camp example and review "social media strategic outline."

Business Activity:

a) Create a social media marketing strategy for a brand or retailer for a launch of influencer collaboration. The presentation should include the digital SWOT analysis from chapter 2. Set clear goals and actionable engaging components.

b) Building Engagement through Social Media: This assignment requires working in teams to investigate how social media marketing is currently being used in the entertainment industry (television programs/movies) to engage with their audience. Each team will select one television show or block buster movie and research their social media strategy to connect with their audience.

Infographics:

Create an infographic based on a successful social media campaign that combines both online and offline collaboration. Review the BCBG Liketoknow.it fashion week collaboration and how they utilized Instagram to reach millions with the help of some top influencers.

Technology Corner:

- Develop a social media strategy plan from strategy to activation of a marketing campaign. Look into software to provide you with the metrics to measure your campaign and compare the features of at least two companies that can provide this insight.
- Explore and share examples of how measurable metrics are used in marketing such as click-through rates (CTR), cost per click (CPC), cost per conversion, and cost per acquisition (CPA).

REFERENCES

Abnet, K. (2015), "Do Fashion Trends Still Exist?," *Business of Fashion*, January, 5. Available online: http://www.businessoffashion.com/2015/01/fashion-trends-still-exist.html

About Us. (n.d.). *In Fohr Card*. Available online: http://www.fohrcard.com/about

Arthur, R. (2015), "British Brands Enabling Fans To Shop-Real-Time #LFW Trends by Leveraging Outdoor Advertising," *Forbes*, February 17. Available online: http://www.forbes.com/sites/rachelarthur/2015/02/17/british-brands-enabling-fans-to-shop-real-time-lfw-trends-by-leveraging-outdoor-advertising/

Brand vs. Influencer Content (2015) [Web log post], January 6. Available online: http://blog.fohrcard.com/post/2015/1/5/brand-vs-influencer-content

Brooke, E. (2013), "For On-The-Go Clothes Stalking, The Hunt Releases An iOS App," *TechCrunch*, November 21. Available online: http://techcrunch.com/2013/11/21/for-on-the-go-clothes-stalking-the-hunt-releases-an-ios-app/

Corcoran, C. (2010), "Marketing's New Rage: Brands Sponsoring Influential Bloggers," *Women's Wear Daily*, August 27. Available online: http://wwd.com/business-news/advertising/marketings-new-rage-brands-sponsor-influential-bloggers-3230386/

DeMers, J. (2015), "The Top 7 Social Media Marketing Trends That Will Dominate 2016," *Forbes*, September 28. Available online: http://www.forbes.com/sites/jaysondemers/2015/09/28/the-top-7-social-media-marketing-trends-that-will-dominate-2016/

Dugan, L. (2011), "Tweet Your Wishes At Barneys NYC, And They'll End Up In A Gaga Constellation On Display," *Adweek*, December 6. Available online: http://www.adweek.com/socialtimes/tweet-your-wishes-at-barneys-nyc-and-theyll-end-up-in-a-gaga-constellation-on-display/457906

eBay and Jonathan Adler Partner to Open "the EBay Inspiration Shop"—24/7 Shoppable Storefront Powered Exclusively by eBay Mobile. (2011, October 20). eBay Press Room.

Retrieved form https://www.ebayinc.com/stories/news/ebay-and-jonathan-adler-partner-open-ebay-inspiration-shop-247-shoppable/

Fratti, K. (2014), "New App Helps you Shop for *Pretty Little Liars* Wardrobe," *Adweek*, September 3. Available online: http://www.adweek.com/lostremote/gandr-in-public-beta-with-pretty-little-liars/47112

Ginsberg, M. (2014), "Colin Firth Spy Movie Inspires Mr. Porter Clothing Line," *The Hollywood Reporter*, June 10. Available online: http://www.hollywoodreporter.com/news/colin-firth-spy-movie-inspires-710984

Graj, S. (2012), "Skill Set of a Brand Curator," *Forbes*, April 16. Available online: http://www.forbes.com/sites/simongraj/2012/04/16/skill-set-of-a-brand-curator/

Harilela, D. (n.d.), "Mr Porter and filmmaker Matthew Vaughn launch Kingsman menswear label," *Post Magazine*. Available online: http://www.scmp.com/magazines/post-magazine/article/1693431/mr-porter-and-filmmaker-matthew-vaughn-launch-kingsman

Indivik, L. (2013), "SoHo Gives a Glimpse of Retail's Future," *Mashable*, June 9. Available online: http://mashable.com/2013/06/09/retail-store-future/#a8nd70bFqEqM

Influencer Marketing—The New Buzzword for Content Marketers [Web log post], (n.d.). Available online: http://www.socialyte.co/above-the-influence/influencer-marketing-the-new-buzzword-for-content-marketers

Instagram (2015), "Get Started with Instagram API," *Instagram Help*. Available online: https://help.instagram.com/554924547867832/

Jones, N. (2014), "Wired Retail Conference Returns to London," *Women's Wear Daily*, November 25. Available online: http://www.wwd.com/media-news/fashion-memopad/gordian-knot-8044111

Karimzadeh, M. (2014), "Marc by Marc Jacobs Gets Social With Fall Campaign," *Women's Wear Daily*, June 30. Available online: http://wwd.com/globe-news/fashion-memopad/real-time-7775379/

"Kate Spade's Mary Beech Talks Brand Storytelling," In *Kate Spade & Company*, (n.d.). Available online: http://www.katespadeandcompany.com/c/journal/view_article_content?groupId=10123&articleId=25276411&version=1.3

"Key performance indicator" (2015), *TechTarget*, November 21. Retrieved from http://searchcrm.techtarget.com/definition/key-performance-indicator

Kissell, R. (2015), "Ratings: '*Pretty Little Liars*' Hits 20-Year Highs With Big Reveal," *Variety*, August 12. Available online: http://variety.com/2015/tv/news/ratings-pretty-little-liars-hits-2-year-highs-with-big-reveal-1201568791/

McDonald, J. (2015), "The Power of Storytelling: By the Facebook IQ," *LinkedIn*, September 2. Available online: https://www.linkedin.com/pulse/power-storytelling-facebook-iq-james-mcdonald

Miller, C.C. (2014), "Shopping on a Phone Is Still Uncommon But Growing Fast," *The New York Times*, November 28. Available online: http://www.nytimes.com/2014/11/29/upshot/mobile-shopping-is-still-uncommon-but-growing-fast.html?_r=1&abt=0002&abg=1

Mobilzed (n.d) Overview of Klout. Available online: http://www.moblized.com/apps/klout

Morrison, K. (2015), "Report: Influencer Marketing Can Yield Big Returns," *Adweek*, March 6. Available online: http://www.adweek.com/socialtimes/report-influencer-marketing-can-yield-big-returns/616512

Oberoi, A. (2013), "Adsense CTR—Everything you need to Know," *AdPushup*, July 26. Available online: http://www.adpushup.com/blog/adsense-ctr-everything-you-need-to-know/

Patterson, M. (2014), "Social Media Manger vs. Community Manager: What's the Difference?," *SproutSocial*, October 30. Available online: http://sproutsocial.com/insights/social-media-vs-community-manager/

Rogers, S. (2011), Rethinking the Marketing Funnel in a World of Social Media [Web log post]. Available online: http://davidrogers.biz/blog/rethinking-the-marketing-funnel-in-a-world-of-social-media/

Sheff, H. (2015), "Mr. Porter Releases Second Spy Thriller-Inspired Kingsman Collection," *MR Magazine*, May 12. Available online: http://www.mr-mag.com/mr-porter-releases-second-spy-thriller-inspired-kingsman-collection/

Sherman, L. (2011), "Banana Republic Launches Mad Men-Inspired Line With Janie Bryant: Here's the Complete Collection," *Fashionista*, June 22. Available online: http://fashionista.com/2011/06/banana-republic-is-launching-a-mad-men-inspired-collection-with-janie-bryant

Shoppable Barricades for Kate Spade New York [Web log post] (n.d.). Available online: http://theaterofretail.tspxyz.com/post/126347361244/the-science-project-end-of-summer-announcements

Social Listening. (2015). In *TrackMaven*, November 21. Retrieved from http://trackmaven.com/marketing-dictionary/social-listening/

Talarico, B. (2014), "Want to Shop the *Pretty Little Liars* Closet? Costume Designer Mandi Line Has Your Back," *People*, January 10. Available online: http://people.com/style/want-to-shop-the-pretty-little-liars-wardrobe-closet-costume-designer-mandi-line-has-your-back/

The Collaboration. (n.d.). In *Kingsman*. Available online: http://www.mrporter.com/content/kingsman_movie

The Science Project (2011) "Gaga Constellation" for Barney's New York. Available online: http://tspxyz.com/our-work/gaga-social-universe

Tsjeng, Z. (2014, November), "Check out Marc by Marc Jacobs Instagram-cast campaign" [Web log post]. Available online: http://www.dazeddigital.com/fashion/article/20587/1/check-out-marc-by-marc-jacobs-instagram-cast-campaign

Tusing, D. (2015), "The Directory: Meet the Kingsman designer," *Gulf News*, February 7. Available online: http://gulfnews.com/life-style/glamour/fashion/the-directory-meet-the-kingsman-designer-1.1452853

Weingarten T. and Brooks, S. (2013), "The Hunt: How Social Media Democratized Fashion," *PSFK*, November 29. Available online: http://www.psfk.com/2013/11/tim-wiengarten-sara-brooks-draft-copy.html

Weiss, A. (2015), "From Catwalks to Conversions: How Bloggers Become Successful Through Affiliate Marketing," *Marketing Land*, March 20. Available online: http://marketingland.com/catwalks-conversions-bloggers-become-successful-affiliate-marketing-121676

What is a URL? (n.d.), in *Indiana University Knowledge Base*. Retrieved November 21, 2015 from https://kb.iu.edu/d/adnz

What We Do. (n.d.), in *Hello Society*. Available online: https://hellosociety.com/whatwedo

Xavier, J. (2014), "How tech startups are taking the fashion runway by storm." *Upstart Business Journal*, March 22. Available online: http://upstart.bizjournals.com/companies/startups/2014/03/22/how-tech-startups-are-remaking-fashion.html?page=all

6.1
The ability to explore the world of
data driven personas and trends.

06

PART 2
**THE BUSINESS OF
MARKETING FASHION**

THE EVOLVING
MEASURABLE IMPACT
OF SOCIAL MEDIA

Chapter Objectives

- Discovering fashion data insight
- Exploring data-driven personas
- Understanding the power of search
- Learning through journey mapping

6.2

INTRODUCTION

Throughout this textbook, we have explored the theory and practice of digital and social media marketing. In this chapter we turn to experts working in the industry to give us further insight into the fields of search engine optimization (SEO), search engine marketing (SEM), and data contextualization. This chapter will evaluate how the industry is challenging new technologies, developing stronger data set algorithms, and changing the way brands market to consumers as a whole. We will also examine how brands utilize data to understand consumer personas, spending habits, and daily routines. Brands that are able to influence their audiences begin by knowing their consumers and generating content that will drive the engagement of those consumers.

Consumers are perpetually online and show no signs of slowing down—the average person spends approximately one hour and forty minutes reviewing the Internet per day (Davidson, 2015). In the United States, consumers check their social media accounts seventeen times a day; they check at least once every hour they are awake, taking up about 4.7 hours of that consumer's day (Chang, 2015). Maintaining an online presence has now become an integral element of people's daily lives. Therefore, social media marketers are now realigning their budgets to craft robust media campaigns that will maximize their interactions with consumers.

How do we begin to measure the data collected from online consumer interactions? As we begin building a buyer's persona, when and how do we contextualize this data and its impact? In this chapter, we will establish the importance of creating a journey map of measurable consumer data points. We will also discover the tools that measure these data points—these tools allow brands to identify trends and better comprehend their target audiences.

6.2
Consumers are connected 24/7 whether it's on their mobile social media accounts or their body monitoring wearable technology such as a Fitbit.

Both brands and retailers seek to understand how their audiences perceive them across the social media landscape. They listen to online conversations and are able to identify consumers who are simply listening or actively driving these interactions. The information gathered from social media data mining allows marketers to drive traffic, strengthen their digital presence, create better content, and influence their target audiences. Marketers are required to report accurate return on investment (ROI) figures and conversion rates in order to justify their overall strategic plan. Hence, measurable impact is becoming less about transactions and more about building and sustaining customer relations. Understanding how to utilize "big data" properly is crucial in enhancing a brand's reputation and providing outstanding customer experiences.

" MASS RELEVANCE: BRANDS HAVE THE DATA AND TOOLS TODAY TO GIVE CONSUMERS WHAT THEY WANT, WHEN THEY WANT IT, AND WHERE THEY WANT IT."
FAST COMPANY CO.CREATE

THE POWER OF DATA

Merriam-Webster defines data as a collection of informative facts that are used to calculate, analyze, or plan something. Big data is a term used to describe extremely large data sets. Industry analyst Doug Laney articulated big data by the "3Vs" framework for both comprehending and utilizing "big data": Volume, Velocity and Variety (Laney, 2012).

Marketers, digital strategists, trends directors, merchandisers, and other members of the fashion business are constantly in pursuit of good contextualized data. Good data is simply thought of as the pot of gold at the end of the rainbow. Collecting data is nothing more than an aggregation of numbers until it is placed in a certain context by uniquely created algorithms. As the fashion industry transitions toward data-driven insights, brands are using analytical services to develop new positions and maintain their customers' interest. Retailers also use accurate, data-driven personas and communication data points to leverage their development of multi-touch marketing strategies. Advanced algorithms and data collection approaches allow the industry to keep up with the high expectations of today's hyper-connected consumers.

The 3Vs framework ("SAS," n.d.)

Volume: the process of organization and collection of data from a variety of sources from social media to machine-to-machine data.

Velocity: the great speed in which data is generated, and the process of managing it.

Variety: data sets come in a variety of formats, from numeric data to financial transaction.

6.3
Fashion and data have become inextricably linked in today's hyper-connected world.
Illustrated by Kathryn Hagen

6.3

Hagen, 16

1011(
0101110100
10010010010010
100100100010001001000
000101110001001000111000
100100111000100100011110(
0100100110010101011101000
0100100100100100100100
01001001001001000
0010010001110C
010 0011111(
110100

Data Contextualization

According to the renowned data team at fashion analytics firm EDITED, data without context is nothing more than a series of numbers that is limited. Companies like EDITED bring billions of data points into focus through data contextualization, whereas firms like Affinio focus on contextualizing data content from social media communities (tribes), based on their social presence (Bezzant).

" CONSUMERS ARE REALIZING THE VALUE OF THEIR DATA. THEIR WILLINGNESS TO SHARE THAT DATA (AND WHAT THEY EXPECT IN RETURN) WILL DEFINE FUTURE BRAND-CONSUMER RELATIONSHIPS. THE BRANDS THAT GET CONSUMERS TO HAND OVER DATA WILL BE THE BRANDS THAT GIVE THOSE CONSUMERS SOMETHING VALUABLE IN RETURN, LIKE PERSONALIZED EXPERIENCES. FIVE YEARS FROM NOW, YOU ARE NEVER GOING TO GET A PRESENT YOU DO NOT WANT. MY HUSBAND WILL PULL UP AN APP THAT PULLS TOGETHER ALL OF MY FAVORITE THINGS FROM ALL OF MY FAVORITE STORES INTO ONE, AWESOME, JUST-FOR-ME CAPSULE.
LISA PEARSON, CMO FOR BAZAARVOICE (2013)

EVOLUTION OF FASHION DATA + ANALYTICS

In chapter 1, we delved into how social media, real time content, and industry gatekeepers have disrupted the business of fashion. The continuous shift of consumer expectations—from basic services to the latest social media trends, and the movement toward a "fashion on demand" industry.

Today, fashion relies heavily on quantitative research facilitated by the systematic collection of information known as big data. However, data interpretation still depends on natural instinct and intuition in order to reveal what consumers will want next. Algorithms, Google Analytics, Radian6, and Facebook Insight are tools that unearth new perspectives about online consumer behaviors. Data insight geared toward fashion can help buyers in purchasing decisions, fashion directors in retail planning, and marketing teams in making better choices to reach customers. Thus, the selling of fashion requires a filtering system that will pinpoint trends, consumer interests, and online content reactions.

Contextualizing data

Innovative forecasting companies that utilize new, data-driven methodologies in trend monitoring have begun to emerge in the current fashion climate. Firms such as WGSN's INstock and EDITED use unique approaches to generate insight about today's digital native/e-commerce consumers. Dataset (big data) collection utilizes social intelligence to collect and analyze all aspects of consumer engagement online. Social media feeds filter conversations around trends, runway images, retail sales numbers, and other fashion buzz. Services such as these allow the fashion industry to read a custom dashboard that monitors the buying, trading, and sharing behavior of its customers. Fashion technology companies have also developed behavior algorithms that have changed the manner in which the business of fashion is run. Offering the right product to the targeted consumer requires listening, observing, and a quick response to the demands of the ever-changing marketplace.

6.4
Fashion insight from the runway and
street fashion can be monitored on social
media platforms and translated into key
trends to watch through data profiling.

Crowdsourcing websites that focus on bringing fashion-minded consumers together enhance the predictability of a trend's success. Geoff Watts, co-founder of EDITED, states that companies need to "capitalize on this willingness to share on social media, taking their customer's shared photos (e.g., from Instagram) and building these directly into their sites. It works on two levels: Generation Y consumers need that pre-purchase validation and retailers need a constant stream of content to compete" (Gibbs, 2013). Fashion brands are currently turning to big data to learn more about their social media audiences.

The global reach of social media, coupled with content sharing, is transforming the speed of fashion trend cycles at a massive scale. The same fashion trends are now selling out across multi-markets, and simultaneously from mass to fast-fashion valued price points. These trends now move concurrently because of social media's real-time access across a transnational market. Watts claims that "all thanks to live-streamed shows, the ability for anyone to generate content, and the power of social sharing of opinion and tastes, although the ability for factories to rapidly reproduce clothing ideas may play a part" (Gibbs, 2013). Because of this movement originating from hyper-connected consumers of today (and tomorrow), it is more important than ever to utilize the data trails left online in order to enable the fashion industry to better predict the behavior patterns of consumers.

THE FUTURE OF FASHION FORECASTING

One company that has changed the fashion forecasting process is the UK company called EDITED. They are a retail technology company that helps leading brands make data-driven buying, merchandising, and design decisions. With more than eighty billion data points and millions being added daily, EDITED is the leading company providing real-time data to apparel retailers worldwide. EDITED's expertise and ability to augment data sets it apart from conventional web crawler companies. The company has found a way to aggregate fashion trends and sale information from a global feed of over fifty-four billion data points from retail sites, social media, runway, and blogs. Everything done at EDITED, be it creating pricing structures or analyzing replenishment rates, is made possible by the contextualization of data. Dealing with an incredible amount of data requires entire teams of individuals (with different specializations) and state-of-the-art equipment working in tandem to generate maximum results.

6.5
EDITED Trend and Market Insight Infograph

6.5

AW14's trends: chosen by you

EDITED runs the world's biggest apparel data warehouse, which global and local retailers use to track the market, align product assortment and trade with competitive intelligence. www.edited.com

Top 5 Designers by Fanbase Growth

1 Sophia Webster ↑ 13.2%
Proof that you don't need a traditional catwalk show in order to create buzz. Webster's 90s dreamworld presentation was an online hit.

2 Daks ↑ 7.5%
With Mulberry not showing, other British heritage brand Daks took opportunity to up their social presence, tweeting backstage, live-streaming and a comp to win show tickets.

3 Emilio de la Morena ↑ 4.7%
De la Morena's velvet rich eveningwear show was a hit with online spectators, earning the brand a social boost despite no Twitter posting, instead using Facebook as a show countdown.

4 Joseph ↑ 4.5%
Miley Cyrus fronted the brand's Valentines campaign, in collaboration with Love Magazine - her face graced their Westbourne Grove store front and brought with it some of her social media appeal.

5 Peter Pilotto ↑ 3.7%
With their first season as Fashion Fund winners, Peter Pilotto's social presence ramped up, building up to the show with snippets of collection inspiration ahead of their Facebook live-stream.

EDITED
The EDITED colour wheel was generated from all LFW catwalk imagery from the last 4 days.

BORA AKSU
DAKS
EMILIO DE LA MORENA
PPQ
CHRISTOPHER RAEBURN
FELDER FELDER

Top Trends by Fanbase Growth

TEXTURE 24% POSITIVE — 3,972 mentions
FRIEDER GOLAN
Fur, shearling, suede and leather; designers got touchy-feely for AW14 and it got consumers buzzing, with this being the week's most talked-about trend.

VOLUME 36% POSITIVE — 3,388 mentions
JACKIE J S LEE
From Jonathan Saunders' form-defying outerwear and Topshop Unique's blown-up puffer jackets, to simply a more fluid trouser shape at Paul Smith; play with volume is pivotal to the new season.

60s 34% POSITIVE — 3,050 mentions
EUDON CHOI
Seek 60s guidance from Markus Lupfer's modish shifts and skirt suits and Richard Nicoll's simple Harrington jackets and pleated skirt combo. The turtle neck top or jumper is paramount to this trend.

90s 27% POSITIVE — 2,756 mentions
NASIR MAZHAR
Whether it's a bomber jacket thrown over a LBD and accessorised with a choker at Marios Schwab or full-blown hip-hop referencing from Nasir Mazhar, the 90s aren't shifting from focus just yet.

Tracking the BFC Vogue Fashion Fund Winning Designers

1. Peter Pilotto (2014)
2. Nicholas Kirkwood (2013)
3. Jonathan Saunders (2012)
4. Christopher Kane (2011)
5. Erdem (2010)

Aug 13 · Sept 13 · Nov 13 · Dec 13 · Jan 14 · Feb 14

18th September 2013 On the day of his SS14 show, Kane announces plans to open a store on London's Mount Street.

MOUNT STREET W1
CITY OF WESTMINSTER

15th December 2013 Following a night out on the tiles with Erdem, Victoria Beckham tweets that she's had "so much fun".

9th February 2014 Peter Pilotto's Target collection goes on sale.

11th August 2013 Selena Gomez wears Nicholas Kirkwood pumps at the Teen Choice Awards.

19th September 2013 Saunders' SS14 collection is well received by fashion critics, as he celebrates 10 years in business.

18th September 2013 Peter Pilotto announce a collaboration with Target which went on to be become their fastest selling collection.

INTERVIEW:
EDITED, Katie Smith, Senior Fashion & Retail Market Analyst at EDITED

Katie Smith is the Senior Fashion & Retail Market Analyst at EDITED. EDITED runs the world's biggest retail data warehouse, underpinning decision making at the world's best apparel retailers. EDITED's software is used on five continents, and leads the market in real-time analytics of pricing, assortment, and deep product metrics for apparel professionals in merchandising, buying, trading and strategy. Customers include ASOS, Gap and Target Australia.

The following interview was conducted by contributing writer Evelyn Chua.

Since EDITED's founding, how have the fashion industry's data-driven strategies evolved? In particular, is the adaptation of data science becoming more of an industry standard and intuition passé?

KS: There is always going to be a place for intuition in everything—data's purpose is not to stomp that out. What it does do, though, is give clarity and certainty around particular aspects of retail.

Data science has not been so much a sudden adaptation as much as it has been an evolution. Retailers have had their own business intelligence systems for a long time but the data was only internal. Plus, the reports were hard to read. And even if you could make sense of them, they were usually distributed anywhere from monthly to bi-annually, which pretty much guaranteed that the data was too old to be actionable. So, that was sort of version one. EDITED today would be a hundred or so versions down the road.

What is different now is that the the retail industry is moving faster. Considering, for example, that some retailers can have a product turned around in three weeks. For that retailer, it makes sense that e-commerce decisions be made quickly and accurately. Online, as opposed to full store rollouts, means there is more flexibility of testing too. Luckily, data science has matured too, and can be accessed by every person within an organization, allowing them to see and gauge their own and their competitors' performance in real-time. That is when it is really powerful.

The significance of data culture has also created an increased demand for data scientists in the greater fashion industry. How did data's increased importance disrupt the fashion forecasting and marketing strategy-planning ecosystem, specifically, functional hierarchies and day-to-day process flows in fashion businesses?

Two things that were previously not expected are now expected at every stage of the retail process. The first is being able to back everything up with facts. The second is a need to have market-wide visibility. The significance of those changes, in an industry where instinct-based decision-making has been the standard for decades, cannot be downplayed.

The world's biggest and most successful brands, like Saks Fifth Avenue, Topshop, Gap Inc., and Marks & Spencer, have made EDITED retail analytics software part of their daily process. It is not just e-commerce retailers that have been quick to adopt; our clients span the value, mass, premium, and luxury markets, globally.

Hierarchically, EDITED is used at every level of the business and data's impact is greatest when everyone in an organization has access to it, because they can all make better-informed decisions. Where once buyers might have spent hours looking at a competitor's site analyzing their offering, or weeks going to stores and compiling what amounted to incomplete reports, that information is now accessible at the click of a button. It creates better product selection, finely tuned and responsive promotional activities, and fewer losses at the end of the season.

INTERVIEW:
EDITED, Katie Smith, Senior Fashion & Retail Market Analyst at EDITED

As dedicated data analytics and consulting practices grow in number, how do you recommend digital strategists and marketing executives to go about choosing the right partners for their firms? What criteria and product/service offerings should they be looking at, and why?

Big data is not necessarily good data. Scale is important, but so are accuracy and the level of insight that the data allows. Real-time analytics is most powerful when used as part of a retailer's daily process; so, the software has to be easy to use, and there have to be actionable outcomes.

Here are some of the big things to look out for:

Quality of data: Since you will want to base strategically important decisions with this, it is important to know that it is correct. Look for transparency behind the numbers.

Retail provenance: The best product is going to be coming from people who understand the retail industry and the types of decisions people will be making when using the service; so, the analytics are relevant to their use case.

Ease of use: Does it communicate the information in a clear, direct way? Just because a tool is powerful, it does not mean that it cannot be simple to use.

Reliability and transparency: Who else uses the product? If your data supplier cannot tell you who else is using its data, and offer relevant testimonials or case studies, stay away.

Support: Bringing new software into your business can be an easy thing to do, but you are going to have some questions. And when you have questions, make sure that your supplier will be around to answer them.

Experience: How long has your data supplier been doing this? Is their engineering team in-house or is the bulk of it outsourced? Knowing who is behind your data and reassuring yourself that they are credible and able is paramount to picking the company.

The increased level of accuracy and expediency with which your clients are able to access comp-related insight is immensely powerful and big ecommerce players have rejoiced at this. However, there is a huge segment of the ecommerce industry that comprises significantly smaller players relative to your more notable clients (e.g., ASOS). Is the company going toward the direction of addressing the needs of these smaller players?

Our customers run the full gamut including, but not limited to multi-brand retailers, department stores, flash sale retailers, and fast-fashion retailers as well as luxury brands, manufacturers, and suppliers. There are definite commonalities across all: the need to have the right product, at the right price, and at the right time. The brand or retailer defines the "right" in accordance to its own consumer and market.

Because of that, we have always made sure that EDITED software is highly customizable. Each user creates its own dashboards—selected views of the marketplace based on their own criteria and filtering. Smaller brands or retailers that may not need access to worldwide data across every segment instead choose to focus on their niche market.

In terms of addressable market, is EDITED looking into developing retailer intelligence for companies that strongly focus on an older demographic (>40)? Given that the aforementioned market segment still prefers retail experiences that involve the traditional brick and mortar model, how has EDITED incorporated data intelligence that relate to this powerful—in terms of aggregate purchasing power—market?

Online data is the only way retailers have full visibility of what their competitors are doing. The way we see it, consumer behavior does not differ much between the online and offline spaces. Consumer confidence has soared online, and that is just as applicable to the 40+ demographic as it is to Gen Y. Evidence of that is the way e-commerce has rocketed for the likes of Nordstrom and Net-a-Porter.

Our software covers everything online, across all markets, globally. So, we are already relevant to the older demographic and have customers who cater to this market, as well as other niches like plus-sized and maternity.

Cross-selling, as an avenue to optimize revenue generation, requires greater attention and more robust algorithms to truly capture consumer behavior, both online and offline. How has EDITED, through its various analytics solutions, been able to highlight the value of cross-selling across different product SKUs?

We capture every bit of information on the product pages of more than fifty million SKUs. That goes right down to the merchandise information. If a retailer pairs it with another item, we will know about it. A popular example of successful cross-selling is the proliferation of co-ord sets in the last three seasons. With close to 5,000 co-ord pieces currently online, they have a 10 percent replenishment rate and take, on average, ninety-seven days to sell out.

What is next for the EDITED team—Any impending acquisition plans or strategic partnerships in the works?

We are a technology company, so, we are literally releasing new things every day. It would be impossible to stay still for long in such an agile industry. We will continue to work closely with brands and retailers to understand their primary concerns and develop technology to address these. We have got a clearly defined roadmap, but we are always conscious to stay flexible enough to cater to the needs of our customers and the rapidly evolving retail industry.

Actionable Analytics

Business intelligence is often described as a technology-driven process that transforms raw data into meaningful and actionable information to help make business decisions. Business intelligence programs can also incorporate forms of advance analytics: data mining, predictive analytics and big data analytics.
("Business Intelligence," n.d.)

CASE STUDY:
Think With Google—Shopping Insight

(Content pulled from the Shopping Insight Press Release. (Adwords, 2015)

Shopping Insights shows the products that people are searching for across cities, time, and devices. While 87 percent of shopping research happens online, 92 percent of goods are still sold in retail stores. By better understanding a user's online shopping intent, retailers can make more informed local merchandising and marketing decisions for their stores (Adwords, 2015).

The Shopping Insights tool estimates popularity and trends for a given product by aggregating keyword data from the millions of searches that consumers are doing to shop for that product. Further, you can see data for every city that is available for targeting in AdWords, and compare mobile to desktop patterns to better serve customers near your stores (Adwords, 2015).

6.6a

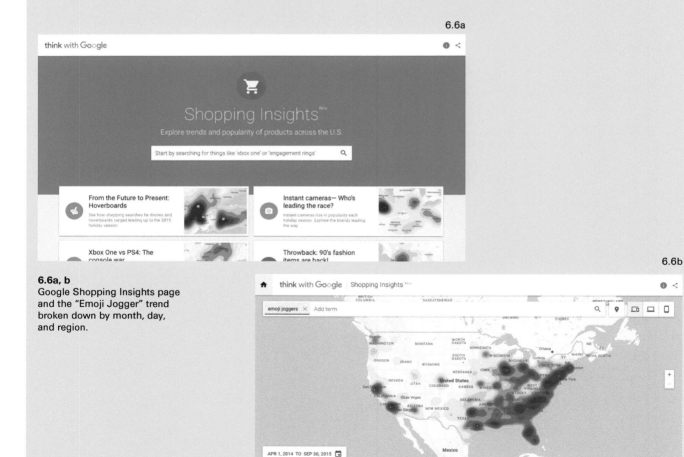

6.6b

6.6a, b
Google Shopping Insights page and the "Emoji Jogger" trend broken down by month, day, and region.

DATA-DRIVEN BRIEFS AND PERSONAS

Brands strive to engage with their social media audiences and, ideally, convert them into customers. While brands sometimes turn to social media influencers to reach their target audience, they also spend a great deal of money on paid advertising campaigns and outreach programs. Advertisers worldwide will spend $23.68 billion on paid media to reach consumers on social networks this year, according to new figures from eMarketer, which is a 33.5 percent increase from 2014. By 2017, social network advertisement spending will reach $35.98 billion, representing 16 percent of all digital advertisement spending globally ("Social Network Ad," 2015). Marketers need to determine how and where they should advertise in order to better connect with consumers online.

How much do brands know about their social media network audience? In the past, brands relied on research firms to better understand their target markets. Big data companies monitor consumers online and create contextualized data reports that enable brands to discover the persona of their customers. These data insights are far more advanced than the traditional demographic formulas used pre-social media.

Hotwire, a public relations communications agency, published a report about the rapid evolution of how brands connect with their customers. The report, based on crowdsourced data from 400 communicators across twenty-two countries, revealed that brands will look to engage consumers with age-agnostic or age-neutral content that emphasizes certain values (Stein, 2015). Johanna Blakely, a researcher from University of Southern California's Norman Lear Center, has spent the last decade studying demographics, and how they affect media and entertainment. Blakely began by focusing on social media users and how this form of community enabled users to avoid marketers' conventional demographic segmentation. While social media clickstream was able to generate valuable insight, the ages of users online were difficult to pinpoint. "We are able to connect with people quite freely and to redefine ourselves online. We can lie about our age online too, pretty easily. We can also connect with people based on our very specific interests," claims Blakely (TED, 2011).

Traditional demographic segmentation has been replaced by the data mining of consumers' online presence, movements, and interactions. Marketers observe online audience behavior in order to determine the target market best suited for a particular brand. "The challenge of accurate and effective customer targeting is being won through new and highly intelligent approaches to segmentation and characterization," said Joe Catalfamo, who served as a director for social media monitoring company Radian6/Salesforce (Rogers, 2015).

CASE STUDY:
Affinio, India White, Content Strategist

INTERVIEW WITH INDIA WHITE BY CONTRIBUTING WRITER EVELYN CHUA

Affinio is an award-winning audience intelligence technology company that extracts deep psychographic insights from social media participants. Their approach breaks down communities into tribes based on shared interests in order to better understand their audiences. Affinio's algorithm analyzes the relationships that exist within an audience, and it groups individuals into passion clusters, based on member affinities and the people, topics, and brands that these individuals choose to connect with. This methodology is a prime example of marketing intelligence that leverages social graphs to understand today's consumer.

In their constant fight for relevance, companies and executives have begun incorporating large, data-driven insights into their immediate strategies.

A study conducted by McKinsey Global Institute (MGI) titled *Game Changers: Five Opportunities for US Growth and Renewal* cited big data analytics as the top-ranked catalyst in increasing business productivity. The greatest benefactors of the rise in big data usage are retailers and manufacturers who are estimated to generate productivity gains of up $325 billion dollars by 2020 (McKinsey Global Institute, 2013). Similarly, a joint study by The University of Texas at Austin and Sybase Company found that every 10 percent increase in data attributes improved retail market productivity (sales per employee) by 49 percent, and increased sales figures by $6.9 billion (Barua et al., n.d.).

The aforementioned dynamics is exactly what drives companies in the actionable digital analytics world and explains the influx of new players in this space. Each of these analytics companies differentiates itself by using proprietary techniques to process raw data and create different story angles on the same subsets of data. India White, Content Strategist of the award winning audience intelligence company Affinio, assures that "[t]here is still plenty of room in the sandbox" for other companies to develop unique data utilization offerings.

In the context of consumer retail, big data is only made revolutionary by the insights derived from the analysis performed against it. The ability to make sense of and transform—what otherwise would be indigestible—data into actionable insights is what is truly relevant for both marketers and management.

Digital strategists often enlist the services of companies that provide hybrid (products and services) data extraction and proprietary methods of synthesizing such data into a digestible consumer insights report. As digital marketers come to terms with the copious amount of data readily making itself available, they realize that the value lies less in the number of data points (observation of a set of one or more measurements) and more in the quality of analysis generated from the respective pools of data. Ultimately, the reports are used for daily merchandising decisions, price strategy calibrations, inventory management, and efficient production runs.

Empathetic Approach

- Think before you speak?
- Who is your target audience?
- What are their interests?
- How can your brand relate to the customer?

~ AFFIANO

Affinio's clients produce audience reports by pulling large amounts of data, thus giving them insight into the persona of their target markets. To enhance overall engagement, brands and retailers must first define who their respective audiences are. According to Affinio, these are the steps that must be undertaken in order to accomplish this (Park, 2015).

• Know who your current social media audience is: Understanding your current audience allows you to recognize common interests and personas, thus boosting the chance to locate similar consumers. This allows brands/retailers to identify the existing personas, preferences, and behaviors within its unique audience.

• Know who their competitors' audience is: Understanding your competitor's key audience segments allows brands/retailers to obtain a better understanding of the overall market and the digital space it resides in.

• Know who in the digital space of social media is sharing their content: Find out who is sharing your content online. Determine the frequency and motivation for this sharing.

• Companies like Affinio generate exceptional, value-added insights by identifying unique relationship attributes within digital audiences. With the aid of its award-winning "Social Affinity Engine" technology, Affinio is able to mine billions of data to develop connections—which they term as tribes/audience clusters—to help clients develop a more thorough and authentic concept of their respective audiences.

The remarkability of Affinio's services is not derived from the type of information or volume of data its able to access. The company differentiates itself by including certain data types (e.g., lurkers) and insights (e.g., tribes and shared interests) in their analysis of chosen datasets. Lurkers are individuals who consume content but refuse to engage with brands and retailers. White claims, "Upwards of 80 percent of the current pool of social media participants are silent . . . these are a substantial group of the audience for any product/brand/companies that are not being given enough attention." Affinio officially defines lurkers as consumers who post less than fifteen times a month on social media platforms.

On average, only about 10 percent of overall social media subscribers engage and/or edit online content. Given the staggering statistics of this latent set of users, it seems almost irresponsible for marketers not to conduct further analyses into the behavior of this particular segment. Doing so will allow them to craft a strategy that will monetize and prompt specific actions from this group.

" AFFINO'S ALGORITHM ANALYZES THE RELATIONSHIPS THAT EXIST WITHIN ANY AUDIENCE AND GROUPS INDIVIDUALS INTO PASSION CLUSTERS BASED ON MEMBER AFFINITIES AND THE PEOPLE, TOPICS, AND BRANDS THAT THESE INDIVIDUALS CHOOSE TO CONNECT WITH"
INDIA WHITE, CONTENT STRATEGIST OF AFFINIO

The Affinio Reports

Affinio produced two reports to show how the marketing intelligence platform is used to better understand latent audiences left out of previous studies conducted by social media monitoring firms. The first report that was examined was by the merging of multiple retailers and their respective social media audiences: Nordstrom, Saks Fifth Ave, Macy's, and Neiman Marcus. The second we will closely examine is the luxury e-commerce retailer Net-a-Porter.

MULTI-RETAILER SUMMARY REPORT

For a two-month timeframe, Affinio examined the Twitter accounts of Nordstrom, including those under the company's umbrella: @nordstrom (31.1 percent), @macys (18.8 percent), @neimanmarcus (24.8 percent), and @saks (25.2 percent). The report shows that only 13.04 percent of Nordstrom's 1,562,430 users actually engaged either through content creation or content sharing. This indicates that almost 90 percent of Nordstrom's Twitter (Fig. 6.8) audience is "lurking" in stealth mode, a fact that has massive implications for the brand going forward.

Despite the dissimilarities in exhibited levels of activity, this user group actually has quantifiable levels of shared interest, affinity, and relevance within the context of their respective tribes. Tribes are clustered according to commonalities in interest as defined by Affinio's proprietary algorithm. The firm is then able to provide a visual on the profile that generates the greatest interest within a specific cluster, making it easier to find a more effective set of influencers.

The images include brands, celebrities, media outlets, social networks, etc. Thus, it is important to develop content that works best within the context of specific clusters. This allows marketers to develop and attach effective content to specific brands.

Nordstrom had clusters that ranged from World Wrestling Entertainment, Inc. (WWE) fans (1 percent) to coupon moms (6 percent) (Fig. 6.9–Fig. 6.10). Profiles that would normally be overlooked by more streamlined consumer insight companies are now treated as contributors due to their online social interactions.

This page shows the share of audience that each account (input to run the report) counts among their followers. This will only show up in reports using more than one account as source. The normalized view takes into account disparities between account sizes of the provided source handles, and adjusts the share percentages accordingly. This makes comparing very large accounts and much smaller ones manageable, according to the Affinio report breakdown.

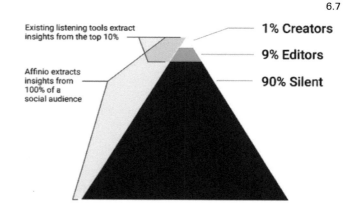

6.7

1% Creators

9% Editors

90% Silent

Existing listening tools extract insights from the top 10%

Affinio extracts insights from 100% of a social audience

6.7
Social audience engagement pyramid demonstrating levels of engagement. Traditional social media software would listen to only the 10 percent of the audience.

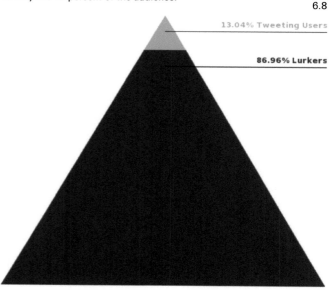

6.8

13.04% Tweeting Users

86.96% Lurkers

6.8
Pyramid chart showing the proportion of active "tweeters" vs. "lurkers."

6.9

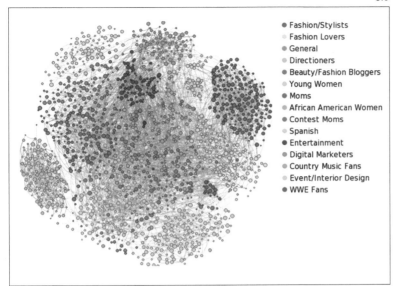

- Fashion/Stylists
- Fashion Lovers
- General
- Directioners
- Beauty/Fashion Bloggers
- Young Women
- Moms
- African American Women
- Contest Moms
- Spanish
- Entertainment
- Digital Marketers
- Country Music Fans
- Event/Interior Design
- WWE Fans

6.9
Audience visualization in an information-mapping format. More lines equates to more common interests.

6.10

6.10
Pie chart displaying the tribe audience cluster size of Nordstrom, Saks Fifth Ave, Neiman Marcus, and Macy's Twitter audiences. The graphic map represents the different tribes within this audience.

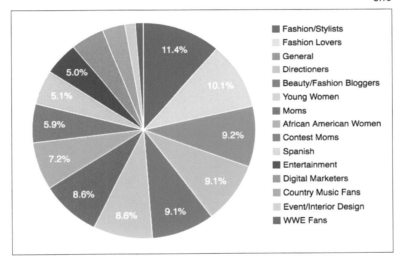

- Fashion/Stylists
- Fashion Lovers
- General
- Directioners
- Beauty/Fashion Bloggers
- Young Women
- Moms
- African American Women
- Contest Moms
- Spanish
- Entertainment
- Digital Marketers
- Country Music Fans
- Event/Interior Design
- WWE Fans

6.11

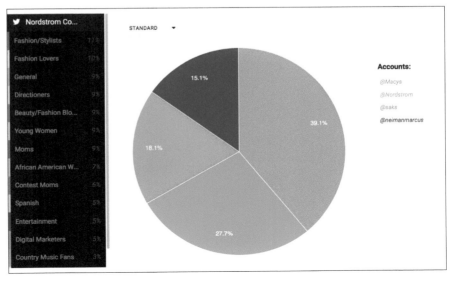

6.11
Affinio's normalized view chart of the compared accounts

Net-a-Porter Summary Report

The global luxury market is stepping up and paying attention to the social space that their audience is embracing. "The pervasive influence of technology on younger consumers underscores the need to focus resources on digital efforts to cultivate the next generation of luxury consumers," says Luxury Institute CEO, Milton Pedraza (Luxury Institute, 2015). Luxury retailers and brands know the importance of understanding their audience personas in order to create actionable strategy in their marketing plans. As hyper-connected millennials are gaining more affluence in the luxury sector, the need to monitor their persona rises. This report by Affinio will help to better contextualize the audience of Net-a-Porter in order to understand how to communicate to this "low-touch" luxury highly social consumer. Low-touch describes consumers who are knowledgeable about the brand and products without the heavy sales hand to ensure the purchase.

In this section, we share the results of the report for luxury e-commerce retailer, Net-a-Porter to take a closer look at the unique tribes of people found in their audience. Affinio analyzed the Net-a-Porter (@netaporter) Twitter account (fig 6.12) for one month to gain some insightful results; 9.53 percent of its audience tweets actively while 90.47 percent are lurkers. This does not rule out the lurkers, but gives the idea of who to look closely through the "relevancy" and "affinity" scores.

Contributing Writer

Evelyn Chua works under the financial restructuring division of Glass Ratner Advisory & Capital Group. She is also the Founder & CEO of The Artistic Bind, a strategy consulting firm focus on Los Angeles' fashion industry. Recently, she served as adjunct faculty at Woodbury University lecturing on Finance and Product Development.

6.12
Net-a-Porter's summary report

6.12

NET-A-PORTER.COM - Summary Report

Affinio analyzes the underlying network connections of an audience to generate an Affinity Graph. The audience is then segmented into tribes based on shared interests and affinities. Affinity Graph based insights help strategists develop data-informed creative, partnerships, and ad placement.

Report Query Source
Followers of: @netaporter

Report Details
Date Range: 09.19.15 - 10.19.15
Size: 759,469
Engagement: 7.06 tweets/month
Interest Similarity: 81.24

Unique tribes of people found within audience:

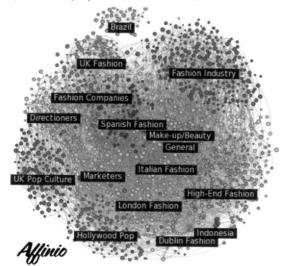

Level of engagement within audience:

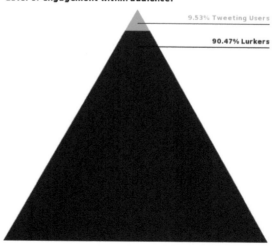

6.13

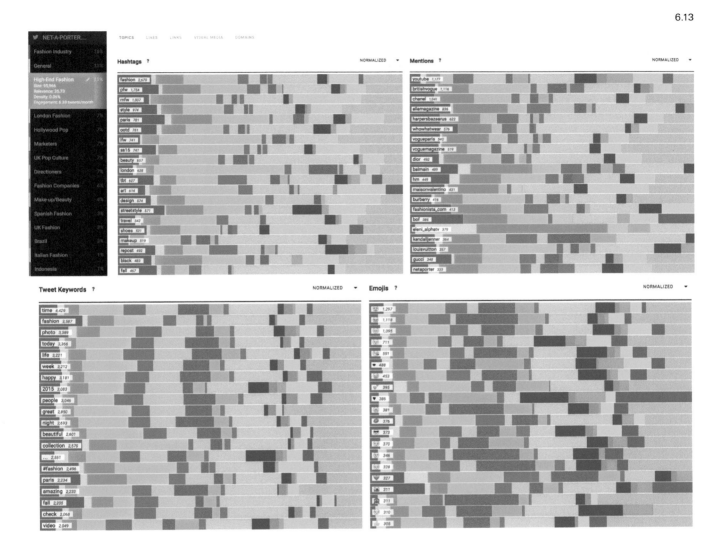

6.13
Affiano's cluster summary of
Net-a-Porter Twitter audience's
communication through
hashtags, mentions, keywords
and emojis.

THE POWER OF SEARCH

The power of search helps in revealing the Internet's endless possibilities. Search is the first thing that consumers do when looking up a restaurant, locating a retail store, or finding other people online. Nothing is out of reach for today's consumers because of the power of search engines such as Google. Consumer exploration of online content is characterized by the personalized self-discovery of endless options and unique finds. Today, a customer does not need to visit a retailer's physical space in order to find a desired piece of clothing; instead, he/she may simply "search" for the item online. While the buzz in digital media is that "Content is King," it is become apparent that Search Engine Optimization has now become the dominant theme in the industry.

Search Engines

One normality for consumers today is the ability to search on one of the most impressive search engines in the world, Google. While Google is the most popular search engine, there are others such as Bing, Yahoo, Baidu (Chinese), AOL, Yandex (Russia), and Lycos (Biswal, 2015). In ten countries, including the United States and Japan in 2015, mobile search (not including tablets) out-numbered the amount of searchers on a desktop (Macmillian, 2015). Today, one in every six people on the planet uses "Google," according to Searchmetrics. Whether consumers want to buy something or are merely looking for an answer to their related queries, the answer always is "Google it" (or Google Scholar it). "Search as we think about it, is fundamentally how you will interact with computing," stated Amit Singhal, senior vice president of search at Google (Macmillian, 2015).

Search topics and key terms are worth their weight in gold when it comes to optimizing how consumers search for brands. Bloglovin', a popular blogger community, connects users with similar interests on a global level. Josh Fischer, Vice President of Product and Analytics at Bloglovin', states, "The interesting thing about Bloglovin' is that a lot of our users are also our bloggers. Seeing that travel is being searched for the most, it makes sense that the content around travel and other "lifestyle" topics will organically grow in popularity" (Suarez, 2015).

In 2015, Bloglovin' decided to find out more about their community of six million users, and uncovered the most commonly searched terms in different parts of the world (Arthur, n.d.): From a user base of ninety-six countries and 750,000 searches made on the platform; the focus of the US and Europe revolved around fashion (Fig. 6.14).

"What was interesting was the emergence of other more "lifestyle" topics such as fitness, yoga, family, and travel. A common trajectory we see for many bloggers is that they start out primarily talking about what they wear, but as they build an audience, people want to know more about them as a person; where they vacation, how they stay fit, etc." Fischer explained (Suarez, 2015).

Tools such as the Google Analytics tabulate how consumers search, shop, engage, and converse online on Google Attribution 360 to measure the effectiveness of the brand's marketing efforts. These types of tools provide a way to optimize data across all touch-point channels to create actionable insights that improve their overall return on investment. Today, the business of fashion requires an ever-faster grasp of consumer demand. The expectation of digital natives (also referred to as digital immigrants) to know and possess every novel style imposes increased demand on fashion producers instantly.

6.14

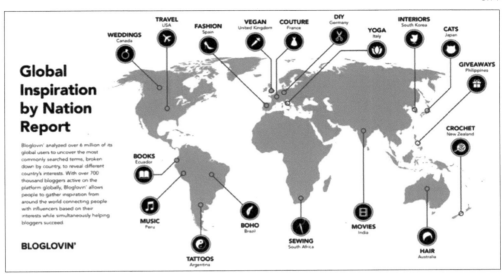

6.14
Bloglovin' Global Inspiration by
Nation Report

How to Navigate Organic vs. Paid Search

CONTRIBUTING WRITER COURTNEY MESSERLI,
GLOBAL SEO SPECIALIST AT ANTHROPOLOGIE

In order to understand how paid and organic search can
be leveraged for any business, one must first understand
their differences. The goal of Google or any other search
engine is to provide its users (searchers) with the most
relevant and accurate listings, based on that user's query.
A search engine results page is comprised of two types of
listings: paid and unpaid. Paid listings are advertisements
paid for by an advertiser and are featured at the top and
right hand side of a search engine results page. These
are distinguished by an "ad" of "sponsored" label, and are
inclusive of both text and product listing advertisements
(PLAs).

" AT 3 BILLION QUERIES PER DAY, THAT HAS
GOOGLE DOING 90 BILLION PER MONTH
OR 1.1 TRILLION SEARCHES PER YEAR."
(SULLIVAN, 2015)

Example of the SERP (search engine results page)

Top paid adverting text and advertising slots are occupied by retailers Nordstrom, LuLus, and Zappos. These top slots on the top and right hand side of the SERP are different from organic listings in that advertisers can pay for these top slots. Advertisers pay for each click on their advertisement that links to their site on a cost-per-click basis.

PLA listings (product image advertisements on the right) are occupied by retailers Bebe, Forever 21, Topshop, etc. These image results are also paid advertising slots. When a searcher clicks on the product image ad, they are linked to that specific product on the advertiser's website.

The first unpaid or organic slots on the Google search are occupied by retailers Forever 21 and Charlotte Russe. Advertisers cannot pay for these organic listings, but they can perform both on-page and off-page optimizations to their website to increase their chances of ranking in top positions.

The paid text and product advertisements, as well as the organic listings, all contain the keyword included in the search query and closely match the user's original query. This is how the search engine serves the most relevant results for each search that passes through the engine. These paid advertisements and organic listings then link directly to category, trend, or featured products on the retailer's site related to the query.

6.15

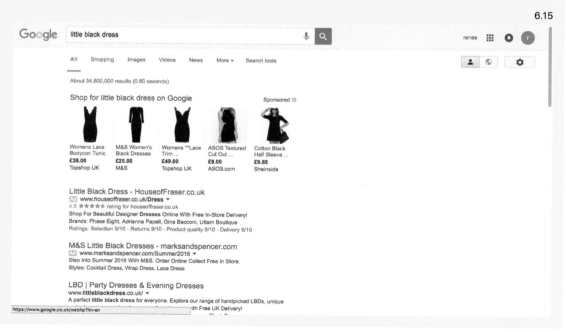

6.15
SERP (search engine results page)

Now that we have seen the differences between paid and unpaid listings on a results page, it is important to understand how the retailers above claimed these top slots through search engine marketing and search engine optimization efforts.

SEM

Paid search or search engine marketing (SEM) refers to the paid advertisements that appear in the top and right hand sides of a search engine results page. Advertisers bid on a targeted set of keywords, which are triggered by searchers' queries and are ranked through a bidding auction. Advertisements are ranked higher in the results based on two criteria: the bid amount in relation to competing keywords in the auction and the quality score of each keyword. Quality score is a value between 1 and 10 (10 being the highest) assigned to each keyword that an advertiser is targeting, which is determined by the relevancy of the keyword to a searcher's query, as well as the forecasted click through rate (CTR) of an advertisement. Click through rate is based on advertisement quality and the relevance of the landing page. This score is then multiplied by the bid for each keyword. This 1 to 10 quality score provides an idea of how the keywords will rank in the results, but does not take real-time bids in the auction into consideration.

Retailers create SEM campaigns in the Google and Bing user interfaces. In the e-commerce space, campaigns are typically broken out by categories, trends, or brands. Campaigns are separate entities, and are optimized accordingly. Advertisers create these campaigns that are devised by a common theme, and these are then broken down more granularly into advertisement groups. Each advertisement group contains its own set of advertisements, which are served for queries that match to keywords that are relevant to that category.

To provide more context, let us say that an advertiser creates a campaign called "Women's Skirts." This campaign would then be broken down into specific advertisement groups for each subcategory falling under skirts. Advertisement groups that fall under the Women's Skirt campaign could include "Mini Skirts," "Lace Skirts," and "Sequin Skirts." Each of these advertisement groups would include advertisements, landing pages, and keywords that are relevant to their specific subcategory or trend. Advertisers then specify the maximum bid amount that they are willing to pay for each keyword, which is referred to as the "Max CPC" (maximum cost per click). Once the Max CPCs are set, the keywords enter into the bidding auction and have the ability to achieve top advertisement slots based on the bid and quality score.

Campaign Structure Example:

Campaign:

Women's Skirts
Lace Skirts
Sequin Skirts
Mini Skirts

Ad Groups:

Mini Skirts	Keywords (Using Mini Skirts Ad Group as an example):
Midi Skirts	
Maxi Skirts	

[mini skirt]	**[black mini skirt]**
[mini skirts]	**[black mini skirts]**

Keyword Match Types

There are several different match types to consider when building out advertisement groups. Match types distinguish how the keywords you are bidding on match searchers' queries. It is important to understand the different options of match types in order to reach your target customer and control the spending of each keyword.

BROAD MATCH

Broad match is the default match type in Google AdWords. It is useful in reaching a larger audience and in determining what your customer is looking for. However, this match type can drive the most irrelevant traffic to your website and can be very costly. Broad match keywords will match to close variations of your targeted keyword, misspellings, and synonyms and can match to queries that contain your targeted keywords in any order. For example:

In the example, not only does "women's hats" match to queries including women's hats, but it also matches to different variations of the term (ladies, girls, etc.)

If "negative keywords" are not used with broad match keywords, broad match keywords can drive irrelevant traffic and be costly. Negative keywords are terms that if included in a search query, your advertisements will not match to them. For example, if you are advertising for strictly women's hats, you would want to include "girls, toddlers, and babies" as negatives to ensure more relevant traffic to your site.

BROAD MATCH MODIFIER

Broad match modifier was introduced in 2010 in order to provide a new option for driving higher visibility of advertisements, but offering more control than broad match. Broad match modifier contains the targeted keyword and close variations in any order but will not match to synonyms or similar searches, ensuring that more relevant traffic will be driven to your website. For example:

Board match keyword	Ads may show on searches
women's hats	women's hats
	buy ladies hats
	womens caps
	hats for girls
	woman's hats
	buy red hats for women

Board match modifer	Ads may show on searches for	Ads won't show on searches for
+women's +hats	women's hats	helmets for women
	buy women's hats	women's visors
	hats for women	

In the example above, +women's +hats matches to close variations of the term, but not synonyms.

PHRASE MATCH

Phrase match keywords help drive more relevant traffic to a website than broad match or broad match modifier, and contain the targeted keyword or phrase or close variations, but in the exact order listed. There can be additional words in front of or following the phrase, but the phrase will only match to a query that is in the exact order specified.

In the example for "women's hats," advertisements can match to the phrase when the word "buy" is featured in the search query, since the phrase is included in the exact order.

EXACT MATCH

Exact match keywords offer more granularity than all other match type options. Exact match will only surface advertisements for searches for the exact keyword. This option offers the best control and the best relevancy of traffic to your site, but can narrow visibility if the exact keyword does not have a high enough search volume. Advertisements only surface for the exact keyword, [women's hats].

" UNDERSTANDING SEO–OR KNOWING SOMEONE WHO DOES–
IS AN ESSENTIAL FOR DIGITAL MARKETERS. WITH SEARCH
ONE OF THE MAJOR WAYS PEOPLE DISCOVER CONTENT,
YOU CAN'T AFFORD TO BE IGNORANT HERE."
THIRD DOOR MEDIA

Phrase match keyword	Ads may show on searches for	Ads won't show on searches for
"women's hats"	women's hats	girls hats
	buy women's hats	women's baseball hats
	woman's hats	
	Women's hats	

Exact match keyword	Ads may show on searches for	Ads won't show on searches for
[women's hats]	women's hats	buy women's hats
	woman's hats	women's hats on sale

Key points and terms for searches

Search engine optimization (SEO) refers to the process of generating organic site traffic from the unpaid section of search engine results on Google or any major search engine (SearchEngineLand.com). Since the goal of Google or any other search engine is to provide its searchers with the most relevant and accurate information for every query that passes through the engine, it has an ever-changing algorithm in place to ensure the most relevant listings are served for each query. Think of Google as the world's largest library or index of information. In milliseconds, it processes a search query and populates the most relevant listings relevant to that specified query.

In order to rank at the top of the organic search results for queries relevant to the web pages that an advertiser desires to drive traffic to, webmasters utilize both on-page and off-page optimization efforts to increase the probability of their site ranking on the first page of the search engine results.

On-page optimization involves making adjustments to a website that triggers search engine algorithms and matches the information on the advertiser's website to search queries. On page optimization is performed to influence higher rankings in the search engine results for targeted keywords that are relevant to an advertiser's offerings. Examples of on-page optimization include making adjustments to URL structure, header tags, meta information, relevant images and alt text, content, and internal links. All of these efforts need to be relevant to the subject of the page.

A **URL** refers to the unique address of your web page. URL best practices for SEO include keeping your URL short length, including keywords relevant to the page's subject, separating keywords with hyphens, and being readable to people.

An **H1 Header** appears as larger visible text in the body of the content on the webpage, serving as the title of a page. These titles are crucial for user experience and preface the subject matter of a webpage, but do not hold SEO value as meta titles.

Meta titles (title tags) are the titles of your webpage that surface when you are listing populates in the search results for relevant queries. These titles describe the content of your webpage and are crawled and indexed by search engines. Meta titles are one of the key factors in search engines determining rank and relevancy. Meta titles also surface in the title bar of your website, but are not as visible to users as the H1 tags.

Meta descriptions tags are the descriptions of your web page that surface under the meta title in the search engine results. Though these are not as important as the meta title to the search engine indexing and ranking process, they are important to influence click-through-rate in the search engine results.

Since search engines cannot read the actual content of an image, image alt text is used as a description of the image. Google also uses alt text to index images in the Google Images section. Also, if an image does not render for any reason, this text will populate and is important for user experience.

Off-page optimization refers to any efforts that are performed beyond an advertiser's website that build authority across the Web, and cultivate higher listings in the search results. Off-page optimization includes, but is not limited to, link building, social media signals, and user reviews.

Search engines use links as a way to navigate through pages across the Web, distinguish how pages are related to one another, and determine the authority of pages. **Link Building** refers to the process of gaining hyperlinks from other websites back to your own and is one of the most important components of SEO, while determining rankings. Search engines essentially treat links as votes for favorability and relevancy. If a web page has many credible websites linking back to its page, the search engines will deem the page as a credible source. Although link building can be one of the most difficult aspects of search engine optimization, it can be the most successful method used in establishing first page rankings.

Contributing Expert: Courtney Messerli is currently the Global SEO Specialist at Anthropologie, formerly the Marketing Specialist for SEM and SEO for Nasty Gal at Los Angeles, California. She is passionate about the search industry and lectures on topics as an industry expert. Messerli continues to extend her collaborating expertise.

6.16

THE PERIODIC TABLE OF SEO SUCCESS FACTORS

Search engine optimization — SEO — seems like alchemy to the uninitiated. But there's a science to it. Below are some important "ranking factors" and best practices that can lead to success with both search engines and searchers.

ON-THE-PAGE SEO

OFF-THE-PAGE SEO

CONTENT | ARCHITECTURE | HTML | TRUST | LINKS | PERSONAL | SOCIAL

Cq +3 Quality	Ac +3 Crawl	Ht +3 Titles	Ta +3 Authority	Lq +3 Quality	Pc +3 Country	Sr +2 Reputation
Cr +3 Research	Ad +2 Duplicate	Hd +2 Description	Te +2 Engage	Lt +2 Text	Pl +3 Locality	Ss +1 Shares
Cw +2 Words	Am +2 Mobile	Hs +2 Structure	Th +1 History	Ln +1 Numbers	Ph +3 History	
Cf +2 Fresh	As +1 Speed	Hh +1 Headers	Ti +1 Identity	Vp -2 Paid	Ps +2 Social	
Cv +2 Vertical	Au +1 URLs	Vs -2 Stuffing	Vd -1 Piracy	Vl -3 Spam		
Ca +1 Answers	Ah +1 HTTPS	Vh -1 Hidden	Va -1 Ads			
Vt -2 Thin	Vc -3 Cloaking					

FACTORS WORK TOGETHER

All factors on the table are important, but those marked 3 carry more weight than 1 or 2. No single factor guarantees top rankings or success, but having several favorable ones increases the odds. Negative "violation" factors shown in red harm your chances.

Written By: **Search Engine Land**
Design By: COLUMN FIVE
Copyright Third Door Media
Learn More: http://sefind.com/seotable

ON-THE-PAGE FACTORS
These elements are in the direct control of the publisher

CONTENT

Cq	QUALITY	Are pages well written & have substantial quality content?
Cr	RESEARCH	Have you researched the keywords people may use to find your content?
Cw	WORDS	Do pages use words & phrases you hope they'll be found for?
Cf	FRESH	Are pages fresh & about "hot" topics?
Cv	VERTICAL	Do you have image, local, news, video or other vertical content?
Ca	ANSWERS	Is your content turned into direct answers within search results?
Vt	THIN	Is content "thin" or "shallow" & lacking substance?

ARCHITECTURE

Ac	CRAWL	Can search engines easily "crawl" pages on site?
Ad	DUPLICATE	Does site manage duplicate content issues well?
Am	MOBILE	Does your site work well for mobile devices & make use of app indexing?
As	SPEED	Does site load quickly?
Au	URLS	Do URLs contain meaningful keywords to page topics?
Ah	HTTPS	Does site use HTTPS to provide secure connection for visitors?
Vc	CLOAKING	Do you show search engines different pages than humans?

HTML

Ht	TITLES	Do HTML title tags contain keywords relevant to page topics?
Hd	DESCRIPTION	Do meta description tags describe what pages are about?
Hs	STRUCTURE	Do pages use structured data to enhance listings?
Hh	HEADERS	Do headlines & subheads use header tags with relevant keywords?
Vs	STUFFING	Do you excessively use words you want pages to be found for?
Vh	HIDDEN	Do colors or design "hide" words you want pages to be found for?

OFF-THE-PAGE FACTORS
Elements influenced by readers, visitors & other publishers

TRUST

Ta	AUTHORITY	Do links, shares & other factors make site a trusted authority?
Te	ENGAGE	Do visitors spend time reading or "bounce" away quickly?
Th	HISTORY	Has site or its domain been around a long time, operating in same way?
Ti	IDENTITY	Does site use means to verify its identity & that of authors?
Vd	PIRACY	Has site been flagged for hosting pirated content?
Va	ADS	Is your content ad-heavy, especially "above-the-fold"?

LINKS

Lq	QUALITY	Are links from trusted, quality or respected web sites?
Lt	TEXT	Do links pointing at pages use words you hope they'll be found for?
Ln	NUMBER	Do many links point at your web pages?
Vp	PAID	Have you purchased links in hopes of better rankings?
Vl	SPAM	Have you created links by spamming blogs, forums or other places?

PERSONAL

Pc	COUNTRY	What country is someone located in?
Pl	LOCALITY	What city or local area is someone located in?
Ph	HISTORY	Has someone regularly visited your site or socially favored it?
Ps	SOCIAL	Has someone or their friends socially favored the site?

SOCIAL

| Sr | REPUTATION | Do those respected on social networks share your content? |
| Ss | SHARES | Do many share your content on social networks? |

6.16
The Periodic Table of SEO Success Factors

JOURNEY MAPPING

CONTRIBUTING WRITER CLAUDIA UKONU

Consumer surveillance is the practice of accumulating specific information about consumers such as age, gender, credit score, and location, which companies use to determine and predict consumer behavior (Steel, 2013). Acxiom and Experian are two major providers of consumer data in the United States. They collect and sell consumer information to individuals, businesses, and the government. This consumer data becomes a strategic asset for organizations as it reveals the behaviors of their end users, which ultimately allows them to develop new products and services that are specifically tailored to target these users.

In an environment where "90 percent of consumers now move 'sequentially' between different screens" (Olenski, 2012), it is essential that brands develop marketing strategies and content that touch each of these devices and the various other touch points or points of contact, such as online reviews, brand websites, social media, and emails that consumers interact with. The multi-touch point of view for developing marketing strategies creates a seamless story or presentation of the brand (Nguyen, 2015). This seamlessness is especially vital for e-commerce brands where consumers in this environment focus much of their attention on the brand's website, social media platforms, and other online channels (Hazan and Wagener, 2012). With online retail sales projected to grow to $512 billion by 2020 (FTI Consulting, n.d.), aligning a brand's messaging to the behavior of their consumers is a major incentive for them to leverage their data as a means for ensuring that they capture a portion of these potential sales.

Consumers nowadays demand exactly what types of products and services they want, which poses a challenge for brands to meet and even surpass those demands. With more and more brands trying to create seamless stories of their key messages, data becomes a vital component, playing the role of an investigator while revealing key insights about the consumer. In addition to this challenge, brands must also determine how to extract meaningful insights from the data and how it can be leveraged to develop a multi-touch marketing strategy that puts the brand in a situation where it is influencing the consumer throughout the consumer's decision-making process.

Goals for the brand can include increasing awareness among new consumers, retaining existing customers, and increasing sales. Once the brand collects and analyzes the data, the information can be used to develop a framework that allows for the tracking and predicting of consumer behavior to be utilized in conjunction with the development of the multi-touch point strategy. Through this process, brands will be able to identify specific triggers at each point of the customer's decision-making process, prompting their users to purchase or react, given certain incentives (Richardson, 2010). Questions that can be answered using this framework include "does offering a new user 20 percent off their first purchase increase the likelihood of conversion" or "does a promoted post on Instagram featuring new merchandise prompt the user to share the post with others?"

Consumer Data

When a user signs up for a new service, subscription, or social media platform, there are clauses in the "Terms and Conditions" and "Privacy Policy" that outline a company's lawful ownership of all information used and uploaded to its platform. For example, Instagram's privacy policy states that they collect information ranging from usernames and passwords to user content, which includes photos and comments (Instagram Privacy Policy, n.d.). In addition to the information collected, Instagram utilizes third-party analytics tools and metadata to track users' engagement and usage on the platform. Lastly, the privacy policy states that Instagram can share your information with any other businesses that are, "…legally part of the group of companies that Instagram is part of…" (Instagram Terms of Use, n.d.), which includes, but is not limited to, Facebook and YouTube. While consumers consent to these terms and conditions upon registration for using platforms such as Instagram, many are unaware of how much of their data is actually being collected, how that information is shared, and who the information is shared with. Associations such as the Digital Advertising Alliance (DAA), American Association of Advertising Agencies (4As), and the Federal Communications Commission (FCC) outline principles for how organizations may collect and use data from consumers. Many of the principles and in some cases laws are often changing due to the fluctuating landscape of technology.

While consumers may not be fully aware of how this data is used, it is a valuable asset to brands. Frequently, the problem with this data is that it comes from multiple channels in different formats and it is difficult to analyze and synthesize into actionable insights. This is why, in many cases, brands will rely on third-party companies like Experian to provide data about their target market.

Buyer Persona

As a brand, it is important to understand and identify the wants and needs of existing customers. By understanding these wants and needs, brands can use this information in their favor to strengthen the loyalty of existing customers while creating awareness for prospective consumers with similar wants and needs. Market research, which can include geographic location, age, gender and buying behavior, can be used to assist in uncovering consumer wants and needs. Formatting these wants, needs, behaviors, and other information into different segment is known as the "buyer persona" or semi-fictional representation of a brand's target customer based on market research (Kusinitz, 2014).

Every customer has a unique set of behaviors and motivations for how he/she shops for goods and services, and within these characteristics, lays the ideal customer for brands. Based on the brand's goals and target market (i.e., sell merchandise to 20-year-olds in Southern California and increase awareness on Instagram), it can begin to build its ideal customer profile or buyer persona. The persona for this specific example would include the gender, age, education level, geographic location, income, and psychographic characteristics such as bargain-hunter or tech-savvy. Brands are not limited to targeting only one persona and in many cases, can segment their total pool consumers into multiple categories with different persona criteria.

The Buyer Journey: Conceptual Framework

Actively listening to the wants and needs of existing consumers is only one part of the equation in developing multi-touch point strategies. Brands must also have an understanding of which channels consumers are interacting with, and have tactics in place for how they plan to fulfill the wants and needs of consumers. Given the overwhelming amount of data collected by brands, it is necessary to apply a framework that can be used to outline how customers purchase products, which data is being collected, how the data can be used, and which touch-points they interact with. "Journey mapping" or the "buyer journey" is a framework that documents how customers experience and interact with a brand (Sorman, 2014).

The buyer journey can be explained in the following four stages (Discover, Learn, Buy, and Advocate) that reveal key information about the "buyer" or consumer ("Understanding, n.d.).

DISCOVER

In a situation where a buyer may be unaware of the existence of a certain brand or the fact that they have a problem or a need to fulfill, it is the role of the brand to create awareness of their offerings in order to spark a buyer's interest. This awareness introduces buyers to a brand and helps them discover that they have a problem or need that requires fulfillment. During the discovery stage, the buyer will research about a brand's offering by utilizing search engines, social media, word-of-mouth, and video sharing sites for product and company reviews. The buyer will also compare the brand's offering with competitors who offer similar products.

LEARN

Once buyers have established what their problem or need is, they learn about the different options available to solve this problem or need. This is the stage where the buyer continues to evaluate the brand's offerings and make comparisons with brands of similar offerings. In instances where buyers visit the brand's website, they may subscribe to the brand's email list, which will provide new information about the buyer. In order to keep the buyer's interest in hopes of prompting them to purchase, brands must ensure that their content and assets are varied and tailored to fit the target persona. Website traffic, email subscriptions, and new followers on social media platforms are some sources from where brands can extract data during the learn stage in the buyer journey.

BUY

After assessing the options of other brands, a buyer selects a brand whose offerings best solve their problem or needs. If the brand's awareness efforts have been successful and their offerings fulfill the buyer's needs, the brand will be able to convert the buyer from a potential to an existing customer. Attributes to a brand's website that allow the buyer to intuitively flow from one section to the next and leading them to complete the purchase process will aid positively in the customer experience that the buyer receives from interacting with the brand.

ADVOCATE

Loyal customers are valuable because they "tend to concentrate their purchases," may be willing to pay more for the received value, and are a good source of "positive word-of-mouth" (Walker and Mullins, 2011). By passing through the first three stages of the buyer journey, buyers now have a clear perception of how they view the brand. In the advocate stage, buyers reach the post purchase stage and begin to discuss their experience associated with the brand. Buyers become advocates by expressing the likes and dislikes of their brand experiences using various mediums such as social media and blogs. This is likely the most crucial stage of the buyer journey for the brand, as it dictates the possibility of retaining the customer. The advocacy stage also reveals gaps in the brand's current strategic marketing efforts. Brands may utilize post-purchase tactics such a referral programs, content, or other incentives to strengthen and reinforce the customer relationship.

CASE STUDY:
Simplified Example of the Buyer Journey*

Patricia is an online user and falls within Topshop's target market of a 20-something living in New York or Los Angeles and either works in fashion or has a desire to do so (Fashion Target Market, n.d.). While browsing the Internet, Patricia sees a Facebook advertisement for Topshop that reads, "Sign up for our email list to receive $20 off your first order." This behavior falls under the Discover stage of the buyer journey. The user then clicks the advertisement and signs up for the email list, browses the Topshop website, adds three items to her "My Bag" but then, does not purchase anything. This behavior moves Patricia through to the Learn stage of the buyer journey.

At this stage, based on the Facebook advertisement, Topshop knows that Patricia either has previously been to their website or was referred by another similar site; they also have her email address and have a good idea of Patricia's likes based on the items in her tote. Topshop would employ the tactic of abandoned cart marketing (Shopping Cart, n.d.) and send out an email blast to Patricia offering for a discount on one of the items she already added to her "My Bag."

After receiving the email with the discount, Patricia decides to purchase all three items she originally abandoned in her "My Bag." Patricia's items arrive to her within the standard four to seven-business days and she is very pleased with her purchase. In fact, Patricia is so pleased that she puts together an outfit using the items she purchased from Topshop and posts an image of her wearing them on Instagram ensuring that she tags the official @Topshop Instagram page along with the hashtags #Topshop, #Topshopstyle, and #fashionlover.

Specific data, such as email open rate, the number of site visits, conversion and retention rates occur throughout different stages of the buyer journey. The email open rate that takes place in the Discovery stage of the journey will tell retailers how successful they were in delivering their intended message, as well as show a direct correlation between an increase in sales and products featured in email. Drawing these kinds of insights at each stage of the journey enables online retailers to influence consumers at each touch point.

*This example is a micro view. On a macro scale, Topshop would look at the aggregate data to identify the common behaviors among their existing and potential consumers and customize their marketing efforts to suite these behaviors.

Putting it into action: developing a strategy with data in mind

A simple way to develop a multi-touch marketing strategy is to utilize the journey-mapping framework to lay out not only the wants and needs of consumers but also to identify the brand's goals for the campaign. Aligning customer touch points with the journey map allows for drawing insight at each stage, ultimately driving the end goals of increasing sales, customer retention, and brand exposure.

Step 1: Defining Goals and Setting Benchmarks

Defining goals is the first step in developing a strategy to target new customers, allowing brands to leverage the data they collect. For the upcoming season, the brand may have a series of new products to offer and want to target a specific persona for these products. Some goals that the brand would want to achieve post campaign are increase sales, increase website traffic, increase conversion, and retain customers. Establishing goals sets the foundation strategy and holds the brand accountable for their projected campaign efforts.

CASE STUDY:
Simplified Example of the Buyer Journey*

Step 2: Audit of Data and Assets

Once the goals are defined, the brand will need to conduct an audit to understand what type of data they are currently collecting, how that data is being stored, and the type of content, assets, and offers they possess. These components are extremely valuable and help drive demand for both new and existing consumers. The current data also acts as a benchmark for how brands can track their progress throughout the campaign lifecycle. In a hypothetical sense, the content, assets, and offers serve as fuel for the brand's demand generation efforts. The audit allows the brand to pinpoint gaps in their existing consumer information and highlights which areas they should invest time and money in for new infrastructure and the creation of more valuable content and assets. While not all gaps will be filled at once, assessing which gaps are greatest and which will have the highest impact, once filled, allows the brand to make incremental changes.

Step 3: Drawing Insights

The third step in developing the strategy is to lay out a customer journey map that is targeted to a specific persona. In instances where the brand is targeting multiple personas, developing more than one journey map can be useful in segmenting the different actions for each profile. Once the journey map is laid out, the brand will want to include which touch points this strategy will focus on, and build their actions based on these points of contact. During the audit of data and assets, the brand will be able to identify gaps in their current setup, which also allows the brand to ask questions about this format. The questions brands ask can include, "During the discovery phase of the buyer journey, what efforts are being put forth to generate demand and satisfy the consumer?" and "What effect have these efforts had on the goals set at the beginning of the campaign?

Step 4: Review and Revise

The execution of the first three steps in developing a strategy (with data in mind) will enable the brand to uncover focus areas for its efforts. The brand will use this information as the basis of the campaign to target a specific persona. For example, during the learn stage of the buyer journey, the buyer subscribes to the brand's email list and follows them on Twitter. The brand will know to focus their efforts on developing relevant content and assets for these touch-points. The implementation and success of the proposed efforts will heavily depend on the maintenance, relevance, and frequency of keeping these efforts current, which is where constant review becomes vital. Proposed tactics will work for some buyer personas while failing for others; brands must be able to recognize the pitfalls and success of their varied marketing efforts. Throughout the campaign, the brand will refer back the original goals and track the performance of the efforts. The performance of the brand's plan must be measured, and this means that standards must be developed against which performance can be evaluated. Revisions should be made accordingly if the established standards are not met to ensure that efforts and investments are not wasted.

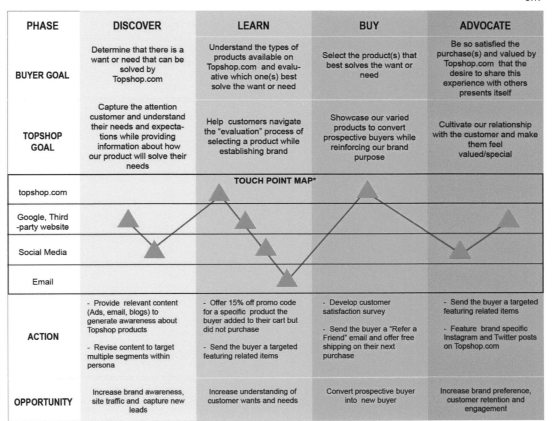

6.17
Topshop's Target Buyer Persona

As the world of e-commerce continues to evolve into an ecosystem that is brand-focused, companies have to shift to a mode of simplification, making an impression with consumers using the simplest messages possible (Fridman, n.d.). Applying a data-driven approach to leverage and uncover insights about consumers will be the key to brands remaining relevant and in demand, as the landscape changes. The role of data across all industries and segments will only continue to gain greater importance as new technologies are created. Brands who fail to utilize and evolve their data collection and data analysis methodologies will struggle to succeed as their competitors take on marketing tactics focused at consumer information. The combination of actively listening to the wants and needs of consumers, mapping actions and goals on the buyer journey, and using data to influence consumer behavior creates the perfect equation for brands to progress into the future. Ultimately, a brand that is focused on actively listening to the buyer while trying to fulfill their needs will have greater viability and longevity. The lifetime value of a customer can always be improved by focusing on loyalty and satisfaction.

Contributing Expert: Claudia Ukonu is the Regional Marketing Leader for Employee Health & Benefits, Asia at Mercer, a global consulting leader. Claudia is based in Hong Kong and her responsibilities include project management support and strategic planning advice on complex and detailed marketing projects across Asia. With a background in B2C marketing, Claudia is always in search of new methods to leverage consumer data specifically in e-commerce environments.

EXERCISES

Critical Thinking: Review the most recent tools of the trade at Google Analytics Academy: https://analyticsacademy.withgoogle.com/explorer

Business Activity: Develop a Campaign Outline—List Your Campaign
1. Select an online retailer such as BCBG.com
2. Develop a campaign outline—list your campaign *(First used for Ad Groups Outline Second used for Ad Group Outline)*
3. Pick two campaigns and develop an Ad Group Outline: minimum five Ad Groups each campaign.
4. Pick one Ad Group from each campaign and develop: Keyword List—minimum ten keywords per Ad Group
5. Pick one Ad Group from each campaign and develop: Ad Copy—minimum two Ad Cop per Ad Group.

Technology Corner
Visit www.google.com/trends/ to see the latest *trends*, data, and visualizations from *Google around the world*. Create a comparable graph for two or more products and services from two or more countries.

REFERENCES

Adword (2015), "What are people shopping for near your stores—and across America?," October 15. Available online: http://adwords.blogspot.com/2015/10/shopping-insights-what-are-people-shopping-for-near-your-stores.html

Approach: Better insights through innovation. (n.d.). In *Affinio*. Available online: http://www.affinio.com/approach

Arthur, R. (2015), "Bloglovin' Data Shows Key Blog Search Terms By Country," *Fashion & Mash*, November 5. Available online: http://fashionandmash.com/2015/11/05/infographic-bloglovin-data-shows-key-blog-search-terms-by-country/

Barua, A., Mani, D. and Mukherjee, R. (n.d.), "Measuring the Business Impacts of Effective Data" [PDF file]. Available online: http://www.datascienceassn.org/sites/default/files/Measuring%20Business%20Impacts%20of%20Effective%20Data%20I.pdf

Bezzant, E. (n.d.), "More Data. With More Data Science Behind It," *EDITED*. Available online: https://edited.com/data/

Business intelligence (n.d.), In *TechTarget*. Retrieved November 21, 2015 from http://searchdatamanagement.techtarget.com/definition/business-intelligence

Biswal, R. (2015), "Top 10 Best Engines in The World," *eCloudBuzz*, July 27. Available online: http://www.ecloudbuzz.com/top-10-best-search-engines-in-the-world/

Chang, L. (2015), "Americans Spend an Alarming Amount of Time Checking Social Media on Their Phones," *Digital Trends*, June 13. Available online: http://www.digitaltrends.com/mobile/informate-report-social-media-smartphone-use/#ixzz3s6hVDYMt

Data (n.d). In *Merriam-Webster*. Retrieved November 21, 2015 from http://www.merriam-webster.com/dictionary/data

Davidson, L. (2015), "Is your daily social media usage higher than average?," *The Telegraph*, May 17. Available online: http://www.telegraph.co.uk/finance/newsbysector/mediatechnologyandtelecoms/11610959/Is-your-daily-social-media-usage-higher-than-average.html

Fashion Target Market (n.d.). In *Topshop*. Available online: https://sites.google.com/site/topshopyellowgroup/fashion-target-market

Fridman, A. (n.d.), "3 Trends Redefining the Future of E-Commerce," *Inc. Magazine*. Available online: http://www.inc.com/adam-fridman/3-trends-redefining-the-future-of-ecommerce.html

FTI Consulting (2014), "FTI Consulting Projects US Online Retail Sales Will Grow to $512 Billion by 2020," *PR Newswire*, December 1. Available online: http://www.prnewswire.com/news-releases/fti-consulting-projects-us-online-retail-sales-will-grow-to-512-billion-by-2020-300002389.html

Gibbs, S. (2013), "Editd aims to spot the trends the fashion world doesn't," *The Guardian*, September 13. Available online: http://www.theguardian.com/technology/2013/sep/13/editd-fashion-trends-big-data

Hazan, E. and Wagener, N. (2012, September). "Get in touch with customer touch points," *McKinsey & Company*. Available online: http://www.mckinsey.com/client_service/marketing_and_sales/latest_thinking/get_in_touch_with_customer_touch_points

Kusinitz, S. (2014), "The Definition of a Buyer Persona" [Web log post], *Hubspot*, March 8. Available online: http://blog.hubspot.com/marketing/buyer-persona-definition-under-100-sr

Macmillion, D. (2015), "Mobile Search Tops at Google," *The Wall Street Journal*, October 8. Available online: http://blogs.wsj.com/digits/2015/10/08/google-says-mobile-searches-surpass-those-on-pcs/

McKinsey Global Institute. (2013, July), "Game changers: Five opportunities for US growth and renewal." Available online: file:///Users/LJFuna/Downloads/MGI_US_game_changers_Full_report_July_2013.pdf

Laney, D. (2012), "Deja VVVu: Others Claiming Gartner's Construct for Big Data," *Gartner*, January 14. Available online: http://blogs.gartner.com/doug-laney/deja-vvvue-others-claiming-gartners-volume-velocity-variety-construct-for-big-data/

Luxury Institute, LLC (2015), "Luxury Institute Survey Shows Big Divide Between Boomers and Millennials in Embrace of New Technology and Relationships With Luxury Brands," Market Wired, March 3. Available online: http://www.marketwired.com/printer_friendly?id=1997131

Nguyen, J. (2015), "Understanding the Multi-Device Consumer" [Presentation]. Available online: http://www.comscore.com/Insights/Presentations-and-Whitepapers/2015/Understanding-the-Multi-Device-Consumer

Olenski, S. (2012), "Consumers Take A Multi-Device Path To Purchase," *Forbes*, December 4. Available online: http://www.forbes.com/sites/marketshare/2012/12/04/consumers-take-a-multi-device-path-to-purchase/

Park, L. (2015), "How to build data-driven Personas to better understand your customer," *Affinio*, November 19. Available online: http://www.affinio.com/blog/how-to-build-data-driven-buyer-personas-to-better-understand-your-customer

Privacy Policy. (n.d.). In *Instagram*. Available online: https://instagram.com/about/legal/privacy/

Richardson, A. (2010), "Touchpoints Bring the Customer Experience to Life," *Harvard Business Review*, December 2. Available online: https://hbr.org/2010/12/touchpoints-bring-the-customer

Rogers, S. (2015), "Affinio raises $4M to help understand social tribes around the globe," *Venture Beat*, November 3. Available online: http://venturebeat.com/2015/11/03/affinio-raise-4m-to-help-understand-social-tribes-around-the-globe/

SAS (n.d.), Big Data, What It Is And Why It Matter, *SAS*. Available online: http://www.sas.com/en_us/insights/big-data/what-is-big-data.html

Shopping cart abandonment (n.d.), In *The Digital Marketing Glossary*. Retrieved November 21, 2015 from http://digitalmarketing-glossary.com/What-is-Shopping-cart-abandonment-definition

Social Network Ad Spending to Hit $23.68 Billion Worldwide in 2015 (2014), eMarketer, April 15. Available online: http://www.emarketer.com/Article/Social-Network-Ad-Spending-Hit-2368-Billion-Worldwide-2015/1012357

Sullivan, D. (2015), "Google Still Doing at Least 1 Trillion Searches Per Year," *Search Engine Land*, January 16. Available online: http://searchengineland.com/google-1-trillion-searches-per-year-212940

Walker, O. C. and Mullins, J. W. (2011), *Marketing strategy: a decision-focused approach* (7th ed.), New York: McGraw-Hill/Irwin.

Glossary

Ambient awareness—social scientists define this as a form of incessant online contact.

Big data—a term used to describe extremely large data sets.

Blog—an online personal journal with reflections, comments, and often, hyperlinks, videos, and photos provided by the writer.

Blogosphere—all of the blogs or bloggers on the Internet regarded collectively.

Brand-driven microsites—or (individual web pages) are exclusively hosted to enable the storytelling communities to create and control a network based on the brand's commonality. A microsite is a dedicated platform that hosts community discussions and is a subset of a brand's main distribution channel (website). Microsites are beneficial because they create spaces for like-minded consumers to connect with each other.

Business intelligence (BI)—is often described as a technology-driven process that transforms raw data into meaningful and actionable information to help in business decisions. Business intelligence programs can also incorporate forms of advanced analytics such as data mining, predictive analytics, and big data analytics.

Business-to-Business (B2B)—the marketing of products to businesses or other organizations for use in production of goods, for use in general business operations, or for resale to other consumers.

Business-to-Consumer (B2C)—these companies focus on selling to individuals and market their products for personal use.

Call-to-action—an instruction to the audience to provoke an immediate response.

Citizen journalism—sometimes referred to as "street" journalism, it puts the public citizen in the active role of being a reporter. This is a volunteer position that enables "real people" disseminate the news or stories they collect, and analyze.

Click through—to click on a link (such as a link for a promotion or advertisement) on a web page that opens a new page or site.

Crowdsourcing—the practice of obtaining needed services, ideas, content, or information by soliciting contributions from a large group of people, especially from the online community, rather than from traditional employees or suppliers. Fashion communities are crowd-sourced websites allowing individuals with a common passion to share content and insights within the group. Users collect and share ideas involving inspiring lifestyle images and organize them based on communal preferences.

Customer relationship management (CRM)—a term that refers to practices, strategies and technologies that companies use to manage and analyze customer interactions and data to better connect with existing customers, with storytelling used to attract potential customers. CRM systems are designed to compile information on customers across different channels, which could include the company's website, telephone, live chat, direct mail, marketing materials, and social media.

Data—a collection of informative facts that are used to calculate, analyze, or plan something.

Digital analytics—according to Google, this the analysis of qualitative and quantitative data from a business and the competition to drive a continual improvement of the online experience that customers and potential customers have, which translates to desired outcomes (both online and offline).

Data mining—the practice of searching through large amounts of usually computerized data to find useful patterns or trends.

Digital curation—the selection, preservation, maintenance, collection, and archiving of digital assets. Digital curation establishes, maintains, and adds value to repositories of digital data for present and future use. Curation enables consumers to express themselves in more meaningful ways; they take great pride in purposefully sharing what they think is funny, interesting, and acceptable to their peers.

Digital SWOT analysis—evaluates the strengths, weaknesses, opportunities, and threats of consumer/audience engagement.

Engagement (intensity of feeling)—on social media, this derived from interactions that occur within online communities. While some forms of engagement are more passive than others, their fundamental goals are to generate traction and drive return-on-investment (ROI).

Fair use—a legal doctrine that portions of copyrighted materials may be used (as by publishing) without permission of the copyright owner, provided the use is fair and reasonable, does not substantially impair the value of the materials, and does not curtail the profits reasonably expected by the owner, such use often being accompanied by fair comment.

Fashion cycle—the amount of time it takes for a fashion trend to emerge, peak, and fall out of style.

Fashion system—a concept that encompasses the business of fashion, the art and craft of fashion, and the production and consumption of fashion. Before the advent of real-time social media feeds, the fashion system followed predictable boundaries of time and space. Fashion collections were set, styles were anticipated, and fashion venues for the collections were globally established, thus setting the tone for the fashion season.

Fast fashion—refers to a phenomenon in the fashion industry, whereby production processes are expedited in order to get new trends to the market as quickly and as cheaply as possible. Fast fashion retailers achieve maximum productivity through efficient planning and manufacturing technologies that increase speed-to-market and thus, the concept-to-commerce process (design, manufacturing, distribution).

Fear of Missing Out (FOMO)—the reason that most people check their phones upon waking up and before going to sleep. Many theories claim that FOMO stems from seeing your peers engage in positive activities on social media, making you compare their lives to yours. FOMO can cause anxiety, stress and, in more extreme cases, depression.

Gamification—the process of adding games or gamelike elements to something (such as a task) so as to encourage participation. It boosts the competitive edge of the "sonic youth generation" who stay connected through their mobile devices. This competitive strategy uses the idea of gamer obsession and converts it to brand marketing through social media interactive campaigns. In a non-gamer context, gamification describes the elements of gaming, including strategy and competition that offer awards to consumers. This marketing strategy prompts users to participate.

Gatekeepers (influencers)—a pre-selected, elite group of fashion editors, collectors, buyers, and celebrities.

Joy of Missing Out (JOMO)—a means by which users can disconnect from the pressures of social media and appreciate their detachment from online communities. By not focusing on others' activities, one can discover and embrace solitude within the digital realm, thus leading to a host of positive outcomes.

Meme—an amusing or interesting item (such as a captioned picture or video or genre of items) that is spread widely on the Internet, especially through social media

On-page optimization—involves making adjustments to a website that triggers search engine algorithms and matches the information on the advertiser's website to search queries. On-page optimization is performed to influence higher rankings in the search engine results for targeted keywords that are relevant to an advertiser's offerings.

Real-time fashion—accessed through top influencers' social media feeds; these live-streamed fashion shows disrupt the classic mode of diffusing innovation, enabling almost any consumer to view merchandise before it becomes available for purchase.

Runway-to-Commerce (R2C)—during some live runway events, attendees can use their smartphones to instantaneously buy items through the event's digital shop. One must be present at the event to buy the merchandise, affording attendees exclusive access to next seasons' fashions, otherwise unavailable until they hit retailers.

Search Engine Marketing (SEM)—refers to the paid advertisements that appear in the top and right-hand sides of a search engine results page. Advertisers bid on a targeted set of keywords, which are triggered by searchers' queries and are ranked through a bidding auction.

Search Engine Optimization (SEO)—refers to the process of generating organic site traffic from the unpaid section of search engine results on Google or any major search engine (SearchEngineLand. com). Since the goal of Google, or any other search engine, is to provide its searchers with the most relevant and accurate information for every query that passes through the engine, it has an ever-changing algorithm in place to ensure the most relevant listings are served for each query.

Share of Voice—a media term that meant how much a brand was outspending the competition to have a presence or "voice" on TV, radio, or print. "Share of voice" is now the activity and volume of conversations taking place in social media.

Glossary

Social confirmation—now measured through engagement and acknowledgment of social media feeds, trends "liked" and commented on, and those shared by the new digital native gatekeepers (digital influencers and fashion bloggers). The "likeability" of a trend can now be measured and evaluated by consumers through social media feeds.

Social currency—acquired from value, insights, and data that result from the collective interaction across social networks and digital communities. Social currency has value to others in social networks, whether it is curated information, opinions, or visual content. This true currency enables social media users to be recognized as impactful on the social communities around them.

Social generations—groups of people who were born in the same date range and share similar cultural experiences (for example: Gen Z or Generation C (1995–2012); iGeneration or Millennials (1986–1994), Gen X (1965–1985) and Baby Boomers (1946–1964)).

Social intelligence—information gathered to create algorithms, enabling it to track trends showing good traction.

Social listening—refers to the assessment and monitoring of what's currently being said about a brand by users of social media networks. Such listening of a select group creates a "skewed perception" of the social audience as well as of the followers as a whole.

Social media marketing (SMM)—a form of Internet marketing that utilizes social networking websites as a marketing tool. The goal of SMM is to produce content that users will share with their social network to help a company increase brand exposure and broaden customer reach. A brand that operates in social media marketing (sharing, comments, networks, blogging, click-throughs) must create a narrative to continuously drive social conversations and brand story movement.

Social transmission—the movement of content across social network channels (e.g. Twitter, Instagram), which drives the process of communication. These encounters are measured by the user's reach and impressions garnered online.

Street fashion—fashion that is considered to have emerged from the grassroots (not studios). Street fashion is generally associated with youth culture and is most often seen in major urban centers

Style-sharing communities—groups of fashion enthusiasts searching and exchanging fashion trends, looks, and inspirations by viewing style portfolios created through user-generated content. Communities can also filter through style-sharers that best match users' style preferences. This "strength in numbers" enables these communities to influence the diffusion of innovation of fashion trends from one market to another. The community looks to others within itself to study, and then incorporate their styles into their own wardrobe.

Trending—to generate or attract a lot of interest or attention especially online and in social media.

User-generated content (UGC)—text and images originating from consumers (users) shared in blogs, wikis, discussion forums, posts, chats, tweets, podcasts, pins, and other digital images. UGC creates a new hybrid of online social community that freely discusses the affirmation or nullification of a brand or product. UGC enables fashion enthusiasts to pool their inspirations and fuel purchases as new users join in with comments or social shopping links. Within the creative community, UGC is one of the most valuable currencies today, ensuring authenticity of shared material within the connected community.

URL (Uniform Resource Locator)—refers to the unique address of a web page. URL best practices for SEO include keeping a URL at a shorter length, including keywords relevant to the page's subject, separating keywords with hyphens, and being readable to people.

Visual marketing—involves the careful positioning and sequencing of a visual narrative with the goal of pushing a brand's context toward its audience.

Word-of-mouth (WOM)—generated by consumers through social media from one consumer to another with the use of social transmission through the vast supply of social media. The spreading of a message through social media characterizes social transmission, which may include verbal and non-verbal communications, actions, behaviors, knowledge, and beliefs.

Index

A

Account Manager, 198
Acxiom, 254
Adaptly, 150
Adidas X Yeezy collection, 51, 66
Advanced Style, 31
advocate stage of buyer journey, 255
Aeropostale, 209
affective response to storytelling, 168
affiliate marketing programs, 29, 33, 188, 196, 204–205
Affinio, 232, 240–243
    Multi-Retailer Summary Report, 242–243
    Net-a-Porter Summary Report, 244–245
Airbnb, 129, 132
Albus, Trina, 196
Aldridge, Jane, 206
Allia, Zach, 81
Almost Girl, 32
ALS Association (ALSA) challenge, 69, 70
Always, 159
Amazon, 85, 129, 205
ambient awareness, 67
Amed, Imran, 34
American Association of Advertising Agencies (4As), 255
AMLUL.COM, 30
Angelou, Maya, 152
Ann Taylor, 88
AOL, 131, 246
Apfel, Iris, 136–137
App Store, 71
ArcLight Cinemas, 133
Art Basel, 158
Arthur, Rachel, 38–39
Art of the Trench (Burberry), 172, 212
ASOS, 48, 77, 114, 235, 236
augmented gamification, 71
authority social proof, 69
Automatic Content Recognition (ACR), 218–219
average-order-value (AOV), 35
Awesomeness TV, 126, 127

B

Baby Boomers, 98, 101, 118, 128, 131, 132, 134–137
Badia, Alex, 15, 50
Bag Borrow or Steal, 129
Baidu, 246
Barbie, 158
@BarbieStyle, 158
bar codes, 223
Barr, Nathaniel, 102
Batliwalla, Navaz, 31
BBH, 48
BCBGMAXAZRIA, 213, 220–221
Bebe, 248
Beckerman sisters, 127
Beckman, David, 131
behavioral science, 69, 70, 71
Berger, Jonah, 67
Bergstein, Jeremy, 224–225
Best, Robert, 158
Beyoncé, 69, 131
Bieber, Justin, 128
big data, 67, 230, 231, 232, 233, 236, 237, 239, 240
Bill Cunningham New York, 2010, 25
Bing, 246, 249
Blair Witch Project, The, 170, 171
Blakely, Johanna, 239
Blanks, Tim, 25, 32

blog, defined, 29
blogger, 18, 30
Blogger Squads, 31
Bloglovin', 246
blogosphere, 28–34
    fashion bloggers' role, 28–29
    fashion blogging movement, 32–33
    innovation changed by, 34
blogrolls, 29
Blonde Salad (Ferragni), 30, 31, 34
Blow, Isabella, 13
BoomAgers, 135
Box, Amber Venz, 31, 221
"Brain in Your Pocket: Evidence That Smartphones are Used to Supplant Thinking, The" (Barr, Pennycook, Stolz and Fugelsang), 102
brand
    awareness through social media tie-ins, 20
    brand-driven microsites, 172–175
    social connection through, 152–153
    voice in story, identifying, 157–159
brand content curators, 213, 214
brand-driven microsites, 172–175
Bremont, 211
Bright.Bazaar, 201
broad match, 250
broad match modifier, 250–251
Brooklyn Circus, 153, 156
Brown, Reggie, 85
Bryanboy, 31
Budget Fashionista, The, 31, 32
Bumpy Pitch, 154–156
Burberry
    Art of the Trench, 172, 212
    "Burberry Dream Team," 163
    digital storytelling success, 172
    runway shows, 20, 48, 52
business intelligence (BI), 15, 34, 235, 237
Business of Fashion, The (BofF), 25, 32, 34, 38, 92, 162
Business-to-Business (B2B), 18, 28, 43
Business-to-Consumer (B2C), 18, 28, 43
buyer persona, 255, 259
buying stage of buyer journey, 255
"Buy Now" button, 48

C

C&A, 71
call-to-action (CTA), 49, 143, 146, 150
Campfire, 170, 171
#CampKateSpade, 199
#CastMeMarc, 212
Catch-A-Choo (#CatchAChoo) Foursquare campaign, 73
celebrity social proof, 69
Chajin, Farah, 154
Chandra, Manish, 10, 27, 216
Chanel, 39, 51, 148–149, 205
Chapple, Ruth, 24
Charlotte Russe, 248
Chen, Eva, 78, 79
Cherry, Alix, 30
Cherry Blossom Girl, 30
Chictopia, 34, 36
Choo, Jimmy, 73, 173
CHOO247 Stylemakers, 173
Christian Dior, 31, 86, 89, 111, 205
"Circus of Fashion, The" (Menkes), 23
citizen journalism, 29, 198, 207, 214
click-through rate (CTR), 207, 249, 252

click-throughs, 62, 128, 146, 205
CNN, 16
Coach, 31
CoachxBloggers, 31
cognitive response to storytelling, 168
Cohen, Ari Seth, 31
Collezioni Donna, 15
comments, 29
commerce on social media, 217
Commission Junction, 205
common thread community, 174
Computers in Human Behavior, 102
consumer data, 255
consumers' expectations, 114–117
content curation, 86
content management system (CMS), 29
Cooke, Justin, 48
Cooley, Charles Horton, 112
copyright/content regulations, 87
cost per acquisition (CPA), 207, 226
cost per click (CPC), 226, 248, 249
costume designers, 208–212
costume-to-e-commerce, 210
Coty Prestige, 68
Council of Fashion Designers of America (CFDA), 13, 20
Coveteur, 31
CP+B, 170
Crawford, Cindy, 16
Crosby, Caitlin, 179
crowd social proof, 70, 71
crowdsourcing, 35, 36, 118, 120, 217, 233
Culmone, Kim, 158
Cunningham, Bill, 25
curators, gatekeeper, 213, 214
Curvy Blogger, 31
Curvy Fashionista, 31
customer relationship management (CRM), 143, 256
Cyberspace, 131
Cypher, Healey, 223

D

Daily Candy Newsletter, 30
Daily Trade Record, 15
Dance of A-Z, The, 174
data, 231–259
    Affinio reports, 242–243
    briefs and personas, 239–245
    contextualizing, 232–233
    defined, 231
    fashion forecasting, 234–238
    journey mapping, 254–259
    Net-a-Porter Summary Report, 244–245
    search, 246–253
    3Vs framework, 231
data contextualization, 232
data mining, 230, 237, 239
Dava, Gregory, 36, 99
Dax, Jürgen, 136
DeAngelit, Meg, 126
degrees of separation, 89
dematerialization, 61
democratization of fashion industry, 22–25
Diamond Cart/DanTDM, The, 126
DIESEL, 174
diffusion of innovation, 17, 36, 43, 148
Digital Advertising Alliance (DAA), 255
digital analytics, 232–233, 240
Digital Brand Architects, 30

digital curation/curators, 6, 7, 188, 213–215
Digital Marketing Coordinator, 197
digital nesting, 101
digital storyboards, 77
digital storytelling
    anatomy of, 144
    areas to focus on, 152
    brand social connection through, 152–153
    brand's voice in story, identifying, 157–159
    case studies, 158–159, 163, 166–167, 175, 179, 182–183
    emotional connection of, with audience, 144
    funnel approach to, 146–149, 150
    hashtags (#), 164–168
    interviews, 154–156, 160–161, 171, 176–177, 180–181
    introduction, 142
    in marketing, 143–161
    neurological response to, 168–169
    perfect story, crafting, 144–145
    role of, 143
    social good marketing and, 178–183
    storygiving, 170–171
    storytelling communities, 172–177
    visual content consumption, 162–163
Digital SWOT Analysis, 64–65
Dior, 31, 86, 89, 111, 205
discovery stage of buyer journey, 255
Disneyrollergirl, 31
DKNY PR Girl®, 82–84
DNR, 15
Dogg, 117
do-it-yourself (DIY) fashion, 19, 29, 120, 122, 126, 132
Dokusha Moderu, 92
Dolce & Gabbana, 45, 51
Domesek, Erica, 206
dot-com commercial in Super Bowl XXXIII, 47–48
dot-com crash, 19
Downing, Ken, 44
Downtown Dava, 36, 99
Drapers, 15
Drybar, 69–70
Dunseth, Brian, 154
Dunst, Kirsten, 32
Dusters California, 161
Duursema, Jan, 222
Dwindle Inc., 160
Dyson, Jenny, 48

E
eBay, 31, 32, 34, 222, 223
Econsultancy, 194–195, 199
EDITED, 50, 110, 232, 233, 234, 235–237
Elle, 18, 30
emoji, 74
empathetic approach, 240
engagement
    defined, 62–63
    disruption, 66
    in influencer marketing, 203
    runway to, 49
    in social media marketing strategy, 189, 191
    trend confirmation through, 50–53
Engle, Mary, 88
Escobar, Ana Maria, 157
Evening Standard, The, 73
exact match, 251
Experian, 254
expert social proof, 69
expiring digital content, 76, 85, 111
extended mind, 102
extended self, 69

F
Facebook, 6, 18, 25, 59, 60, 77, 82, 87, 149, 156, 173, 197, 198
    Baby Boomers on, 136
    BCBG on, 220
    Beyoncé on, 69
    "Buy Button," 217
    in buyer journey, 257
    #CastMeMarc casting call announcement on, 212
    check-ins, 73, 103

degrees of separation and, 89
    digital nesting and, 101
    digital storytelling and, 180–181
    disruption of social media and, 206
    f8 conference, 71
    friends, average (mean) number of, 89
    Gandr app and, 218
    generational adoption of social media and, 118
    Gen X on, 131, 133
    Gen Z girls on, 161
    Insight, 232
    IQ study, 150
    Krochet Kids intl. on, 180–181
    leveraging on, 196
    "likes" on, 60, 71, 212
    Live, 33, 48, 49
    MAGENTA on, 196
    marketing funnel and, 149
    marketing strategies, 192
    micro-blogging and, 78
    Millennials on, 128
    My Social Book, 133
    "News Feed," 103
    rainbow filter, 166
    runway shows on, 33
    sequence approach to advertising, 150
    social behavior impacted by, 59
    social proof and, 71
    "Terms and Conditions" and "Privacy Policy," 255
    tipping point phenomenon and, 74
    "Trainer Hunt" check-ins on, 73
    visual culture and, 162
    Zuckerberg and, 71, 89, 131, 166
Face Hunter, 34
fair use, 87
fair use restrictions, 87
Fashion and Mash, 38–39
fashion bloggers, 28–34
    fashion blogging movement and, 32–33
    first fashion blogger association and community, 33
    innovation changed by, 34
    role of, in fashion industry, 28–29
    timeline, 30–31
fashion blogging movement, 32–33
fashion communities, 36
fashion cycle, 6, 7, 11, 17, 20, 22, 48, 59, 99, 120
Fashion Data + Analytics EDITED.com, 49
fashion forecasting, 234–238
fashion industry
    bloggers and, 28–34
    consumer-directed news about, 16
    democratization of, 22–25
    disruptions that changed, 26–27
    online engagement, 50–53
    runways of the future, 40–49
    before social media, 11–15
    traditional coverage of, 16
    user-generated content, 35–39
FashionNet.com, 18
fashion on-demand consumerism, 216–222
    case studies, 222–223
    interviews, 218–221
    real-time commerce, 216–217
Fashion Revolution Day, 182–183
FashionSpot.com, 18
fashion system
    defined, 17
    evolution of, 18–21
    before social media, 11–15
    social media's influence on, 52, 216
#FashRev, 182
Fast Company Co. Create, 230
fast fashion, 22, 208, 233
Fear of Missing Out (FOMO), 20, 70, 86, 103, 105, 149, 179
Federal Communications Commission (FCC), 255
Federal Trade Commission (FTC), 30, 88
Ferragni, Chiara, 30, 31, 116
Filipowski, Ed, 21
Finney, Kathryn, 31, 32
Firth, Colin, 211
Fischer, Josh, 246

Fitbit, 132
Flickr, 31, 77
Flipbook, 76
Forbes, 38, 39, 128
Ford, Tom, 135
Ford Motor Co., 179
Forever 21, 22, 208, 248
Forrester Research, 135
found footage, filmmaking style, 170
4D presentation, 37, 47
Foursquare, 73
Fredrickson, Julie, 32
French Toast, 31
FreshNetworks, 73
friending, 106
friends' social proof, 70, 71
Furstenberg, Diane von, 20
Future of Retail Report (PSFK), 23

G
Gabifresh, 31
Galliano, John, 13
Game Changers: Five Opportunities for US Growth and Renewal (MGI), 240
gamification, 71–72, 122, 126
Gandr, 217, 218–219
Gap, The, 201
GARAGE Magazine, 25, 32
Garbo, Greta, 25
gatekeepers (influencers)
    bloggers as, 28, 32, 33
    content shared by, 52, 53
    curators, 213, 214
    defined, 11
    disruption caused by, 198, 232
    example of (Anna Wintour), 13
    storytelling funnel, 148
Gates, Bill, 135
Gaultier, Jean-Paul, 18
generation gap, 117–137
    Baby Boomers, 118, 128, 131, 132, 134–137
    behavior/aptitudes, 117–118
    generational adoption of social media and digital space, 118–120
    Gen X, 118, 131–134
    Gen Z, 118, 120–127
    Millennials/Gen Y, 118, 122, 128–130
Generation X (Gen X), 101, 118, 131–134
    adapting online content to offline, 133
    community-supported workouts and health monitors, 132–133
    focus on social media, 132
    Pinterest, 132
Generation Y (Gen Y). *see* Millennials/Gen Y
Generation Z (Gen Z), 77, 85, 98, 109, 112, 118, 120–127
Gentleman Blogger, 30
George Cleverley, 211
Gevinson, Tavi, 31, 123, 125
Girl Is NOT a 4 Letter Word (GN4LW), 160–161
Givenchy, 37, 43
Giving Keys, 179
Gizmodo, 117
Gladwell, Malcolm, 72
God & Beauty, 204
Godin, Seth, 152
Goidel, Melissa, 150
Gonzalez, Cuit, 213, 220–221
Gonzalez, Gala, 30
#GoodIsWinning, 176
Google, 246, 247, 248, 249
Google+, 196, 197, 198
Google Analytics, 246
Google Attribution 360, 246
Google Image Search, 23
Google Play, 71
Googling, 75, 106
GoPro, 161
GQ, 25, 36
Graceffa, Joey, 127
Grammy Awards, 23
Green, R. Kay, 107

Greenfield, Lauren, 159
Griffin, Christopher, 206
Groundswell tool, 90
Gucci, 17, 51
"Guides Concerning the Use of Endorsements in
        Advertising" (FTC), 88
Gunn, Tim, 70

H
halo effect, 69
Hanson, Bailey, 180–181
Harvard University, 31, 90–91
Harvey, Branden, 176–177
hashtag activism, 182
hashtags (#), 164–168
haul video, 77
HeartIFB.com, 33
HelloSociety, 200–201, 214–215
Hermés, 156, 157, 190
Hjelmeseth, Kyle, 204–205
H&M Loves Music collection, 72
H1 Header, 252
Hooper, Ben, 154–156
House of Style, 16
Hubbell, Peter, 135
Hummingbird Bakery, 73
hyper-connected consumers, 99–110
        case study, 110
        digital nesting, 101
        extended mind, 102
        Fear of Missing Out, 103
        interview, 104–105
        Joy of Missing Out, 103
        "Look at Me" culture, 107–109
        measuring moods, 103
        psychological impacts of social media, 102
        social communities, 106

I
"ideal self," 109
iDisorder: Understanding Our Obsession with
        Technology and Overcoming Its Hold on Us
        (Rosen), 104–105
i-D Magazine, 123, 174
i-D X DIESEL, 174
image/sound recognition technology, 217
Immersive Media Entertainment, Research, Science &
        Arts (IMERSA), 168
Independent Fashion Bloggers (IFB), 30, 33
influencer marketing/marketing agencies, 198–212
        case study, 199
        costume designers, 208–212
        interviews, 200–206
        pitch, 208
        social metrics, 207
        of today, 208
Influencer Score Card, 60
Infographics, 168
innovation, diffusion of, 17, 36, 43, 148
Instagram, 6, 7, 20, 23, 28, 30, 31, 38, 59, 60, 181, 197,
        200, 233, 254, 257
        affiliate marketing and, 205
        Baby Boomers on, 136
        BCBG on, 220–221
        Bethany Mota on, 77
        Beyoncé on, 69
        brand voice through, 158, 159
        Chen's announcement on, 78
        crowdsourcing and, 217
        digital curation and, 213
        digital nesting and, 101
        digital tipping point phenomenon and, 72
        disruption of social media and, 206
        Fall/Winter Valentino show, 2015, 42
        Ford's public service announcement on, 179
        Gen X on, 131, 133
        Gen Z girls on, 161
        influencer marketing and, 203
        Instapurge, 80–81
        leveraging on, 196
        limited-time content, 111
        MAGENTA on, 196

Michael Kors' first sponsored content on, 78
        micro-blogging and, 78
        Millennials on, 128
        Pretty Little Liars on, 209
        runway shows on, 33, 47, 49, 220–221
        selfies, 110
        social behavior impacted by, 59, 60
        Stories, 85
        storygiving and, 170
        "Terms and Conditions" and "Privacy Policy," 255
        trend confirmation and, 50
        visual culture and, 162
INstock, 232
Intel, 101
iPhone, 11, 61, 161, 218
iTunes, 48, 69

J
Jacob, Jennine, 31, 33
Jacobs, Marc, 31, 39, 68, 89, 135, 212
Jak & Jil blog, 25
Janette, Misha, 92–93
Japan Times, The, 92–93
J. Crew, 136
Jenner, Kylie, 110
Jimmy Choo brand, 73
J-Lo, 23
Jobs, Steve, 135
journey mapping, 254–259
        buyer persona, 255, 259
        conceptual framework of, 256
        consumer data in, 255
        example of, simplified, 257–258
Joy of Missing Out (JOMO), 103
Juice Served Here, 202

K
Karan, Donna, 16, 20–21, 82–83, 84
Kardashian, Kim, 131
Karp, David, 31
Kate Spade, 114, 151, 225
Kate Spade Camp, 199
Kate Spade Saturday, 222
Kenzo's tiger sweatshirt, 24
keyword match types, 250–251
        broad match, 250
        broad match modifier, 250–251
        exact match, 251
        phase match, 251
        quality score of, 249
Kia, Raman, 151
Kickstarter, 117
Kill the Night (Lim), 222
Kingsman: The Secret Service, 210, 211
Kjaer, Anne Lise, 23
Klensch, Elsa, 16
Klum, Heidi, 70
Kozinets, Robert, 106
Krochet Kids intl., 180–181

L
Lady Gaga, 77, 167
"Lady Gaga Constellation" window display, 225
Lagerfeld, Karl, 123
Lantz, Ed, 168
Lau, Susanna, 18, 30, 207
laws and regulations for social media, 87–88
        applicability of FTC law to online advertising, 88
        copyright/content regulations, 87
        fair use restrictions, 87
learning stage of buyer journey, 255
Leave Your Mark (Licht), 84
Leave Your Mark, LLC, 82, 84
Leon, Humberto, 165
Leverage New Age Media, 75, 76
LGBT community, 166
Licht, Aliza, 82–84
"Like A Girl" campaign, 159
LikeToKnow.it, 31, 52, 205, 217, 220, 221
Lim, Phillip, 222
limited-time content, 111–112
Line, Mandi, 209

Link Building, 252
LinkedIn, 78, 197, 198
Linkshare, 205
LiveJournal, 18, 29, 30
Loft, 88
London Fashion Week, 13, 40–41, 48, 49
"Long Boarding for Peace," 161
"look at me, I'm just like you," 111
"Look at Me" culture, 107–109
Lookbook.nu, 23, 34, 35, 36
Looking Glass Self, 112
Louis Vuitton, 51, 86
Lounge Lover, 73
#LoveWins, 166
low-touch luxury market, 86, 244
Lucky magazine, 78
LuLus, 248
Luxury Institute, 244
Lycos, 246

M
Mackintosh, 211
Macy's, 136, 242, 243
Madonna, 130, 210
MAGENTA, 196
Man Repeller (Medine), 30, 31, 34
marketing funnel, 146–149, 150
Marks & Spencer's Shwop, 128
Mashable, 117
Massenet, Natalie, 131, 210
MATTE BLACK, 188, 202–203
Mattel, Inc., 158
Matthews, Chelsea, 188, 202–203
Max CPC (maximum cost per click), 249
MayBaby, 126
McDonald, James, 206
McKinsey Global Institute (MGI), 240
McNeill, Caitlin, 167
McQueen, Alexander, 13, 30, 39, 40
media, defined, 75
media sharing, 77
Medine, Leandra, 30, 31
meme, 38, 191
Menkes, Suzy, 20, 24
Messerlin, Courtney, 247
meta descriptions tags, 252
meta titles (title tags), 252
Michael Kors, 78
micro-blogging/blogs, 67, 78
microsites, brand-driven, 172–175
Middleton, Daniel, 126
Milan Fashion Week, 158
Milgram, Stanley, 89
Millennials/Gen Y, 39, 77, 85, 118, 122, 128–130
Mindcraft, 126
Minkoff, Rebecca, 49
Mr. Porter, 210
MJ Daisy fragrances, 68
mobile storefronts, 223–225
Molin, Janelle, 86
Monello, Mike, 170, 171
moods, measuring, 103
Moore, Booth, 29, 35, 63
Mortons, 73
Moss, Kate, 131
Mota, Bethany, 77, 126
motion-tracking devices, 132–133
MTV, 16, 120, 130, 131
Multi-Retailer Summary Report (Affino), 242–243
Murphy, Bobby, 85
"Museum of Me," 101
My Social Book, 133
MySpace, 18, 60, 74

N
Naggiar, Caroline, 175
Nasty Gal, 129
Neely, Rumi, 31
Neiman Marcus, 44, 242, 243
Net-a-Porter, 210
        Summary Report, 244–245
Net Generation. see Generation X (Gen X)

Netiquette, 115
netnography, 106
networks, social media, 75–86
neurological response to storytelling, 168–169
"new" factor, 113
New York Fashion Week, 25, 27, 30, 31, 32, 37, 66, 92, 116, 158, 220
New York Times, 25, 32, 43, 82, 105
"Next Season Now, The," 40
Nike, 157
Nike+ Friends, 133
NikeFuel band, 133
Nordstrom, 69–70, 165, 237, 242, 243, 248
Nuttall, Lindsay, 48

O

Oakley, Tyler, 126
Obama, Barack, 166
off-page optimization, 252
One for One Promise, 128
on-page optimization, 252
Onstrander, John, 222
Open Diary, 30
Original Winger, The, 154
Oroton's, 157
Oscars, 63
outfits of the day (#OOTD), 28
Oxford Circus, 49
Oxford Dictionaries, 74
Oxford New Monitor corpus, 74

P

paparazzi, 27
Peacocking, 25
Pearson, Lisa, 232
Pedraza, Milton, 244
Pepperjam, 205
periodic table of content marketing (Econsultancy), 194–195
Periscope, 161, 200
Pernet, Diane, 30
Pew Research Center, 89, 115, 116, 117
phase match, 251
Phillips, Arianne, 210–211
Picaboo. *see* Snapchat
Pinterest, 17, 20, 23, 35, 38, 52, 173, 181, 197, 198, 200
    "Buy Button," 217
    digital nesting and, 101
    fair use restrictions and, 87
    Gen X on, 132
    MAGENTA on, 196
    pinning images on, 87, 149
    "Popular on Pinterest" tags, 70
    social bookmarking and, 76
    social proof and, 70
pitch, 208
Platinum Edition (Beyoncé), 69
Pokémon GO, 71
Poland Snapchat gamification (urban chase) campaign, 72
#PolyData, 50
Polyvore, 17, 35, 38, 50, 52, 76, 77, 106, 198
Pomerantz, Lisa, 78
Poshmark, 10, 27, 106, 129, 216
"Power of Storytelling: Taking a Sequenced Approach to Digital Marketing, The" (Facebook IQ), 150
Prada, Miuccia, 123
predictive analytics, 237
Pret-a-Reporter, 29, 35, 63
Pretty Little Liars, 209, 218, 219
Prince and Princess of Wales, 130
"Privacy Policy," 255
Procter & Gamble, 159
product listing advertisements (PLAs), 247
Project Runway, Mercedes-Benz Fashion Week, Spring 2015, 70
PSFK, 23, 224
P.S. I Made This, 206
psychological impacts of social media, 102
"public-audience project," 43

Q

QR (Quick Response Code), 223

R

rainbow filter, 166
Ralph Lauren, 37, 47
Ramsey, Stewart, 180–181
Rana Plaza, 182–183
R.E.A.L.L.Y. framework, 91
"real self," 109
real-time commerce, 216–217
real-time fashion, 22–23, 43, 216
Rebecca Minkoff NYC, 71
Refinery29, 150
Rent the Runway, 129
return on investment (ROI), 62, 194, 230
RewardStyle, 31, 205, 220, 221
Rhodes, Matt, 73
Rigby, Darrell, 114
RJK Project, 151
Robbins, Brian, 126, 127
Rodic, Yvan, 34
Rodin, Linda, 136
Rogers, Carl, 109
Roman Originals, 167
Rookie Magazine, 125
Rosen, Larry, 74, 104–105
runway shows, 21, 22, 23, 26, 31, 32, 33
    Adidas X Yeezy collection, 51, 66
    Alexander McQueen Spring 1999, 40–41
    brand awareness through social media tie-ins at, 20
    Burberry's, 20, 48, 52
    as entertainment, 47–48
    first ready-to-shop, on Instagram, 220, 221
    4D presentation, 37, 47
    future of, 47–49
    Givenchy Spring/Summer 2016 collection, 37
    Kanye West's, 51, 66
    live-streaming, 17, 20, 22, 40, 44, 48, 66, 148, 233
    luxury, 86, 111
    Project Runway, 70
    real-time, instant access to, 217
    Runway-to-Commerce (R2C), 48
    "See-Now-Buy-Now" and, 40, 52
    shoppable, 26, 48, 218, 221
    for social confirmation of a trend, 50
    before social media, 15, 17
    social media engagement and, 49
    Spring 2015 collection from Polo Ralph Lauren, 37, 47
    Tokyo Girls Collection, 46, 48
    2015 Fall/Winter Valentino show, 42, 43, 44
    Victoria's Secret Fashion Show, 47
    Vogue website runway, 51
Runway-to-Commerce (R2C), 48

S

"safe zone" of social media, 111
Saks Fifth Avenue, 235, 242, 243
same-sex marriage, 166
Samii, Leila, 90–91
Sarin, Tania, 28
Sartorialist, The, 30, 172
Sauvaire, Sheena, 48
Scandal, 219
Schiffer, Claudia, 16
Schmidt, Eric, 23
Schulman, Joshua, 73
Schuman, Scott, 30, 172
Science Project, 224–225
Scoglio, Damian F., 218–219
Seal, Moorea, 201
Sea of Shoes, 206
search, 246–253
    key points and terms for, 252
    keyword match types, 250–251
    organic *vs.* paid, 247, 249
    search engine marketing, 197, 230, 249
    search engine optimization, 67, 230, 246, 249, 252, 253
    search engine results page, 248
    search engines, 246
search engine marketing (SEM), 197, 230, 249
search engine optimization (SEO), 230, 246, 249
    defined, 252
    periodic table of SEO success factors, 253

social currency and, 67
URL best practices for, 252
Searchmetrics, 246
secret application. *see* expiring digital content
"See-Now-Buy-Now," 40, 48, 51, 52
"self," 109
self-destructing application. *see* expiring digital content
selfies, 45, 63, 107–110
self-published blogs, 29
Sensor Tower Store, 71
Sephora, 196
sequenced approach to digital marketing, 150
SERP (search engine results page), 248
Seven Super Girls, 126
Shaded View on Fashion, A (ASVOF), 30
Share a Sale, 205
share of voice, 190
sharing economy, 129
"shopability" of website, 77
Shopping Insights, 238
ShopTheFloor, 206
Short, James E., 72
Sin City (Lim, Onstrander, and Duursema), 222
Singer, Lori, 68
Singhal, Amit, 246
Six Degrees of Separation Theory, 89
skewed perception, 63
"small-world experiment," 89
smartphones, 61, 72, 74, 102, 223
Smith, Katie, 235–237
Snapchat, 6, 85–86
    Brandon Harvey on, 176
    digital tipping point phenomenon and, 72
    expiring digital content, 76, 85, 111
    filters, 166
    Gen Z girls on, 161
    influencer marketing and, 203
    Live Story, 86
    luxury market and, 86
    MAGENTA on, 196
    Millennials on, 128
    Pretty Little Liars on, 209
    read receipts, 102
    runway shows on, 33, 42, 44
    storygiving, 170
    tipping point phenomenon and, 72
    unedited sharing on, 111
    urban chase and, 72
social, defined, 75
"Social Affinity Engine" technology, 241
social behavior on social media, evolution of, 111–117
    consumers' expectations, 114–117
    limited-time content, 111–112
    "look at me, I'm just like you," 111
    Looking Glass Self, 112
    "new" factor, 113
    "safe zone" of social media, 111
    unedited sharing, 111
social bookmarking, 76
social communities, 106
social confirmation, 22, 50, 53, 70, 71, 110, 128, 157, 174
social currency, 67–69
social engagement, 62–63
    disruption, 66
social exploration, 64–67
    ambient awareness, 67
    Digital SWOT Analysis, 64–65
    social engagement disruption, 66
social good marketing, 178–183
social intelligence, 23, 232
social listening, 63, 64
social media
    comparison infographic, 75, 76
    defined, 11
    directional flow of trend before, 17
    fundamentals of, 59–61
Social Media and the Cost of Caring (Pew Research Center), 115
social media channels, 75–79
    comparison infographic, 75, 76
    media sharing, 77
    micro-blogging, 78
    social bookmarking, 76

Social Media Community Manager, 198
Social Media Copywriter, 197
Social Media Director, 197
social media marketing
    affiliate marketing programs, 29, 33, 188, 196,
        204–205
    competitive, 192
    consideration set, 190
    conversation, 192
    cost reduction, 192
    customer service, 192
    digital storytelling in, 143–161
    education, 192
    engagement in, 189, 191
    global perspective of, 89–93
    goal, 191
    influencer marketing/marketing agencies, 198–212
    interviews, 90–93
    leadership, 192
    listening campaign, 191
    MAGENTA, 196
    measurement, 194
    objective, 191
    periodic table of content marketing, 194–195
    real-time marketing strategies, 190–196, 197
    research, 192
    return on investment (ROI), 194
    search engine marketing, 197, 230, 249
    sequenced approach to, 150
    social good marketing, 178–183
    social media strategic outline, 189
    strategy activation, 191
    strategy foundation, building, 190
    strategy plan, developing, 190–191
    successful, tips for, 193
    tactics and phases in, 191
    timing, 192
Social Media Marketing Manager, 197
social media marketing team, 197–198
    Account Manager, 198
    Digital Marketing Coordinator, 197
    Social Media Community Manager, 198
    Social Media Copywriter, 197
    Social Media Director, 197
    Social Media Marketing Manager, 197
    Social Media Strategist, 198
social media networks, 75–86
Social Media Strategist, 198
social metrics, 207
social phobia, 102
social proof, 69–71
Song, Aimee, 30, 31
Song of Style, 30, 31, 34
sonic youth generation, 71
Spiegel, Evan, 85, 111, 128
Spotify, 132
#SquadGoals, 31
Stefani, Gwen, 131
Stiller, Ben, 43, 44
storefronts, mobile interactive shoppable, 223–225
Storify, 76
storyboards, digital, 77
storygiving, 170–171
storytelling brand community, 172–177
    approach/setting goals, 173
    case study, 175
    common thread community, 174
    interview, 176–177
    motivation/incentive to co-create, 174
    reaching, 173
Stratmann, Jo, 73
Strava, 132
Strogatz, Steven, 89
StumbleUpon, 76
"Style at Every Age" program, 136
Style Bubble, 18, 30, 34
Style.com, 25, 32, 52, 53, 149
Style Feed: The World's Top Fashion Blogs (Lau), 18
Style Rookie, 31, 123
Styles, Harry, 128
Style Sharing Communities, 26, 35–39
StyleSight.com, 19

Style with Elsa Klensch, 16
Stylus Fashion, 24
subscriptions, 29
Sutton, Jacob, 174
Swift, Taylor, 167
SWOT Analysis, Digital, 64–65
Sybase Company, 240
Systrom, Kevin, 78, 131
Szumowski, Wojtek, 170

T
Takada, Kenzo, 92
Take My Picture (GARAGE Magazine), 25, 32
Target, 70
Teana Nails, 165
TechCrunch, 67, 117
Ted Baker, 201
"Teen Vogue Blogger Lounge," 206
Teen Vogue Magazine, 206
"Terms and Conditions," 255
#TheDress, 167
Theodore, Ouigi, 153
third party curators, 213
3Vs framework, 231
Tiffany & Co., 175
tiger sweatshirt, Kenzo's, 24
Tipping Point, The (Gladwell), 72
Tisci, Riccardo, 43
TokyoFashionDiaries.com, 92–93
Tokyo Girls Collection, 46, 48
TOMS, 128
Ton, Tommy, 25
Topshop, 48–49, 52, 114, 235, 248, 257, 259
trackbacks, 29
traditional media, 11, 16, 33, 38, 162
"Trainer Hunt" check-ins, 73
Treacy, Philip, 13
Treasure Chest Vintage, 31
trendboard collages, 77
trend confirmation, 50–53
trend forecasting, 17, 19. see also fashion forecasting
True Love, 175
Tumblr, 31, 78, 87, 167, 217
Turnbull & Asser, 211
Tweet Shop, 68
Twitter, 6, 18, 180, 181, 192, 197, 198, 220
    Affinio reports and, 242, 243, 244
    ambient awareness and, 67
    Baby Boomers on, 135
    Bethany Mota on, 77
    Beyoncé on, 69
    "Buy Button," 217
    buyer journey and, 258
    #CastMeMarc casting call announcement on, 212
    disruption of social media and, 206
    DKNY PR Girl and, 82–84
    fair use restrictions and, 87
    Gandr app and, 218
    generational adoption of social media and, 118
    Gen Z girls on, 161
    impact on social behavior, 59, 60
    "Made to Order" function, 48
    MAGENTA, 196
    micro-blogging and, 78
    Net-a-Porter account, 244
    Polyvore data tweets, 50, 77
    Pretty Little Liars and, 209
    retweeting, 87, 109, 122
    runway shows on, 31, 44, 48
    selfies on, 63
    TopShop on, 48, 52
    "Trainer Hunt" check-ins on, 73
    trend confirmation and, 50
    Twitter TV, 209

U
Uber, 129, 132, 218
Ulta, 196
unedited sharing, 111
Università degli Studi di Milano, 89
University of Texas at Austin, 240
urban chase, 72

Urban Outfitters, 114
URL (Uniform Resource Locator), 252
user-generated content (UGC), 35–39, 60, 77, 78
user social proof, 69–70

V
Valentino, 24, 42, 43, 44, 51, 86
variety, in 3Vs framework, 231
Vaughn, Matthew, 210–211
Vaynerchuk, Gary, 100
velocity, in 3Vs framework, 231
Versace, Gianni, 16, 23
V for Vendetta (Lim, Onstrander, and Duursema), 222
Victoria's Secret Fashion Show, 47
Vimeo, 77
Vine, 78, 111, 200
visual content consumption, 162–163
visual culture, 162
visual marketing, 153
vloggers, 43, 77, 214
Vogue, 13, 24, 30, 32, 51, 77, 89
volume, in 3Vs framework, 231

W
Waldron, Zoe, 200–201
Warby Parker, 129
Watts, Geoff, 233
WEAR, 93, 217
Web 2.0, 11, 78, 153
web logs, 29
WeChat, 128
Weibo, 78
West, Kanye, 51, 66
WhatsApp, 128
What Social Media Analytics Can't Tell You
        (Samuel and Reid), 63
White, Constance, 32, 34
White, India, 240–241
Whitehead, Cindy, 160–161
#WhoMadeMyClothes, 182
Wilson, Owen, 43, 44
Wintour, Anna, 13, 20, 30, 32, 123
Wiseman, Eva, 125
Wistia Video Analytics, 112
Witherspoon, Reese, 32
Women's Wear Daily (WWD), 7, 15, 20, 31, 32, 44,
        198, 224
word-of-mouth, 17, 34, 64, 69, 149, 159
WordPress, 31, 32
"world-scale social-network graph-distance
        computation," 89
World Wrestling Entertainment, Inc. (WWE), 242
Worth Global Style Network (WGSN), 19, 38, 232
WWDMAGIC, 15, 202, 206, 208

Y
Yahoo, 246
Yamamoto, Yohji, 92
Yambao, Bryan Grey, 31
Yandex, 246
YouTube, 160, 192
    Bethany Mota on, 77
    #CastMeMarc casting call announcement on, 212
    Gen Z on, 122, 126–127
    haul video on, 77
    MAGENTA on, 196
    media sharing on, 77
    social behavior impacted by, 59, 60
    social media strategies and, 200
    "Terms and Conditions" and "Privacy Policy," 255
    tipping point phenomenon and, 74
    vloggers, 214
    "webisode" series, 126

Z
Zappos, 248
zeitgeist, 7, 15
Zoolander 2, 42, 43
Zorpas, Matthew, 30
Zuckerberg, Mark, 71, 89, 131, 166

Acknowledgments

This book is dedicated to my loving husband Greg, my daughters Morgan and Samantha, and to my father John. Thank you for supporting me throughout this journey with your endless love and support.
#MyFamily

Special honor to my mother Kay who taught me to laugh often and enjoy life's moments.

Many thanks to all who have helped me bring an idea together–to create a textbook that I could proudly share with the next generation of students venturing into the digital-driven world of fashion. I learned that it truly takes a village to generate all the academic research and industry insight that goes into creating a textbook. There is no way to thank the many people who deserve acknowledgement into of couple pages, but do know that all who have helped, I am forever grateful and promise to pass it on to others.

I feel overwhelmed by the support from all, especially from Mine Üçok Hughes, my first academic research partner and the woman who encouraged me to complete this book after many long nights of research; the entire Woodbury University School of Business community for continuous encouragement and support along the way. Special thanks to Keith Nishida, from Woodbury's fashion marketing department, for his insightful direction and late night debates about the world of social media; Teri Thompson whose industry knowledge and academic guidance and late night calls encouraged me along the way; three research assistants who went beyond the call of duty and took on many long hours to bring this book to life, including Kallie Hoxter and Mallory Quiroa who inspired me with their point of view of the fashion industry.

I would also like to thank those who have helped me in my career. My interest in the world of computer science and the fashion industry began in the early 1990s when I started college. While that may not sound like an unusual collaboration nowadays, back in the early 1990s, this was not the normality. I would like to thank the Woodbury University fashion marketing department chair at that time, Karen Kaigler-Walker for letting a little girl take on technology and write computer codes while most girls wanted to sew. **My love of fashion and computers led me to a fashion forecasting office where I worked for over twenty years as their European correspondent. It was there I met the owner of the company, Bill Glazer, who forever changed my life. He has been my mentor, a true friend, and someone I could depend on through the years. The road of forecasting and technology led to contributing as retail reporter to the first on-line trend service, WGSN, where I worked for over eight years and led their fashion research in Los Angeles, San Francisco, and Seattle. Special thanks to WGSN for providing me with new approaches in the future of digital and consumer insight.**

Additionally, I would like to thank the various professionals from the fashion industry who have contributed, through interviews and advice, of what was necessary for the next generation to understand. One who stands out is Aliza Licht, who has not only supported me as a mentor but who also open-heartedly gives back to the next generation of fashion innovators. Imran Amed, CEO of *The Business of Fashion*, whose support of academics is beyond gracious, and through his guidance, changed the path I took in covering the ever-changing digital landscape. Highlights from the research process of this book will have to be when connecting with the Burberry digital and communication team on the future of fashion and their insightful presentation. I will be eternally grateful to the Burberry marketing team and their visionary approach to the digital world of fashion retail and customer experience.

The data science segment of this book is where I discovered companies that were gracious with their time and resources. One key contributor was Affinio, where India White helped me understand the elements of data while taking a glimpse into what type of contextualized data can be gathered by extracting deep psychographic insights from social media participants. Special thanks to their marketing director, who spent hours with me to ensure that I had accurate industry insight. The team at EDITED, and their endless openness to work with me on interviews and new data analysis has also been a highlight, especially the London team and of the founders, Geoff Watts. He was kind enough to share how they fused the power of *data* science with contextualized apparel retail insight. When it came to insight on SEO content, I feel most blessed to have met this young lady who was more than giving with her time. Thanks to Courtney Messerli for your never-ending support. Thanks to Jeremy Bergstein from The Science Project for opening my eyes to the future of fashion experiences.

It was an honor to have featured one of the big game-changers in women in sports, Cindy Whitehead, a.k.a. @SportStylist, who taught me to take on the biggest challenges head on. A big thank you to Gregory Dava (Downtown Dava) for your endless support while still traveling around the world and inspiring the next generation of men's lifestyle trends. Dear-to-my-heart is my thanks to my alumni students, Tania Sarin (@Tania_Sarin), Emily Cholakian (@stilettobeatss), Gina McFinch, Leo Funa and Kelsey White, all kind enough to share their industry insights.

Last but not least, I would like to acknowledge my past, present, and soon-to-be students, who have no idea how much they encourage me to continuously explore the future of fashion. My students tend to share my enthusiasm for the area of fashion and technology and make lectures more of an open platform dialog between us. I truly cherish my role in academia as a contributor to the knowledge of tomorrow.

Thank you all!
Wendy K. Bendoni
@BendoniStyle
@FashionMarketing

Picture credits

Cover:
Top Row: Mallory Quiroa, Kelsey White, Natasha Lloyd, Emily Cholakian, Chanelle Laurence. Second Row: Tania Sarin, Emily Cholakian, Gregory Dava, Chanelle Laurence, Fabio Duma. Third Row: Cindy Whitehead photographed by Ian Logan, Getty Image, Gregory Dava, Jessica Matlock West, Tania Sarin, Eric Christian. Fourth Row: Marla Verdugo, Kimberly Luu, Lauren Messiah & Luke Storey, School of Style, Vanessa Rosales, Morgan Bendoni. Fifth Row: Natasha Lloyd, Gina McFinch.

1.1 Getty Images (various). 1.2 Bertrand Rindoff Petroff/Getty Images. 1.3 MJ Kim/Getty Images. 1.4 Archivio Cameraphoto Epoche/Getty Images. 1.5 Dave Allocca/DMI/The LIFE Picture Collection/Getty Images. 1.6 George Rose/Getty Images. 1.7 Adapted from 1.bp. blogspot.com/-9ZHx5wn-zsc/UFltyMvNv6l/AAAAAAAACpY/hTlluuGcuuQ/s1600/fashion+cycle.jpg. 1.8 Kirstin Sinclair/Getty Images. 1.9 Pierre-Yann Dolbec, Eileen Fischer. "Refashioning a Field? Connected Consumers and Institutional Dynamics in Markets." Journal of Consumer Research, 2015; 41 (6): 1447 DOI: 10.1086/680671/By permission of Oxford University Press. 1.10 Kristina Nikishina/Getty Images for Mercedes-Benz Fashion Week Russia. 1.11 Nick Harvey/WireImage. 1.12 Selin Alemdar/Getty Images. 1.13 Scott Gries/ImageDirect. 1.14 Kirstin Sinclair/Getty Images. 1.15 Cindy Ord/Getty Images for NYFW: The Shows. 1.16 Tim Whitby/Getty Images. 1.17 GABRIEL BOUYS/AFP/Getty Images. 1.18 Tania Sarin. 1.19 Monica Schipper/Getty Images. 1.20 IFB Media LLC. 1.21 Courtesy of Gregory Dava. 1.22a Peter Michael Dills/Stringer/Getty Images, 1.22b Joshua Lott/Getty Images. 1.23 Guy Marineau/Conde Nast via Getty Images. 1.24, 1.25 Antonio de Moraes Barros Filho/WireImage. 1.26 Kiyoshi Ota/Getty Images. 1.27 Based on EDITED images (see 3.6). 1.28 Randy Brooke/Getty Images.

2.1 William West/Staff/Getty Images. 2.2 Adapted from barrydalton.com/wp-content/uploads/2013/08/Social-Media-Insights.jpg. 2.3 D'Marie Group, Inc. (March 8, 2016). 2.4 © Cato Institute. Used by permission. 2.5 Todor Svetkov/Getty Images. 2.6 Ellen DeGeneres/Twitter via Getty Images. 2.7 Adapted from defensecontractormarketing.com/wp-content/uploads/2014/09/SWOT-Analysis.pnghttps://defensecontractormarketing.com/wp-content/uploads/2014/09/SWOT-Analysis.png. 2.8 Theo Wargo/Getty Images for Adidas. 2.9 Ben Hider/Getty Images. 2.10 Thomas Concordia/WireImage. 2.11 Justin Sullivan/Getty Images. 2.12 common.wikimedia.org. 2.13 Bettmann/Getty Images. 2.14 Courtesy of Matt Kreikemeier/leveragenewmedia.com. 2.15 Ben Gabbe/Getty Images. 2.16, 2.17 Courtesy of Zach Allia. 2.18 Astrid Stawiarz/Getty Images. 2.19 Patrick T. Fallon/Bloomberg via Getty Images. 2.20, 2.21 Courtesy of Misha Janette.

3.1 Scott Barbour/Getty Images. 3.2a Borut Trdina/Getty Images. 3.2b Rolf Bruderer/Fuse. 3.2c Courtesy of Gregory Dava. 3.3 Caiaimage/Getty Images. 3.4 Courtesy of J Pierce @ iamjpierce. 3.5 Petar Chernaev/Getty Images. 3.6 Courtesy of EDITED. 3.7 Universal History Archive/UIG via Getty Images. 3.8 Timur Emek/Getty Images. 3.9 Nick Dolding/Getty Images. 3.10 Westend61/Getty Images. 3.11 Wendy Bendoni. 3.12 Heather Charles/Chicago Tribune/MCT via Getty Images. 3.13 Bethany Mollenkof/Los Angeles Times via Getty Images. 3.14 Kevin Winter/Getty Images. 3.15 Wendy Bendoni. 3.16 Georgie Wileman/Getty Images. 3.17 Andrew Harrer/Bloomberg via Getty Images. 3.18 Astrid Stawiarz/Getty Images. 3.19a Princess Diana Archive/Getty Images. 3.19b Michael Putland/Getty Images. 3.19c Michael Ochs Archives/Stringer. 3.20 Wendy Bendoni. 3.21 David Paul Morris/Bloomberg via Getty Images. 3.22a, 3.22b Wendy Bendoni. 3.23 Andreas Kuehn/Getty Images. 3.24 Vivien Killilea/Getty Images. 3.25 Wendell Teodoro/WireImage.

4.1 Westend61/Getty Images. 4.2, 4.3 Wendy Bendoni. 4.4 Adapted from chrisohara.files. wordpress.com/2012/12/top_funnel.png?w=531&h=306. 4.5 Adapted from The Network is Your Customer by David Rogers. 4.6a, 4.6b Courtesy of Bumpy Pitch. 4.7 ERIC PIERMONT/AFP/Getty Images. 4.8 Ronald Martinez/Getty Images. 4.9 Ryan Miller/Getty Images. 4.10 Wendy Bendoni. 4.11a Courtesy of Cindy Whitehead/Girl is NOT a 4 Letter Word. 4.11b Photograph by Ian Logan. 4.12 Dimitrios Kambouris/WireImage for Burberry. 4.13, 4.14a Wendy Bendoni. 4.14b Courtesy of @TeanaNails. 4.15 © Keith Nishida. 4.16 Trendsmap.com. 4.17 Adapted from infograph by Wendy Bendoni. 4.18 © 2014 OneSpot, designed by Erica Boynton and Adam Weinroth. 4.19 Henry S. Dziekan III/Getty Images for Tiffany. 4.20 Photograph by Gregory Woodman. Hand-lettering by Judson Collier. 4.21a, 4.21b Courtesy of Stewart William Ramsey/Krochet Kids Intl. 4.22a, 4.22b FashionRevolution.org/Photographer: Stephanie Sian Smith @stephaniesiansmith.

5.1 Bernhard Lang/Getty Images. 5.2 Caiaimage/Tom Merton/Getty Images. 5.3 Econsultancy. com. 5.4, 5.5 Courtesy of Hello Society. 5.6 Chelsea Lauren/Getty Images. 5.7 Laura Cavanaugh/FilmMagic. 5.8 Rachel Murray/Getty Images for LACMA Costume Council. 5.9 Dave J Hogan/Getty Images. 5.10 Courtesy of Hello Society. 5.11a, 5.11b, 5.11c, 5.11d gandr App. 5.12 Courtesy of Cuit Gonzalez/Wendy Bendoni. 5.13 Stephen Lovekin/Getty Images for eBay. 5.14a, 5.14b, 5.14c Courtesy of The Science Project.

6.1 Enamul Hoque Rod Steele/Getty Images. 6.2 Chris Jackson/Getty Images. 6.3 © Kathryn Hagen. 6.4 Catherine Farrell/Getty Images. 6.5 Courtesy of EDITED. 6.6a, 6.6b, 6.15 Google and the Google logo are registered trademarks of Google Inc., used with permission. 6.7, 6.8, 6.9, 6.10, 6.11, 6.12, 6.13 Courtesy of Affinio. 6.14 Courtesy of Bloglovin'. 6.16 Courtesy of Danny Sullivan/Searchengineland.com 6.17 Courtesy of Claudia Ukonu.